C000006333

How to...

NT® Server 4

seven™

Matthew Strebe

San Francisco Paris Düsseldorf Soest London

Associate Publisher: Guy Hart-Davis
Contracts and Licensing Manager: Kristine O'Callaghan
Acquisitions & Developmental Editor: Maureen Adams
Editor: Brianne Hope Agatep
Technical Editor: Robert Gradante
Book Designer: Bill Gibson
Graphic Illustrator: Tony Jonick
Electronic Publishing Specialist: Bill Gibson
Project Team Leader: Shannon Murphy
Proofreaders: Blythe Woolston, Jeff Chorney
Indexer: Blythe Woolston
Cover Designer: Ingalls + Associates
Cover Illustrator/Photographer: Ingalls + Associates

SYBEX, Network Press, and the Network Press logo are registered trademarks of SYBEX Inc.

24seven and the 24seven logo are trademarks of SYBEX Inc.

Screen reproductions produced with Collage Complete.
Collage Complete is a trademark of Inner Media Inc.

TRADEMARKS: SYBEX has attempted throughout this book to distinguish proprietary trademarks from descriptive terms by following the capitalization style used by the manufacturer.

The author and publisher have made their best efforts to prepare this book, and the content is based upon final release software whenever possible. Portions of the manuscript may be based upon pre-release versions supplied by software manufacturer(s). The author and the publisher make no representation or warranties of any kind with regard to the completeness or accuracy of the contents herein and accept no liability of any kind including but not limited to performance, merchantability, fitness for any particular purpose, or any losses or damages of any kind caused or alleged to be caused directly or indirectly from this book.

Library of Congress Card Number: 99-61308
ISBN: 0-7821-2507-7

Manufactured in the United States of America

10 9 8 7 6 5 4 3 2 1

To Christy

Acknowledgments

I'd like to thank all the wonderful people at Sybex for making this series a reality, especially Maureen Adams, Brianne Agatep, Neil Edde, Guy Hart-Davis, Bob Gradante, Shannon Murphy, Bill Gibson, Blythe Woolston, Jeff Chorney, and Tony Jonick. I'd also like to thank Michael Moncur, Charles Perkins, and James Chellis, without whom I would never have been a technical writer. Most of all I'd like to thank my wife, whose constant support sustains me.

Contents at a Glance

Table of Contents

Introduction

Windows NT is an amazing operating system. It can also be a very frustrating operating system at times. Supporting NT can be easy with the right planning, or it can be difficult when you make architectural decisions that cannot be sustained as your network grows. This book will help you make the right decisions about Windows NT networks, and it will steer you away from the pitfalls administrators (including myself) often fall into. Windows NT is the most advanced, most highly evolved software produced by any company ever—it is the flagship product of the largest software development company in the world. Its complexity is both a blessing and a curse, but with proper management, you can maximize the blessing and minimize the cursing. This book will show you how.

About This Book

This book contains the essence of my six years of Windows NT experience as an NT consultant—both my successes and failures. This book is formatted for ease of use and maximum clarity. It is not an encyclopedia of Windows NT; it is an operator's manual. It is based mostly on those problems that I've seen affect more than one customer. I've avoided fluffing the book up with the minutia of every discovered bug in NT. This book does not explain every esoteric Windows NT problem; it explains how to avoid them en masse. It does not toe the Microsoft line; it approaches NT with the clarity of skepticism. You'll find solutions to large-scale problems (for example, server rollout and network software design) as well as small-scale problems (automatically shutting down the NTVDM after exiting a 16-bit program). This book covers problems where Microsoft's documentation either leaves off or is unclear.

Microsoft's TechNet information CD is my constant companion in my consulting practice and during the writing of this book, and it should be yours as well. If you don't have a subscription to TechNet, get one. Without authoritative technical information from the manufacturer of the operating system, you'll be poking around in the dark when you try to fix esoteric problems—no matter how long you've worked with NT. Think of this book as a companion to TechNet rather than a replacement for it.

Who Should Buy This Book?

This book is for active Windows NT system administrators or for those who would like to become system administrators. Although it is written for those who already consider themselves to be expert Windows NT administrators, you do not need to be an expert to learn from it. However, you should at least be an MCSE or have equivalent understanding of NT, because I assume you understand the architecture of Windows NT, networks protocols, and networks in general. To benefit from this book, you should also run Windows NT in your company. This book is designed to be useful to both large enterprises and small businesses.

Assumptions

This book is primarily about Windows NT Server 4. It covers earlier editions of the operating system only so far as they are the same. It covers other editions of the operating system only inasmuch as they are similar to the services of NT Server 4, except for an occasional note about a feature that is different between versions. For the most part, this is adequate for troubleshooting purposes, because the various editions of NT are remarkably similar, varying only in the included services and a few minor Registry settings.

I've also assumed that you are running Windows NT on the Intel platform. I do not have access to an Alpha server and have only worked with one once, so I'm not really qualified to write about them. Other platforms are now completely obsolete, so if you haven't migrated from them to Intel, you should consider doing that now. Sadly, there doesn't seem to be room for more than one microprocessor in the world.

I've also assumed that you are working from NT Service Pack 4 (or at the very least, Service Pack 3). If you aren't, consider upgrading your servers now. Service Pack 4 has some issues with installed applications, so check with the vendors of your major applications before applying it. Service Pack 3 is very stable—I know of no complications it causes.

How This Book Is Organized

This book is divided into four parts in the order that you will work with NT in the field throughout its service life. Part I, "Planning for NT," covers those things you should have in place before you install your system. Part II, "Up and Running," covers issues you'll run into when you bring Windows NT online, such as installation and initial security setup. Part III, "NT Everyday," discusses long term maintenance of NT and your support organization. Finally, Part IV, "When Things Go Wrong," details procedures you can use to repair Windows NT.

The sides of this book are tabbed by section to make it easy for you to refer to these parts as a reference.

Part I—Planning for NT

This section discusses the design and use of Windows NT in a networked environment. The emphasis is on proper planning and architecture to support the remaining sections of the book.

Chapter 1, "Starting with Windows NT," discusses the architecture of Windows NT. Chapter 2, "Designing NT Networks," covers proper design principles—from the physical plant to the services that you will eventually provide. Although this chapter is written primarily for new installations, it can be used as a guide to overhaul an existing network as well. Chapter 3, "Installing Windows NT (the Right Way)," discusses how to install Windows NT quickly and easily in even the most difficult environments.

Part II—Up and Running

This section covers the establishment of higher-level services in your operating network. You have NT running, and now you want to make it more useful, more secure, and more stable. This section tells you how to accomplish these goals.

Chapter 4, "Storage and Fault Tolerance," discusses how to use mass-storage devices for storage and archiving. The chapter also deals with Windows NT's built-in fault tolerance mechanisms and discusses which are useful and which are more trouble than they're worth. Chapter 5, "Network Protocols," discusses network protocols and routing, along with the architectural differences between switched and routed networks. Chapter 6, "Network Services," covers the services included with Windows NT with an emphasis on which you should use and why. Chapter 7, "Securing Windows NT," discusses both the built-in security mechanisms of Windows NT and those security measures that should be but aren't. Chapter 8, "The Internet and RAS," covers connecting your network to the outside world.

Part III—NT Everyday

This section is about the long-term maintenance of both your network and your network support operation.

Chapter 9, "Supporting Clients," discusses how to manage the client computers in your network—no matter how many you have or what sort of clients you use. This chapter covers establishing a four-tiered support structure for rapidly responding to and fixing problems with client computers. Chapter 10, "Supporting Servers," discusses how to manage multiple servers in your network. Issues like domain management and high availability are covered in depth. Chapter 11, "Information Technology Management," discusses your IT support organization and how to troubleshoot it to keep your computers running well.

Part IV—When Things Go Wrong

This section shows you the fastest ways to deal with a wide range of problems, covering both the theory and practice of optimization and troubleshooting.

Chapter 12, "Performance Optimization," covers not only performance theory but which optimizations make the most sense. Chapter 13, "Troubleshooting Theory," covers the basic tenets of troubleshooting that apply to all systems. Chapter 14, "Practical Troubleshooting," is a troubleshooting guide written specifically for Windows NT that will help you narrowly define what's wrong and how to fix it. Chapter 15, "The Registry," discusses that holy grail of NT gurudom: the Registry. This chapter will help you decipher its cryptic contents and make it a tool you use rather than a problem you fear.

Appendix A—The Registry

This encyclopedic reference to the Windows NT Registry is as complete as I could possibly make it. You will find valuable information that will assist you throughout your practice and as an NT administrator. Important Registry keys are highlighted for easy reference.

Watch the 24seven Web site, `www.24sevenbooks.com`, for a comprehensive Registry database that you can help to maintain. See you there!

Part 1

Planning for NT

Topics Covered:

- Explaining Windows NT architecture

- Major variations of Windows NT

- Selecting core network technologies

- Estimating client load on servers and networks

- Designing the physical plant

- Network architecture choices

- Installing Windows NT under difficult circumstances

- Explaining the boot process

1

Starting with Windows NT

Windows NT is an amazing operating system; it is in rare company among the most sophisticated operating systems ever developed. Most amazing is the relative simplicity of NT's basic architecture. From a few simple design decisions springs an operating system capable of running the most complex software available across a number of processors in a single machine on virtually any processor architecture.

Before we dive into the complexity of Windows NT, let's take a look at those simple precepts upon which all the complex services of NT are based. Once you understand the architecture of Windows NT, its sometimes inexplicable behavior becomes quite explicable.

Although I wrote this chapter primarily for administrators migrating from other operating systems like Unix, it explains the inner workings of Windows NT in a concise manner that even the most seasoned NT administrator should appreciate. It also sets the stage for the rest of the book and explains terms that will be used throughout the book. This chapter is broken up into the following sections:

Design Goals for Windows NT   Explains why Microsoft developed NT

Incarnations of NT   Compares the various packages of Windows NT so you can choose the version you need

Basic Services   Explains what Windows NT Server can do for you straight out of the box

Planning Fundamentals   Explains a planning methodology you can use to design and implement networks of any size

Buying and Licensing Windows NT   Demystifies Microsoft's somewhat complicated method of extracting money from you and your organization

---

NOTE   This book is primarily about the most important package of Windows NT: Windows NT Server. However, nearly all the information in this book applies to all packages of Windows NT, so throughout this book, the term NT and Windows NT are used interchangeably to refer to any current version of Windows NT. More specific terms, such as Windows NT Server or Terminal Server Edition, are used to refer to specific packages when a feature is available only in that package.

Windows NT Design Goals

Microsoft created Windows NT to compete directly against OS/2, NetWare, and Unix in the file server and small application server market. Since then, microprocessors have become as powerful as traditional mainframe processors, and the mini-computer and mainframe markets have nearly been replaced by the microcomputer platform upon which NT runs, so it now competes as an application server as well.

To succeed as a *network operating system* against strong competition, Microsoft designed Windows NT to support some important computing technologies that none of its prior operating systems supported. Those core technologies are

- Multithreading
- Huge applications
- Multiprocessing
- Platform independence
- Pervasive security
- Backward compatibility

Many functions of Windows NT, such as disk security and network connectivity, are actually the functions of services and drivers that run on top of this basic architecture. They are discussed in the next section.

Multiprocessing

Multiprocessing refers to using more than one microprocessor in a single computer—in other words, all the microprocessors are attached to a single memory space. This functionality provides multiple microprocessors that can work on a single problem, which is useful for tasks limited by processor performance (like graphical rendering or trajectory calculations) or to provide more processing power for heavily loaded application servers (like Web or database servers). NT implements *symmetrical multiprocessing* (SMP), meaning that all processors are loaded as equally as possible.

Multithreading

Multithreading allows more than one program to run simultaneously and allows single programs (*processes*) to have more than one simultaneous thread of execution. The "Windows NT Architecture" section describes multithreading in complete detail.

Reality Check: Multithreaded Applications

The Web service of IIS is an excellent example of a multithreaded application. When you start a Web server, code that runs in a single thread listens on TCP port 80 for connection attempts. When a Web browser sends a connection request, that monitor thread immediately spawns a new thread, which runs code that answers the connection. This frees the monitor thread to continue listening for new connections without interruption and provides a dedicated process for every individual Web connection to the server. Multithreading makes it easy to write server applications, and all multi-user services in Windows NT work this way.

Linear Address Space

Huge applications that use enormous amounts of memory efficiently require a "flat" or linear memory space of 32 bits (or 4GB). However, NT uses the high bit to separate system processes from user processes, so only 2^{31} bits are actually available for user processes (2GB).

The developers of Windows NT didn't feel the need to exceed a 32-bit address space for applications, because when Windows NT was developed, 2GB hard disks didn't exist, much less dynamic memory modules large enough to provide 4GB to a single machine. However, new software development always seems to be able to use up the resources provided by new hardware development, and NT runs best with copious amounts of RAM. Due to these two factors, some enterprise applications need more memory space than NT can provide, and some large corporate users have begun to complain about NT's 2GB limitation. Windows NT Server Enterprise Edition was developed to solve this problem. Windows NT Server Enterprise edition can provide 50 percent more RAM to user applications as described in the "Incarnations of NT" section.

Reality Check: Farewell Flat Memory

Remember MS-DOS and the 640KB limit? Ever wonder why there was a 640KB limit? The 8086 processor divided RAM into 16 banks of 64KB (1MB total) because the 16-bit processor could only address a 16-bit address space (64KB bytes). Intel added a "page" register of 4 bits (16 unique values) to indicate which bank of 64KB the computer was working on at that moment. A special processor instruction was required to switch banks, and no other processor instructions could address memory outside the current bank. This was a major pain for program developers who had to make sure their code either fit within a single 64KB bank or always correctly handled the bank switching. The first 10 banks of memory were dedicated to user memory (640KB) and the remaining six banks (384KB) were dedicated to BIOS ROM routines and to I/O hardware plugged into the ISA bus. This problem was further compounded by the 80286 architecture, which added another four bits of page space to increase the total available memory to 16MB—still segmented into 64KB chunks.

The flat memory architecture of Windows NT prevents all of these bizarre problems—but it's limited to just 32 bits of address space (4GB). While that seems like plenty for most functions, there are a number of applications that could make good use of more memory. Windows 2000, the next version of Windows NT, will use the same bank register scheme to address up to 64GB in sixteen 4GB blocks. Individual processes will still be limited to a 32-bit address space, so those that need more than 4GB of address space will have to work around the 4GB limitation just the way MS-DOS programs had to work around the 64KB bank boundaries. It's déjà vu all over again.

Platform Independence

Platform independence allows Microsoft to quickly target emerging machines as platforms for Windows NT and to keep from being tied to any specific hardware manufacturer (namely Intel). Windows NT runs on an abstract virtual machine (the Hardware Abstraction Layer, or HAL) that translates hardware accesses from NT to whatever is required by the hardware machine. This feature allows Microsoft to quickly port NT to any machine architecture by creating a unique HAL for the new target machine and recompiling Windows NT for the microprocessor used by the machine.

> **NOTE**   Windows NT actually only supports microprocessors capable of operating in the little-endian byte order mode used by Intel microprocessors. Endian refers to the byte order of a stored 32-bit word: Storing a word with the most significant byte first is big endian; storing a word with the least significant byte first is little endian. Most modern processors (except those made by Intel) can switch between big-endian and little-endian modes but an actual computer may be hardware limited to one mode or the other. For example, while the PowerPC processor can run in either mode, it's probable that the processor is hardwired in the big-endian mode on the Apple Macintosh, which would make it impossible to port Windows NT to that platform.

At one time, Microsoft supported four microprocessor architectures for Windows NT:

MIPS   NT was originally developed on MIPS computers, but MIPS development has now been abandoned.

Intel 32-Bit Architecture   Including the obsolete 386 and 486 processors, and the current Pentium, Pentium Pro, Celeron, Pentium II, Pentium III, and Xeon processors.

Digital Alpha   Now that it is owned by Compaq, its future is uncertain.

IBM's PowerPC   PowerPC development has been abandoned despite the fact that PowerPC G3 processors are faster than the fastest Intel processors.

Microsoft has since dropped support for the MIPS and PowerPC processors for Windows NT due to lack of demand. The future of the Alpha processor is now uncertain following the acquisition of Digital's semiconductor divisions by Compaq, so Windows 2000 may not support the Alpha processor. Even though future versions of NT may only run on one processor, Microsoft will retain the hardware abstraction layer so they can quickly jump to future platforms as they arise.

Pervasive Security

Pervasive security provides an environment wherein an application can be certain that its data has not been modified by another application on the same machine. Applications running on the same machine cannot violate the memory space of other applications, which prevents both accidentally crashing them and malicious theft of data. Despite recent news about holes in Windows NT's security implementation, the architecture remains secure and Windows NT is no less secure than any other mass-market, high-end operating system.

Backward Compatibility

Windows NT supports backward compatibility with existing applications and standards. It also supports a number of application subsystems that provide backward compatibility to various earlier Microsoft and third-party operating systems. Various subsystems provide compatibility with the following:

- DOS (NT Virtual DOS Machine, NTVDM)
- 16-bit Windows applications (Windows on Windows, WoW)
- OS/2 1.3 (OS/2 subsystem)
- POSIX (POSIX subsystem)
- OpenGL (OpenGL API)
- Win32

Programs that are written to these specifications, which do not try to access hardware directly or require the services of drivers that do, should work correctly under Windows NT. The OS/2 subsystem is obsolete and the POSIX subsystem is not used by the vast majority of users, but the MS-DOS and Windows on Windows subsystems are used frequently, especially by users of Windows NT Workstation. The Win32 subsystem is required for the operation of NT and for that reason is sometimes not considered to be a subsystem.

Windows NT Architecture

Windows NT is a *preemptive multitasking* operating system, which means it can do more than one thing at a time whether or not the individual processes are written to cooperate with one another.

The scheduling of these various processes is the domain of the Kernel, as is the allocation of memory and communication with I/O devices. The Kernel manages the three basic components of a computer: memory, processor time, and I/O.

The physical (if you can call it that) implementation of Windows NT is as a series of dynamic link libraries that are loaded during the boot process. For example, basic Kernel services are contained in the file `ntoskrnl.exe`, and the hardware abstraction layer for your machine is contained in a file called `hal.dll`. Each specific system service or driver has its own file associated with it. When a service is dependent upon another service, such as the `cdfs.sys` CD file system's dependency upon the `cdrom.sys` device driver, the dependent module will fail to start if the dependent driver isn't already running.

The Kernel and all drivers and services (which form the executive when combined) share a single memory address space—they are protected from other processes but not from each other. This process memory space is called the *Kernel mode*. The Kernel is non-pageable, which means that it's always available in RAM and is never paged out to disk. The Kernel cannot be paged out, because it contains the code that controls paging and the disk drivers. It is also a performance optimization since the Kernel is frequently used. Drivers and services in the executive are pageable because they're less often used and are not critical to the paging function.

TIP   Since drivers share the same protected space as the Kernel, they can crash Windows NT. Blue screen crashes are usually caused by drivers that are either poorly written or that are trying to drive malfunctioning hardware.

The Kernel is divided into distinct components:

The Process Manager   Creates threads and processes upon request. A *process* is simply a unique virtual address space consisting of one or more threads. *Threads* are unique chains of execution within a process that represent the fundamental scheduled entity in Windows NT. Threads have their own Kernel stack, user stack, and environmental variables. (A *stack* is a scratchpad area available to thread for quick storage and retrieval of data during calculations.)

Interrupt Handlers   Act when called upon by hardware events such as page faults or I/O calls. The Kernel establishes an interrupt handler for each possible interrupt call. The Kernel handles some interrupts itself, others are handled by drivers running in the Kernel space.

The Hardware Abstraction Layer   Makes all computers appear the same to Windows NT, whether they are based on the industry standard PC architecture, the Advanced RISC Computing (ARC) platform, or any other machine. The hardware manufacturer provides the HAL for machines other than standard PCs.

TIP   Think of the HAL as a device driver for the computer's motherboard.

The Object Manager   Provides a namespace for various components of Windows NT, such as files, ports, processes, and threads—virtually anything that the system would need to keep track of. Processes can use the services of the object manager to refer to other objects in the system.

TIP   Using the Performance Monitor, you can view many of the objects managed by the Object Manager.

The Virtual Memory Manager   Controls the paging of memory to disk.

In addition to the typical processing functions, all modern microprocessors include a device called a *Memory Management Unit* (MMU) which is crucial to the architecture of preemptive multitasking operating systems including Windows NT.

MMUs facilitate three crucial functions:

Address Abstraction   Creates a unique address space for each process. This allows processes to assume they have control of the entire computer's memory space without conflicting with the memory of another process.

Page Protection   Prevents processes from accessing memory that is assigned to another process (which results in the familiar access violation error message). This ensures that one process can't crash other processes on the machine.

Virtual Memory   Allows the operating system to use I/O storage as memory by recording pages of memory on an I/O device (such as a hard disk drive) and recalling them whenever the memory is accessed. This operation is entirely hidden from the process, so the computer appears to have more RAM than it actually has.

TIP   Use the System applet in the Control Panel to specify how you want virtual memory set up on your computer.

The Local Procedure Call Facility   Passes messages between processes; since processes cannot violate the address space of another process, they use the local procedure call facility to transfer information. The LPC facility acts as the interface between the Kernel mode and the user mode. In concert with the remote procedure call service, it provides the abstraction necessary to interface with processes on remote computers over a network.

The I/O Manager   Presents a uniform interface to which all drivers can attach. The I/O manager handles the passing of data and messages between device drivers, similar to the way the LPC mechanism handles interprocess communication. Drivers can depend upon the services of other drivers through layers called dependencies. For example, basic drivers that communicate directly to hardware are called device drivers. Higher level drivers like the NTFS file system depend on hard disk device drivers to store data. This layering of drivers allows the abstraction of specific purpose for drivers; e.g., various storage mediums can use the same file system, and multiple file systems can use the same storage medium.

TIP   The Devices Control Panel allows you to control the functionality of the I/O Manager.

The Cache Manager   Optimizes file access by using RAM to store frequently accessed files. The cache manager acts much like a driver layered between the file system driver and user-level processes. When a user requests a file, if that file is in the cache the cache manager returns it rather than accessing the slower storage medium. The cache manager works closely with the virtual memory manager to use otherwise unused RAM. Whenever the VMM needs memory, it de-allocates cache memory before paging active processes out to disk.

Drivers   Provide the interface to I/O devices through a layered system of dependencies upon more basic drivers. The next section explains drivers in detail.

The Security Reference Monitor   Enforces security by limiting which objects can access other objects. When an object makes a request to access another object, the accessing object provides a security identifier that the SRM checks against the access control list of the referenced object. If the object's security identifier is not present in the control list of the referenced object, access is denied. Through this mechanism, user-level security is implemented pervasively throughout Windows NT. Chapter 7, "Implementing Security," describes this mechanism in detail.

Drivers

Drivers are used to control (or drive) I/O devices such as hard disks, serial ports, or video displays. Every piece of hardware that can work with NT ships with a piece of software that NT can use to control the functionality of the device. (In reality, NT comes with a number of drivers for common devices).

This driver allows Windows NT to control any type of I/O device—not just those devices that existed when Windows NT was written. Drivers also provide a convenient abstraction for various low-level services—for example, file system drivers allow a single computer to use more than one data structure for file storage to more closely fit the characteristics of a specific device.

Drivers are all pretty much the same, but there are a few important classes of drivers that are made distinct by the importance of their function to the operation of Windows NT:

Device Drivers Control hardware directly. These include hard disk controller drivers, video device drivers, etc.

File System Drivers Control the structure of stored data on a storage device and allow chunks of data, called files, to be referred to by a given name. File system drives control the device drivers for storage devices in order to perform this function.

Network Drivers Perform the various functions necessary to transmit data over data links. These layered functions include such functions as chopping up data into addressed packets, providing named storage retrieval, and driving network adapters.

Services

Services differ from drivers in that they run outside the Kernel and cannot, therefore, directly affect the operation of Windows NT (in the theoretical version of Windows NT that is bug free, of course)—they can only make calls to the executive within the Kernel. Many services are started automatically at boot time with various security permissions as required by their purpose. Other services are started upon demand.

Services operate within the protected mode security environment of the Kernel but outside the executive and the Kernel.

Basic Services

Now that you know more than you wanted to about Windows NT's internal details, let's take a look at the practical services that foundation provides. This list doesn't include every esoteric service available—it lists only those services that would make a compelling argument to purchase Windows NT. Without paying for extra software, Windows NT Server provides the following services:

File and Print Service Fundamental to network operating systems, file service provides the ability for a server to act as a large shared hard disk, so that many clients have access to a vast amount of shared storage space. This provides the ability to share files ubiquitously in an organization and provides a platform for basic multiuser applications. Print service allows clients to share printers by transmitting their documents to a server which queues them up and prints them one at a time.

File and Print Service for Macintosh Clients   File and print service for Macintosh clients was an early market opportunity for Windows NT since Apple had never come up with a compelling server operating system despite many attempts. Microsoft implemented Apple's AppleTalk network protocol and packaged it with a service to provide file and print services to Macintosh clients. Because the service emulates an Apple file share, no software installation is necessary on the Macintosh client. For this reason, Windows NT is the preferred network operating system in most Macintosh installations.

Dynamic Host Configuration Protocol (DHCP)   DHCP address assignment is included so TCP/IP clients can dynamically obtain their IP address and other TCP/IP configuration data from a central server. This eliminates a lot of hassle for network administrators and is easy to use.

Remote Access   Remote access dial-up networking provides a way for modem users to attach to a Windows NT network to access any of its service features or applications. Windows NT supports up to 256 simultaneous dial-in users as well as dial-out connectivity and automated services to connect to the Internet or other networks.

NetWare Connectivity and Gateway Services   Client and gateway services for NetWare allows Windows NT to operate seamlessly with NetWare file servers. NT can operate as a client to a NetWare server and can act as a gateway to "reshare" NetWare shares to other Microsoft clients to ease the migration between systems.

Domain Name Service   DNS provides resource location through name resolution to clients by returning the IP address of named resources on the Internet or the local network.

Remote Boot   This service allows diskless workstations to receive their operating system from a central server. Read-only memory located on the network adapter makes a plea for an address assignment and then loads its operating system files automatically. This can lower the cost of client computers somewhat, although hard disks are now generally less expensive than the special network adapters required for this function.

Routing   Routing TCP/IP and IPX packets allows NT servers to act as routers in an internetwork. Although generally less efficient than special purpose routers, the function adds no additional cost and is an effective way to increase overall network throughput when you use it judiciously.

File Transfer Protocol (FTP)   FTP allows Windows NT to act as an FTP server to FTP clients. FTP is a very simple protocol for transferring files; it does not provide the services of a true file sharing protocol because it doesn't handle file and record locking, but it's a very efficient way to distribute software to a number of clients running virtually any operating system. FTP is a service of IIS provided with the Windows NT Option Pack.

HyperText Transfer Protocol (HTTP)   HTTP is the protocol of Web service. Windows NT makes an excellent Web server and is especially compelling when combined with other BackOffice applications and the dynamic features of Active Server Pages to create e-business solutions. HTTP is a service of IIS provided with the Windows NT Option Pack.

Network News Transfer Protocol (NNTP)   NNTP provides message board browsing and posting functions for an Intranet. This function is handy for providing technical support or customer service forums on your server, but the NNTP service provided with Windows NT is not capable of participating in the Usenet Internet-based NNTP group. NNTP is a service of IIS provided with the Windows NT Option Pack.

These services are detailed throughout the remainder of this book.

Incarnations of NT

Microsoft currently maintains two major versions of Windows NT: Server (NTS) and Workstation (NTW). They are the same operating system, but the two packages are differentiated in the following ways:

- Cost
- Included services and utilities
- Default Registry optimizations

The following sections describe the major differences between the two packages.

Software Differences

The following list of services, drivers, and applications are not included with Windows NT Workstation but are included with Windows NT Server:

- Dynamic Host Configuration Protocol (DHCP) server provides TCP/IP addresses for network clients. Both NT Server and Workstation support the client for DHCP to request TCP/IP addresses from DHCP servers.

- Windows Internet Naming Service (WINS) provides Windows name resolution across TCP/IP domains in routed environments.

- Software fault tolerance in the form of disk mirroring (RAID 1) and striping with parity (RAID 5). Workstation supports striping (RAID 0), which does not improve fault tolerance.

- The Remote Access Server service accepts up to 256 simultaneous connections. Workstation is limited to 1.

- Gateway Services for NetWare(GSNW) allows an NT Server to connect to a NetWare server and "reshare" its file and print services to assist in NetWare-to-NT migrations.

- Services for Macintosh supports Macintosh clients for file and print services and allows all clients to print to AppleTalk printers on the network.

- The Network Client Administrator allows administrators to create installation packages for network clients.

- Server Manager allows limited remote administration of NT Servers, Workstations, and Windows 95 or 98 clients

- User Manager for Domains allows administrators to manage global user accounts and groups.

- Remoteboot service allows diskless clients to boot their operating systems over the network.

Registry Optimizations

In addition to the services and tools listed in the previous section, the following differences are affected by various changes to default Registry settings between the two products:

- Windows NT Server and Workstation both contain secret Registry keys that identify the platform license. It is possible to (illegally) patch this Registry value to make the product appear to be the other.

- More of the server service in Windows NT (SRV.SYS) is kept in RAM, thus increasing server performance on a heavily loaded RAM-limited machine. Workstation optimizes to keep more RAM available and therefore is less suited to file service.

- Write throttling, which is the timing values used to determine when write-back disk caches are actually written to disk, is different. The default values for NT Server are optimized to reduce disk head movement in an extremely busy environment. Workstation writes back data more immediately and is optimized for fewer open files.

- NT Workstation loads the NTVDM virtual DOS machine at boot time for improved application launch time. NT Server only loads the NTVDM when necessary. Your software will be more stable if you load the NTVDM individually for each 16-bit application as described below.

TIP   Have a separate virtual machine for each running 16-bit application by setting the DefaultSeparateVDM value in HKEY_LOCAL_MACHINE\SYSTEM\ CurrentControlSet\Control\WOW to *yes*. This improves application stability and shuts down the NTVDM when no 16-bit applications are running.

- The number and priority of system and blocking threads differ. NT Server is optimized for fast response, and Workstation is optimized for maximum processor and memory resources.

- Windows NT comes with a tuning Control Panel to optimize for file service or application service. NT Workstation is optimized for application service only.

- NT Workstation will accept only 10 client connections to its srv.sys service, thus limiting its usefulness as a server.

- Windows NT Server supports up to four microprocessors simultaneously as packaged. Workstation supports two. Both can be updated using special hardware abstraction layers provided by the various multiprocessor motherboard manufacturers.

Internet Information Server (IIS) will only accept 10 simultaneous inbound connections when running on NT Workstation, but this limitation is implemented in IIS rather than in NT. Originally, Microsoft had intended to hard limit Workstation's TCP/IP stack to communicate with a maximum of 10 foreign machines at a time, but outcry from the user base forced them to enact their 10 Web-users limit for NT Workstation in IIS.

Minor Versions of Windows NT

Other versions of Windows NT exist. These versions are packaged for specific business environments, so they sell considerably less than the general versions of NT Server. These versions include the following:

- Small Business Server
- NT Server Terminal Server Edition
- NT Server Enterprise Edition

Small Business Server

Small Business Server (SBS) is packaged with the following limited versions of Microsoft BackOffice applications:

- Exchange Server is an SMTP, POP3, IMAP, and MAPI mail server. Exchange supports virtually every popular mail format. The SBS edition includes enhancements to RAS to allow auto-dialing to check for mail at specific intervals.

- SQL Server provides support for structured query language databases. Unfortunately, the version included with SBS is limited to five concurrent work loads and 1 gigabyte of data and table space, so it's arguably less useful than a standard copy of Microsoft Access.

- IIS is Microsoft's Internet server and includes services for the Web, FTP, and news. IIS is also available for free with any version of Windows NT, but it's included by default with SBS.

- Proxy Server provides the ability to share a single connection to the Internet among a number of machines and provides some security for Web clients in that all access appears to be coming from a single machine. Proxy server also caches frequently accessed pages to provide faster subsequent access time.

SBS also includes various utilities to make managing a single server easier for non-professionals, for sharing a single modem connection to the Internet among a group of users, and for providing common services like shared faxing.

SBS is limited to running 25 concurrent services, but many services for SBS (Seagate Backup Exec, for example) patch that limit so they can install and run on the SBS platform.

SBS is firmly limited to 25 concurrent user connections. The license manager is disabled, so licenses can only be added through the SBS Add License Pack function of the Manage Server application provided only with SBS.

SBS installs only as the primary domain controller of a new domain, and trust relationships are disabled. For these reasons, SBS doesn't work well in multiserver environments. Support for user groups has been removed. Users are either grouped as users or administrators.

Terminal Server

NT Server Terminal Server Edition (NTS/TS) integrates the services of a package formerly known as Citrix WinFrame to make Windows NT Server a truly multiuser operating system. Terminal Server allows diskless windows terminals (known as "thin clients") to create multiple user sessions on a single server.

A multiuser operating system is an operating system where more than one person can be logged on locally to the same machine. In traditional mainframe or Unix environments, these "extra" users would be connected via text terminals attached to serial ports on the actual computer. These terminals are "dumb terminals" in that they don't have any processing power, RAM, or disk drives.

Windows NT Server Terminal Server Edition supports a "smarter" dumb terminal called a thin client or a NetPC. These devices usually have microprocessors, but they aren't used to work on your work problems. Thin clients use their processors to transmit keystrokes and mouse-clicks to the terminal server, to connect to the network, and to interpret the windowing commands sent back from the terminal server. The software applications in use are actually run on the terminal server, not the client. So, for instance, if 15 users are all running Microsoft Word, 15 copies of Word are running on the terminal server.

Users on a thin client will experience much the same environment as users of a full-function computer, except that their applications will seem to be a little more sluggish than they would on a normal computer under heavy load conditions.

Terminal servers and thin clients are appropriate for situations where only low bandwidth is available, where maintenance costs are extreme, or where actual computers are too expensive. However, powerful Pentium-class computers are usually cheaper than thin clients because of their mass-market appeal and product maturity, so cost alone is rarely a good justification to use terminal servers and thin clients.

Enterprise Edition

NT Server Enterprise Edition (NTS/E) adds support for clustering, which is running a single application across more than one computer. Enterprise Edition also supports up to eight processors by default, double the number supported by the regular version of NT Server.

Unfortunately, Microsoft's current implementation only allows clusters of two machines and isn't useful for improving the performance of an application, because the overhead that is required to manage the cluster wastes the performance gained by using two machines. Because applications must be specially written to support clustering, very few clustered applications exist.

Enterprise Edition also allows RAM tuning to free up an additional gigabyte of memory for user applications by allocating the top two bits of the address space to check for system processes and to use three of the four possible values of those bits to indicate a user process. This means that 3GB of RAM are available for user processes rather than just two. However, this is only an interim solution. Windows NT5/2000 supports a new, segmented 64-bit memory architecture that will allow for much larger applications. This architecture is not "flat"—it still provides just 4 gigabytes to each process. Hopefully, it is also just an interim solution until a future flat 64-bit architecture can be developed which would last the entire useful lifetime of Windows NT.

Evaluation Editions

Microsoft releases special versions of both Windows NT Workstation and Server for evaluation purposes. These evaluation editions are available from the Microsoft Web site for around $30 U.S. and are ideal for experimenting with Windows NT or for training purposes.

Evaluation editions expire after 60 days. After the 60-day evaluation expires, the machine will crash once per hour. You can reinstall the evaluation edition for another 60 days of uninterrupted use or purchase and install a full version of Windows NT.

WARNING   Don't use the evaluation boot floppies to install a full version of Windows NT. If you do, the timeout function will be applied to your full version.

NT On Site: Licensing Windows NT

Licensing Windows NT is easier than it seems, especially if you follow some simple rules. Here's how it works:

Every server running Windows NT requires an NT Software license. These licenses cost about $600 retail. In addition to that cost, you'll need client access licenses for the number of users you want to support. Small Business Server and other versions of NT work the same way, but they require their own special client access licenses. For instance, you can't apply Windows NT Server licenses to a Windows NT Small Business Server; you must purchase Small Business Server licenses. SBS has a firm limit of 25 clients.

- Every computer or simultaneous user that connects to an NT Server requires a Client Access License.

- Client Access Licenses can work in one of two ways:

    Per Server   You may apply the licenses to a specific server to limit the number of simultaneous users that the specific server allows.

    Per Seat   You may apply the license to a specific client computer, allowing that client to access any number of NT servers.

NT On Site: Licensing Windows NT *(continued)*

You should always use Per Seat licensing to simplify your costs and make your network most flexible. Using this method, you simply purchase an NT Server software license for each server in your business and a Client Access license for each client. Compliance is easy, and you don't have to worry about who needs access to which server.

Planning Fundamentals

Now that you're familiar with NT's architecture and what it can do for you, I'm going to digress for a moment to talk about planning—a critical component of successful networking that is often ignored. Any effort to create a new system requires the following:

- A budget to constrain choices
- A goal to achieve
- A plan to achieve the goal within budget constraints

These fundamentals don't have the glamour (well, for us geeks anyway) of the more technical work to follow, but any attempt to start building a network without first laying this groundwork will only achieve its goals by accident.

Small networks will require proportionally less planning than large networks. In fact, if you've designed small networks in the past, you may not need to do any specific planning work at all.

Budgeting

The budget is the overwhelming constraint on your network. In the face of an unlimited budget, there's little need for design; you could simply buy the largest and fastest of everything, connect it all, and be done. Unfortunately, unlimited budgets are not common.

Budgeting changes considerably from organization, and no two organizations are in exactly the same financial position. Chances are, you already have an idea which general category your budget position fits into: constricted, normal, or nearly unrestricted. These categories depend largely on your organization's overall financial strength and the importance of the network to your organization.

The best way to request a budget is to design what you would like to build under ideal financial circumstances. Create categories of equipment and software; for instance, one category might be the components that support dial-in remote access. Determine the overall price of the network and request that budget. After your finance people recover from their heart attacks, you will at least have prepared them for what it will cost to get at least a working network. You'll be ready to scale down your requirements to meet your financial reality by eliminating specific categories of goals that are less important.

Total Cost of Ownership

Total Cost of Ownership (TCO) is financial jargon for the complete cost of a resource (like a network) throughout its entire useful life. Calculating the TCO for a resource is theoretically simple and is described by the following formula:

$$
\begin{array}{r}
\text{Initial Cost} \\
+\quad \text{Maintenance Cost} \\
-\quad \text{Sale Value} \\
\hline
=\quad \text{Total Cost of Ownership}
\end{array}
$$

Installation cost is straightforward: Determine the cost of the equipment and services necessary to install the network, and you're done. Sale value is also easy for computer and network equipment: Assume you'll use everything until it breaks or is completely worthless, so just plug in a zero. Since you'll assume that every piece of networking hardware and software will be worthless in five years, assume that you'll bear the installation cost at least once every five years. Anything that lasts longer is a bonus.

Maintenance cost is the big unknown. It includes:

- Salaries of network staff (this usually includes you)
- Consultants
- Outsourcing services (ISP, communication charges, etc.)
- Replacement hardware (estimate 20% of the initial cost per year, 100% in five years)

The industry rule of thumb for estimating the maintenance costs for medium to large networks is six times the initial purchase price of the network per year. Smaller networks fare better; two to four times the purchase price is considered normal. Your estimates should be between three and six times the initial purchase price per year.

Because of the enormous recurring cost of maintaining a network, you should make maintenance cost your primary consideration when purchasing equipment. Time is money. Save both by choosing equipment and technologies that are easy to support and not likely to fail.

How do you estimate the maintenance cost of a network component? There's no standard method. Some components, like bridges, seem to last forever and require no care. Others, like servers, often seem to require constant attention and intervention. The following sections will give you a sense of what to look for in hardware and software. They are all variations on the same theme: Stick to the mass-market, low-priced equipment by avoiding small niche-market products and custom solutions.

> ***WARNING***   Be suspicious of any product that touts, as its primary advantage, a "lower total cost of ownership." Remember that the TCO for that product and the TCOs of its competitors in the ad you're reading was calculated by the manufacturer's marketing department. It's basically an admission that the initial purchase price is way higher than the competition and there's no other significant feature to talk about.

Choose Software that Is Easy to Install and Maintain   Ease of use is the mantra of low total cost of ownership. This is what makes Windows NT such a stellar performer compared to NetWare and Unix, and why Macintoshes are still less expensive to own than similar Windows machines. Because most maintenance costs are tied directly to the payment of humans for their time, easy-to-use devices cost less.

Maintenance cost is what makes the TCO for Windows NT lower than Linux, for example. Maintaining Linux requires consultants or specialized staff due to its cryptic Unix command-line interface and its difficult installation and customization. Clerical staff can be trained to maintain Windows NT Servers in small networks.

Avoid Applications that Require Programming or Specialized Configuration   This includes GroupWare packages (such as Lotus Notes, GroupWise, and Exchange Server), highly customizable database applications (such as PeopleSoft), and any other sort of database application. The custom development required by these applications makes sense for only the very largest businesses—those with a billion dollars in sales or more— or for businesses where the passing of information forms the foundation of the business, so its handling is crucial. Even then, it's common in the development industry to present the best case budget when competing for a job. The honest and meticulous consultant will always present a higher bid cost than less honest consultants, and therefore lose the consulting contract—so those willing to underestimate the costs always win in a typical lowest bidder selection. Cost overruns are typical for this reason, and most development efforts cost more than your entire network infrastructure combined.

Most standard business problems can be fulfilled by existing applications. I know it's heresy to make this suggestion, but if you have any control over operations, you should consider modifying your business practices to fit software rather than modifying software to fit your business practices. It's far easier to train people than to develop applications, and you'll probably find that the way you work now is less efficient than the way a mass-market application makes you work.

Try to plan for standard technologies like Internet e-mail, Web pages, and Usenet newsgroups rather than expensive GroupWare. These standard technologies are far easier to customize and have a much larger group of competing consultants, which drives down consulting prices. Of course, your business may actually require customized applications, but always scrutinize the need strongly; push for simpler technologies whenever possible. Remember: Everything will be obsolete in five years. Will you even be done customizing by then?

If you must use a customized GroupWare application, define your requirements closely and stick to those things you actually must have—don't waste effort adding frivolous features that only a few people will actually use. Once you have a detailed requirements document, create a list of test conditions that will satisfy the requirements, (for example, "Edited document must be automatically forwarded to production department upon completion," and so forth). These test conditions explain quite clearly to everyone involved what the system must be able to do when it's finished, and leave little room for "that's an extra feature at extra cost" haggling when the consultant wants to deliver incomplete software.

The requirements and test condition documents will form your request for quotes in your search for consultants. Make certain all candidates understand that the bid is a fixed price and that they must be able to complete the test conditions at the price they return. You don't have to be pushed into paying for cost overruns if the consultant has agreed in writing to a specific price.

Don't select the low-bid consulting group. Select the consulting group with the longest list of satisfied customers who has shown that it can develop a system according to a limited budget.

Reality Check: Notes from the Front

I was actually hired to arbitrate a disagreement between a customer of mine and their Lotus Notes developer. Both parties were to blame for the shoddy manner in which work proceeded.

Reality Check: Notes from the Front *(continued)*

The company gave a vague requirement to the consultant: "We want a work flow system." The consultant, with no understanding of their business, returned a very encouraging price: $50,000. So they entered into a contract to develop the system. The developer returned an initial product that did little more than e-mail; users could pass information amongst themselves. They also installed a Domino e-mail server to integrate this system with the Internet.

The company demanded "more work" and gave the consultant many new requirements: The system should automatically forward certain messages to various groups of people and should be capable of storing a "knowledge base" of IS resources. The consultant performed the work and presented another bill: $200,000.

I was called in as a sort of expert witness to help the arbitrator determine how much, if any, additional money should be paid to the developer. Rather than stick the customer with an incomplete hodgepodge of functions and stick the consultant with six months of work without pay, I encouraged the arbitrator to recommend that the company perform a complete design specification for the system they wanted with the help of the consultant. The consultant would then complete that design "at cost" so long as the customer paid the current bill.

Upon completion, the customer had a very functional work flow system that cost them $500,000—10 times the originally estimated price.

Never, Ever, Ever Develop Custom Software   Software development is an arcane art that is best left to large software publishers. Unless you are a software development house, you'll throw so much money at a custom software development effort that you'll probably lose your job before it's finished. It takes so long to develop applications that they're usually obsolete before they're finished. And even in the best case, the software quality is always lower than a mass-produced application. Think of software like a vehicle. Would you even consider building your own car? Of course you wouldn't. You shop for what's available and chose the model that comes closest to meeting your needs. Treat software the same way. Look at the software market and select the existing application that comes closest to meeting your needs. Then modify your existing practices to match the software.

Use Rapid Application Development Tools   If you absolutely have to develop your own software, use Rapid Application Development (RAD) tools. The idea is not to reinvent the wheel. If you feel you must develop software, use the tools that make it as quick and easy as possible. For example, there's no faster way to put together a database front end than with Microsoft Access or similar products, such as Alpha 5. Use these visual tools rather than developing a custom front end in Visual C++. If you outsource programming, always negotiate a firm, fixed price up front and pay based on the achievement of easily identifiable milestones. Never get into a situation where you pay on a time basis for software, because the more time it takes, the more your developer gets from you, so your software will never be finished.

Avoid Specialized Hardware (and Software)   If you can't buy it off the shelf at a local computer store, think twice about purchasing it. Get your servers from a major national vendor (such as Dell, Compaq, or Gateway) that can provide replacements in a day or two. Avoid hardware that is so esoteric that it's hard to find, like the machines mentioned below. Avoid the temptation to demand customized computers that will be difficult to replace. Of course, nobody sells routers and bridges in town, so you'll have to order that equipment specially. Don't feel like you have to order everything from a single vendor, though—I've never seen a case where one vendor competes well in the market for all the components of a network.

Forget using esoteric hardware like Digital Alphas, Sun Ultras, and other high-end workstation and server hardware. Now these machines are not much faster than standard Intel-based computers, they cost far more than their slight advantage justifies, and there's no easy way to repair them when they break. Because of their limited sales, consulting costs are high.

Avoid the Temptation to Build Your Own Computers and Servers   We all do it on occasion, and sure, you can get exactly what you want, but it takes more time than it's worth, the resulting computer has no system warranty, and it doesn't come bundled with any software. By the time you add up the costs of the individual hardware components, the OS, and the installed applications, you'll find that a national direct marketer like Dell is extremely competitive.

Existing Conditions

If you're lucky enough to be starting from scratch with your network, you're in the enviable minority. Most networks are born from at least an installed base of individual computers and office applications, which means that the network is handled less as an installation than a migration.

Existing conditions often will precipitate certain requirements (for example, to support specific applications, platforms, or work methodologies). Survey your organization to determine the following information:

> **How many computers are in use?**   The answer will determine the size of your network, the number of servers you will need, and the quantity and type of datalink equipment you will require.

What types of computers are being used?   This answer will define the network operating system you should use, the transport protocols you can use, and some of the services you will need.

What special computing equipment, such as printers, are in use?   This step will identify additional special equipment, such as print servers, that might be required.

What contracted services, such as Internet or private wide area network connections, are in use?   This step will further isolate which network operating system you should use, as well as help you identify any third-party software that might be required.

What software is currently being used?   Some network-ready software will operate only under certain network operating systems. If your network is using this type of software, your choice of network operating systems may be limited.

Will existing local area subnetworks have to be integrated into the new network?   These existing networks will have to be compatible with the network you install, or they will have to be migrated to technologies that are compatible.

Goals

When starting a network installation contract, I ask clients why they want a network. The answer to this question gives me the information I need to start planning for applications, services, and desktop requirements.

It always amazes me how many respond by saying that they don't know or that everyone else has one, so they must need one, too. Neither are good reasons to install a network, but answers like that really indicate that many people simply don't know what a network can do for their business.

If they don't know themselves, you must determine what the network needs to do by interviewing the people who will be using it and who will be responsible for it. Common goals include:

- E-mail
- Web access
- Sharing files and printers
- Group scheduling
- Work-flow management
- Customer support resources
- A Web site
- E-business

NT On Site: Interviewing Clients

Here are a few questions I ask clients about their networks in the planning phase:

- About how many computers will be attached to the network?

- What is more important: security or ease of use?

- Do you want to use the Internet? How (Web site, e-mail, e-commerce, etc.)?

- Will you be retaining a consultant, hiring employees, or maintaining the network with existing staff?

- What are your budget limitations?

- Will you be connecting to remote offices?

- Are there any specific applications you know you want to use?

Determining Your Requirements

Networks are the platform for providing shared computer-based services. So to determine your requirements, you simply need to determine which shared services you need, what platforms those services need to be compatible with, and how many users you need to support.

Forget about specific components like Windows NT, Cisco routers, Lotus Notes, and Compaq servers while you define your requirements—get down to basic services and general applications. You may find that your preconceived notions about what you thought you needed go by the wayside when you let your requirements guide you. Never let a salesperson define your requirements for you—the resulting system will only be ideal for their cash flow. Use the following questions as a guideline to developing your own requirements:

Compatibility   Is the network supposed to replace any existing systems? If so, you'll need to plan for migration from one platform to the other, which usually means that both platforms have to be available during some transition phase. Software to interface to or emulate existing systems is one of your network's requirements.

Applications   Is there a database to support? Are there specialized applications such as planning packages for materials requirements? Is GroupWare required? Will you need to host a Web site or e-mail?

Users   How many users will get networked computers? This number provides the magnitude of your network and will ultimately decide both your architecture and budget. Are there remote users, and if so, what is the ratio of local to remote users?

Connectivity   Will you need to connect to distant offices? How about the Internet for e-mail and Web service?

Platforms   What platforms need to be supported? Windows machines, DOS clients, Macintoshes, Unix machines, and perhaps terminals attached to minicomputers are all clients you might expect to support. Esoteric clients may need special software or emulators to connect to the network—expect substantial additional cost in that case.

Services   What basic network services are required? File sharing is usually a must, as is print sharing. But what about shared faxing? Paging? Computer telephony?

Security   Does the business have proprietary secrets to protect? How about government contracts? Security will affect your choice of software and constrain your ability to provide or access some services.

Once you've got all your requirements down on paper, try to assess a vague cost for each one: expensive, valuable, inexpensive, easy, etc. Assign a numerical priority to all of the goals from most important to least important. This will help you determine what to axe when your budget can't support it all.

Now that you've got your requirements down on paper, you'll have to do a bit of research to determine exactly what networked resources are required to fulfill your goals. We will present specific methods for quantifying hardware resources in the following section.

Planning

Now that you've got your goals on paper, you'll need to create a network plan. Without getting into any specifics just yet, you should consider using a visual design tool like Visio or SysDraw to help you plan.

By visually laying out servers and clients, you'll be forced to think deeply about the connectivity of each client, which will help you quantify all the necessary hardware and software to complete your network. Figure 1.1 shows a network laid out with Visio.

Figure 1.1 A Visio Network Diagram

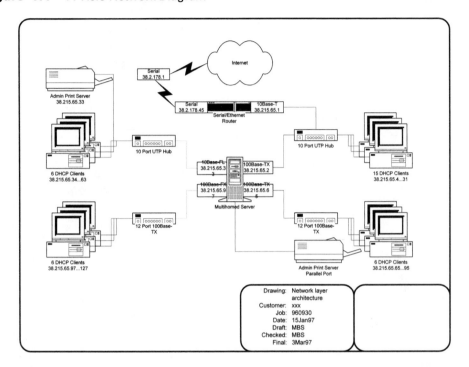

When finished, you'll have a diagram that can precisely explain your intentions to hired contractors and consultants, leaving little room for misunderstandings. You'll also have a handy check-off list to track progress with and a source for documenting the system as it is installed. Once the network is finished, you'll have a map to your network that anyone can use to locate resources during troubleshooting.

Some of these software design tools are capable of connecting directly to inventory data-bases, which is a great way to make sure your maps are up-to-date and consistent with reality.

Finally, you can use your design schema as a data source for systems like HP-OpenView and CA-UniCenter, which are both great tools for keeping track of large networks.

Choosing a Network Operating System

As a practicing network integrator, my clients rely upon me to design and manage the installations of their networks. In one case, a small business customer needed its 10 computers set up on a network. They used Macintoshes to perform graphic design work for Web sites, so strong support for Macintosh networking was crucial. They knew nothing more than that they needed to connect their computers together and to participate on the Internet. Their networkless configuration required each computer to dial into their remote Web server individually to upload files into their Web sites, so sharing a high-speed Internet connection was their primary concern.

When designing their networks, the first decision to make was which network operating system to use. In today's market, there are three choices:

- Windows NT Server

- Unix (Usually Linux or Solaris)

- NetWare

These three operating systems are all very different. NT Server is, by far, the easiest to use and administer. Linux is compelling because it's free and has no per-client licensing cost. Solaris is fairly easy to use for a version of Unix. Net-Ware is more difficult to sell these days because it's as difficult to administer as Linux and costs as much as Windows NT. Given these options, clients generally dismiss NetWare quickly. Clients rarely see

any reason to buy Solaris when Linux provides largely the same functionality for free, so it, too, does not fare well in the competition.

So the question then becomes NT versus Linux. Both are 32-bit multitasking operating systems—in fact, their underlying architecture is surprisingly similar. Both support a vast array of service applications. Both support Windows and Macintosh clients fairly seamlessly, and Linux supports Unix clients natively as well. Both make excellent platforms for Internet services.

For this customer, the answer lay in the recurring costs: They were not willing to hire at least one employee or permanently retain the services of a network integration company to manage their servers. Linux only appears to be free. Support costs for Linux servers typically outstrip Windows NT in a matter of months. Windows NT in a small business environment can be managed by nearly anyone as a collateral duty that doesn't consume much time. Managing a Linux server takes months of training and practice, even for those already familiar with network operating systems. When compared to an additional $50,000 per year salary, Windows NT is very inexpensive. The customer chose to install Windows NT even though the up-front costs were considerably higher than Linux.

Designing NT
Networks

Building a network from scratch can be a daunting task, even for experienced administrators. But there's no need to reinvent the wheel—network integrators have been building networks of all sizes for a decade. You can draw from their experience to design and build a network of any size.

Network design can be approached methodically. Design a network in the following order:

- Select core technologies
- Estimate network requirements
- Map the physical plant
- Plan the network connectivity
- Specify service and resource provision
- Plan a network management scheme

These design elements are approached on three scales, distinguished by the speed and distance at which the network must operate. By handling each scale of networking somewhat independently, the complete network design is broken down into manageable tasks. The three scales are:

Subnetwork A single LAN of usually 2–100 clients. Subnetworks are defined by the fact that all computers communicate on the same medium and can therefore address each other directly.

Network   Usually a network of 100–1,000 clients. Networks are defined by the requirement for data-link bridging between individual media, and the network broadcasts are forwarded to all participating computers.

Internetwork   Usually networks of more than 1,000 clients that are defined by necessary routing between networks and that broadcast forwarding, so some name resolution protocol is required.

The following sections describe each of the scales in more detail. These scales are fluid—there's no reason, for instance, that even a small network could not use routers for connectivity.

Subnetworks   The basic shared media connections between computers, subnetworks operate as the data links between computers. A subnetwork consists of a single Ethernet, Token Ring, ARCnet, or FDDI Ring. The important characteristic of a subnetwork is that every device participating in the subnetwork can communicate directly with every other device and that the total bandwidth of the subnetwork is divided by the number of devices on the subnetwork, because only one device can transmit at a time. Subnetworks form the smallest accumulation of computers in your network, and they are physically limited by the distance that the link technology supports—100 meters for Ethernet over twisted pair, for example. In order to create networks larger than the physical distance limitations of the network media, bridging and routing must be used to create networks and internetworks.

Networks   Formed by bridging more than one subnetwork together. Bridges are hardware devices that sit between two networks that are attached to both. Whenever a packet address to a computer on the foreign network is received, the bridge retransmits the packet on the foreign network. You can think of a bridge as a person standing in the doorway between two rooms, relaying bits of the conversations in each room to the other. Broadcast packets reach all recipients on the network. Broadcasts are used to locate computers on the network, to announce participation and network names, and for other protocol purposes such as transmitting error messages. In networks of more than about 2,000 computers, broadcasts consume far too much bandwidth, making it difficult for computers to transmit useful traffic. For this reason networks must be split and reconnected into internetworks.

Bridges rely upon the addressing mechanism of the data-link layer to distinguish between computers. Since the addressing mechanisms are different between different shared media types, bridges are only able to connect like subnetworks together. Because bridges can only connect like subnetworks (Ethernets to Ethernets, Token Rings to Token Rings), the entire network can consist of only one network type. For example, an Ethernet client cannot directly address a Token Ring client through any type of device, because their addressing schemes are not compatible. That function requires a higher-level protocol with a secondary addressing scheme like IPX or TCP/IP. However, one protocol could be used to encapsulate packets of another protocol type and forward them between two similar networks. This sort of functionality is called *protocol encapsulation.*

Switches are multi-network bridges. A switch can simultaneously participate in many subnetworks and switch frames between them as necessary. Switches are easy to use and require little or no setup, but they are rarely ideal—in more complex networks they tend to retransmit more information than is actually required.

Internetworks These are networks connected together by routers, which operate at the network layer and are therefore free from the constraint that only like networks can be connected. Routers can be used to connect any type of network together: Ethernets to Token Rings, leased lines to ATM networks. For this reason, routing is generally more popular than bridging and is often used to connect subnetworks together directly. Routers are also less expensive than switches, and servers can perform double duty as routers if you are on a constricted budget.

Selecting Core Technologies

Selecting the various technologies you'll use before you make specific design decisions is crucial, because each element of network design is too closely tied to the others to independently make these decisions. It's extremely difficult to design a physical plant without knowing which data-link technology you'll be using, for example.

The following sections present pragmatic solutions for each of the elements of design rather than exhausting the list of available options, because the market has made most of these decisions for you. Varying from these solutions is expensive, and you should only do so when requirements clearly call for an alternative solution.

Physical Plant

Physical plant decisions are easy right now: Install the highest-grade unshielded twisted pair (UTP) available for your subnetworks, and connect the subnetworks together using optical fiber. Single-mode optical fiber is ideal, but multi-mode is acceptable for smaller networks and shorter distance runs (less than 2 kilometers).

These design choices are obvious because earlier physical plant technologies have all been made obsolete by the versatility and low cost of UTP. In the past, you had to select a data-link technology and then install the physical plant mandated by that technology. This meant that premises wiring could not be installed when the building was originally constructed, because the architect could not make network design decisions.

Because UTP is inexpensive and supports Ethernet, it became the premises wiring of choice. Other data-link technologies soon adapted to UTP, so that now all common-shared media data-link technologies can operate over UTP. UTP supports only two devices per link, so a cable must be run from a central location to each station location. Each of these cable runs is referred to as a *drop* in the industry, because the cable is typically run through ceilings and dropped down to the wall outlet for termination. The central locations are generally referred to as either *distribution frames* or *closets.*

Optical fiber links between subnetworks are necessary because UTP attenuates signals too rapidly to allow its use over more than about 100 meters. Most UTP data link technologies are designed to limit transmissions to 100 meters, so distances greater than that require a different cable type. Although it's possible to use coaxial cable to link closets, optical fiber is no more expensive than coaxial cable and allows much greater bandwidth and flexibility. Accordingly, all medium area network technologies run over optical fiber, including Ethernet, Fast Ethernet, FDDI, Gigabit Ethernet, and ATM.

Optical fiber to the desktop will eventually replace UTP as the cabling methodology of choice for two simple reasons: Sand, the source material for optical fiber, is cheaper than copper, and optical fiber has vastly better data-transmission characteristics than copper wire. When economies of scale shift in favor of optical fiber, its significant bandwidth advantage will cause a sudden abandonment of copper wiring, and the recommendations I'm making will sound as dated as a 19th-century textbook on electrical wiring. When this will happen is difficult to gauge, but we're probably still about 10 years away. At the moment, optical cabling is about four times the price of UTP cabling, and optical network devices are about 10 times the price of copper network devices.

Connectivity

Ethernet is the king of data-link technology. No other data-link technology is even remotely as inexpensive for the bandwidth, and there's no reason why any ever will be. Ethernet's simplicity makes it easy to work with, highly tolerant of faults (except when run over coaxial cable), and easy to design for. Ethernet is simple, cheap, and easy. Ethernet comes in three speeds:

- Ethernet (10Mbps)
- Fast Ethernet (100Mbps)
- Gigabit Ethernet (1000Mbps)

10Mbps Ethernet is considered obsolete for new installations but is still required for connectivity to lower speed devices, such as older computers, print servers, routers, and other network devices. Until 1996, 10Mbps Ethernet was the standard for connecting networks.

100Mbps Fast Ethernet is now the workhorse of networking. All your new designs should specify this data-link technology, because it is vastly cheaper than its equivalent technologies and is highly reliable. 100Base-TX is the UTP variant; 100Base-FX is the optical fiber variant, which is useful for connecting closets closer than 400 meters apart. Most 100Base-FX cards support a full-duplex mode that allows greater distance connections.

Beware the evil twin of Fast Ethernet: 100Base-VG AnyLAN. 100Base-VG AnyLAN is the mutant result of a number of silly compromises designed to make Ethernet incompatible with previous devices, harder to correctly install, and more expensive. Okay, granted that's not what the design specification called for, but that's what happened. 100Base-VG had some technically interesting ideas, like guaranteed bandwidth (called Demand Priority), collision avoidance arbitration rather than collision-based arbitration, and other technical improvements, none of which were necessary and all of which added cost, complexity, and incompatibility. Fortunately, nobody bought 100Base-VG, so it's as expensive as all the other esoteric data-link technologies.

1000Mbps (Gigabit) Ethernet is a point-to-point technology designed to link closets together over optical fiber while retaining protocol compatibility with standard Ethernet. 1000Mbps Ethernet is not useful for connecting directly to clients because the protocol is not shared, so clients cannot be connected together into shared media collision domains. I thought Gigabit Ethernet would remain expensive for some time, but adapters are already available at retail stores for under $300 each. Because you can build routers and even switches out of standard PC hardware with just these devices, Gigabit Ethernet is already inexpensive enough to use as a standard data-link technology.

You will probably use other network technologies, such as Frame Relay or ATM, to connect to a wide area network. Your WAN service provider will mandate these decisions; you'll have to support whatever type of network they have.

In rare cases, other data-link technologies like FDDI might be more appropriate than Ethernet for network and backbone data links, but the extremely high cost of these options makes those cases rare.

Network Protocols

Once you've selected your data link, decide which network protocols you will support on your network. There are four common network protocols:

- TCP/IP is by far the most common, and the protocol of the Internet and Unix networking.
- IPX/SPX is the protocol developed by Novell that was the standard in local area networks until the Internet made TCP/IP more popular.

- NetBEUI is the original Microsoft/IBM LAN protocol for small workgroups.
- AppleTalk is required for file sharing among Macintosh computers.

Other less popular networking protocols exist, but they are so rare that they don't need to be discussed. The NetBEUI protocol also included in Windows NT cannot be routed, so it is not a true network protocol and not worthy of serious consideration in any but the smallest networks or as a troubleshooting protocol.

Nearly all routers support both TCP/IP and IPX/SPX, so your choice of network protocols is mitigated by only a few choices:

- TCP/IP is required for Internet Access.
- IPX/SPX routes broadcasts, which can be problematic in large networks but makes name resolution much easier in small to medium networks. IPX/SPX is faster and easier to configure.
- AppleTalk is required if you intend to support Macintoshes, otherwise it's not necessary.

That's all there is to it. If you aren't going to connect your network to the Internet, use IPX/SPX. If you are, use TCP/IP. If you have Macs, add AppleTalk.

Sage Advice: Protocol and Etiquette

Use IPX/SPX for all your servers and clients even if you intend to support Internet connectivity. IPX/SPX is faster, easier to configure, has no name service issues through routers, and is immune to attack from the Internet.

Install TCP/IP on clients that need it to access the Internet and on Web and mail servers outside your interior firewall.

Service and Resource Provision

Service and resource provision describes the applications your network will provide and the servers required to provide them. Service and resource decisions are answered when you ask yourself why you are installing a network. For example, if you need a database, then you'll need a database server. That database server is a network resource. Common network resources include:

- File servers
- Network Printers

- Web servers
- Firewalls
- Database servers
- E-mail/GroupWare servers

These service providers are a key element of your network and belong in your initial network designs. Why? Because they are the destinations for network traffic—the clients are all trying to communicate with these resources, so network traffic is shaped by their presence.

List each service provider in your network by the network operating system and applications it runs. If you have only vague ideas about which specific products you'll use to solve certain problems, stop and decide. Don't wait until after you have a network in place, because some service decisions can change the architecture of your network.

Network Management

Network management practices should also be finalized before starting on a network, because it often changes the specific equipment you'll use in your network. The specific decision you need to make is whether you'll be using SNMP-managed devices.

SNMP-managed devices are connectivity hardware (hubs, routers, bridges, and switches) that have small computers built into them to respond to SNMP queries. Adding SNMP management typically adds about $500 per device.

I have never found SNMP to be worth the expense for troubleshooting or managing a network of 1,000 clients or less, but it becomes very useful for extremely large networks. Medium to small networks can certainly be easily managed without the automation provided by SNMP.

Enterprise management solutions like CA-UniCenter and HP-OpenView can work with managed or non-managed devices, but they are most useful when used with managed devices.

Estimating Network Requirements

If you were going to build a warehouse to store engines, you could simply measure the size of each engine, determine how high you can stack them, quantify the maximum number of engines you'll ever need to store, add floor space for access, and build a warehouse of the exact size you need. Most architects also add room for expansion. Another method is to simply buy more space than you will ever need, but this approach obviously requires deep pockets.

Both techniques are used in networking, and, unfortunately, the second is more common. Many organizations waste a tremendous amount of money on hardware to guarantee that they will not have a capacity problem. In very small networks, buying more hardware than you need can actually make financial sense, because network architects may charge more to design a network of the proper size than the extra equipment will cost. We will assume, however, that you intend to spend as little as you can to create a well-designed network.

The method presented below is based upon the client load placed upon two capacities: network and server. When you set out to design a network, the only information you bring with you is the scope of your problem as measured by a planned number of clients of each specific client type to support. A useful method must be able to take this information and answer the two important questions: How many servers will it take to serve these clients? And how should the network be laid out to handle the load? This method will help you answer both of those questions.

You will use this system both in the initial design stages to get an idea of how many servers will be required and later in the physical plant and service design stage to lay out network resources and locate servers physically.

Estimating Client Load

To estimate load capacities of networks, you need a system with which you can compare very different network technologies and relate them to client computer requirements, often without the benefit of knowing exactly how those client computers will be used.

Although no simple method will replace an experienced network integrator, experience can be distilled into methods that are useful for planning and estimating. A good working methodology will serve a number of roles:

- It will be useful for comparing data-link technologies.
- It will be useful for planning the network's physical layout.
- It will be able to predict the amount and type of hardware necessary to implement the network.

I've developed a simple method that will help you plan your network based upon the client load limit of various current data-link technologies. For instance, a single 10Mbps Ethernet network can support a maximum of approximately 50 DOS clients. The same Ethernet network can be relied upon to serve 20 or so Windows NT workstations. These numbers provide the basis of a useful formula for estimating how many Ethernet collision domains you'll need, which in turn tells you how many hubs to buy, how many routers to connect them with, and so on.

Of course, these estimations are not absolute—the way the client is used will greatly affect their load on the network, and as technology changes, so will the load estimates for various clients. However, the law of averages comes to our aid by smoothing the usage characteristics of a single computer over the number of computers attached to the network. Unfortunately, averaging doesn't always work well. Consider the case of a diskless Windows computer that must boot its operating system from a network server. This client will usually demand far more from a network than a typical client because even its memory page file is being sent over the network.

You can use the method presented here if your operations conform to the common business uses of computers. If you are doing something you know will require more bandwidth, consider revising the load values for clients presented upwards. We have presented worst-case capacities in this method, so resist the temptation to revise them downward.

Load Requirements of Typical Network Clients

The client load requirements shown in Table 2.1 were determined by dividing 100 by the maximum useful number of clients of that type that could operate on a single Ethernet segment.

Table 2.1   Load Requirements of Network Clients

Client	Metric	Explanation
Macintosh	1	Macintoshes usually require very little from a network, so we used a typical Macintosh client as the basis for our network formula.
DOS	2	MS-DOS machines tend to run simpler application software that does not demand much from a network.
Diskless DOS Client	6	Diskless MS-DOS clients are much more demanding. These computers must use the network for every I/O command that would normally go to a local hard disk drive.
Windows 3.x	3	Windows is a more complex platform than is MS-DOS, and applications built to run on Windows are more complex and network aware.

Planning for NT

Table 2.1   Load Requirements of Network Clients *(continued)*

Client	Metric	Explanation
Power Macintosh	3	Macintosh computers based on the PowerPC micropro-cessor are very fast. Although Macintoshes demand less from a network than most PC file-sharing schemes demand, these computers can hit the network pretty hard because of their speed.
Diskless Windows	9	Diskless Windows clients are extremely demanding of network bandwidth—more so than any other type of computer.
Windows 95	4	Windows 95 is a powerful multitasking operating sys-tem that typically runs on fast client computers.
OS/2	4	OS/2 is very similar to Windows 95 in most respects. It runs on similar hardware and runs similar applications.
Windows NT Workstation	5	Windows NT Workstation is the most powerful operat-ing system available for PCs. Its ability to multitask multiple network applications smoothly requires much from a network.
Unix Workstation	5	Unix workstations are usually used by bandwidth intensive users like programmers, graphic artists, and CAD operators.
Unix X Terminal	3	X terminals are diskless, but they operate as simple displays. Screen updates are sent from a compute server that actually performs the work requested by the user.
NetPC (Windows Terminal)	2	Windows Terminals are similar to X terminals in their use of bandwidth but are more efficient.

Load Capacities and Requirements of Servers

A single server can only handle only so many requests before it becomes bogged down. This typical load capacity can be used to determine how many servers of a specific type you'll need in a network.

To determine the load value your clients will place on servers, sum their client load numbers. Then, for each service you'll provide, multiply that sum by the service multiplier found in table 2.2 to determine how much service capacity will be required to solve that problem. Finally, sum those service loads into a total service capacity requirement to get an idea of how many servers you'll need. Later in the planning process, you'll assign various services to specific servers based on the load that a specific service creates.

Table 2.2   Service Load Multipliers

Service	Multiplier	Explanation
File service	1	Loads are based on file service.
Print service	.5	Printed documents are transmitted twice on the network: from client to server and from server to printer. But printing is fairly rare on most networks, so this traffic tends to be "bursty"—it's uncommon, but when it happens, it bogs down the network.
Terminal service	10	Acting as a compute server places a substantial load on a server. Use this value for Windows Terminal Servers or X clients.
Database service	0.5	Database service is typically more efficient than file service.
Web service	0.1	Web service is a fairly light load for a server.
E-mail	0.01	E-mail generates very little load on a server. Often a single e-mail server can serve an entire organization.
Router	0.2	Depending upon a server's place in the network, routing can be demanding.
Firewall	0.25	Firewalling is similar to routing but causes more CPU load.

Once you've determined the total service load your clients will place for all combined functions, find the server hardware you're most likely to use from Table 2.3 and divide your total service load by the load capacity of that server. The result (rounded up of course) will tell you approximately how many servers you will need.

The following table shows the load capacities of various generations of server hardware. Each generation is twice as powerful as the previous generation. Use these figures as guidelines to interpolate the capacity of your hardware. For example, a Pentium-II 300 with 96MB of RAM and a 6GB disk would be directly between the Pentium Pro and the Pentium II listed, so it would have a load capacity of 480.

Table 2.3   Load Capacities of Common Server Hardware

Server Class	Metric	Explanation
386-33/16M/.5G	40	Serves approximately 20 DOS clients
I486-66/32M/1G	80	Handles 40 DOS clients
Pentium-120/64M/2G	160	Handles 40 Windows machines
Pentium Pro-200/128M/4G	320	Handles 80 Windows machines
Pentium II-400/256M/8G	640	Handles 128 NT Boxes
Xeon-400x2/512M/16G	1280	Sufficient for 60 NetPCs

Reality Check: A Server Capacity Example

Determining service capacities using this method can be a little confusing, so let's break for two extended examples.

Standard Network

Let's say you have a client sum of 800, which represents 200 Windows machines. These machines create the following service loads:

- File service: 800
- Print service: 400
- Web service: 80
- E-mail service: 8
- Firewall service: 200
- Total server capacity: 1,488

Reality Check: A Server Capacity Example *(continued)*

Consulting table 2.3, we find that we can break our problem down into a single Xeon file, print, e-mail, and Web server and then install a Pentium Pro firewall. This is probably not wise, however, because our network is probably going to be partitioned into multiple Fast Ethernets. We'll probably want at least two file servers, so two Pentium IIs will be more appropriate.

Windows Terminals

In this case, let's compute how many terminal servers it will take to operate a group of NetPCs. We have 32 NetPCs for a total client load of 64. Multiplying this by the server load factor for terminal service (10) gives us a total server load of 640 to support this function. Looking at our server hardware, we find that a Pentium II-400 class machine should be up to the task of serving this many NetPCs. Does this match reality? Based on my experience with Citrix Winframe (the product upon which NT Server TSE is based), it's stretches a little thin (I'd call 25 a maximum for this hardware), but Microsoft claims in the guidelines set forth in Windows Terminal Server Capacity Planning and Performance Analysis that this should be well within the capacity of Windows NT TSE. Windows Terminals compute loads are extremely sensitive to the type of client software in use. For word processing, Microsoft's numbers might make sense, but browsing the Web would be a burden, even using our more conservative estimate.

When calculating load versus capacity, remember that these numbers are maximum capacity estimates. Erring on the side of excess capacity is preferable to being tied to a slow network. You should try to avoid coming within 25 percent of the maximum values presented here if you want your servers to run smoothly at all times.

Load Capacities of Data-Link Technologies

Data-link technologies use various methods to arbitrate the sharing of media, which makes them difficult to compare. For example, although Token Ring has a faster bit rate than Ethernet, a client must wait for the token before transmitting, which can make Ethernet seem more responsive. Adding clients to a Token Ring will slow the network in a simple deterministic manner, whereas overloading an Ethernet can cause it to suddenly cease operating all together. These differences make comparisons based on simple bit rate meaningless.

I chose to use the worst-case number of clients I felt could be usefully attached to a single shared-media network rather than a comparison of raw throughput. I then applied this same value to the capacities of other types of networks that are not shared media, such as asynchronous transfer mode (ATM), to show how these networks can be aggregated into large internetworks.

When creating internetworks, the capacity number used for a subnetwork becomes its load. For instance, a Fiber Distributed Data Interface (FDDI) ring with a capacity rating of 1,000 can be expected to handle up to 10 Ethernet networks, each with a capacity rating of 100. Network data-link technology capacities are shown in Table 2.4.

Table 2.4   Load Capacities of Network Technologies

Network	Capacity	Explanation
Ethernet	100	Ethernet was used as the basis for comparison, because it is the most common network data-link technology. You can expect to attach 50 DOS clients to a single Ethernet subnetwork before it bogs down.
Token Ring (16Mb)	200	A single Token Ring can support roughly twice as many computers as a single Ethernet subnetwork. Because Token Ring degrades gracefully, you can continue to load a Token Ring past this point, but your network will slow considerably.
Fast Ethernet	500	Although the bit rate for fast Ethernet is ten times the rate of Ethernet, it cannot handle 10 times the traffic because of the delay involved in resolving collisions.
Fiber Distributed Data Interface	1,000	You can reasonably connect 10 Ethernet networks together on a single FDDI ring. This arrangement depends greatly upon where you've chosen to place your servers—centralized servers demand more from the backbone.
Gigabit Ethernet (1Gbps)	10,000	Gigabit Ethernet operates over FiberChannel at 1 gigabit per second. Although gigabit Ethernet retains the Ethernet name, it is full duplex point-to-point and does not have collisions. It is perfect for a backbone technology in campus environments.

Table 2.4   Load Capacities of Network Technologies *(continued)*

Network	Capacity	Explanation
T1/E1	24/32	T1 (1.5Mb, U.S.) and E1 (2Mb, Europe, MX, South America) are telephony trunk standards commonly used for data transport. Frame Relay typically operates over these circuits but is sold in fractions of 56KMb (U.S.) or 64K (Europe). For Frame circuits, consider each fraction useful for one client.
T3/E3	672/512	T3 (45Mb) and E3 (32Mb) are aggregates of T1 and E1 circuits used in the same manner for higher capacity trunks.
ATM-155 OC-3	1,000	ATM is a switched-network technology; it is not shared. For this reason, you can count on being able to use about 80 percent of the bit rate for useable traffic so long as you maintain constant connections between servers.
ATM OC-12	4,000	ATM bandwidth increases linearly with speed. At 622 Mbps, ATM OC-12 is sufficient for the most demanding backbone applications.
ATM OC-48 and (SONET)	16,000	ATM at OC-48 (2.2 Gbps) is typically used for metropolitan area networks. This capacity is appropriate for metropolitan area high-speed links.
ATM OC-192	48,000	ATM at OC-192 (8.8Gbps) is used by the telephone companies for major trunks between metropolitan areas.

When calculating load versus capacity, remember that these numbers are maximum capacity estimates. Erring on the side of excess capacity is preferable to being tied to a slow network. You should try to avoid coming within 25 percent of the maximum values presented here if you want your network to run smoothly.

Physical Plant Design

To properly design the physical plant, you must determine the physical location of network resources and determine which data-link technology you will use. With that information, you'll be able to design both the physical plant and the network connectivity. Use the following procedure to design the physical plant:

1. Map the locations of each network resource.

2. Group the resources into subnetworks as limited by the distance and connectivity limitations of the selected data-link technology.

3. Lay out the premise's wiring that is necessary to link the resource on blueprints.

4. Link the subnetworks together using a high-capacity medium.

It is easiest to map the physical location if you use a copy of the blueprints for your building. You should be able to acquire a set from your architect, landlord, or facilities group. In exceptionally rare cases, you may even be able to get them in an online format that can be imported into your design software. Figure 2.1 shows a blueprint in the first phase of design.

Figure 2.1   Starting a network design

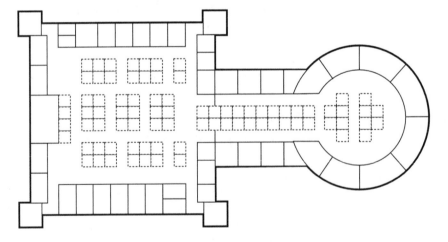

Often you may not know precisely where computers will be located in a new network. In this case, you should plan network drops as if they were power or telephone outlets—simply install at least two network drops per office (a similar frequency to telephone jacks) and more for larger rooms. EIA/TIA guidelines for the length of installed cabling are 80 meters maximum; leave 10 meters on each end for jumpers from the wall or patch panel to the computer or hub.

Open bay cubicles can present a special challenge because there's no industrially accepted method for wiring through them to individual computers and because office furniture will probably not be installed when you design the network. Myriad options exist to solve this problem, from cubicle-mounted patch panels to pre-wired office furniture. None work well in my opinion, and they're all considerably more expensive than they are worth.

The easiest way in my experience to design for open-bay cubicles is to mount high-density, surface mount patch panels or wall boxes in the fixed locations closest to the cubicles. These locations could be in columns or in walls adjacent to a cubicle group. Sometimes no fixed wall is available and hollow power poles must be used to bring the networking cables down from the ceiling. In this case, specify surface mount wall boxes on the power poles. When the furniture is installed, you can then use long (20 meters) jumpers that are run through the wire ways of the cubicle furniture to connect individual computers to these high-density patch panels. When you install runs to open bay cubicles, your installed wiring should run no longer than 60 meters to allow for extra long connection jumpers through the cubicles.

Map the location of NetWare clients by marking a symbol on your blueprints that specifies the client load value as shown in Figure 2.2.

Figure 2.2   Mapping the location of network clients

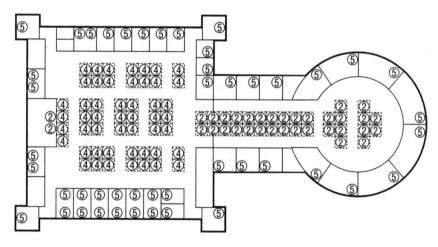

Grouping the individual units is an optimization problem for which there is no single solution. Different integrators will often select different routes and accumulations of computers based on their slightly different requirements and preferences. You should keep the following requirements in mind when grouping clients:

- Each client must be within the data-link distance limit of the closet (80 meters for Ethernet)

- Group clients by natural physical boundaries like buildings, areas, and rooms. No grouping should cross large open areas like atriums or halls.

- Try to group clients according to the number of ports on the hubs you'll be using.

Figure 2.3 shows clients grouped into both closets and Ethernet collision domains.

Lay out the premises wiring as mandated by the location of units and the link technology that has been selected. This step is fairly obvious once you've grouped computers together, but selecting where to put the wiring centers (called closets or distribution frames) isn't always obvious. In existing buildings, you may have to make trade-offs like sharing space with a mop or using cabinets installed in otherwise occupied rooms. Figure 2.4 shows an example of laying out premises wiring.

Figure 2.3   Grouping clients by closet and collision domains

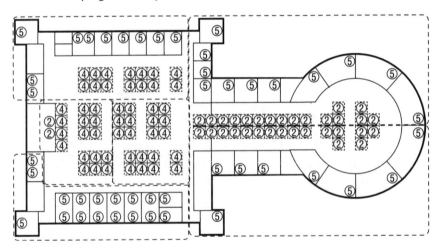

Figure 2.4   Laying out premises wiring

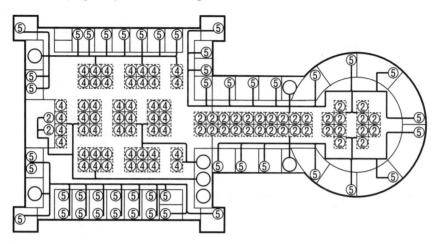

Link the subnetworks together using optical fiber—a medium capable of handling the combined traffic of the subnetworks. You can always select a backbone technology later, because all campus area backbone technologies operate over fiber. There are two types of optical fiber in use today: lower grade multi-mode fiber, which was originally used for local area networking, and higher grade single-mode fiber, which was designed for long distance telephony and costs about twice as much as multi-mode. Both types of fiber work well for the majority of campus area networking needs, but single-mode is more appropriate for backbone runs. Figure 2.5 shows an example of connecting closets.

Figure 2.5   Connecting closets

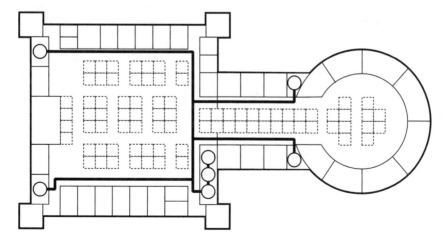

You will often have to connect buildings together in your network, which often presents unusual challenges. If you happen to own the path between the two buildings, you can simply trench, install conduit, and pull the fiber through. Often it won't be that simple—you may be leasing the office space and have no ability to modify public areas. Or you may have a public street to cross. For these situations, you should consider wireless transports. A number of wireless options exist, but for backbone connections you won't want to use anything slower than 10Mbps Ethernet or perhaps 4-channel T1 microwave radios. In some circumstances, laser or infrared LED transceivers will work, but these options are easily obscured by smoke, fog, or rain and have serious line-of-sight constraints.

Data-Link and Protocol Design

Data-link and protocol design is easy if it's handled in the proper order. Once you have the premise's wiring laid out and your closets designed, it's obvious where you will need to place hubs. To determine exactly how many hubs you'll need, you can simply count the number of clients you have in each closet and divide by the number of ports on the hubs that you'll be using.

One of the following methods you'll use to connect closets together depends somewhat on the level of efficiency you want to achieve, your budget, your ultimate design goals, and your level of expertise.

Use Switches to Connect Closets Together   This option is quite easily implemented and can be ideal for situations where clients will access a broad number of servers frequently. Figure 2.6 shows a network that uses a central switch to manage network access. This configuration is frequently called a *collapsed backbone* because the high traffic connection occurs on the back-plane circuit board of a single device. Remember that if you use this option, all data traffic in your network will go through this single bottleneck, which means you will have to have a very high-speed switch. Larger organizations cannot use collapsed backbones for this reason.

Use Routers to Connect All Closets Together   This option is harder to implement, but is ideal when it client access patterns are unknown or when link redundancy is a requirement. This option is ideal in a number of circumstances and scales reasonably well to large organizations. The fact that the Internet is based on this model shows that it functions on a large scale. Figure 2.7 shows a routed network.

Figure 2.6   A switched network

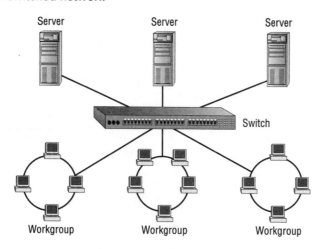

Use Servers as Routers   This option is very inexpensive and can be ideal for situations when most users will access only their primary server. For situations where users frequently access multiple servers, this configuration causes significant load on the server and is slower than dedicated switching or routing options. This solution can scale indefinitely, because if it is used properly, most traffic will stop at the server. Figure 2.8 shows a network where servers are used as routers.

Figure 2.7   A routed network

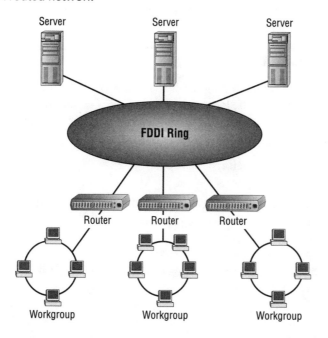

Figure 2.8   Distributed servers

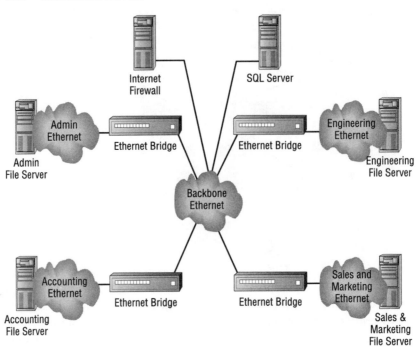

If you can't tell which method is right for your situation, go with routers. They work reasonably well in all cases and can be reconfigured to work well in growth environments.

Service Design

Service design refers to the provision of network services such as file service, e-mail service, or database service. The location of these servers defines the routes that data traffic will have to take on your network, so plan carefully to prevent network bottlenecks.

You need to determine where you will locate your servers once you've grouped your clients into subnetworks but before you've determined how you will link those subnetworks together. There are two options:

- Centralizing all servers on the backbone
- Distributing servers to subnetworks

Many large organizations place all their servers in a central location and then build massive network infrastructures to route client data to and from these servers. This model has the advantage of centralizing the administration problems for servers to a single location. It makes it easy for functions such as archiving to take place and provides a single point of physical security. When these advantages are more important than cost, you should use this model. Keep in mind that it can become very difficult to keep the network operating at full speed using this model. Because all client traffic must be routed in and out of one location, your network can become bogged down. Figure 2.9 shows centralized servers in a switched network.

Distributing servers refers to placing servers on the subnetworks or networks in which they are primarily used. This means that most clients will have a direct non-routed connection to their primary server. Distributing servers creates administrative problems. Archiving is problematic if you have tape drives in every server, and it usually means you'll have to travel to different servers to perform routine administration. If you use distributed servers, plan on centralized archiving the hardware and software and incurring additional costs for network management. You'll want to use SNMP management, and you'll probably want some sort of remote management software installed on servers so you can manage them from a central location.

With this model, you can use your servers as routers by connecting them to both their local networks and the backbone with two network interface cards. This puts additional load on the server, but it eliminates the cost of a router.

Figure 2.9   Centralized servers

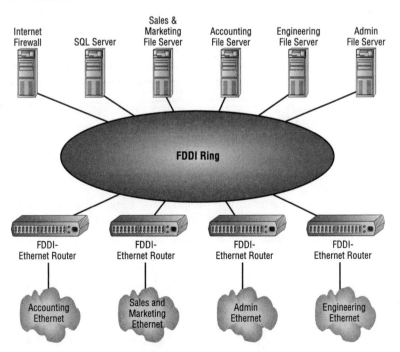

This model is far more scalable than the centralized server model. Whenever you add new clients, you add a server with them. The only client traffic that gets routed to the backbone is connectivity to enterprise servers such as e-mail and database machines or Internet traffic. By eliminating typical file, print, and authentication traffic from the backbone, you'll find that you won't have nearly as much to worry about when you increase the size of your network. Therefore, you should prefer this method when cost outweighs administrative convenience and physical security.

TIP   Choose centralized servers if you have a large budget and administrative convenience is more important that cost. Choose distributed servers if you are on a budget or if labor is more available than capital.

Implementation

By this point, you should know exactly what equipment you'll need to build your network, and you should have made layout for premises wiring. To complete your network, you need to contract for the installation of premise's wiring, purchase your equipment, and, if necessary, hire integrators to put it together.

When you hire cabling contractors, be certain to put the bid out to at least three companies of various sizes. Cabling costs vary widely. Make absolutely certain that the cabling company will provide test results for every individual station location. Insist on TDR (time-domain reflectometer) cable scans that shows the length and whether or not the cable's electrical performance is within its expected rating for each drop. Do not accept simple wiring continuity checks or "toning" as an adequate test. Bad wiring is frustrating for integrators, because it's difficult to tell from other types of hardware failure.

When you select network hardware, don't worry about getting name brands. As long as the hardware is solid state and actually works when you get it, it's not likely to fail. Name brands like 3Com, Bay Networks, and Cabletron are far more expensive than second tier brands like Linksys, Allied Telesyn, and Bay's NetGear brand for lower-cost equipment.

When you select servers, however, you should avoid generic machinery and go with pre-installed software on hardware from national distributors. Generic computers can be plagued with minor compatibility problems. Servers from major vendors are designed to run Windows NT and are certified by Microsoft.

When you purchase equipment, check prices from Internet-based distributors like shopper.com or buy.com. These distributors are often far less expensive for the same equipment than national distributors like Anixter, Ingram Micro, and GBC/Vitek—and they'll sell to anyone with a credit card, not just to account holders who guarantee yearly minimum purchases.

When you hire network integrators, always negotiate a firm, fixed price for the equipment setup and server installation. Never hire anyone on an hourly basis—hourly maintenance puts the wrong motivation behind contracted service.

If you'll need routine maintenance on a regular basis, find a network integrator that will set up a fixed "per incident" charge or a monthly retainer rather than charging by the hour. Less competent integrators always take longer to fix problems—there's no point in rewarding them by paying them more.

Redesigning a Massive Network

A large metropolitan hospital requires an upgrade to an existing network. In this case, a contractor won a bid to install a network that subsequently did not perform as planned. The contractor then preµsented a proposal for additional contracting to implement the network correctly; the hospital rejected it.

Budget Constraint

$100 per user, 4,000 users ($400,000).

Existing Conditions

The entire hospital has a single 10-megabit Ethernet network with 4,000 client computers attached. Obviously, the network is extremely slow, taking hours for clients to login.

This network has the unusual requirement that every client is able to access every server directly because patient records are stored across all the servers. Since there are no preferred servers for subnetworks of clients, distributing servers would provide no significant reduction in traffic on the backbone.

The network is divided into 25 distribution frames so that all connect to a single computer room where 50 Windows NT Servers are located. Each distribution frame handles between 100 and 200 clients, averaging at about 160 clients. Thirty-two Port Ethernet hubs are used for all client connectivity. Hubs in each distribution frame are directly cascaded together to form a single subnetwork and then bridged to the backbone link that runs to the computer room. All installed cabling between clients and distribution

frames is category five, unshielded twisted pair. All cabling between distribution frames and the computer room is four pair multi-mode optical fiber.

All 4,000 clients run MS-DOS and a proprietary healthcare application. They are attached to the network and have all requisite software installed.

Goals

Implement an architecture that can satisfy the traffic demands of this network.

Plan

Split the network into multiple networks, and then connect networks together with a high-speed backbone.

To accomplish this goal, the following must be done:

- Implement a high-speed transport between the distribution frames and the computer room.

- Upgrade the connection speed between the servers and the backbone. Ideally, this will be the same technology as the distribution frame links.

- Split distribution frames into multiple subnetworks. One subnetwork per 32 port hub is ideal.

Perhaps the best way to accomplish this goal is to use Fast Ethernet over fiber as the data link from the distribution frames to a Fast Ethernet switch in the computer room, and to use Fast Ethernet over twisted pair to connect the servers to the same switch.

The following table breaks down the cost to implement the solution

Qt	Component	Cost	Sum	Use
25	8 Port Ethernet to 1 Fast Ethernet Switch	$6,500	$162,500	Connects individual hubs in distribution frames to switch in computer room
50	Fast Ethernet Network Adapters	$200	$10,000	Installed in servers to connect to switch
1	Enterprise fast Ethernet Switch (8GB backplane)	$25,000	$25,000	Hosts individual switch modules
7	4-Port Fiber switch module	$5,000	$35,000	Connects distribution frames to switch chassis
9	6-Port UTP switch module	$3,000	$27,000	Connects servers to switch chassis
	Total Cost		$259,500	

As you can see, this solution comes in well below the budgeted $400,000 dollars and provides a slick resolution to the traffic problem. The high cost of the fast Ethernet switching hardware is offset by the number of computers supported.

24seven CASE STUDY

3

Installing Windows NT
(the Right Way)

The Windows NT installation process has two faces—on some hardware platforms it's a painless 10-minute process, while on others installation simply is not possible without third-party software to assist. Windows NT is an excellent operating system, but I will be pointing out a number of serious problems with its boot loader and installation processes in this chapter. I have wasted at least 100 hours on problems that are easy to solve in other operating systems, because Microsoft ignores how important the boot and installation processes are to the people who have to deal with NT on regular basis.

The difference between an easy and a difficult installation is standard hardware—especially the hard disk controller. Any ATAPI/IDE compatible hard disk will install easily, as will any SCSI controller supported by drivers already on the Windows NT installation CD. SCSI controllers that are not supported on the CD-ROM present special problems, and many RAID devices are either obnoxiously difficult or impossible to get working correctly using NT's installation software.

There are other problems. Microsoft chose to use a 16-bit installation program that uses the BIOS for disk access, which would be okay except that it's limited to working with just 1024 hard disk cylinders. That means you can only install Windows NT in a partition of 4GB or less, no matter how big your disk is, and that you'll have to have at least two partitions on larger disks (but, later in this chapter, I'll explain a workaround for you single-partition purists). This wouldn't be an issue if the NT installation CD-ROM booted Windows NT, and if NT could load and start drives after the completion of the boot process.

NT's ridiculous boot loader causes another major problem. With SCSI controllers that have a BIOS, the boot loader sometimes chooses to create the boot.ini file using the SCSI ARC path and other times the MULTI path—and sometimes it changes its mind between the installation and the first boot, leaving you with an unbootable installation and a headache trying to figure out how to work around the problem.

Fortunately, you bought this book, which shows you how to make short work of any NT installation and even how to get past NT's egregious shortcomings. If you haven't run into problems with NT's installation process, you haven't installed it on any esoteric hardware.

TIP Use IDE/ATAPI/UltraDMA hard disks for a trouble-free NT installation. Keep one handy for your tough installations, too.

The Installation Process

This section describes a standard installation on generic hardware to provide a foundation for the rest of the chapter. I'm not going to describe the installation process in excruciating detail—on standard hardware it's a fairly straightforward process. Feel free to grab a computer and follow along—preferably a computer you don't need for anything else.

A generic computer for the purposes of this discussion is any platform with a hard disk driver and Ethernet adapter supported by drivers that come on the Windows NT CD-ROM. Generally this means an Intel-based PC with an IDE hard disk, but many common SCSI controllers and a few other base platforms also fit the definition.

Installation Source Options

You can choose to begin a normal installation from one of the following sources:

- Boot floppy disks
- A boot CD-ROM
- A running installation of MS-DOS or Windows
- A running installation of Windows NT

These four methods are broken down into two types: Booting the installation program or running the WINNT or WINNT32 setup program. Other source options, such as installing from the hard disk drive or from over a network, are just special cases of the last two options.

When you run the WINNT or WINNT32 programs to install NT, the WINNT program simply installs the NT Boot loader and the setup program, copies the NT source files on your hard disk, and then reboots. When your computer reboots, it's running the setup program as if it had booted the CD-ROM. So in fact all standard installations of Windows NT run through the normal setup program no matter what the source media is.

Sage Advice: Easy Standard Installs

Here's the easiest way to perform nearly any standard installation:

1. Partition and format your disk using an MS-DOS boot floppy.

2. Copy the contents of the \I386 directory onto the local hard disk.

3. Use the following command to install NT: `C:\i386\WINNT /B`.

The advantage of this method, besides speed, is that you'll never have to forage around for your NT CD-ROM when you change networking options later because the installation files are located on the hard disk and the Registry is aware of their location.

Starting an Installation

This example installation will be easy. Booting from CD-ROM, we will install Windows NT Server on generic new hardware. The only difference between an upgrade from another operating system and a new installation is that you should back up the computer before you install NT. Although it's possible to install NT over other versions of Windows on a FAT partition, you should always plan for disaster by backing up first.

Sage Advice: Fast Backups for Migration

Backing up to FAT-formatted removable media like Jaz or SyJet cartridges is usually the fastest and easiest way when you want to migrate a significant number of files from a previous operating system. You can also backup a machine over a high-speed network easily. The problem with backing up to tape is that every tape backup program seems to have its own data format—so you likely won't be able to retrieve your data in NT once you've got it installed if you wrote the tape in a different operating system.

Once your machine is prepared, you're ready to begin. By setting the computer's BIOS to boot from the CD-ROM, you can simply insert the NT CD and go—no boot from floppy is required. The CD-ROM boots quickly, and you're ready to begin by inserting the CD-ROM and powering up the computer. If your BIOS or CD-ROM is not capable of booting, you'll have to boot from floppy disks.

NT's initial setup load phase is a 16-bit process that was created just to support loading NT. During this phase, drivers for generic devices and hard disk controllers are loaded. This phase is necessary for its compatibility—Windows NT cannot start until the appropriate HAL and disk drivers are loaded, which must of course be specified somehow. The setup program also is capable of probing hardware resources to determine what hardware is installed.

Press F2 during the initial setup load to specify a different HAL for your computer if a special one is required before NT switches to 32-bit mode. Your hardware vendor will have supplied a floppy containing these files if they are necessary.

Once the screen switches to the 50-line character mode Windows NT banner, the Kernel has been started and the setup program is ready to begin.

Hard Disk Drivers

If you have a SCSI, RAID, or an unusual IDE hard disk controller, you're in for a somewhat more harrowing installation experience. The device driver for your hard disk controller must already be in memory when the NT installation program starts for the Windows setup program to install to it. Although you can specify additional hard disk controllers during the normal installation process, you cannot install to a drive managed by any loader that isn't loaded prior to starting the NT Kernel.

There's an undocumented method to load disk drivers before the setup program starts. Press F6 during the initial NT load to specify an alternate hard disk driver for the installation. This method is an imperative for many RAID hard disk controllers. If you get an error stating that NT cannot find any drives to install to, you need to use this method of loading the disk driver. The disk containing these drivers should have been provided with the hard disk controller.

Some hard disk controllers can appear to be different controllers to NT when it loads during the setup program, because they return the same signature codes when NT probes the device using a driver included on the NT CD-ROM or boot floppies. This means that NT will load the wrong device driver and subsequently will not be able to access the controller or any drives attached to it. Specifying the driver as mentioned will not solve this problem because NT doesn't look for specified drivers until it has already tried the built-in drivers. You'll have to make a set of boot floppies for NT, erase the file that's loaded erroneously, copy the correct driver to those boot floppies, and then start the installation by booting from that set of floppies to get around this specific problem.

> **NOTE** The term "built-in driver" simply refers to a driver that ships on the Windows NT Installation CD-ROM and is available when the setup program probes for hardware. There is no other technical difference between a driver that comes with NT and one provided on a floppy disk or CD-ROM.

Windows NT's setup program is only capable of loading device drivers from the primary floppy drive. This means that if you use a device other than a floppy as your A: drive (for example an ATAPI removable media drive such as an LS-120 SuperDisk), your BIOS must be capable of handling it as a floppy disk drive or you won't be able to load drivers during the setup phase. The only workaround to this problem, if your BIOS cannot emulate a floppy with the device, is to install an actual floppy drive.

Sage Advice: Installing to Any Hard Disk

If after attempting to use the F6 method to introduce a device driver to the setup program, you still cannot successfully use your disk controller under NT, use the following method to install NT:

1. Install a standard IDE hard disk drive on the motherboard controller, and install NT to that controller.

2. Once NT is up and running, install the disk controller driver for your special hardware using the SCSI applet in Control Panel and reboot.

3. Edit the boot.ini file to add entries that will allow you to boot from the other partition.

4. Copy the hard disk driver for your hard disk controller to the system partition on the IDE disk and rename it ntboodd.sys.

5. Format a floppy from within Windows NT.

6. Copy the following files from the root directory of the system partition to the formatted floppy disk: ntldr, ntdetect.com, boot.ini, and ntbootdd.sys.

7. Use the Disk Administrator to mirror the system partition that is located on the IDE disk onto the disks attached to the special controller.

Sage Advice: Installing to Any Hard Disk *(continued)*

8. Once the mirror partition has completed, shut the computer down and remove the original IDE disk.

9. Reboot and select the boot.ini option that will load NT from the special hardware.

10. If the computer cannot find the operating system when you attempt to reboot, insert the floppy you created and boot from that. When NT is up and running, use Disk Administrator to mark the system partition active.

Partition Decisions

Eventually you'll have to decide how large you want your boot partition to be. I suggest making it as large as the installation program will allow. Nearly every application you install will put DLLs in the system directory, and many programs simply require being installed on the C: drive. Both of these problems require a large boot partition.

Unfortunately, the setup program is only capable of formatting partitions of up to 4GB because it is limited to seeing 1,024 cylinders, similar to the FAT file system in MS-DOS.

Sage Advice: Creating Large System Partitions

Contrary to Microsoft's support documentation, Windows NT can be installed on larger partitions if the partition is formatted before running the Setup program. You can use your large disk as a single partition by using another running copy of Windows NT on a different hard disk (usually in a different computer) to partition and format the drive before installing NT.

Install a hard disk removable carriage system in your administrative PC so you can easily install new hard disks and format them to their full capacity with a single NTFS partition. These carriages install in a typical 5.25-inch drive bay and can handle typical 3.5-inch hard disk drives. Put the carriage on its own IDE bus so you don't have to muck with jumper settings on the drives.

Networking Installation Options

Once the correct hard disk driver is installed, NT will reboot at least once (more if you're converting a hard disk partition to FAT), and then return to a second phase of the start-up program that runs graphically. During this phase, you'll set up networking options for your computer.

It can be problematic to install networking during the initial installation. You may often find your network adapter driver is out of date and won't work with the version of NT that you have. In a new network, the network infrastructure or cabling may not be complete, so computers may not be able to talk on the network. Other services such as DHCP may not yet be available, or you may have a hardware conflict that prevents your network adapter from being detected properly. You may be working from the other end of a wide area network link that is not completely reliable, or you may be rolling out a large number of computers using a disk-to-disk cloning technique that might have different adapters. For a number of reasons, it may not be convenient to install networking during the installation process, but sometimes you must.

If you aren't having problems with your hardware or your network, there's little reason to delay the installation of networking. But if the network fails to start and you don't know why (and you aren't installing a domain controller), you can simply skip the networking installation by clearing the check boxes for both participation options in the Installation Wizard, and then troubleshoot the problem once you've got your server up. With a primary domain controller, you can install all generic network components and the MS-Loopback adapter to achieve similar results.

There are four roles your computer can take on the network, some of which must be determined at installation time:

- Primary Domain Controller
- Backup Domain Controller
- Domain member server
- Stand-alone server

Chapter 7 discusses the effects of these options. What you need to know here is that you must install networking during the installation process if you are working on a domain controller. Domain members, stand-alone servers, and workstations do not require the installation of network services during startup.

Primary Domain Controllers

Primary Domain Controllers (PDC) create the security information used by the entire domain. The networking services are an integral part of those security structures, so networking must be installed during the installation of a PDC. However, the PDC does not actually need to communicate on the network for its own installation, so you can install a PDC by using the MS-Loopback adapter if you have problems with the installed network adapter or driver. Using the MS-Loopback adapter will allow you to get through the installation completely and deal with hardware or driver issues once you have a running NT machine.

Backup Domain Controllers

Backup Domain Controllers (BDC) must communicate with a Primary Domain Controller during the installation process, which means that you have to get them all the way up on a functioning network without any supportive troubleshooting tools. If you are on a new network that isn't 100 percent validated, you may find it easiest to install Backup Domain Controllers on the same Ethernet collision domain (hub) as the Primary Domain Controller, and then place them in their ultimate locations after the installation is complete.

Domain Member Server

Domain member servers are simply servers that participate in a domain. You do not need to install networking during the installation process for these computers. It's often easiest to skip the networking installation portion during the installation, then apply the networking components once you have a running NT machine. You can join the domain at any time after the networking services and drivers are installed.

Stand-Alone Server

Stand-alone servers are servers that are not members of domains. Like domain member servers, these servers do not have to have networking installed during the installation process.

Finalizing the Installation

After network support has been installed, you can specify a video adapter. It's nearly always easier to simply let the computer restart using the default VGA adapter driver and install the video driver once the machine is running. In fact, most modern display controllers must be installed this way.

After installing (or skipping) the video adapter installation, you'll have to set the time zone and then you're finished. The next time you reboot your computer, you'll have a running Windows NT installation.

Using Install to Fix Problems

Problems with a Windows NT server are often caused by a corrupt installation or Registry. What exactly does *corrupt* mean in this case? Quite simply, it means that one or more things—either a component of the operating system or a Registry setting—is either missing or not behaving as expected.

What causes corruption? Well, mucking around deleting files or Registry keys is one obvious cause, but sometimes corruption is caused by more typical and necessary practices:

Patches   Software vendors often feel free to patch an operating system when they need an extra bit of functionality. This patch might work fine with a very specific version of a DLL, but after installing a service pack, it can begin to cause problems. This sort of corruption is especially common with firewall software. Service packs themselves have been known to cause corruption problems.

Installing or Removing Software   Occasionally, an uninstall program can be a little too aggressive in removing Registry keys and files that might be used by other programs.

Incompatible Applications   Applications and drivers often change operating system Registry settings when they're installed, and, on occasion, applications may need to set the same Registry setting to different values or install a DLL with the same name but different functionality in the same location. These applications cannot safely exist on the same computer, but they aren't easy to identify, so you may not know that. Strange problems result.

Poorly Written Programs   Vendors frequently fail to thoroughly test software before it ships. While it probably worked fine on their hardware, there may be compatibility problems with your hardware. Just because the software fails to function and you remove it, it doesn't mean the entries it made in the Registry are gone or that the files it installed in system directories have been removed.

Hardware Failure   Disk controllers and hard disks that are going bad can cause an amazing amount of corruption in a very short time. Writing incorrect data to the disk can cause pernicious problems with an install. You'll usually know about these problems soon after they start happening, but probably not in time to do anything about it.

Old Configuration Information   Changing the hardware on a server requires installing new drivers, but administrators often fail to remove old drivers, services, and software. These obsolete bits of code still try to start and usually fail, but they still soak up time and memory in the effort. In some cases, they can also cause compatibility problems or Kernel crashes (blue screens), too.

Reinstalling Windows NT can solve all these problems. I don't want to sound cavalier here—reinstallation can also introduce problems and is, at the very best, a time consuming process. But there are many problems that simply can't be solved any other way, because files and Registry settings must be restored to their original state or at least a known-working state for the computer to function. Unless you happen to possess a complete and correct diagnosis of the exact problem, you won't know exactly which files or Registry settings are needed or where they should go.

Reinstalling NT is similar to an original installation except that you choose the Repair option rather than the New option during the initial setup. When you select the New option, you'll be presented with a screen that asks which areas of the Registry should be replaced. You opt to replace a hive by selecting the option, which will cause the setup program to replace that section of the Registry with default information. The options and their consequences are:

System   This is the hardware configuration of the computer. Use this option when you have a problem with a device that's preventing normal operation. This is the hive I've most often replaced when troubleshooting malfunctioning computers. Be prepared: You must reinstall all device drivers if you select this hive.

Software   This hive contains the software settings maintained by applications on the computer. Use this option when a malfunctioning application is preventing normal operation of the server. Be prepared: You must reinstall all applications on the computer if you select this hive.

SAM   This hive stores user and security information. Overwriting this hive will eliminate all account and group information on the machine. I've never seen a good reason to overwrite it. Be prepared: You must recreate all user and group accounts and re-establish security on all shares and file system resources if you overwrite this hive.

Replacing a hive should not be done lightly and is usually not necessary—merely restoring the original NT setup files can often fix problems. Always run through a restoration without replacing any hives first to see if the problem goes away. Replace hives only as a last resort.

When an NT installation goes completely south, you may not have a Registry remaining to work with. In this case, the setup program will inform you that it cannot find an existing NT installation. If this happens, you have two options: Either reinstall Windows NT completely, create all new user accounts, and reinstall all applications, or provide a recent copy of the emergency repair disk for this computer. This disk contains backup copies of the Registry hives mentioned above and can be used to make a completely new installation equivalent to a prior installation that is now corrupt.

Sage Advice: Emergency Repair Disks

Save yourself a lot of time by keeping your emergency repair disks up-to-date. Create a new emergency repair disk every time you install a driver, application, or new user or group. If physical security is not a concern, leave the ERD disk in the floppy drive so you'll always have it. But watch out—hackers can glean account names and passwords from the information stored on the ERD, so do not let it fall into the wrong hands.

Installation Alternatives

You have to use the Microsoft installation method to install Windows NT for the first time, but you don't have to use that method for your remaining installations.

For years computer geeks have been using a method called *disk-to-disk sector* copying (also known as disk cloning) to copy the contents of a hard disk from one computer to another when they had to install a number of systems. When you buy a new computer from Dell or Compaq, the software that comes on the computer's hard disk was put there using this method. Disk-to-disk copying is handy for migrating from a smaller to a larger disk as well.

This method is amazingly handy for installing Windows NT. Using the CD-ROM boot installation method on a fast computer, you might install Windows NT in 30 minutes. After getting all your drivers loaded, service packs applied, and applications installed, you'll be another two hours down the road if everything goes well. With direct disk-to-disk copying, all these functions can be performed in 10 minutes for your second machine and those that follow.

But there's a problem: When you copy an installation of Windows NT from one disk to another, you get an exact clone of the first installation. Windows NT relies upon the installation process to create a unique security identifier for each computer. Since you've copied the Windows NT installation from another installation, the computer's SID is not unique. If left uncorrected, this can cause strange security problems in a networked environment. For example, the local administrator on one machine would have the same SID as the local administrator on another and would therefore be able to access resources inappropriately.

Solutions to this problem exist. A number of utilities can apply new unique security identifiers to an existing Windows NT installation. This solves the problem with disk-to-disk copying of Windows NT installations and makes it a viable method for performing rollouts of several machines. It also makes it technically possible to promote any computer to the role of Primary Domain Controller or Backup Domain Controller because those roles are determined by the SID of the machine—but that's a hairy hack fraught with peril and not all that useful. I'll just mention that it's possible and recommend that you stick with the normal method of reinstalling if you actually need to change the role of a machine.

These utilities typically work under extended versions of MS-DOS. After booting to MS-DOS, these utilities sector copy the contents of the hard drive you select either directly to another hard disk, an image file, or a file containing data to reconstruct the source partition, which may or may not be compressed. That image file may be stored on a second hard disk or transmitted over the network if you've got a network available from DOS.

Sage Advice: The Easiest Way to Install Windows NT

The most flexible way I've found to do quick and easy NT installs is to create a generic NT image file using your favorite disk-to-disk copying utility and a boot disk containing MS-DOS, a generic ATAPI CD-ROM driver, your disk-to-disk copying utility, and a SID changing utility. Using Adaptec's EZ-CD Creator and a CD-ROM burner, create a bootable CD-ROM that contains the image file. Then you can simply boot the CD-ROM in a brand new computer and copy the image file from the CD-ROM to the hard disk. Change the SID and you're done. It's fast, flexible, and doesn't require swapping hard disks or a network connection.

You needn't install every operating system component prior to creating your source image—in fact, you're better off installing as few specific drivers as you can get away with because this makes your source image applicable to many different hardware configurations. You can always install specific drivers after an image has been copied to your computer.

Once your image is installed, you must reboot the computer to change the security identifier. During this first boot, you also can install the correct video, sound, and network drivers for the specific platform, as well as any other drivers specific to the machine. Remember to reapply the latest service pack as the last step of your installation.

Methods for Disk-to-Disk Copying

So how do you perform a disk-to-disk copy? There are two ways: Purchase a third-party disk-copying utility or use Windows NT's built-in mirroring to create the copy for you and download a freeware SID-changing utility to apply a new security identifier.

The mirroring method has the advantage of being free, easy, and bulletproof—you aren't going to mess anything up doing it this way. However, it requires opening up your computers to switch hard disk drives each time.

Third-party utilities are fast and flexible. They allow you to connect to an image server, a machine that stores files containing complete hard disk images, and download and install over the network. This method is the easiest and fastest because you don't have to open up machines and swap hard disks around—just boot an MS-DOS floppy with network support and download the image file from an image server. The third-party utilities cost between $30 and $50 for individual use, increasing to about $250 for network-enterprise use.

Windows NT Utility

Microsoft originally didn't support the use of disk-to-disk copying, going so far as to say that it simply wouldn't work because of the SID issue. This, of course, deterred no one, and eventually Microsoft got on the bandwagon and even released their own disk-to-disk copying utility and SID management software.

The Microsoft System Preparation Tool is free for large customers. You have to request a license to use the tool and prove your license levels to get it though, so I recommend going with DriveImage or Ghost for these sorts of roll-outs. Microsoft's site mentions that "many customers were concerned about the safety of using generic disk cloning tools until the Microsoft System Preparation Tool came along." That's not true. They all work the same way, so use any of them—just don't forget to apply a new system security identifier once the machine is up and running.

You can request a copy of the System Preparation Tool at www.microsoft.com/ntworkstation.

DriveImage

DriveImage is my personal favorite. It costs about $30 and does everything it's supposed to do without much hassle. It's from PowerQuest and should be available at your local software store. It's an indispensable part of any NT administrator's toolbox, in my humble opinion. It supports disk-to-disk copying and disk-to-file creation, so that images can be stored on other local disks or the network. DriveImage also supports creating and resizing NTFS partitions during the copy process so you can use the entire disk rather than be limited to a partition of the same size as the source. Check out DriveImage at www.powerquest.com.

Ghost

Ghost is the classic disk-copying software—the company pretty much invented the industry. Their software was and is available for download from the Internet for free. Ghost was recently purchased by Symantec, so the name has changed to Norton Ghost. A demonstration version can be downloaded from the Symantec Web site. Download an evaluation edition at www.symantec.com.

Mirroring

Mirroring two disks is easy, but it cannot be performed over a network or to image files. When you mirror a hard disk, you're using NT's NTFS disk driver to create a sector copy for you. Once the mirror operating is finished, the mirrored drive can be moved to another computer and booted.

NT will not assign an active partition on a disk other than the boot hard disk, so you may need to use an MS-DOS disk with fdisk or another partitioning utility to set the partition on the mirrored drive to boot. You can also create a Windows NT boot floppy to boot the disk initially, and then use Disk Administrator to set the partition active.

Finally, a mirrored partition must be the same size as the original source partition. This is only a minor annoyance.

Sage Advice: Create a Generic Source

Disk-to-disk copying is sometimes maligned because some people believe the destination machine and the source machine must have a somewhat similar hardware configuration to run NT. In fact, that's not the case at all.

- The HAL must be the same. This is not generally a problem because 99 percent of all NT machines use the uniprocessor HAL for standard PCs.

- The video display driver must be the same. This is not a problem because all NT machines can run with the default VGA driver, so you simply shouldn't install a video driver on your source installation.

- The hard disk driver must be supported by the installation. This is easy: Simply install the driver for every hard disk adapter you need to support with your source partition. Whichever driver is correct for a specific machine will start, and the others will fail. You'll get a Device Driver Failed to Start dialog box when NT finishes booting due to these extra controller drivers. You can then use the device's applet in the Control Panel to shut off all the non-functioning disk device drivers that don't match that machine.

Sage Advice: Create a Generic Source *(continued)*

Other issues, like dissimilar LAN adapters, sound cards, or other drivers can be handled in a similar fashion—either don't install them at all or install the complete set and let the ones not actually present fail upon the first boot. You can remove them once the installation is running.

Installing Applications

The second major advantage to using disk-to-disk copying, aside from installation speed, is the fact that you can copy entire installations, including installed applications, policy settings, configuration information, and anything else you want. Basically, the copy proceeds from the point you decide you're finished customizing the source computer. And none of this extra information takes much longer to copy.

You can also remove the excess baggage (such as the Channel bar of Internet Explorer or those start-up tip dialogs) installed by applications, so your users don't have to do it themselves. Make desktop settings and configure the user policy for your network before creating your source image, too.

> **TIP** Install all of your organization's typical applications before you create your master source. Disk-to-disk copying can be used to copy any fully installed set of applications.

Service Packs—Good and Bad

At some point during the installation of applications (especially if you install Microsoft Office), you'll probably have to install a service pack. Service packs are a necessary evil: They fix often-serious problems with Windows NT, but they also cause a serious problem.

Once you install a service pack, you can't go back except by using the service pack uninstaller. Many of the original source files are not compatible with later versions from the service pack. Unfortunately, whenever you change certain components (especially network components), NT requests your original start-up disk and copies old, original files, replacing newer service pack files. This can cause version conflicts that will cause NT to become unstable under very unusual circumstances and may even prevent it from rebooting. Always reapply service packs after any change of hardware configuration on an NT machine.

Sage Advice: Service Packs as a Troubleshooting Tool

Version conflicts with service packs cause strange problems that are difficult to troubleshoot. I've seen problems such as a server service failing to start, the remote-procedure call service failing, and the remote access server causing blue screens—all because of service pack version problems. Whenever you run into an unusual problem on an NT server, reinstall the latest service pack first to see if the problem doesn't just go away.

The Boot Process

Windows NT's first-stage boot loader is always contained in the boot sector of the primary partition on the first hard drive on your computer (no matter where NT is located, which is a silly flaw). When you boot your computer, the master boot record loads the NT boot loader into memory. The NT boot loader reads the contents of the boot.ini file (which must be located in the root directory of the first hard disk) and displays a menu of boot options based on its contents. By default, that file contains a reference to the standard NT installation and a reference that enables some debugging options.

The NT boot loader is capable of loading just two operating systems: Windows NT and everything else. I'm actually not kidding—it knows how to load Windows NT, but for all other operating systems it relies on a special file called bootsect.dos which must contain a valid image of a boot sector for the operating system. When you install Windows NT on a machine that already has an OS, the installation program automatically creates that image before it replaces the boot sector. If you select the original OS in the boot menu, the boot loader chains to that file and expects it to handle loading the foreign OS.

That covers operating systems installed before Windows NT, but how about operating systems installed after Windows NT? Microsoft apparently decided not to support loading other operating systems after NT, so you are left with some choices, none of which are particularly easy. You can hope the next operating system's boot loader supports chaining to Windows NT, use whatever native fdisk utility is available to switch the active partition every time you want to change operating systems, hack NT's boot loader, or install a third-party, multi-boot utility such as System Commander.

If you enjoy hacking, you can use sector-editing tools to "lift" the boot sector for foreign operating systems and create bootsect.dos files so you can select operating systems installed after Windows NT. I've done it to support dual booting a Linux system that was installed after Windows NT.

Problems with Removable Media

Ever had a Mac user laugh at you because she can boot her operating system from a Zip disk or a CD-ROM if she needs to repair her computer? Ever notice how Mac users can simply copy their system folder from hard disk to hard disk to Jaz cartridge, or any other media, and boot it at will from a seemingly endless variety of devices? Well, they can and you can't because Microsoft doesn't care to expend any energy on fixing their lousy boot loader.

Until recently, computer BIOSes have only been programmed to read a boot sector from either a floppy disk or the C: drive. Since 1995 or so, most BIOSes also have been able to boot any ATAPI device, such as CD-ROMs, and removable media cartridges like LS-120 and Zip cartridges. Unfortunately, Microsoft wrote their boot loader to work from just the floppy drive and hard disks, instead of the more compatible method of using the BIOS to load the complete OS into memory.

It is technically possible to low-level copy the contents of your boot and system partitions to removable media and, if your controller BIOS supports it, simulate a hard disk to boot that removable media. Unfortunately, the process is so Byzantine that it's not worth the bother—especially since it'll only work on that one computer or its hardware clones. I don't have a good solution to this problem (other than to point out your operating system's ability to perform preemptive multitasking to your laughing Macintosh friends).

OS Installation Order

The order in which you install operating systems is extremely important if you want them all to coexist peacefully with their multitude of boot loaders. Since I can't go through every operating system on the planet, I'll just stick to those people actually use (and OS/2, since I have a copy).

First, you can't install MS-DOS or Windows on top of NT and still boot NT. You can't install NT to work with an existing Linux installation unless you know how to write your own Linux boot loader. Finally, OS/2s can't be loaded by any other boot loader that I know of. Given these constraints, I've determined that the following installation order actually works:

1. MS-DOS/Windows/95/98
2. Windows NT
3. Linux (using the master boot record method)
4. OS/2

Of course, when you're done, you get this really strange "chain-o-boot-loaders" effect where the OS/2 boot loader lets you select OS/2 or Linux, the Linux boot loader then lets you select Linux or NT, and finally the NT boot loader lets you select NT or MS-DOS/Windows.

Sage Advice: Power Multi-Booting

One easy way around the OS installation order, if you have to have more than one OS, is to buy a copy of System Commander by PowerQuest, the authors of much useful software. Recent versions of System Commander have become bloated with features though, so it requires a FAT partition—annoying if you didn't plan on having one. And I've had it chew up an NTFS partition or two for some reason during installation. Make sure you put System Commander on first and let it detect operating systems as you install them.

The SCSI/MULTI Problem

The last problem with NT's boot loader is the stupid SCSI/MULTI ARC path syntax in the boot.ini file. ARC (which stands for Advanced RISC Computing) paths are supposed to be a universal standard for locating hardware on all computers. The problem is that they are neither universal nor standard. The idea was cooked-up in the early '90s as a way to have the new RISC computers boot any operating system. (Remember when RISC was going to save the world from Intel? Those were the good old days.)

Microsoft supported the idea so that the RISC computers NT ran on could locate their boot hardware using a standard method. (This was in the days when NT ran on a variety of RISC computers.) Because Intel BIOSes didn't support ARC paths, Microsoft wrote the Intel boot loader to support them instead. With the ARC path, the NT Kernel would know where to find the rest of the operating system once it started. The Boot loader just uses the BIOS to find the files. Why the Kernel can't do the same is beyond me.

But Microsoft added a feature. Unlike the RISC machines, which always needed a specific device driver to speak to the hard disk, most Intel machines can use the BIOS embedded in the hard disk controller to talk to the machine in a generic fashion, thus obviating the need for a specific hard disk controller driver in the initial load. To indicate that the BIOS should be used, rather than a specific driver, Microsoft invented the MULTI device, which is like the standard SCSI device except that it doesn't require a specific hard disk driver.

This is all fine and good except for one thing—if you install from an ATAPI CD-ROM onto a hard disk that is attached to a SCSI, RAID, or non-standard IDE controller, the setup program will write the BOOT.INI file for a MULTI device, because that's what it detects you booted (the CD-ROM). When you try to reboot for the first time, your actual hard disk controller (which requires the SCSI syntax and a hard disk driver) won't be found and the computer will display a Stop: Operating System Not Found error message.

The only way to prevent the problem from happening is to install from floppy disks. If it has already happened and you want to salvage the installation, you can install the hard disk in another NT machine, fire it up, and correct the ARC paths. You may also need to copy the disk controller's device driver from C:\winnt\system32\devices to the root partition and rename it ntbootdd.sys.

There's another problem with the ARC naming convention. ARC conventions prevent you from booting removable media. If you sector copy a working NT installation to an LS-120 floppy and change the ARC paths to boot the A: drive, the boot loader will actually bring the entire NT Kernel into memory. But when the Kernel starts, it will fail because without a valid ARC path it can't find the rest of the operating system. And since there's no ARC method to refer to the LS-120 drive, you can't fix the problem using an ARC path name. ARC paths also will fail if you change the drive hardware ID of the disk with Windows NT on it.

TIP   Format a floppy disk and copy the ntldr, ntdetect.com, boot.ini, and ntbootdd.sys files from the root directory of the boot partition to the floppy. You can use this floppy to boot Windows NT if something happens to your master boot record or the boot files of your NT machine.

Planning for NT

PART 1

24seven **CASE STUDY**

Using Disk Cloning In Different Environments

The following two case studies show the different sides of disk-to-disk copying: reproducing several identically configured machines and using a single, generic image to perform a number of vastly different disk-to-disk installations.

A Server Roll-Out

A large corporation needs to install 12 identical NT servers, all configured as terminal servers that are members of an existing domain. I solved the problem as follows:

1. Windows NT Server Terminal Server edition was installed and configured on the first machine. Because all machines are identically configured, the drivers for the hard disk, video adapters, and LAN adapters were installed.

2. The source machine was rebooted to MS-DOS and an image of the system/ boot partition was created using DriveImage on a specially created FAT partition.

3. The source machine was rebooted to NT and configured to serve the image file.

4. An MS-DOS boot floppy was prepared to connect to the network using the smallest available networking protocol, NetBEUI.

5. All 12 machines were connected to a temporary network comprised of a 16-port hub and category 5 UTP jumper cables.

6. The 11 remaining machines were booted to MS-DOS and logged into the source server.

7. DriveImage was used to create a single large system partition, download the Image file, and copy it to the local disk.

8. Each of the 11 remaining machines was rebooted to Windows NT and a unique SID was applied using the utility supplied with DriveImage.

9. The 12 identical terminal servers were disconnected from the temporary network and placed on the production network.

All 12 servers were brought up in the time it normally takes to install just two.

Saving Time with NT Installs

As an active networking consultant, I needed to save time during NT installations for a wide variety of customers and individual machines. Here is how I solved the problem:

1. I created two installations of Windows NT in separate 1GB partitions on an Intel uniprocessor machine with an IDE hard disk drive. One machine was created as a domain controller, and the other was created as a member server.

2. I installed networking using the MS-Loopback adapter. Up-to-date service packs and the NT Option Pack containing Internet Information Server 4 were installed. I copied the contents of the I386 directory onto the partition, along with other useful tools (such as the Service Pack source files).

3. I downloaded numerous hard-disk controller drivers from the Internet sites of their various manufacturers and installed them onto both disk images, thus creating a library of up-to-date disk controller drivers that would be able to operate on the vast majority of servers.

4. Using DriveImage, I copied both installations into compressed image files. With compression, both files came to approximately 300MB.

5. I prepared an MS-DOS boot disk with a generic ATAPI CD-ROM driver installed, and I installed Microsoft Networking using the NetBEUI protocol.

6. Using Adaptec EZ-CD Creator and an HP CD-ROM writer, I created a bootable CD-ROM containing the boot floppy, a copy of Drive Image, a SID management tool, and the image files.

7. To validate the process, I booted the CD and used it to recreate a member server.

The CD has become my preferred method of installing Windows NT as it takes mere minutes to perform. All customers must purchase a copy of NT for licensing purposes, and I provided a licensed copy of DriveImage to the customers for their own use later.

Part 2

Up and Running

Topics Covered:

- Effective Backup and Archive strategies
- Working with RAID
- Effective CD-ROM service
- Third-party fault tolerance solutions
- Network protocols explained
- Routing
- Services of Windows NT
- Windows NT name resolution
- User account management
- Windows NT security mechanisms
- Internet security
- Remote Access Service

4

Storage and Fault Tolerance

There now exists an array of storage options that tout faster or more secure ways to store your data than the traditional single hard disk method, which has been used since the dawn of computing. Some of these options are effective, while others add more complexity than value and wind up causing more problems than they solve.

This chapter will help you filter the wheat from the chaff in today's rather confusing storage market. Choosing the correct storage devices and fault tolerance methods will make your server rock solid, while choosing incorrectly can make your server a maintenance nightmare.

I'll review disk storage technology, basic concepts, and features built into Windows NT before opining on methodologies and explaining the more esoteric fault tolerance options that you'll find in the market. The first quarter of this book may seem a little simplistic for those of you with a hardware background. Persevere—the chapter picks up quite a bit once we've got everyone up to speed.

Sage Advice: Fault Tolerance Axioms

Implementing fault tolerance in your network can either be a breeze or a nightmare. Here are some tips to make it work:

- Keep it simple. Complexity is the enemy of fault tolerance.

- Avoid single points of failure through redundancy.

- Plan for the worst case.

- An ounce of mirrored disks is worth a pound of backup tape.

- Humans are unreliable. Automate everything.

Storage Basics

Many different media are used to store data, but they all fall into just three categories of technology:

Magnetic   Hard disk drives, floppy disk drives, removable cartridge drives of various sizes, including Zip, Jaz, LS-120, SyJet, and SparQ

Optical   Compact disc read-only memory (CD-ROM), CD-Recordable (CD-R), CD-ReWriteable (CD-RW), and digital video disc (DVD)

Semiconductor   Random access memory (RAM), read-only memory (ROM), erasable programmable ROM (EPROM), and Flash-EEPROM, which is now available on PCMCIA cards to simulate small removable cartridge disks

Some esoteric removable cartridge media devices use both optical and magnetic technologies at the same time, but these devices provide no serious advantage, so they have never made much impact in the market.

This chapter doesn't discuss semiconductor devices because they are not used for permanent user-data storage except in the case of flash memory devices, which are so expensive that they don't (yet) constitute a significant development for the server market.

Disks

Hard disk drives are the workhorses of data storage. A hard disk drive (also called a fixed disk drive, a hard drive, or simply, a disk) consists of one or more spinning metal (usually aluminum) discs coated with a ferric metal oxide. The coating can be magnetically aligned in minute areas to either the north or south magnetic polarity to indicate a one or zero value for a bit of data storage. Data is read or written to this coating as the disc passes beneath the head (a magnetic coil transducer) located at the end of a swing-arm that can span the radius of the disc. Modern hard disks have heads on both sides of the disc and usually contain multiple discs. If you've never seen the insides of a hard disk, find an old low-capacity model that you no longer use and take it apart.

Terminology

Disc   Anything round and flat.

Disk   A disc with a magnetic coating that stores data. Hence, CD-ROMs are called "discs" because they are not magnetic (and because they come from the audio market), while hard disk drives, floppy disk drives, and even magneto-optical drives are called disks. It's okay to be confused about this.

Up and Running

PART 2

Low-Level Format

Low-level formatting is the process of applying data to a new, empty hard disk to provide points of reference for the retrieval of information, to "zero-out" any random data existing on the disk, and to test each individual bit of storage so that any anomalous areas on the disk that fail to store data correctly can be marked out of use. All modern hard disk drives are already low-level formatted from the factory, so you shouldn't need to worry about this process. However, some controller manufacturers (like Adaptec) don't always conform to industrial standards for low-level formatting, so they may recommend low-level formatting the disk with their controller. You may also need to perform this function with RAID controllers or other esoteric devices.

Finally, drives tend to accumulate errors as they age (these accumulated errors are called "grown defects"), so a low-level format might sometimes be required to get an older drive working correctly.

Low-level formatting utilities are not provided with any operating system because they're usually specific to a certain controller. The low-level formatting utility should be embedded in the BIOS of the controller or provided on a set of utility floppies with the controller. IDE hard disks should never need to be low-level formatted throughout their useful life.

TIP   Disks are cheap. Rather than reformatting an old disk, consider replacing it. Chances are the disk is relatively small compared to contemporary drives by the time it begins to fail enough to require a low-level format.

Partitions

Partitioning is the process of apportioning a hard disk for use by multiple operating systems. When hard disks first appeared, there was no way to use more than one operating system on them because the operating system installed first would apply its boot sector, tables, and indexes (a *high-level format*) in the same place all the other operating systems would need to install their own. So you had to have a different hard disk for each operating system that you wanted to install.

Microsoft and IBM developed a standard method for partitioning the hard disk drives of IBM PC-compatible hard disks into partitions that could each hold a different high-level format. A new *master boot record* would store a small table of partitions that allows four entries and would contain a small boot loader that could determine which partition was marked active for booting, and then chain to the boot sector for that partition. This way, you could store multiple operating systems on a hard disk and determine which one you wanted to boot by marking that partition active.

Partitioning also became handy when hard disks became larger than certain operating systems could address. MS-DOS could originally handle only 12 bits of sector address information, which meant that only 16MB of hard disk space could be used for a FAT partition. Disks larger than 16MB had to be partitioned and formatted separately to access their full size. Microsoft then created a 16-bit version of the FAT file system that could access up to 2GB of disk space and recently created a new 32-bit version of the FAT file system that accesses up to 4TB of disk space.

Because Windows NT's setup program suffers from a similar limitation as MS-DOS, it can only format partitions up to 4GB in size. However, from Windows NT itself, you can format partitions up to 4TB in size.

Mirrors

Mirrors are exact copies of the data in another partition, generally on another disk. Disk mirroring is considered a fault tolerant strategy, because in the event of a single disk failure, the data can be read and written to the still working mirror partition. Mirroring also can be used to double the read speed of a partition, since data can be read from both disks at the same time. RAID Level 1 describes mirroring. Windows NT Server supports RAID 1 mirroring.

> **TIP**   Because the Windows NT system and boot partitions can be mirrored, you should use this form of fault tolerance to protect your NT system files.

Volumes

Volumes are the directory and index structures applied to one or more partitions during the process of high-level formatting, which allows files to be stored on the disk and referenced by name. Volumes, unlike partitions, can only be read by or written to the specific file system to which they are formatted. Windows NT supports NTFS volumes and FAT volumes, and it used to ship with support for HPFS volumes until version 4. Version 5 (Windows 2000) will support the 32-bit version of the FAT file system included with Windows 95 OSR/2 and Windows 98.

> **TIP** If for some reason you need to support FAT32 under Windows NT 4, you can buy a driver for it from www.ntinternals.com.

Stripe Sets

Stripe sets are volumes that span across multiple disks and are read and written to simultaneously. This makes disk accesses considerably faster if the disk traffic is handled correctly and if all the disks are synchronized correctly (meaning they are all exactly the same size and make).

Stripe sets with parity (RAID 5) can be used as a form of fault tolerance. The parity information, which is equal to the size of one member of the set, is spread across all disks and contains the mathematical sum of information contained in the other stripes. The loss of any disk can be tolerated because its information can be recreated from the information stored on the other disks and in the parity stripe.

RAID level 0 is striping without parity and is supported in software by Windows NT Workstation and Server. RAID 0 reduces fault tolerance, because the loss of any one disk causes the failure of the volume.

RAID level 5 is striping with parity and is supported in software by Windows NT Server. RAID 1 increases fault tolerance over a single disk solution because the failure of any single disk can be tolerated. Mirroring (RAID 1) can be considered a form of striping with parity across only two disks, although mirroring is implemented differently.

> **NOTE** Neither the NT system nor boot partitions (they are usually the same) can reside on a stripe set, because the format of the actual data on a stripe set cannot be read by the computer's BIOS to load it.

Up and Running

PART 2

Volume Sets

Volume sets are volume structures that are conjoined across two or more partitions, which usually means across two or more disks. Volume sets make it easy to "add space" to a full volume, which is especially handy on Windows NT servers when they run out of space.

Because volume sets often involve more than one disk, they make your volume set less fault tolerant—the failure of any one disk in the set will cause the entire volume set to be inaccessible. Frequent backup can help insure that you won't lose data in this event. Figure 4.1 shows the differences between a mirror set, a volume set, and stripe sets.

> **TIP**   The Windows NT Boot partition (the partition containing your system files) cannot be made part of a volume set. This is one argument for isolating the system files into their own partition. If your user shares are located on their own partition, you can use volume sets to add space to the shared volumes whenever you need to.

Removable Media

Removable media is an entire category of storage that can be removed while the computer is operating. This is its most important characteristic. Because it can be removed, the operating system cannot rely on the presence of the data stored on it, so it cannot be write-cached and active system files cannot be stored on it.

Magnetic Tape   Used since the beginning of time to store computer data. Modern versions are simply smaller, faster, and denser applications of the same old technology.

Floppy Drives   Revolving tapes that use the same magnetic powder-coated mylar, but the media revolves around a central axis so rewinding is never necessary. Data from any portion of the surface of the disk is available every time the disk makes a single revolution. Because floppies added the element of quick access to any portion of the stored data, they quickly became very popular in the workstation market.

CD-ROM   Born of audio compact disc technology and adapted to store any type of digital information instead of just digital audio.

Removable Cartridge Hard Disks   Developed during the mid-eighties, removable cartridge hard disks applied high-capacity hard disk platter technology to the removable market. They operate much like floppy disk drives, but with much greater capacity.

Modern variations of removable media are based on these four basic technologies.

Figure 4.1   Mirror sets, volume sets, and stripe sets

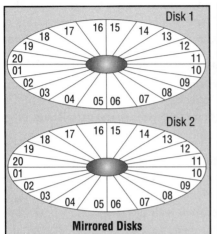

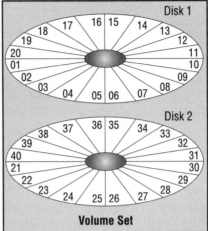

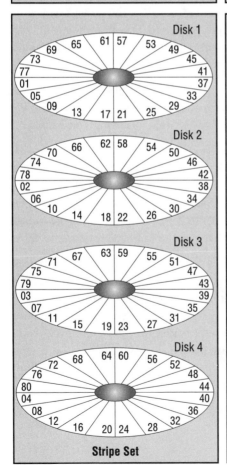

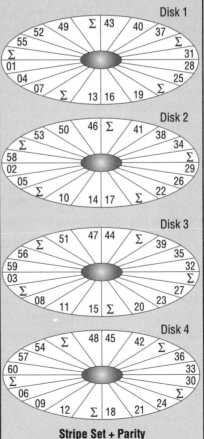

Tape

The original form of removable media was mylar tape, similar to audio tape. (Earlier technologies, such as paper punch cards, were used to load data into memory, not as online storage.) These tapes were booted and used to store the data for mainframe systems.

Tape suffered from the problem of sequential linear access—the tape had to be forwarded and rewound to find specific data. To make data easier to find, timing marks (called a format) were applied to the tape at specific intervals, which the read head could find while spooling the tape at high speed. The advantage to tape is that length is not important, so more storage can be had by using longer tapes.

Tape was difficult to handle because it frequently looped off the reels that held it, and it had to be threaded through the tape-reading machines every time it was mounted on the tape reader. To solve these problems, tape cartridges were created that are roughly similar to audiocassettes. Each cartridge contained two reels and a specific length of tape, and could be easily mounted and removed from the tape reader. The most popular form of early tape cartridge was the quarter-inch cartridge (QIC), the direct predecessor of the modern mini-QIC and Travan backup tapes. QIC and Travan tapes are (currently) capable of handling up to 10MB of data with compression, enough for small servers or workstations.

Digital Audiotape (DAT) is a high-capacity format for digital audio that was adapted for computer use. The significant increase in capacity afforded by the more modern DAT helical recording method made it a natural fit for data archiving and backup.

Finally, Digital Linear Tape (DLT) was developed by Digital as a high-capacity medium for backing up their VAX minicomputer. DLT is similar to DAT but uses a thicker tape for higher capacity. DLT also comes in longer lengths than can be stored in a small DAT cartridge, so it is suitable for even the largest of servers. Quantum now owns the DLT specification, and they are currently releasing SuperDLT that has uncompressed capacities up to 500GB per cartridge. With compression, that's about 1TB—plenty for any server.

Tape auto-changers are devices that use some mechanical method to change tapes among a library of installed cartridges. When one tape is filled to capacity, the next tape in the changer is installed, and the archive operation proceeds. With auto-changers, literally any amount of data can be archived. They suffer from the problem that the archive operation takes as long as there are cartridges to be used because the operation is sequential and the mechanical devices used to change tapes are (as are all moving devices) subject to failure. Auto-changers frequently can take more time to perform an archive than time allows because of the volume of information involved and their sequential nature.

Redundant Arrays of Independent Tapes (RAIT) is the latest development in archiving technology. This technology, also called TapeRAID, is a fairly simple adaptation of disk RAID technology. RAIT uses as many tape devices in parallel as your backup problem requires. RAIT is usually cheaper and always faster than tape auto-changers because auto-changers are low-volume devices that are always expensive, and individual tape units are relatively inexpensive. They are faster because the archival operation is parallel. It takes only the time that a single tape archive takes, no matter how many devices are involved.

Various drivers are used to read or write from tape depending upon the device involved. No file system driver is provided by Microsoft, so you can't access individual files on a tape without using a backup program. The tape device's Control Panel is used to install tape devices, and Microsoft provides `ntbackup.exe`, a tape backup program, for simple archiving.

Up and Running

PART 2

Sage Advice: Tape Technology

DAT is the most convenient and reliable form of tape storage that I've found. The cassettes are more protected than QIC/Travan cassettes, and they are considerably more available than DLT—they can often be found on the shelf at larger computer stores. DAT devices cost more than Travan devices, but the media is cheaper per megabyte.

Select RAIT (or multiple tape devices) over auto-changers whenever possible. Tape auto-changers cost far more than they are worth, depreciate rapidly, and tend to break more often.

Floppy Drives

Mylar tape provided the technology to make mylar discs—floppy disks. Floppy disks were a superior format for online storage because data can be accessed quickly at any point on the medium. They became the preferred form of storage in early computers and provided the original medium for software distribution before the CD-ROM. As such, every computer built contains a floppy disk drive (with the notable recent exception of the iMac—the harbinger of a trend, I think).

Three sizes of floppy disk exist: the completely obsolete 8" size used in older mainframes and workstations, the all-but-completely-obsolete 5.25" format used in the original PC, and the staring-obsolescence-in-the-face 3.5" format that debuted on the Macintosh and then became the standard for PCs. These media ranged in capacity from 360K to 1.44MB (a 2.88MB standard exists, but nobody uses it) and are useful for moving files from computer to computer. All computers are still capable of booting from floppy disk, and for many PCs, they are the only removable media that can be booted.

Two new types of floppy disks exist called LS-120 (120MB, Imation) and SuperFloppy (200MB, Sony), which use laser servos (the LS in LS-120) to precisely align a standard magnetic read head. Although these devices can read and write normal floppy disks, they interface through the hard disk bus like a removable media cartridge technology.

Sage Advice: Don't Rely on Floppy Disks

Floppy disks are the least reliable storage medium. Their reliable life is only about two years, and because they usually move from place to place in shirt pockets through various electromagnetic fields, the data on them tends toward a random state. Don't rely on floppy disks to store any important data.

If you have data you must get off a floppy that your disk drive can't read, try reading it in an LS-120 drive. LS-120 drives are more sensitive than regular floppy disks and can read data from a disk long after the magnetic image is too faint for a standard drive to read.

Floppy disks cannot be formatted with the NTFS file system without installing third-party software. Microsoft decided that it would not support the NTFS file system on floppies because NTFS has a relatively high overhead. But with compression, the media could actually store more than a FAT-formatted floppy.

CD-ROM

CD-ROM is the most important form of removable media. Nearly all software is distributed on CD-ROM, and the entire software industry is based on it as a distribution medium.

A single CD-ROM holds 650MB of data in the ISO9660 industry-standard CD-ROM format. The CDFS device driver is responsible for reading data from CD-ROMs.

Recordable and rewritable CD-ROM is a recent and very interesting development in removable media. Recordable (CD-R) devices and media allow you to master your own CD-ROMs to distribute software. The low cost of the media (about $1 per disc in bulk) makes it practical to use the medium for permanent archiving. Rewritable (CD-RW) devices and media can be erased and reused, but the media is considerably more expensive

($30 per plate) and cannot be read in normal CD-ROM readers, so its primary use is periodic backup.

Digital video disc (also called digital versatile disc by people who can't leave well enough alone) is the next generation of CD-ROM. DVD-ROM increases the format of the medium to a maximum of 17GB per platter through a combination of double-density recording and using both sides of the plate. DVD-ROM can change the focal point of the reading laser to access both an interior and an exterior data track. DVD-ROM is the medium of choice for the digital distribution of movies, and it's obvious practicality for software distribution will be utilized, when DVD-ROM readers are ubiquitous, for applications or data that are too large for distribution on a single CD-ROM.

> **NOTE** DVD-RAM cartridge technology is currently available. True DVD-R is not available, and may never be if movie and music production companies get their way, because they don't want people to be able to copy DVD movies. These groups killed the application of digital tape to audio music in order to prevent music piracy. Resist efforts by these evil empires to make laws that restrict the availability of these truly useful data technologies.

Hard Disk Cartridges

Hard disk cartridges are fixed disk drives with removable platters. Because the platter cannot be as precisely aligned in a removable cartridge as a fixed hard disk, the data tracks must be wider and, therefore, less capacious as a fixed disk.

No clear standard has emerged in hard disk cartridges, and many proprietary formats have arisen. Various sizes, even from the same manufacturer, are usually not interchangeable. Currently available popular technologies include:

Zip 100MB per cartridge, recently a 250MB version was released. Zip disks are actually a mylar film floppy disk that uses a laser servo to precisely align the read/write head. Zip drives are, by far, the most popular form of removable cartridge disk.

LS-120 120MB per cartridge. These devices can read and write standard floppy disks. Like Zip disks, LS-120 disks are a mylar film floppy disk that uses a laser servo for head alignment. Contrary to popular opinion, they are not magneto-optical or related to the now obsolete 20MB floptical technology. LS-120 drives can be used instead of floppy drives and are supported by the ls120 driver in Windows NT. Sony has an incompatible 200MB version called the SuperFloppy.

Up and Running

PART 2

Jaz   Originally a 1GB format, a 2GB version now exists. Jaz is made by Iomega, the manufacturer of the Zip drive and the sole major survivor of the volatile removable media market.

SyJet   A 1.5GB format that is both smaller and quieter than Jaz.

SparQ   A 1GB format related to (but incompatible with) SyJet drives. The manufacturer (SyQuest) has recently gone bankrupt, so this medium will probably disappear.

Orb   A 2GB format that is new to the market by Castlewood. Orb disks use a proprietary magneto-resistive technology to achieve high data density and reliability.

Effective Storage Management

Now that we've exhaustively covered the existing market of technology and devices, let's talk about what works and what doesn't in storage management.

The primary rule of storage management is to stay in the mass market—don't get esoteric. Unusual solutions are harder to maintain, are more likely to have buggy drivers, and are usually more complex than they are worth.

Every hard disk will eventually fail. This bears repeating: Every hard disk will eventually fail. They run constantly in servers at high speed, and they generate the very heat that destroys their spindle lubricant. These two conditions combine to ensure that hard disks wear out through normal use within about 10 years. Early in the computer industry, the mean time before failure (MTBF) of a hard disk drive was an important selling point.

The real problem with disk failure is that hard disks are the only component in a computer that can't be swapped out because they are individually customized with your data. To tolerate the failure of your data, you must have a copy of it elsewhere. That elsewhere can be another hard disk in the same computer or in another computer, on tape, or on removable media.

Some options don't work well—any medium that's smaller than the source medium will require more effort than it's worth to swap media. Usually this means you must either use another hard disk of equivalent or greater size or tape, which can be quite capacious.

Archiving and Backup

Archiving and backup are not the same thing. Archiving refers to the permanent storage of information for future reference, whereas backup refers to the storage of information for the sole purpose of restoration in the event of a failure. The effective difference is that you can reuse backup tapes but not archive tapes.

Backup and archiving are most effectively approached separately—solutions that do both will do neither well. For example, image backup software is better for backups and restoration in an emergency than file-based backup software, which is better for archiving permanently on cheap tape or CD-R media. There is no reason to choose one or the other when you can have both.

The scope of failures that cause data loss falls into four categories:

Disk Failure   Happens when a single drive fails in a computer. Mirroring and parity striping effectively handle this problem.

Machine Failure   Happens when all the storage on a single machine fails for an environmental reason. Tape backup with rotation or server replication effectively handles this problem.

Site Failure   Happens when a meteorite the size of a refrigerator slams into your headquarters at night and destroys all the data at a single site. Fire, flooding, and theft can cause this sort of problem as well. Offsite media storage or network-based remote backup effectively handles this problem.

User Failure   Happens when your CEO tells you he deleted a file four months ago—and that he needs it back. Only archiving with tape or CD-R is inexpensive enough to effectively handle this problem. Because of the depth of difference between this failure mode and the others, I recommend handling archiving as a separate process from backup.

It's technically possible for multiple sites to fail simultaneously, but in this event, you'd be hard pressed to find anyone who cared about your backup problem, so there's no need to worry about it.

The Trouble with Tape

The problem with using tape for archiving and backup is that it is not reliable—in fact, it's highly unreliable. You may find this shocking, but fully 67 percent of attempts to completely restore a system from tape fail. That's two thirds—an awfully high number, especially for how many people rely upon tape as their sole medium of backup.

Tape software really sucks. From disk-based "catalogs" that can grow so large they fill the very volume they're supposed to backup, to arcane interfaces that are supposed to manage "media sets" of tape and refuse to function if you insert the wrong tape, enterprise-based backup software all seems to have been written by people who hate network administrators and want to kick them when they're down. Of course, I'm exaggerating a tad, but anyone who has worked with Cheyenne Arcserve or Seagate BackupExec knows what I'm talking about. These programs are the opposite of intuitive. In my opinion, everyone should be able to figure out how to do an emergency restoration from scribbles jotted on a Post-it note, and that's just not possible with traditional tape backup software.

Traditional Backup   Traditional backup works like this: Every night, you insert a fresh tape into your server. The next morning when you arrive at work, you remove the tape, mark the date, and store it in your tape vault. At larger companies, you'll never use that tape again—it's a permanent record of your network on that date. In smaller companies, that's the same tape you use every Wednesday, and you only keep tapes made over the weekend or perhaps once a month.

Here's a nifty feature of most tape backup software: It won't backup open files. Think about this for a moment: If a file is open, that means it's being used, which means it's an important file, which means it should be backed up. In fact it is your busiest, most important documents that get skipped the most because they are open quite frequently or because they've been left open overnight.

Traditional archiving is okay, except that it has a major failure component: humans. Humans have to change that tape every day. This means that in any organization that doesn't have a dedicated tape archivist, the overburdened IS team is bound to forget. And if you've tried to train a non-IS employee to change the tape, you probably feel lucky if it happens at all.

One of two things will occur when the backup software detects that the tape has not been changed. Poorly designed or configured software will refuse to run the backup in a misguided attempt to protect the data already on the tape. Better-configured software will simply overwrite the tape assuming that a more recent backup is better than no backup at all. So in many cases, the same tape may sit in a server (wearing out) for days or weeks on end while business goes by, and everyone forgets about the backup software.

It is a combination of tape wear, truculent backup software, and this human failure component that contribute to the high failure rate of tape restorations.

Nearly all operating systems, including all Microsoft operating systems, support a backup methodology called archive marking, which is implemented through a single bit flag attached to every file as an attribute on the computer. The archive bit is set every time a file is written to and is only cleared by archive software. This allows the system to retain a memory of which files have changed since the last backup.

Most backup software offers a variety of backup options:

> **Full Backup**   Archives every file on the computer and clears all the archive bits so that all future writes will be marked for archiving.

Copy Backup Archives every file on the computer without modifying the archive bits. Copy operations proceed faster and can archive open files since the file does not have to be opened for write operations to reset the bit.

Incremental Backup Archives every file that has its archive bit set, meaning it has changed since the last full system backup and resets the bit so that the next incremental backup will not rearchive the file.

Differential Backup Archives every file that has its archive bit set, but it does not reset the bit; therefore, every differential backup tape includes the complete set of files since the last system backup.

Periodic Backup Archives all files that have been written to since a certain date.

A typical restore operation is even more Byzantine. Assuming the worst—you lost your storage system completely—here's what you have to look forward to: After installing new hard disks, you must reinstall Windows NT from scratch. Then you must reinstall your tape backup software. Once you've finished these tasks (after a frantic search for the BackupExec installation code that is required to reinstall BackupExec and a panicked call to their tech support to beg forgiveness, mercy, and a new code number), you're ready to completely overwrite all that installation effort with a full restoration from tape. You now get to sit in front of your server providing all the base system tapes, then the Monday incremental tape, the Tuesday incremental tape, and so forth until you hit the current day of the week—the whole time cursing your decision to use daily incremental backups. Once you're completely finished, and assuming that all six tapes involved worked flawlessly, you're ready to reboot your server—an entire work day after you began the restore operation.

Image Backup Because software vendors have begun to realize how badly tape sucks, a new type of tape backup called image backup has become available. In an image backup, a complete sector copy of the disk is written to tape, including all the information necessary to reconstruct partitions. Because the backup occurs below the file level, image archives are capable of archiving open files.

Restoration is where image backup shines. The image backup software will create a set of boot floppies for emergency restoration. By inserting the emergency restore boot floppy and an image tape, the computer will boot a proprietary restore program that simply copies the image on the tape back to disk. One reboot later and you're looking at your old familiar computer.

Image backup is not for archiving—file access is not as good as traditional backup software. But there's no reason you can't use different software for archiving and backup.

Sage Advice: Tape Backup Best Practices

Don't let some policy document written in the early seventies bind your hands when it comes to backup and archiving. If you are the person who will lose their job when a restoration fails, you should mandate the backup policy that works for you. For tape backups, here are the best practices to work with:

- Backup is a critical security component of any network. Allocate a large enough budget to do it correctly.

- Use tape devices and media large enough to perform an entire backup onto a single tape. In the unlikely event that this is not possible, use RAIT software to allow the simultaneous unattended backup of the entire system.

- Always set your tape backup software to overwrite, without asking, media that may have been left in the machine.

- Choose image backup software rather than file-based backup software. Restorations are far easier and faster with this software.

- Turn off storage-based catalogs. They take up far more space than they're worth, and they're never available when the computer has crashed. Use media-based catalogs that are stored on tape.

- Perform a full-system backup every day. Differential, incremental, and daily backups that don't create a complete image cause headaches and complications during a restoration operation and increase the likelihood of failure by adding more components to the process. If your backup system is too slow to backup your entire data set in the allotted time, get a new one that is capable of handling your data.

- Use the Copy feature to backup opened files or force them closed if you perform your backup at night. Use NT's force system logoff user policy to shut down user connections at night and force files closed.

- If you reuse tapes, mark them each time they've been written to. Discard tapes after their 10th backup. Saving a few dollars on media isn't worth the potential for loss.

- Pull out a full system backup once a week or once a month at the longest and store it permanently. You never know when a deleted file will be needed again.

Enterprise Backup

Enterprise backup is the problem of backing up all the servers and workstations in a company with some centrally managed resource. As complex as enterprise backup can be, there are some easy ways to make it simple.

Don't bother backing up workstations. Rather, get users comfortable with the idea that no files stored locally on their computers will be backed up—if it's important, put it on a network file server. This reduces the complexity of your backup problem considerably. Workstations should contain operating system and application files only, all of which can be restored from the original software CD-ROMs.

Use enterprise-based backup software that is capable of transmitting backup data over the network to a central backup server. Watch for network capacity, though, because that much data can often overwhelm a network. Schedule each server's transmission so they don't conflict when running over the same shared media. You should put your archive server on your backbone or at the central point of your network.

You don't have to spend a lot of money on esoteric archive servers, even for large environments. When you consider that a good 20GB DAT drive is going to cost $2,000, adding another $1,000 for a motherboard, hard disk, RAM, network adapter, and a copy of NT Workstation isn't all that big of a deal. The software you have to install is likely to cost more than all the hardware combined anyway. So feel free to have six or eight computers dedicated to large backup problems. They can all run simultaneously to backup different portions of your network without investing in expensive RAIT software or auto-loading tape devices. You'll save money and have a more standard solution that you can fix.

Alternatives to Tape

There are alternatives to backing up with tape. They fall into two major categories: backing up to another disk on the same machine or backing up to another computer over a network. These options are detailed below.

Hard Disks, Removeable Media, and Other Computers   Simply storing another copy of your data is an effective form of backup and archive. That other location could be another hard disk in the same machine, a removable cartridge hard disk, or another computer.

Storing to another hard disk (via mirroring) is an excellent primary method for backup and fault tolerance, but it suffers from the problem that any environmental cause for the failure of the first disk will affect it, too. Fire, flood, theft, or a disgruntled employee will kill both drives, leaving you with no recourse if it's your only method of data protection.

Removable cartridge hard disks suffer from always being smaller than the source you're backing up, and so they require human intervention or the selection of a smaller set of backup data. This method of backup is most appropriate for workstations.

Another computer is a really good idea. So good, in fact, that we'll deal with it later on under the "Fault Tolerance" section.

Internet Archiving   An interesting new backup medium has recently emerged: the Internet. A few companies have begun offering remote archiving and backup via the Internet so that your data is stored (presumably safely) off site. By downloading their backup client and customizing a backup plan to suit your needs, your computer will archive automatically over a constant Internet connection to the disk and tape farms of the backup provider.

They promise encryption, protection, and security—but, of course, they won't be held liable in the event that you actually do lose data. Interesting indeed. This field is so new that it cannot be wholeheartedly recommended by anyone as the sole means of protection for a network—but it is an interesting alternative worth serious consideration and possible implementation as a secondary form of data protection.

Can they promise security? The site I visited touts their use of DES—the government's preferred form of encryption. It has been long suspected (though never proven) that a backdoor exists to DES and that the NSA knows how to exploit it. It's also been shown to be vulnerable to a key-space decryption in short order. There's no doubt that if the government wanted to see your data and knew that an online archive company had a copy of it, they could get it, and they could decrypt it. Other than that, you're probably pretty safe.

Finally, if you think a tape restore is slow, sit behind one proceeding at 28.8Kbps over a modem. Unless you have a high speed Internet connection available, Internet backup is not for you. You'll also have to deal with archiving only user information. In the event of a restore, the operating system and all applications will have to be restored from original media, because Internet archive services charge per megabyte stored, and you'll want to minimize that cost as much as possible.

Disks Are Cheap

Until computers became a household item, hard disks were expensive. The idea of buying extra hard disks just to back up data didn't make sense, and tape was the only cost effective solution. Because the market for computers (and therefore hard disks) has recently expanded by an order of magnitude or two, hard disks have become cheap. They are now cheaper than tape devices and their media, and they are cheap enough to use for archiving. Hard disks are highly reliable until they fail, and for that reason, they make good archival media.

Use Mirroring

Mirroring is the easiest way to protect your computer from hard disk loss. With two disks, you are protected from normal disk failure, because only one disk is likely to fail at one time, unless the reason it fails is environmental or, though unlikely, one failure causes the next device to fail.

When you use mirroring, put the second drive on a different bus. This will prevent an electrical failure on one disk from affecting the other, because they won't be on the same cable.

You may decide to use a different controller altogether so you can tolerate the failure of a controller, but disk controller failure is extraordinarily rare.

A side benefit of mirroring is that it doubles allowable read speed. It's also the only fault tolerance method available for use on the boot partition where NT files are stored, and it is the only way to increase the boot speed of an NT server without using hardware RAID controllers.

Avoid Stripe Sets

Stripe sets are a good idea—too bad they don't work that well. Striping to increase performance only manages to double read and write performance at four disks—you can achieve the same performance increase with mirroring—but without worrying about the decrease in fault tolerance that striping causes. Stripe sets with more disks are faster, but if you're going to spend that much money on your disk subsystem, you should get a RAID controller to go with it.

Stripe sets with parity have even more overhead—write operations are considerably slower than mirrored disks. It takes fewer users to burden servers that rely on stripe sets with parity than servers that rely upon mirroring. Beyond the overhead, stripe sets across disks that aren't exactly the same suffer from severe timing problems.

Finally, NT does not support booting from a stripe set, so your system files (about 50 percent of normal disk access) won't see any read improvement. Also, NT allows you to create stripe sets on partitions that contain other volumes—but accessing those other volumes causes your stripe-set access to fall out of sync and take even more time.

Disk Controllers

Disk controllers are problematic because of the way NT supports (or doesn't support) them. If a manufacturer has provided Microsoft with a driver for their controller to include with the distribution of Windows NT, you'll have no problems. Most likely, NT's setup program will automatically detect the controller and will have loaded the driver early enough to support installing NT on a disk controlled by the controller.

Up and Running

PART 2

If their disk driver doesn't ship with NT, you'll have to go through the rigmarole of providing a driver floppy. And if you intend to install NT through that controller, you'll need to provide the floppy through a secret method described in Chapter 3, "Installing Windows NT (the Right Way)." Unfortunately, some disk controllers don't even work using this method, and you'll have to disk copy the partition from a more supported controller to them if you ever want to boot NT on them.

Sage Advice: Selecting Disk Controllers

Use standard disk controllers, such as UltraDMA IDE controllers or common SCSI adapters like those from Adaptec. Consider checking the NT setup disk for supported controllers to provide a pick list from which to shop if you want to use something more esoteric (like a RAID controller). This is important, because when your server crashes in four years, you'll find the floppy with the driver you need to reinstall has also gone bad. The NT setup program supports common controllers from the following manufacturers:

- Most IDE Controllers
- Adaptec
- AMD
- AMI
- BusLogic
- Compaq
- Dell
- DPT
- Future Domain
- IBM
- Intel
- Matsushita/Panasonic
- Mitsumi
- Mylex
- NCR

Sage Advice: Selecting Disk Controllers *(continued)*

- Olivetti

- Qlogic

- Sony

- Symbios Logic

- UltraStore

- Zenith

Check for individual models by going to the SCSI Adapters Control Panel, selecting the driver tab, and clicking Add. A list of supported drivers will appear. Then you can just click cancel to exit.

Hardware RAID: Use Caution

Hardware RAID is both the fastest and most fail-safe method of storing data when downtime cannot be tolerated. Hardware RAID is expensive, is hard to configure correctly, and can easily cause data corruption when failures occur.

Considering these contradictions, you should approach RAID with caution. It's fantastic and a real ally when configured and used correctly, but it's easy to use incorrectly. There are quite a few companies touting RAID solutions that are incomplete at best.

When speaking of RAID in general, most people are actually talking about RAID 5, the most commonly implemented form of RAID that provides both a speed improvement and a measure of fault tolerance. You can assume that whenever someone doesn't specify a RAID level, they're talking about RAID level 5, and that assumption holds true with this book.

Here's a list of things that I've seen go wrong with RAID:

- The RAID adapter can lose its RAID configuration and suddenly "forget" the configuration of the RAID pack. Many adapters don't include forensic utilities to remedy this problem, and it's most likely to happen after a power-related shutdown.

- A hard disk can have timings that are slightly out of sync with the rest of the pack, causing serious slowdowns of the entire array.

- Hard drive cables can be of lower tolerance than the data bus requires, causing drives to be incorrectly marked bad and forcing the RAID pack to go into fault-tolerance mode.

- Common RAID operations, such as rebuilding a healthy pack, require rebooting to a BIOS-level program or the running of a special utility that requires the server be taken offline for hours.

- Solutions touted as hot-swappable cause the server to crash because the server vendor used the wrong type of bus termination or the adapter is actually more sensitive to termination impedance than it should be to actually tolerate disk insertion.

- The heat from many disks operating in close proximity actually causes the very failures that RAID is supposed to remedy, thus requiring frequent drive replacement.

The real problem with RAID is its snake-oil appeal—once it's installed, everyone seems to think they're protected against all loss and no other backup measures are necessary besides the occasional archive tape. This false sense of security is pernicious in the industry—RAID should be considered nothing more than a high-availability, fault-tolerance measure—it is certainly not a replacement for backup or archiving.

The first thing you should do when you install a server with RAID is simulate failure by (at least) removing the power plug from one of the hard disks in the pack while the computer is running. You won't damage any hardware doing this. If everything doesn't keep humming along smoothly, you don't really have a RAID system. RAID systems simply can't be trusted to operate properly unless they can pass this test.

You should also make certain that every disk is installed in an individually removable carriage. Taking down a server to replace a failed drive causes the downtime you paid so much to avoid. Pay a little extra to do it right.

Be certain the RAID adapters you use are capable of tolerating failure, hot-swapping disks, and rebuilding the failed drive—all without rebooting the computer. Rebuilding a large RAID disk can take hours, so you'll want to make sure you are online while it happens. Many RAID systems recommend using an extra "hot spare" disk that can be spun up and rebuilt whenever any disk fails. This is an excellent idea because the rebuilding begins as soon as the failure is detected and the failed disk is marked out. When you replace the new empty drive, it becomes the hot spare.

Finally, make sure your adapter or software has some method of making you quite certain which drive has failed. (Usually this works by flashing the drive's built-in LED or a LED in the removable carriage.) Nothing will make you feel stupider than pulling one of the good remaining drives out of your RAID pack by accident and watching your server drop like a rock.

Serving CD-ROMs

You will often find a need to serve catalogs of rather static information at your site, and CD-ROM jukeboxes usually seem like a good way to do that. They work well, but they're usually an unnecessary expense. Two other less expensive methods exist, and one of those methods is technically superior.

When you need to serve a number of CD-ROMs, you have three options:

- Use a CD-ROM jukebox to serve them.
- Use Virtual CD-ROM emulation software.
- Use the vast number of CD-ROMs that came with all the PCs at your site.

The first option entails using a server specially configured with a number of CD-ROM drives, usually between 7 and 16, and leaving the CD-ROM media in the CD-ROM drives. This suffers from a few problems:

- Multiple users accessing the same CD-ROM at the same time makes it terribly slow because CD-ROM readers can't seek very quickly.
- CD-ROM jukeboxes are always expensive and usually two or three generations behind in speed. I recently saw 4x CD-ROM jukeboxes being sold in the same catalog that sold 40x CD-ROM readers.
- Your original source discs are in use—not stored for safekeeping.

Virtual CD-ROM emulation software solves all of these problems. Virtual CD-ROM emulation software installs a special driver in Windows NT that can make CD-ROM image files look like CD-ROM devices to NT. By recording the contents of a CD into these compressed CD-ROM image files, the computer will act as if that CD is permanently mounted in it's own drive—the virtual CD-ROM reader even gets its own drive letter. You can generally serve as many CDs as you need to from a single machine with the right software. Multiple users accessing the same CD-ROM image file are no more of a problem than any other multi-user function. And because only a few users generally access CDs at once, you can usually get away with using a copy of NT Workstation to serve the files if you're on a budget.

Finally, the absolute simplest method to serve a large number of CD-ROMs in an enterprise is to serve them from the workstations that already have CD-ROM drives. Of course, this method suffers from many of the problems that jukeboxes suffer from, but at least it's free.

Up and Running

PART 2

If you use any 32-bit version of Windows or Unix on your workstations, you should be able to serve the CD-ROMs from the workstations that have CD-ROM drives without many hassles. It does mean you have to trust your users not to mess with things, but I've found an effective solution to even that problem: Mount the CD-ROM farther back in the case and put a blank face plate in front of it. Then you simply have to trust users not to initiate an eject or shut their computers off.

Fault Tolerance

Now that we've discussed ways to keep a server up, we'll move out a level to the server's purpose: the application. It doesn't matter much that a server runs if the application it serves has crashed. Conversely, it doesn't matter much that a server has crashed if the application it serves still runs. We'll look at solutions that cover both of those eventualities in this section.

Service Monitors

Service monitors are small software applications that run on servers and continuously monitor the state of a software application, such as Exchange or SQL Server. The service monitors simply check to see if the service is responsive to service queries on a periodic basis.

In the event that the service fails to respond to a service query within a given time frame, the service monitor will stop the service and start it again (in exactly the same manner as allowed by the Service Control Panel). This is basically equivalent to shutting down and restarting a crashed word processor.

This method of fault tolerance, of course, assumes that whatever caused the service to crash isn't going to happen again and that the service can actually be stopped and restarted (a number of application errors will prevent that).

Sage Advice: Service Monitors

Rather than hacking on a kludge to stop and start Exchange all the time (the service these little utilities were really designed for), toss it and look for a better mail server for NT. POP and SMTP mail services aren't difficult even when you've got hundreds of thousands of users to support. Don't throw good money after bad to try to prop up bloated and buggy side applications for servers.

Server Replication

One step above mirroring and stripe sets is server replication—keeping an entire redundant server. This provides complete fault tolerance, since you're protected from any disaster up to and including the complete destruction of a single server.

Windows NT provides an extremely basic service, called the directory replicator service, for data replication between servers. This service supports the copying of files and directories between servers, with some (serious) limitations:

- This service can't copy open files.
- It only copies files—it doesn't compare and synchronize versions between the servers.
- You can only specify one directory path to replicate.

Since Windows NT's built-in data replication service isn't very useful, third-party vendors have stepped in to provide sophisticated server replication products.

Vinca makes StandbyServer for NT. It is a server replication system that uses a dedicated network link between two servers to handle the mirroring traffic. It installs as a device driver, so from Windows NT's point of view, you're simply creating a mirror set—one of the partitions just happens to be in another machine.

Since it uses (and requires) its own network link, this product doesn't increase network traffic. StandbyServer also has the ability to automatically switch the backup machine into place when the main server goes down. Check out StandbyServer at www.vinca.com.

Octopus Technologies, a division of FullTime, currently produces two server replication products for Windows NT. Octopus DataStar allows you to create mirror copies of NT volumes, or selected files, on one or several servers across the network. OctopusHA+ is an enhanced version that provides the same data-replication capabilities but also has the ability for a backup server to automatically take over when the original server goes down. Check out Octopus at www.fulltime.com.

Vinca replicates servers on a sector-by-sector basis, whereas Octopus replicates on a file-by-file basis. File-by-file replication provides better flexibility while sector-by-sector replication is more reliable.

Clusters

Clustering is the running of a single application on multiple machines at one time. This allows you to apply the resources of many machines to one problem, and when properly implemented, it is an excellent way to handle large problems like enterprise databases, commercial Web sites, and serious scientific applications.

Too bad NT's clustering isn't handled correctly, yet. Currently, the clustering that ships in Windows NT 4 Enterprise Edition is only capable of handling two machines in a cluster, and because the overhead of handling the clustering problem is just about 50 percent, it actually isn't as fast as a single machine for most problems.

NT's clustering also requires applications that are written for it—even Microsoft's own BackOffice applications like Exchange and IIS4 don't support it. Considering the market for clustered applications is small and it's dubious value, no applications will be written to support it until it can show some advantage.

NT's clustering (known as Wolfpack during its development) is not as good as the high-availability solutions presented in the previous section. Although those solutions also have problems with switching applications, they can be used with many common applications, such as e-mail, as long as a client connection can be interrupted without causing data corruption.

NT's clustering will probably improve as Microsoft works on it. When you can put 32 machines in a cluster, the overhead for clustering may be insignificant enough to make the effort worthwhile. But for the time being, no clustering solution for back-end storage applications works well on Windows NT.

My advice is to avoid clustering like the plague.

NT's clustering in its current incarnation is tremendously complicated and without serious merit. Use solutions that work, like those from Vinca and Octopus, before considering Microsoft's solution.

Windows Load-Balancing Service

There is another form of clustering that works quite well for certain problems: load balancing. Load balancing is quite simple; it allows multiple machines to respond to the same IP address and balances the client load among that group. For problems such as Web service, this makes all the servers appear to be one server that can handle a massive number of simultaneous connections. Microsoft recently purchased a company that made a load-balancing service for NT and has announced that they will roll this product into Windows NT Server Enterprise Edition to shore up their use of the word *clustering*.

Stateless clustering doesn't work for problems such as file service, database, or e-mail, because there's no standard way to replicate data stored on one server to all the rest of the servers. For example, if on your first session you stored a file to the cluster (meaning one of the machines in the cluster) and then connected to the cluster at a later date, there's only a small chance that you would connect again to the machine that had your file. Stateless clustering works only with applications that don't maintain any data transmitted by the client—you can think of them as "output only" applications. Examples of this sort of application are Web and FTP services.

There is a solution to even that problem, though—all the clustered machines can transmit their stored data to a single back-end storage or database server. This puts all the information in one place, where any user can find it, no matter which clustered server they're attached to. Unfortunately, it also means that the cluster is no faster than the single machine used to store everything.

Stateless clustering works well in the one environment it was designed for: Web service for large commercial sites. The amount of user information to store for a Web site is usually miniscule compared to the massive amount of data transmitted to each user. Because some Web sites need to handle millions of simultaneous sessions, this method lets designers put the client-handling load on frontline Web servers and maintain the database load on back-end database servers.

Building Fault Tolerance from Scratch

High availability and clustering solutions are all expensive—the software to implement them is likely to cost as much as the server you put it on. There are easy ways to implement fault tolerance, but they change depending on what you're doing and exactly what level of fault tolerance you need. I'll present a few ideas here to get you thinking about your fault tolerance problems.

The first question to ask about fault tolerance is whether you need it. Upon visiting Vinca's Web site, you'll find a downtime cost calculator that uses this method to calculate the cost of downtime:

Employees x Average Payrate x Down Hours = Downtime Costs

Sounds reasonably complete, but it's based on the assumption that employees in your organization become worthless the moment their computers go down. Sometimes that's the case, but often it's not. I'm not advocating downtime, I'm merely saying that the assumptions used to cost downtime are flawed, and that short periods of downtime aren't nearly as expensive as data loss or the opportunity cost of lost business if your business relies on computers to transact.

If you can tolerate 15 minutes of downtime, a whole array of less expensive options emerges. For example, manually swapping an entire server doesn't take long, especially if the hard disks are on removable cartridges. For an event that might occur once a year, this really isn't all that bad.

The following inexpensive methods can achieve different measures of fault tolerance for specific applications.

The DNS service can assign more than one IP address to a single domain name. If there's no response from the first address, the client can check, in order, each of the next addresses until it gets a response. This means that for Web service, you can simply put up an array of Web servers, each with their own IP address, and trust that users will be able to get through to one of them. Because with Web service, it rarely matters which server clients attach to as long as they're all serving the same data, you have fault tolerance.

Another way to solve the load-balancing problem is with firewalls. Many firewalls can be configured to load balance a single IP address across a group of identical machines, so you can have three Web servers that all respond to a single address behind one of these firewalls.

Fault tolerance for standard file service can be achieved by simply cross-copying files among two or more servers. By doubling the amount of disk space in each server, you can maintain a complete copy of all the data on another machine by periodically running a script to copy files from one machine to another. In the event that a machine has crashed, users can simply remap the drive letter they use for the primary machine to the machine with the share that you have backed everything up to. By using the archive bit to determine which files should be copied, you can update only those files that have changed, and you can make the update period fairly frequent—say, once per hour.

There is a time lag based on the periodicity of your copy operation, so this method may not work in every situation. Since it's not completely automatic (users have to recognize the problem and manually remap a drive letter), it's not appropriate for every environment. You reduce the automation problem by providing a desktop icon that users can click to run a batch file that will remap the drive.

Fault tolerance doesn't mean you have to spend a boatload of money on expensive hardware and esoteric software. It means that you must think about the problem and come up with the simplest workable solution. Sometimes that means expensive hardware and esoteric software, but not always.

Amok Tolerance

Unlike most case studies in this book, I'm going to present a negative example—a real incident when a number of in-place fault tolerance methods failed. The point of this is not to decry the various methods; rather, it is to say that organization and planning are far better fault tolerance tools than esoteric hardware and expensive software. In this specific case, the operating system was NetWare 3.12 rather than Windows NT, but the effect would have been the same with NT.

Clustering, RAID, and Tape

A client of mine used two identically configured servers set up to mirror one another through a common high-availability system. In the event that the primary machine failed, the secondary machine would immediately step in and take up the load without dropping client connections or losing data.

These servers stored information automatically generated by scientific recording equipment. Each day's results depended upon the results from the previous day as the study progressed through time.

Each server contained six hard disks configured in a RAID pack. Five volumes participated in a RAID 5-volume and a sixth disk stood by waiting to be made part of the pack in the event that another disk failed.

Tape backups were performed rigorously and without fail, with a full system backup made once per week on three tapes (the tape system was smaller than the RAID pack), and a daily incremental backup performed each night.

A UPS system the size of a walk-in freezer provided smooth uninterruptible power for the system and, in the event of power loss, could power both servers for days.

The system performed flawlessly and ran for years without serious incident until one night when a new employee decided to clean up some space on the servers (which were dangerously full—a fault none of the in-place fault tolerance methods could handle). He wrote a batch file to delete files in a temporary directory and ran the batch file.

Unfortunately, he mistakenly included a switch to traverse subdirectories, so the delete operation proceeded to remove study data after it erased the files in the temporary directory. The employee didn't realize he had erased study data, and the operations continued for two more days until the error was discovered. By then, the deleted files had been over-written by new data. Not even NetWare's highly forgiving delete methodology could bring it back.

Of course, the RAID pack and high-availability solutions worked perfectly—they efficiently deleted the data on both machines as requested by the user.

When the error was discovered, we pulled up NetWare's undelete tool and determined that the files were, in fact, gone. So we decided to pull the primary machine out of operation and let the secondary

24seven **CASE STUDY**

server take over. We would restore the primary machine from tape and then figure out how to merge the data from that day's run which would be stored on the secondary server.

Being a Thursday, seven tapes composed the complete restore set. We reinstalled the weekly backup and the Monday tapes without incident, but ran into errors with the Tuesday tape. It seems this client had been writing to the same set of weekly tapes for two years. At that point, we realized there was no way to restore the lost data, and since the study was sequential, it would have to be rolled back three days to proceed from the prior Monday.

Three failures contributed to this event:

- The servers were allowed to become full, as no systematic method of detecting or correcting this specific fault existed.

- A human error caused the actual event (but really only highlighted the impending failure due to the full servers).

- A backup system failed due to systematic improper use.

As you can see, not even the most sophisticated fault tolerance equipment will replace proper design, vigilance, and training.

5

Network Protocols

Network protocols define the way data is transported between computers in a networked environment. Network protocols completely hide their functionality from higher-level services and protocols, which can simply assume that, by providing the assigned name of another computer, they can transmit a message or open a continuous communication stream without dealing with the intricacies of data transport. This is analogous to mailing a letter or calling—you don't care or even need to know the technical minutiae of how the message is sent or the call is connected. Protocols handle these functions in a network.

Understanding network protocols is necessary in order to quickly isolate problems in a network. First I'm going to explain network theory and then describe the two major protocols of Windows NT in detail. After that, I'll discuss the best ways to set up networking in your environment.

Network Theory

Early computer communications were fairly simple: Two computers attached to both ends of a digital transport (such as RS-232 serial) communicated by writing data to the serial port. The serial port automatically transmits the data to the receiving computer, which can read the same data in its serial port. Because only two computers participate, there's no real need to address each other—identity is implied by the connection. This simple but effective method of networking remains useful today—it's how dial-up modems work.

But connecting a number of independent computers together represents a serious problem. A direct circuit must exist to talk to a computer. The circuit between the computers is dedicated just to their conversation—no other computers can participate on that channel, and the medium cannot be shared. This requires significantly more communications resources for any computer that needs to talk to more than one device.

The number of circuits required to connect computers together increases exponentially as the number of participating computers increases. The exponential increase in circuits required to connect computers together made it obvious that some method to pass messages among computers was required to implement a large-scale network. But a simple data link between computers was not sufficient to implement a message-passing system because there was no way for a computer to address a computer to which it is not directly attached, even if a connected path of computers exists. Some sort of unique identifier for each computer must exist for a message to be transmitted to its ultimate correct recipient.

Network protocols solve these problems. They provide a mechanism whereby multiple computers can transmit data using the same channel and can uniquely address one another given any connected path of intermediate computers.

Network protocols utilize two fundamental methods:

Packaging   Packages data in small independent messages, which alleviates the problem of the dedicated circuit. More than one computer can participate on the same transport medium because the link is only dedicated during the time a packet is actually transmitted.

Addressing   Addresses packets to computers using an addressing scheme that uniquely identifies each computer in the network. Without unique addresses there is no way to ascertain which of the many computers attached to a shared medium should receive a packet.

The simplest protocols stop at this point. More useful protocols add the following features:

Routability   Identifies both a destination network and client to which a packet should be transmitted. Routability must be able to identify the sequential route to get to that network.

Guaranteed Delivery   Determines when data has been lost in transit and negotiates for its retransmission.

Multiplexing   Uniquely identifies more than one connection into the same computer to allow for multiple simultaneous services on the same machine.

Sockets   Maintain bidirectional streams of traffic seamlessly so the entire network infrastructure is abstracted away from the application. In this way, networks can be handled much like opened files.

Error Detection   Determines when a packet has become corrupted and discards it.

Bandwidth Throttling   Senses the rate at which data is being transmitted most effectively and tunes the transmission times to maximize the effective use of network resources.

Name Resolution   Automatically accesses an index of names to address so networked resources can be identified easily. In some protocols this table is built dynamically through a name broadcast mechanism (browsing), in others it is maintained statically by accessing a name database with a known address (DNS or WINS).

Finally, session layer interprocess communications support even more complex application support mechanisms such as the following:

Establishing and Terminating Sessions   Automatically provides security and accounting context for a series of datagrams between two communicating systems. Sessions allow packet-based networks to simulate the earlier connection-oriented networks.

File Management   Includes opening, closing, and deleting files or performing other tasks. By creating semaphores for common functions of file system management, these operations can be performed efficiently over a network.

Streaming Transmission   Used for copy operations or other bulk-data communication.

File System Services   Include seeking a specific point in a remote file, reading or writing blocks of data, and locking blocks of data so that data integrity can be maintained when multiple users are accessing the same file.

All of these functions are explained in the following sections.

Anatomy of a Data Exchange

Data exchanges between computers takes place using a number of different protocols, each protocol having a specific purpose in the exchange. Higher-level protocols with more specific purposes like name resolution are contained within lower-level protocols that provide more generic services, such as network delivery and addressing.

The following series of figures elucidates this fundamental concept of encapsulation. Figure 5.1 shows a frame capture of a DNS name request. The lowest-level protocol involved in this exchange is the data-link protocol, Ethernet. I chose to display a DNS name request because the exchange is simple and embodied in a single packet. More complex exchanges, such as reading a file, require far more complicated protocols—TCP, SMB, NetBIOS, and so forth. While more complicated in their expression, these protocols are fundamentally the same as the process described here.

Figure 5.1   An Ethernet frame

The frame capture displayed in Figure 5.2 shows the IP datagram contained within the Ethernet frame. The IP packet provides only the addressing between computers and other delivery-based information, most of which are actually unused in modern systems.

Figure 5.2   An IP datagram contained in an Ethernet frame

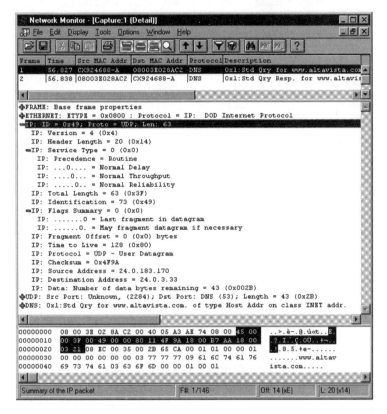

The UDP packet contained within the IP packet is shown in Figure 5.3. The UDP protocol adds port information, which is additional information that is necessary to route the packet to a specific service on the receiving computer and to retain information about the requesting application on the source machine.

Figure 5.3 A UDP packet contained within IP

Finally, the most specific protocol contained within this entire message is the DNS request shown in Figure 5.4. In this exchange, DNS uses UDP to specify the service port to connect to. UDP uses IP to add addressing information. IP uses Ethernet to be transported to the next router in the path to the destination address.

Figure 5.4   A DNS request

The Transport Protocols

The higher-level services of Windows NT are not affected by the particular protocol you choose to use in your network. As long as the protocol exposes the Windows NT Transport Driver Interface (TDI), which is a superset of the NetBIOS Frames Protocol used in LANs since IBM's introduction of NetBIOS in 1983, the protocol can be used to carry Windows NT session information between clients and servers.

At the lower end, a device driver must support the Network Driver Interface Specification (NDIS) in order to connect to a transport driver. All network adapters that support Windows NT do this, so it isn't much of a real-world issue. Figure 5.5 shows a diagram of the Windows NT networking architecture.

Figure 5.5   Windows NT networking architecture

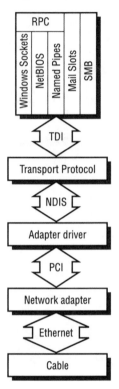

Four transport protocols are popular enough to warrant default support by Windows NT:

- TCP/IP
- IPX
- NetBEUI
- AppleTalk

These protocols are compared below and then detailed in sections of their own.

TCP/IP   Transmission Control Protocol/Internet Protocol (TCP/IP) is the protocol of the Internet. TCP/IP is required by computers that communicate directly with the Internet and is recommended by Microsoft for use in all networks. NBT is the NetBIOS compatibility layer for TCP/IP. TCP/IP is the slowest of the protocols supported by Windows NT.

Hosts in TCP/IP are uniquely numbered in their network; networks are uniquely numbered within an internetwork and globally unique within the Internet. The host and network address are combined into a single 32-bit number with the division between host and network defined by a 32-bit network mask.

The largest chunk of this chapter discusses TCP/IP, because it is both the most popular and the most complex of network protocols.

IPX/SPX   Internetwork Packet eXchange/ Sequential Packet eXchange (IPX/SPX) is the protocol of Novell Networks and is implemented by the NWLink TDI driver in Windows NT. NetBIOS compatibility is provided by the NWBLink compatibility layer. IPX is useful in its own right as a simple, fast, and fairly secure routable protocol and when connectivity with Novell servers is required. IPX is the fastest routable protocol supported by NT.

Hosts in IPX are numbered by their unique media access control identifier (Ethernet MAC address). Servers and routers must be additionally programmed with network identifiers, known as network numbers, which are attached to packets routed between hosts until they reach their ultimate network.

NetBEUI   Network Basic Input Output System Extended User Interface (NetBEUI), the protocol designed by Microsoft and IBM for small networks. NetBEUI cannot be routed, but multi-homed NT servers can "gate" NetBEUI requests between networks. Since NetBEUI implements NetBIOS natively, no compatibility layer is required. NetBEUI is the fastest network protocol for use with Windows NT.

Hosts in a NetBEUI network are identified only by their data-link layer MAC address. There is no network number, so the protocol is not routable.

AppleTalk   AppleTalk is the protocol built into Macintosh computers for file and print sharing. AppleTalk is necessary to support Macintosh clients under Windows NT but is not useful for supporting PC clients.

Of the four protocols, AppleTalk is implemented as a device driver that is not TDI compliant—no NetBIOS functionality is available, so the driver does not work with the standard Server and Workstation services. A congruent service, Services for Macintosh, is provided to facilitate file and print sharing for AppleTalk clients. AppleTalk cannot be bound to other services or protocols using the networking control panel in NT 4. (Windows 2000 will support AppleTalk as a true TDI compliant network protocol.) Other limited function protocols are also supported, but their use is too rare to bother discussing and none of them can be bound to higher level services such as the Server or Workstation services. Because AppleTalk is not a TDI compliant protocol, it is not further detailed in this chapter.

Up and Running

PART 2

NetBEUI

NetBEUI is small and fast. Those are its only benefits. Since it cannot be routed, it's useless except in networks that consist of a single Ethernet collision domain or where a single multi-homed server connects all domains. The NBF TDI compliant protocol driver implements NetBEUI in Windows NT.

Since NetBEUI is non-routable, it's virtually free from security problems. Nobody who isn't already on the network can gain access to your network.

Practical NetBEUI Networking

NetBEUI's only practical uses are derived from its small size and simplicity. Although it is technically the fastest networking protocol included with Windows NT, it is not fast enough to warrant its use on that merit alone.

Contemporary hardware is capacious enough that small size is rarely useful, but there is an important case when small size is important—booting MS-DOS from a floppy. The routable protocols are comparatively large, but NetBEUI provides enough remaining MS-DOS memory to perform useful work. By supporting it on your NT Server, you can use MS-DOS boot floppies to connect to a drive share on your network from PCs that do not yet have operating systems. You can then run a copy of disk copying software, download a stored installation image file, and easily perform network-based OS installs. Other network protocols take up so much conventional DOS memory that there's no room left to run an application.

Simplicity is also a benefit. You may run into situations where, for whatever reason, you can't get one of the more complex protocols to work correctly—for instance, when setting up a PPTP tunnel over RAS. NetBEUI's simplicity provides a protocol that will nearly always function given the existence of a connected data link. This can make NetBEUI an important troubleshooting tool.

Windows NT Server also supports a feature called the NetBIOS gateway, whereby an NT Server will act as a sort of proxy to connect two computers from different segments. Although it doesn't provide the complete services of routing, it can be used to attach to machines across different network segments when a multi-homed NT server connects the segments together.

IPX/SPX

IPX, the protocol developed by Novell for use in NetWare, was originally implemented in Windows NT to support connectivity with NetWare networks. It became the recommended protocol for use with NT until Microsoft perfected their implementation of

TCP/IP. IPX is implemented by the NWLink transport driver interface protocol driver in Windows NT.

IPX   Performs the functions of addressing and includes the data elements necessary for routing, as well as packet reordering. In this respect it is equivalent to IP except that it adds port information, providing the same functionality as UDP over IP.

SPX   Performs flow control functions to ensure that packets arrive to a specific destination in order and do not need to be reordered for purposes such as network printing. SPX is equivalent to TCP, but is used less often because IPX is complex enough to use for many services.

IPX is nearly configuration-free because it uses the media access control unique identifier as the host number, so clients do not need to have a unique address assigned. In the case of Ethernet, this identifier is globally unique and programmed into the adapter at the factory. For other data-link technologies, the address may be factory assigned or assigned during installation, but it must always be unique or the data link will not function. Network numbers are assigned to each shared media network, but this information is programmed only into routers and servers.

IPX has no name-resolution facilities; instead it relies upon higher-level services like NetBIOS or the NetWare Core Protocol (implemented by the NetWare File and Print Services add-on package for Windows NT) for name resolution.

Practical IPX Networking

IPX is a fairly fast, fairly small, routable protocol that was originally included in Windows NT to support migrating from NetWare. In the early days of NT 3.5, IPX was popular because Microsoft's TCP/IP implementation was buggy and incomplete and because the Internet wasn't a huge deal yet.

Since that time, TCP/IP has surpassed IPX as the protocol of choice for NT Servers. This is somewhat shortsighted. TCP/IP is larger, slower, more difficult to configure, and far more vulnerable to security problems than IPX. Its only two benefits are its massive scalability (IPX begins to bog down large networks) and its seamless Internet connectivity.

IPX has some substantial benefits you should consider closely when choosing a primary network protocol:

- It's fast—about 20 percent faster than TCP/IP over the same connections. It has lower overhead and fewer software translation layers to go through. Because it's not subject to Internet attacks, its code contains far fewer time consuming consistency checks than the code to support TCP/IP.

Up and Running

PART 2

- It routes broadcasts, which means that all named resources on your network appear correctly and automatically without the necessity for name services like WINS or DNS.

- It uses MAC layer (usually Ethernet) addresses as network layer addresses, so you don't have to assign a unique client number to each machine, and routing pretty much takes care of itself.

- It does not require much specific configuration on either clients or servers, so proper connectivity is nearly guaranteed.

- It can't be routed over the Internet, so machines running only IPX are (almost) completely immune to attack from the Internet.

IPX does have two problems:

- It can't be routed over the Internet, so Internet servers and clients also need TCP/IP.

- It routes broadcasts, so networks larger than 2,000 clients begin to bog down due to excessive broadcast traffic. This problem is somewhat intractable—IPX becomes useless in large networks for this reason.

Since you'll often use TCP/IP to supplement these shortcomings with IPX, most network administrators feel that installing only TCP/IP is easier. This opinion is not usually correct. Because IPX functions well with the built-in NetBIOS naming services, your clients will have a much easier time finding each other across the routed connections in your network. Even if you run TCP/IP in addition to IPX, using IPX as the primary protocol will result in faster inside network connections and easier name resolution. In fact, you won't need to run WINS or DNS on your servers with IPX. Establishing TCP/IP connections may take slightly longer, but if you only use TCP/IP for Internet connections, you won't notice the difference.

Most importantly, you can secure your inside servers against most Internet attacks by simply not running TCP/IP on them. Without a TCP/IP stack installed, those servers are immune to the vast majority of possible security breaches. You need only install TCP/IP on clients who need to use Internet services, multi-homed servers that route TCP/IP, and Internet servers. Even if your server routes TCP/IP or provides Internet services, higher-level services such as Server and Workstation do not need to be bound to it.

TCP/IP

The Transmission Control Protocol (TCP) and the Internet Protocol (IP) are two distinct protocols that form the basis of most Internet communications. Recently they have come to form the basis of most local area network communications. The two protocols are so tightly bound together in their function and purpose that they are often referred to singularly as TCP/IP; however, they can, and often do, function independently of one another.

In common usage, the entire suite of Internet protocols is referred to as the TCP/IP protocol suite. Those protocols include low-level protocols, such as IP, ARP, UDP, and TCP, as well as higher-level protocols, such as HTTP and FTP, which rely upon the services of the lower-level Internet protocols. This chapter is concerned only with the low-level protocols.

The Internet Protocol

The Internet Protocol (IP) is the foundation upon which all other high-level Internet protocols operate. IP provides the basic mechanism for the forwarding of data between two computers on separate networks. IP can fragment packets if they are too large for some older networks to forward, but this feature is largely obsolete because all routers built during the past decade are able to pass large IP packets.

IP packets are simply handed from computer to computer until they reach their destination. The computer sending the packet and the computer receiving the packet are called *end systems* because they are at the ends of the communication session. The computers between the end systems are called *intermediate systems*. Intermediate system is a generic term for computers more commonly called routers, gateways, or multi-homed hosts.

IP provides the functions of addressing and fragmentation only to support packet forwarding—no other functionality is presumed or implemented. Therefore:

- IP cannot guarantee that a packet will reach its destination.
- IP has no ability to perform flow control.
- IP performs no error correction.
- IP performs no error detection for the data payload.
- IP does not guarantee that packets will arrive in order and does not order them sequentially.

IP relies on the data link (such as Ethernet or frame relay) to transmit data in an error-free condition and does not attempt to provide any guarantees of service. Other protocols, which are transported within IP packets, add information such as packet serial numbers and error-correction codes. The destination system can check to see if all the packets have arrived, arrange them in the correct order, and request that any missing packets be sent again based on this additional information. (TCP performs all these functions, as explained in the next section.)

IP treats each packet as if it existed alone, unrelated to any other packet being transmitted. For this reason, IP packets are often referred to as *datagrams*, which, like a telegram, implies a short but complete transmitted message. IP does not have logical or virtual connections, circuits, sockets, or any other mechanism to provide associations between packets. These functions are all provided by higher level protocols, such as TCP, or occasionally by lower-level protocols, such as ATM.

IP does not perform error correction. IP does, however, implement limited error checking to verify that the header information is correct. Damaged header information could result in the packet being forwarded to the wrong address. If a router on the path between the sending computer and the receiving computer detects at any time that an IP packet's address header has become damaged (by comparing the header with the header's checksum), the router will simply discard the packet without notification of any kind. Again, higher-level protocols will determine what data is missing and generate a request for retransmission. This header checksum does not detect errors that may have crept into the data portion of the packet. That function is also left up to higher-level protocols.

IP does include information about how many times and for how long a packet should continue to be forwarded in a routed system. Every IP packet contains a *time-to-live indicator* that is decremented each time a router forwards the packet or whenever one second of real time elapses. The time-to-live indicator usually starts at around 128, with a maximum possible value of 255. When a packet's time-to-live indicator reaches zero the packet is discarded. This event can occur in three (rare) cases:

- When the network is too busy to forward packets in a timely manner
- When a circular route exists and packets are simply being passed around it
- When the route between two computers is simply too long to be useful

In all three cases, the route is not usable, so communications should not continue.

Internet Addresses   All computers attached to an IP network (such as the Internet) are uniquely identified by a 32-bit number, usually expressed in decimal notation and with each byte separated by a period. Because each portion of the address specifies 8 bits, the decimal range is between 0 and 255 for each of the 4 bytes. For example:

    10.191.31.10

NOTE   You'll often see bytes referred to as *octets* in other network documents. In this book, a byte is always eight bits long, and an octet is eight singing barbers.

This address must be unique to the specific computer to which it is assigned—no other computer can have this address if it is attached to the same network (usually the Internet). If two computers ever do have the same address, unpredictable routing errors will result. IP addresses are analogous to house addresses in that no two are ever the same and each element (in the case of house addresses, elements would be states, cities, streets, and numbers) is increasingly specific—they become more specific as you read to the right.

IP addresses contain two elements of data: the network number and the host number. The network number is the unique code assigned to your network. This number functions much the way a ZIP or postal code functions for routing mail; it gets the packet to the general area—the network. The host (or station) number determines the specific host on that network to which the packet is address. This is similar to your street address.

Internet addresses were originally segmented on byte boundaries. Large networks on which the first byte specifies the network number and the last 3 bytes specify the local addresses are called *Class A domains*. Medium-size networks on which the first 2 bytes specify the network number and the last 2 bytes that specify the local addresses are called *Class B domains*. Smaller networks on which the first 3 bytes specify the network number and the last byte specifies the local addresses are called *Class C domains*.

Before the advent of classes interdomain routing (CIDR), specific address ranges were implied by the Internet domain class. The network number and host number were separated based on the address range rather than the network mask. As the Internet grew, this system became rapidly obsolete and was replaced by CIDR. Classes, as applied to Internet networks, now only specify the network size if it happens to be evenly divisible on byte boundaries.

Class-based subnetting is fairly simple. It is also possible to subnet at any point within the 32 bits of the IP address, not just on byte boundaries. This method of dividing network numbers from local addresses is known as *classless addressing*.

Originally, most Internet addresses were segmented on byte boundaries simply because it was easy, but as IP addresses became scarce, CIDR, the more conservative practice of segmenting based on the actual estimated size of a network, became common.

Eight bits can provide 256 addresses (because 2 to the 8th power is 256), but in this case two addresses in every subnet are reserved. The "all zeros" address is used to specify the entire subnet. The "all ones" (binary 11111111 = 255) address is used to specify an IP broadcast, so sending an IP packet to 10.191.61.255 means that all computers should receive it. Therefore, to calculate the number of available addresses in a subnet, you raise 2 to the number of bits in the subnet portion of the address and then subtract 2.

Each additional bit of address space doubles the number of hosts allowed on a network but divides the number of possible networks in half. So by adding 1 bit to an 8-bit subnet, we can address 510 computers ($2^9 = 512 - 2 = 510$). Adding another bit doubles that to 1,022 ($2^{10} = 1,024 - 2 = 1,022$).

Up and Running

PART 2

TIP When you determine how large an address space should be, add an extra bit to allow for future growth.

Every IP address has two portions:

- The network number
- The local host address

Because both numbers are contained in the same 32 bits and because the size of the network varies greatly from organization to organization, some method is required to determine which part of the IP address is the network number and which is the host's unique identifier. The subnet mask determines which portion of the IP address is the network number and which portion is the local host address. The subnet mask is a 32-bit number—consisting of all ones to the left and all zeros to the right—that specifies how large the network number is. The switch between ones and zeros occurs at the bit size of the network. The following subnet shows an example of a subnet mask for a network with eleven bits of address space:

```
11111111.11111111.11111000.00000000= 255.255.248.0
```

The ones mean that the network number is 21 bits long, and the zeros mean that an 11-bit range is available for host addresses.

The subnet mask determines whether the destination computer and the source computer reside on the same local network or whether the transmission will require routing. When a computer creates an IP packet, it masks off the host address of the destination computer, leaving only the network number. It compares this network number to its own network number, and if the two are equal, the computer transmits the packet directly to the destination computer because the two computers are on the same local data link. If the two numbers are not equal, the client transmits the packet to its default gateway. The default gateway performs a similar comparison. This process continues until the packet eventually reaches the data link to which it is local and is finally received by the destination computer.

Routing

Routers, gateways, and multi-homed servers perform the *routing* function. Routing is the process of forwarding packets among intermediate systems between two end systems. Routers forward datagrams received on one network to another network that is closer to the destination. This process repeats until the datagram reaches its destination. Consequently, routers must be attached to both networks and have an Internet address that is local to each network. (Obviously, the devices need more than one IP address.)

IP addresses are assigned to each network interface, not to each computer. If a server has two network interfaces, each attached to a different network, then it is a multi-homed server. Since most clients have only one network interface, clients have only one IP address and can be referred to by that IP address. Multi-homed servers, routers, and gateways all require more than one address; they are generally referred to by the IP address of the adapter through which the default gateway for that multi-homed host is reached.

NOTE   You may see the term *host* used to describe either a server or a client. Host means any computer attached to the Internet—either client or server.

Figure 5.6 shows a small portion of a very large Internet. Each interrupted ellipse represents a network. The network number portion of that network is shown in bold face, and the host number portion is shown next to each host. The complete IP address for a host is formed by appending the host number to network number—for instance, host number 1.3 on network number 10.191 has an IP address of 10.191.1.3.

Figure 5.6   An IP network showing the path between two hosts

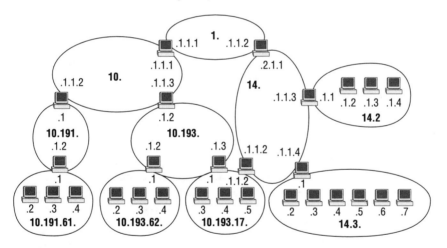

The computers that sit between two networks are multi-homed hosts acting as routers—they have more than one IP address. Notice the following about the figure:

- Multi-homed computers have an IP address for each network to which they are attached.
- Multi-homed hosts connect the networks by forwarding data between them.

- Bottom-tier networks have larger network numbers, usually 3 bytes long. Host identifiers on these networks are only 1 byte long.

- Medium-tier networks have 2-byte network numbers and 2-byte host identifiers.

- Top-tier networks have 1-byte network numbers and 3-byte host identifiers.

- Multi-homed hosts are usually attached to networks with somewhat similar network numbers, but this is not a requirement.

- More than one path can exist between any two-end systems.

A trace route using the `tracert.exe` utility from host `10.191.61.4` to host `14.3.1.7` could produce the following IP address list:

1. `10.191.61.4`

2. `10.191.1.2`

3. `10.1.1.2`

4. `1.1.1.1`

5. `14.2.1.1`

6. `14.3.1.1`

7. `14.3.1.7`

This trace shows that seven routers are involved between the two end systems—an average size for any typical Internet connection. Routers are shown by the network port that the packet travels out of, not by the port that the packet travels into.

The Default Route   In the absence of more specific routing information, the default route specifies which router to send packets to. A router may have any number of network interfaces. For each interface, the router will maintain lists of routes, called *routing tables,* about the network that interface is attached to and the networks that are reachable from that network. The router will forward a packet to the network port (and, therefore, to the network) that is closest to that packet's destination.

If there is no information in a router's routing tables that tells it where a packet should specifically go, the router sends the packet to a default gateway. This route is called the *default route,* because data with no better addressing information is forwarded there. The default route can be followed until the packet reaches a high-level router that has no default route, because it is at the top of the routing hierarchy. The final router either knows where to route the packet, or the packet is dropped and the route is unreachable.

Sage Advice: Default Routes

Due to an obscure bug, Windows NT allows you to specify a default route for every adapter installed in a multi-homed server but uses only the default route established for the first bound network adapter. If the first bound adapter is not the network interface on the same data link as the router that connects to the Internet, your server will not route packets to the Internet. Never specify more than one default route for a multi-homed computer. Assign a default gateway only for the adapter on the same data link as the router that routes to the Internet.

Routing Update Protocols   Routing update protocols are used to exchange information among routers (also known as Internet gateways) about routes, their availability, and their relative congestion. This information provides each router with enough information about its own network environment to make routing decisions for packets. For instance, a router may determine that a certain link is not functioning correctly and send packet traffic to another router attached to a working link. The various routing protocols have evolved through time into two basic groups:

Interior Gateway Protocols   Good at managing small- to medium-scale networks

Exterior Gateway Protocols   Used on the Internet backbone for sophisticated traffic management

Four common routing protocols are in use today:

- Routing Information Protocol (RIP)
- Border Gateway Protocol (BGP)
- Open Shortest Path First (OSPF)
- External Gateway Protocol (EGP)

Windows NT 4 supports only RIP, because it is designed for small-to-medium–scale networks of the sort Windows NT was designed to support and it is the most commonly implemented of all routing protocols. Windows 2000 supports OSPF.

Routing Information Protocol (RIP) is an Internet protocol that routers, gateways, and multi-homed hosts use to trade routing information. RIP was originally developed by Xerox for the Xerox Networking System and adapted for use in IP networks. On Unix systems, RIP is implemented by the *routed daemon*.

RIP is a distance vector protocol, meaning that a router sums the distance cost metrics programmed into each routing interface and selects the route with the lowest sum. A *cost metric* is simply a number assigned by a network administrator that indicates the resources necessary to use that route. Usually, it's just "1," meaning one hop. The cost metric assigned to each interface could be assigned based on the cost of a leased line, the expected congestion, speed, or any other factor the administrator wishes to use.

Periodically, routers send RIP messages to all directly attached routers informing them of their current routing costs. For each route, routers typically remember only the minimum cost seen in RIP updates for that route. Whenever a shorter route is seen in a RIP update, this new route replaces what was formerly the shortest route.

A router may transmit a change in its own cost metric that is higher than its former value, and, in this case, the routers will increase the cost associated with that router. If a router is not heard from in some period of time, that router and the routes associated with it will be invalidated, so another route will be automatically chosen. The router, of course, will be automatically added when it again begins sending RIP updates. This provides a modicum of fault tolerance in case a router fails.

RIP is built into Windows NT 4 and can be added to Windows NT 3.51 by installing the Multi-Protocol Router package on the Windows NT 3.51 service pack CD-ROM. With RIP for IP installed and more than one network adapter, your Windows NT Server can act as a fully functional multi-homed host by automatically updating its routing tables based on information received from other routers.

RIP has a number of significant limitations:

- By design, RIP is limited to covering 15 hops.
- Circular routes can cause RIP to consume inordinate amounts of bandwidth and time trying to resolve a path.
- RIP relies upon programmed metrics involving an administrator's judgment of routing cost rather than real-time metrics, such as current load, capacity, delay, or reliability. This virtually ensures that in a large network, routing will not be optimal.
- RIP has no security mechanisms to prevent bogus updates.

RIP unfortunately allows anyone to send RIP updates to your router. Denial-of-service attacks have already occurred due to bad RIP updates (albeit by accident) and have taken down large portions of the Internet. Using RIP, anyone could use a router, multi-homed server or custom IP stack to essentially reprogram your router.

> **NOTE** Windows 2000 will support Open Shortest Path First (OSPF) for greatly improved routing reliability.

Transmission Control Protocol

Transmission Control Protocol (TCP) provides a reliable connection using an unreliable transport mechanism by supplying the services that IP is missing. Those services are

Reliable Delivery   TCP will request lost packets until the transmission is complete or will return a valid and useful error message. TCP guarantees that as long as a data path exists between two end systems, a reliable stream of data can be transmitted.

Sequencing   TCP will put out-of-order packets back in order so a sequential stream of data is maintained.

Constant Connection   TCP makes data streams act somewhat like files that can be opened, read, and closed. It abstracts the packet-based protocol away from the user's application.

Error Detection and Correction   TCP adds a checksum to the data payload. If the checksum shows that a packet is damaged, the packet is discarded and retransmitted automatically.

Flow Control and Handshaking   TCP implements mechanisms to adapt to the reliability of lower-level systems and improve throughput based on current data-link conditions.

Multiplexing   TCP uses the concept of sockets and ports to create many simultaneous streams of data between the end systems.

TCP does not need any guarantees of service from lower-level protocols. It can use any packet-switched or connection-oriented network protocol as long as two-way communication actually exists between the two end systems. The ability to provide a reliable stream of communication between two systems from an unreliable packet-based transport makes TCP the perfect foundation for higher-level services that require error-free communications.

The TCP specification also provides a modicum of security, but those security mechanisms are obsolete (because they don't really work), so they are not discussed here. Encryption services that work above the TCP layer provide true security by reimplementing the socket services with encryption. These services are collectively referred to as *tunnels* and at the TCP layer they make up the Secure Socket Layer (SSL).

Up and Running

PART 2

Ports and Sockets   As mentioned earlier, TCP provides a multiplexing mechanism to allow multiple data streams to be transmitted between end systems. This multiplexing feature is implemented through ports, sockets, and connections. The ability of a computer to provide different services, such as Telnet service, FTP service, Web service, and Net-BIOS service is dependent upon this multiplexing ability. Without multiplexing, a server could not tell the difference between different higher-level protocols connecting from the same client computer.

A *port* is a TCP connection number. TCP has 16 bits for port numbers, so two end systems may establish up to 65,535 simultaneous separate communications streams. A *socket* is a port, and the IP (or other protocol) address of the end system that is necessary to form a complete path to data; it is usually specified in the form 10.191.61.2:80, where the first 4 bytes are the IP address and the number after the colon (:) is the port. A matched pair of sockets between a client and a host forms a connection.

> **NOTE**   The transmission and reception ports are not the same in a connection. For instance, when a connection to port 80 on a server is established, the client may inform the server to respond to port 15543 on the client. This allows the same client to connect to the same service on the same server multiple times.

Once a connection is established, data can be transmitted between systems bidirectionally until the connection is closed. TCP connections are full duplex, or bidirectional. When you attach your Web browser to an Internet host, the Web browser knows which port to use because the developers of the HTTP service agreed to use the same port number for HTTP servers and clients. This is known as the convention of *well-known ports*.

The well-known port convention specifies that Internet servers of a certain type should "listen" on a certain TCP port for connection requests from client software. The various server software components (such as the Internet Information Server component services) simply open up their socket (the local IP address and the well-known port for that service) and wait for connection attempts from remote clients. Table 5.1 lists some common (and some silly) services and the well-known port that each service uses.

Table 5.1   Some Well-Known Ports

Port	Service	Function
17	Quote	Quote of the Day
21	FTP	File Transfer Protocol

Table 5.1   Some Well-Known Ports *(continued)*

Port	Service	Function
23	Telnet	Telnet
25	SMTP	Mail Transfer
37	Time	Time
53	DNS	Domain Name Server
67	BOOTP	BootP Server
70	Gopher	Gopher
80	HTTP	World Wide Web
110	POP3	Post Office Protocol 3
135	RPC	Remote Procedure Call
139	NBSession	NetBIOS Session

Many well-known ports are in use, but the majority of them are of little consequence except in special systems. Those listed in Table 6.1 are general in nature and used by most Internet hosting systems. A complete list of well-known ports is contained in the Internet Assigned Numbers document defined in RFC 1700.

The Internet Assigned Numbers Authority of the Internet Engineering Task Force assigns all well-known port numbers below 1024. Port numbers above 1024 are available for public use in any manner. Users of some non-official protocols, like Internet Relay Chat (IRC), have simply chosen their own port numbers (in this case: 8000). By convention, everyone knows to use port 8000 for IRC, so it has become a de facto standard. After all, this type of usage is how the well-known port numbering system came to be.

Dynamic Host Configuration Protocol

The Dynamic Host Configuration Protocol (DHCP) makes implementing a TCP/IP network considerably easier than it used to be. DHCP allows computers to request an IP address from an address server, along with other network protocol configuration information like the subnet mask, default gateway, and addresses of important resources (such as name servers).

NOTE   The default gateway is also called the default route.

Dynamic allocation makes it easy to reconfigure network addresses across an entire network by simply changing the addresses served by DHCP servers. DHCP also allows you to reuse IP addresses for pools of computers that are only occasionally attached, such as for dial-up users.

DHCP is an outgrowth of the early BootP protocol, which was somewhat limited in that it provided only an IP address, subnet mask, and default gateway. More complex networks require additional information, such as the address of a WINS server, or additional gateways. DHCP evolved from BootP to provide these (and any other) automatic configuration protocol addresses. DHCP can be forwarded by routers that forward BootP requests, thus removing the requirement that a DHCP server exist on each local network.

DHCP is a client/server protocol in that the booting client requests network information and a server provides that information. The DHCP server is responsible for allocating network numbers so that no two clients get the same IP address. If you have multiple DHCP servers, you must configure them so that no two servers can provide the same address to different clients.

DCHP supports three models of IP allocation:

Automatic Allocation   Assigns a permanent IP address to a host. Whenever a client boots, it will get the same automatically generated but permanently assigned IP address. The DHCP server identifies the client by its MAC address (usually an Ethernet address).

Dynamic Allocation   Assigns IP addresses for a limited period of time (lease duration) or until the client relinquishes the address. This model does not guarantee that the same address will be provided to that client in the future.

Manual Allocation   Assigns a specific IP address to a specific host permanently. This model assigns IP addresses for resources whose IP addresses must be known because they provide some service to the network, such as a file or name server.

The three allocation methods can be used on the same network, as needs dictate. Dynamic allocation is often the most useful because IP addresses can be conserved. With dynamic allocation, IP address assignment is based on the number of clients actually attached, rather than on the number of clients that exist. In other words, dynamic allocation can reserve IP addresses for those clients that are actually using the network at any one time without reserving them for clients that are not in use.

DHCP will automatically avoid manually assigned addresses already in use on the network. If you have a router with an assigned IP address, DHCP will not assign that IP address. Proper implementations of DHCP provide service to BootP clients. (The Windows NT implementation of DHCP currently does not. Microsoft has said it is committed to fixing this problem.)

IP addresses are assigned in ranges called *scopes*. A scope is simply a range of IP addresses that the DHCP server is allowed to assign along with the DHCP options that go along with that range. DHCP options are IP parameters (such as the default gateway, WINS server, and DNS server) that would normally be assigned manually. These parameters can also be set as global DHCP options if the same parameters apply to each of your DHCP scopes. That way, you only have to set the parameter information up one time.

You can also specifically exclude IP addresses or ranges when you set up a DHCP scope. Exclusion prevents DHCP from assigning IP addresses in the excluded range. This is useful for situations when more than one DHCP server may assign the IP address, when you want to reserve a range for future expansion, or when you have clients that cannot support DHCP (like older print servers or obsolete computers).

Internet Control Message Protocol   Internet Control Message Protocol (ICMP) is an integral part of all TCP/IP implementations. As the name implies, it is used specifically to send messages (about the routing of datagrams) between Internet hosts. Essentially, ICMP is the error messenger of the Internet protocols.

ICMP communications are transmitted between gateways (routers) and hosts (servers) under the following circumstances:

- When a gateway cannot reach a destination because a route path does not exist or because the time-to-live indicator of a packet has expired en route.
- When a packet has been discarded because its header information is erroneous.
- When a gateway can't buffer as much information as the host is sending. This controls the rate at which a host transmits TCP/IP information.
- When a shorter route exists.
- When an echo reply has been requested, as in a Ping request.

It's important to note that ICMP messages are only transmitted regarding fragment zero of a fragmented IP packet. Hackers can prevent ICMP error messages from being sent about bad packets by creating fragmented packets that have no zero fragment. Until the release of Windows NT 4 Service Pack 3, NT did not check for a zero packet and simply reassembled packets in order until a fragment with the final fragment flag set arrived.

Since ICMP has no authentication capability, hackers are able to exploit it for a number of denial-of-service attacks. ICMP redirection messages can be hacked to hijack an existing TCP/IP connection, but this is difficult to accomplish seamlessly, and the data must be sent along generally the same route. Inordinately large ICMP ping packets (about 64K) will crash most TCP/IP implementations by overrunning buffers, especially on Intel-based computers. Service Pack 3 fixes most of these problems (except ICMP redirection, which is necessary for the proper operation of TCP/IP and can't be fixed.)

> **WARNING**   ICMP attacks are difficult to prevent because many ICMP messages are crucial to the proper operation of TCP/IP. However, you should set up your firewall to block any access to machines not specifically involved with the external Internet, and make certain you are running the latest version of the TCP/IP software on all your equipment.

Sage Advice: Read the RFCs

The Internet Requests for Comment are the source documents developed by and for the loosely-organized Internet community. They describe the specific details of every Internet related protocol. They are unevenly edited and speak to various levels of reader sophistication, but they are required reading if you ever truly intend to understand TCP/IP. Read at least the following RFCs:

- RFC 791 describes the Internet Protocol.

- RFC 792 describes ICMP.

- RFC 793 describes TCP.

- RFC 768 describes UDP.

A reliable source for RFCs in HTML format can be found at http://www.cis.ohio-state.edu/htbin/rfc/INDEX.rfc.html.

Practical TCP/IP Networking

The benefits of TCP/IP are obvious—it provides the ability to connect massive networks together, and you can't participate on the Internet without it. Less obvious are the dangers of TCP/IP—it is very easily hacked because there's no guarantee of authenticity or even data integrity. Add to that the fact that the evil agents of destruction are attached to the Internet with you, and you have a full-fledged security problem. The Internet is public. Most networks are not.

The largest aspect of practical networking with TCP/IP is security—allowing the users you want to have access while denying access to those you don't. Implementing TCP/IP security is most easily and rigorously accomplished with a sophisticated firewall and a strong firewall policy.

But there are a number of practical security measures you can implement in addition to strong firewalling to further shore up security in your environment, as detailed in the following sections.

Stay Up-to-Date   Keep current on the latest service packs and hot-fixes for computers exposed directly to the Internet. Microsoft releases bug fixes and security improvements routinely in service packs. The latest service pack can be downloaded at www.microsoft.com/ntserver.

> **WARNING**   Unfortunately, there are two serious problems with service packs. Microsoft has, on occasion, released service packs that cause more problems than they solve. Case in point: NT 4 Service Pack 2, which caused serious disk corruption problems. You should generally stay about two months behind the release of a service pack for servers so you'll hear about any problems a release may cause.

Because services packs update system files, they can cause bizarre problems when the versions of system files don't match. This condition can be caused by reinstalling original system files (especially network drivers and services) from the CD-ROM after a service pack has been installed. The various problems you might see in this circumstance are a failure to boot normally or the failure of certain services. To prevent this problem, always reapply service packs before you reboot a computer after software installations.

Use NT's Internal TCP/IP Security   NT's internal TCP/IP security can be used to disallow all services except those the server is specifically configured to serve. NT's TCP/IP stack can be configured to ignore datagrams from specific host addresses and to refuse connections from specific TCP ports. For servers open to a firewall, you should generally disallow all TCP ports except those you explicitly intend to serve.

You can configure TCP/IP to block addresses using the following tactics:

- Unbind TCP/IP from higher level services, such as Server and Workstation. This will prevent unauthorized users from attaching to the server as a normal logged on client and reduces the number of attack vectors down to TCP/IP services, such as FTP and HTTP, which are harder to exploit and easier to secure.

- Install TCP/IP only on Internet hosts that must participate on the Internet—Web servers and clients. Use IPX on internal servers. This option requires that you base your network on IPX rather than TCP/IP and configure IPX as the first bound protocol as explained in the section on IPX. You then install TCP/IP on clients and on Internet servers. Because internal servers do not have a TCP/IP stack installed, any attack on them from the Internet must be vectored through a client having both TCP/IP and IPX, which is very difficult to do and can easily be secured against.

- Use a separate network that is not directly attached to your internal network for Internet connectivity. This is both the most easily implemented and most secure form of TCP/IP security, but it's not that convenient. Users must travel to an Internet-connected client rather than using their desktop PC. However, this can have the effect of reducing casual browsing.

The Interprocess Communications Protocols

Interprocess Communications (IPC) protocols are used to perform higher level functions such as opening files, connecting to servers to see what services are available, and resolving names to addresses in the network. Windows NT supports a number of protocols to perform these services:

- NetBIOS
- Windows Sockets
- SMB/CIFS
- Named Pipes
- Mailslots
- Remote Procedure Call

Each of these protocols is detailed in the following section. You'll notice that I don't cover these protocols as much as others, because there's no configuration information for an administrator to tune, which means these protocols are transparent to the operation of your computer.

NetBIOS

NetBIOS is the basic set of network APIs that perform client-to-server connectivity in a Microsoft network. NetBIOS is a primitive interface that provides the following functionality:

- Name management (add group, check for used, respond used, and report conflict)

- Messaging (datagram and broadcast)
- Session management (locate named resource; establish, transmit, terminate, and flow control)

The data communications facility of NetBIOS is not suitable for many modern applications, but Windows NT still uses the name management services of NetBIOS to find networked resources on the network. This is why the unique name of a computer is often referred to as its NetBIOS name.

NOTE Because the term NetBIOS originally referred to both a network transport and a session protocol, some confusion exists about its correct use. In Windows NT parlance, the transport protocol is NetBEUI, and NetBIOS alone refers only to the session-layer protocol.

Sage Advice: NetBIOS Names

Avoid using common real words (like the name of your company) as NetBIOS names for computers, workgroups, or domains. Users who set their own computers up may often choose the same name for their computer as you've used for a domain or workgroup. This can result in numerous strange errors, such as users of a particular network segment being denied access to a domain. Use prefixes or postfixes to keep names unique, such as "DACCOUNTING" and "CUSERNAME."

Windows Sockets

Windows Sockets provides a mechanism whereby client/server applications can communicate over a network using an interface compatible with the TPC/IP Berkeley Sockets interface. However, Windows Sockets (WinSock) does not require the use of TCP/IP; WinSock applications can operate over any TDI compliant transport protocol. Microsoft Proxy Server uses WinSock to proxy information from IPX interior clients to TCP/IP exterior hosts, for example. WinSock was originally created to facilitate the porting of Unix-based client/server applications to Windows NT but remains important for Internet applications like Web browsers and servers.

Server Message Blocks (SMB)

SMB, alias Common Internet File System (CIFS), is a more complex messaging service to implement client server communications in a Microsoft/IBM network. Windows NT uses

SMB as its core file and print protocol in Windows NT. Microsoft recently renamed SMB to CIFS when it submitted the protocol to the IETF as a draft RFC for open support by a number of vendors as an Internet file system. CIFS actually performs remarkably well as an Internet file system, especially considering its small, local area network origins.

SMB provides interfaces for the following functions:

- Connections (start, end)
- Directory management (create, delete, rename)
- File management (create, delete, rename, get/set attributes, search)
- File access (open, close, commit caches, read, write, seek)
- Record locking (lock block, unlock block)
- Printer control (create job, write job, close job, get queue data)
- Messaging (send, broadcast)
- Name Service (get machine name)

You can play around with various SMB functions directly using various methods in Windows NT. For example, in the Server control panel, when you select an in-use connection and click Close, you are issuing an SMB Connection End command. Similarly, when you type the following at the prompt:

```
Net send administrator "Hello World!"
```

An SMB message sends the data across the network.

Named Pipes

Named Pipes is a connection-oriented interprocess communication interface designed for more complex multi-user functions (such as GroupWare and database connectivity) than SMB will support. For example, MS-SQL server uses Named Pipes to transmit data between clients and servers.

Named Pipes provides a functionality similar to the sockets functionality of TCP/IP. But rather than relying upon well-known ports for services, each service is addressed directly by a known service name. This mimics somewhat the functionality of a traditional disk-oriented file system—so much so that Named Pipes is actually implemented as a file system in Windows NT.

Mailslots

Mailslots is a message-oriented (rather than connection-oriented) interprocess communication protocol. It is used for services that do not require maintaining state (remembering the previously sent data) with a connected computer. For example, Windows NT's browsing mechanism is implemented using the Mailslots interface. Mailslots is somewhat similar to Named Pipes in that it provides a socket mechanism addressed by name and is implemented as a file system.

Remote Procedure Call

Remote Procedure Call was originally developed by Sun as an early attempt at parallel processing to allow certain procedures in a program to be spun off to other machines. RPC was designed to be nearly transparent to the programmer. By compiling an application using a library of "stub" procedures that mimic the interface of standard I/O libraries, client/server functionality could easily be added to any application. The stub procedures took care of identifying resources, connecting sessions, issuing parameters, and collecting results. All of this activity is completely transparent to the original application.

Remote Procedure Call is unique among interprocess communications mechanisms supported by Windows NT, because it relies upon other IPC mechanisms (either Named Pipes, NetBIOS, or WinSock) as its transport. It assumes a fully functional guaranteed transport below it, rather than implementing one.

A Local Procedure Call exists to allow functions to operate transparently on the same machine even if they're written to the RPC interface. The network logon mechanism in Windows NT is handled using Remote Procedure Call (or the Local Procedure Call facility if you are logging on locally).

Up and Running

PART 2

Cheap Security

A customer of mine had a tiny budget to implement their network—they could barely afford a dedicated server, much less complex firewall software, but they needed a direct connection to the Internet. Because they were located in a neighborhood where cable modems were available, they could get a direct Internet connection at 10Mbps for about $150 per month.

But they could not afford a firewall. Although I warned them sternly not to connect their network directly to the Internet without a firewall, the business manager made the decision that they could tolerate being hacked more than they could tolerate not utilizing the Internet.

So we set up the network to run IPX as the internal protocol and use a client station to run proxy software to connect to the Internet. Since all internal machines, including the server, ran only IPX, it would be difficult for a hacker to penetrate beyond the boundary machine—they would have to remotely install a Trojan horse on the proxy machine to penetrate the network beyond.

We installed low-cost proxy software on the receptionist's computer, which was attached both to the cable modem and the local network. We did not use the server as the proxy, because installing TCP/IP on the server would make it vulnerable to Internet attack.

We also installed port monitoring software on the receptionist's machine. This software would detect a "port scan" originating from the Internet (the first strike in a hacking attempt), send a warning message to all users, and immediately break the Internet connection by logging out from the cable modem service provider. Although somewhat inconvenient in the event of an attack, this tactic was effective in preventing penetrations into their network.

We were able to implement this solution for less than $500. In the course of a year, the network resisted four hacking attempts.

6

Network Services

Services provide the network personae of an NT machine. For example, Windows NT's file and print services provide the interface for sharing files and printers on a network. The Workstation service provides the ability for an NT machine to remotely retrieve shared files from another machine. Services are programs designed to provide specific support to other applications running on any computer in the network.

Services provide support to applications, usually on any computer on the network. Drivers provide support to the operating system on the local computer. Services are unlike drivers in that they neither control hardware nor are they necessary for the local operation of the computer—an NT machine can function perfectly well without any services running.

The following services are installed by default in Windows NT:

Alerter   Generates messages about the local computer, which are transmitted via the messenger service.

ClipBook Server   Transmits the contents of the cut-and-paste clipboard over the network to be viewed by remote clipboard viewers.

Computer Browser   Maintains a list of the NetBIOS names of machines the computer is aware of and provides that list to services that request it. The Network Neighborhood displays the known list of computers maintained by the computer browser service.

Directory Replicator   Replicates a specified directory to another computer automatically and receives replication requests from other computers.

Event Log   Records events posted by other services and applications in the event log.

Messenger   Transports messages sent by the Alerter service or the Net Send command.

Net Logon   Performs or passes through logon authentication and synchronizes the security accounts manager among domain participants.

Network DDE   Transports Network Dynamic Data Exchange requests.

Network DDE DSDM (DDE Service Data Manager)   Manages multiple NetDDE streams.

NT LM Security Support Provider   Allows NT LanManager clients such as Windows for Workgroups computers to log on over the network.

Remote Procedure Call (RPC) Locator   Provides a service to check for the existence of named RPC procedures on the local machine over the network.

Remote Procedure Call (RPC) Service   Provides the remote procedure call interprocess communications service.

Scheduler   Maintains and executes a list of time-triggered events such as a nightly tape backup.

Server   Shares files, printers, and IPC mechanisms such as named pipes and mailslots.

Spooler   Receives network-printed documents, queues them, and transports them to local or network printers in order.

UPS   Listens to a locally connected uninterruptible power supply on a serial port for power events and instigates appropriate emergency actions as necessary.

Workstation   Redirects network requests to the appropriate server in a network. Workstation provides the client side of a file, print, or IPC communication.

The following services can be optionally installed in Windows NT Server:

DHCP Client   Transmits a plea for an IP address to a DCHP server and assigns the received information to the appropriate network adapter.

DHCP Relay Agent   Forwards DCHP requests and responses between two networks on a multi-homed host.

Gateway (and Client) Services for NetWare   Provides the redirector service for NetWare networks and a "resharing" mechanism so that NetWare shared directories can be provided to clients of the NT Server. In NT Workstation, Gateway functionality is disabled.

License Logging Service   Records the number of simultaneous user sessions for licensed software on the machine and generates event log messages when installed license numbers are exceeded.

Microsoft DHCP Server   Responds to pleas for and assigns IP addresses from DHCP clients.

Microsoft DNS Server   Responds to domain name queries from TCP/IP clients.

Microsoft TCP/IP Printing   Creates local printer ports that transmit print data to an IP address for final printing by a networked printer.

NetBIOS Interface   Provides a NetBIOS interface for programs written to the NetBIOS interprocess communication specification.

Network Monitor Agent   Shares network monitor data collected on the local machine to a remote viewer.

Plug and Play   Enables activating certain Plug-and-Play ISA devices in Windows NT.

Remote Access Service   Allows modems and other point-to-point data links to be used as network connections.

Remoteboot Service   Allows diskless clients to request boot files from a server.

RIP for Internet Protocol   Shares IP routing information between routing computers in an IP network.

RIP for NWLink IPX/SPX Compatible Transport   Shares IPX routing information between routing hosts in an IPX network.

RPC Support for Banyan   Allows RPC applications to interoperate with Banyan VINES-based networks.

SAP Agent   Publishes network resource availability over the network.

Services for Macintosh   Provides file and print services for Macintosh computers by implementing the AppleShare file sharing protocol.

Simple TCP/IP Services   Provides legacy simple TCP/IP services like chargen, echo, and daytime.

SNMP Service   Provides an interface for Simple Network Management Protocol applications to probe the server for configuration information.

TCP/IP NetBIOS Helper   Passes NetBIOS information between NetBIOS and the Sockets interface for certain TCP/IP services.

Telephony Service   Provides an interface to the TAPI telephony programming interface for applications that work with telephones or call centers.

Windows Internet Name Service   Provides name services for NetBIOS names in a TCP/IP Internetwork. WINS is required, because the browser service cannot normally pass through routers.

And the following optional components are available in the Option Pack for Windows NT Server 4:

Content Index (OP)   Indexes the document text of HTML and other registered file types and provides a search interface to receive and respond to content search queries.

FTP Publishing Service (OP)   Shares files using the FTP TCP/IP protocol.

IIS Admin Service (OP)   Provides an HTTP interface for controlling Internet services (FTP, Web, SMTP, NNTP).

Microsoft SMTP Service (OP)   Provides SMTP mail send, receive, and relay functions. Note that SMTP does not include the POP3 service required to differentiate users of the mail service and separate inbound mail into various e-mail boxes.

Microsoft NNTP Service   Provides Usenet News protocol support for an NT server.

MSDTC   The Distributed Transaction Coordinator manages the transmission of transaction messages between message queues.

Protected Storage   Used by the certificate authority and other secure services for the storage of encryption keys.

World Wide Web Publishing Service   Shares HTML files using the HTTP protocol to support Web browsers.

In the following sections, we'll discuss the pragmatic use of the important services of Windows NT, concentrating on the heavily used services that most administrators deal with. Many of the smaller services are neither configurable nor applicable to most problems, so they do not represent much of an administrative burden. These services are not discussed further in this book, but you may find additional documentation on them in TechNet or Microsoft's KnowledgeBase.

Third-party programs, like license managers, backup software, proxy services, and so forth should install as services. It is also possible to have any program that does not require user input to run as a service using a program available in the Windows NT Server 4 resource kit. This is useful for software (such as Lotus Notes for NT) that should run as services but do not do so by default.

> **WARNING** Windows NT has a hard coded limit of 100 services. You will not be able to install more than this number of services on a single machine, so if you're near this limit, consider removing services or offloading services to other machines. Small Business server is further limited to 25 simultaneous services.

Services Explained

Before we talk about specific services, let's discuss services in general. I'm not going to provide a lot of pretty lines and boxes covering Windows NT's services architecture, because (despite the pretty lines and boxes you may have seen in Microsoft documentation) there really isn't much of an architecture to talk about.

Services in Windows NT are implemented as executable files (`*.exe`) that run in the Executive—that mysterious and poorly defined area that shows up between the Kernel and user space in Microsoft's drawings of how they think Windows NT works. Services are really just executable files that are automatically loaded by the system during the services load phase of the boot process. The services use specially designated security identifiers rather than the security identifier of the system or the logged on user. This view is supported by the fact that any executable can be run as a service as long as it does not require a graphical or user interface.

The only thing that separates services from normal user mode applications is the fact that they're started automatically by Windows NT at boot time. Since they run outside the Kernel, they require a security identifier to run. The identifier is provided by assigning a user account when the service is installed.

Sage Advice: Service Accounts

Create a separate user account for each service (or group of highly related services) you install so that you can fine tune the permission and rights for that service rather than simply providing wide access to your machine. Most BackOffice programs do this for you—don't override their settings. Using the local administrative account is not wise, because it has no authority outside the local domain, and most services in larger organizations will need to connect to relate services in other domains. Using other user accounts may provide more rights than the service account needs, creating a security problem, or they may provide less rights than the service needs, creating a problem that is unusual and difficult to troubleshoot.

The Service Control Manager

Services are started by the Service Control Manager (`services.exe`), which actually also contains a few basic services of NT including Alerter, Messenger, Event Log, and Scheduler.

The Service Control Manager Control Panel (Services) allows you to define the how each service will start (automatic, manual, or disabled) and how to start, pause, and stop a service. The Service Control Manager also allows you to specify which user account should be used to provide a security context for that service.

Stopping a service unloads it from memory and frees up the memory space dedicated to it. Pausing a service merely freezes it to prevent connections to it while maintaining its state and memory allocations.

Sage Advice: Services Best Practices

When a service seems to be unavailable over the network, but the server is operating correctly, try stopping the service and then restarting it. Either the problem will go away, or you'll get a dialog box explaining that the service could not be started, which indicates that something is seriously wrong. Although every third-party service could fail for many different reasons, the default services of Windows NT usually fail for one of four simple reasons:

- The driver the service depends on has not started (due to a hardware malfunction or misconfiguration). This can happen "out of the blue" if a PCI reconfiguration has put two devices on the same IRQ, if termination of a SCSI bus makes devices fail to appear, or if the assignment of high memory has caused a device to fail to allocate enough memory to operate. Or, of course, the driver can fail, because some hardware has actually broken.

- The computer is out of memory or disk space. Make sure the page file is operating correctly and that you have enough memory to support the services you are running on the machine.

- The password for the user account assigned to the service has changed. Watch out for the passwords of accounts assigned to services. If the password of a user account assigned to a service changes, the next time the computer is booted the service will hang. To prevent this problem, always check the Password Never Expires option and the User Cannot Change Password option for the service user account in the User Manager.

> **Sage Advice: Services Best Practices** *(continued)*
>
> - OS files are mismatched due to inconsistent application of a service pack. This is especially likely to show up as failures of the Server service or the Remote Access service. Reapply the most recent service pack to solve this problem.
>
> - A security problem prevents the service's user account from accessing necessary files. Never assign a user account to a service that is actually used by a real user, because the security permissions and passwords for that account could change during the normal operation of the server, which will cause bizarre problems for that service.

Minor Services

There are four minor services actually contained within the `services.exe` Service Control Manager executable. Why Microsoft didn't roll these services out into their own executable files is unknown, especially since fairly common problems with the Event Log service can cause the Service Control Manager to crash and leave the entire machine in an unstable state. These minor services are:

- Alerter
- Scheduler
- Messenger
- Event Log

Each service is detailed in the following sections.

Alerter

Alerter generates text messages from various system services that are transported using the messenger service.

Scheduler

Scheduler maintains a list of commands to be executed at specific times. When the system clock matches a given time, the related command is executed using the security permissions assigned to the Scheduler service.

The Scheduler service was originally included to make nightly backups automatic. The AT command line program is used to add and remove list entries from the schedule.

The Scheduler service can be used to start a program using the permissions of the system, thereby effectively bypassing normal security in a Windows NT system. This is not considered a security problem, because schedule entries can only be made by members of the administrators group. Any program started with the /interactive command line switch can be manipulated by the console user, but it runs with the security identifier of the system or whichever other security account the scheduler program is set to use. If that interactive program can be used to start other processes (for example, taskmgr.exe or explorer.exe) then those other processes inherit the system security identifier and have full system access to the machine, including the ability to stop or start any running process and full access to all secured files. This can be useful in certain cases to shut down a hung process that cannot be stopped otherwise due to denial of access.

Messenger

Messenger uses NetBIOS to transmit small text messages to specific NetBIOS named resources, which can be users, computers, or groups such as workstations or domains. The Alert box of the Server Control Panel uses the messenger service, as does the command line net send command.

Event Log

Event Log receives and stores events from applications running on the local machine, and provides a networked user interface for attaching an event log viewer from a local or remote machine.

Event logs can become corrupted under unusual circumstances, which will cause services .exe to hang upon startup. The solution is technically simple; delete the corrupted event log files. This condition, unfortunately, cannot be corrected from the affected machine without booting a different instance of Windows NT. You have three options at that point: install a new fresh version of Windows NT to the same disk, install the disk in a different unaffected NT computer, or boot an alternative operating system (MS-DOS) that can access the drive and delete the corrupted event log files.

Event logs are stored in the following three files contained in the %systemroot%\system32\ config directory:

- sysevent.evt
- secevent.evt
- appevent.evt

These files cannot be manipulated while the Event Log service is running because they are opened for exclusive use.

Authentication Services

There are two authentication services included with Windows NT: the NetLogon service, which controls authentication between NT machines in a domain, and the Windows NT LanManager security support provider, which allows clients to log into NT servers.

The NetLogon Service

The NetLogon service implements Domain security among Windows NT computers in a network. When a user logs on to a Windows NT machine using an account local to that machine, the logon request is passed directly to the local security accounts manager on the machine. When a user logs on to a Windows NT machine using a domain account, the NetLogon service establishes a secure connection to a domain controller to pass the logon account information and receive authentication.

NetLogon provides the following services:

- Discovers domain controllers upon startup using the browser service
- Establishes secure connections to domain controllers
- Processes domain logons
- Periodically synchronizes the domain security accounts database among domain controllers
- Establishes trust relationships and passes through trust account information

Without the NetLogon service running, NT machines cannot participate in domain security.

Updates to the user accounts database with the User Manager for Domains or the machine accounts database with the Server Manager in a domain occur on the Primary Domain Controller and must be replicated to the Backup Domain Controllers. Although the NetLogon service performs this synchronization automatically, some network and service conditions can prevent full synchronization, which results in failed logon attempts and failed computer connections. You can force complete synchronization using the Server Manager.

NT LM Security Support Provider

NT LM Security Support Provider (NTLMSSP) allows LanManager clients including MS-DOS, OS/2, Windows 95/98, and even Windows NT (when not participating in Domain security) to log onto Windows NT Servers. The NTLMSSP must be running for these clients to log onto an NT server.

Name Services

Name services resolve network addresses given the network name of a resource like a computer or a printer. For example, to access www.altavista.com or a computer called NTDOM01, a client must have a network address to connect to. Name service providers provide the address of named resources that are known to them.

Windows NT Supports numerous NetBIOS name resolution methods:

- NetBIOS name cache (formed by browsing)
- Windows Internet Name Service (WINS)
- Local data-link broadcast query
- LMHOSTS file entry
- HOSTS file entry
- Domain Name Service (DNS)

Name Resolution Process in NT

When you request a named resource on your network, the redirector must resolve the name into a network address for the resource. Since the early days of NetBIOS, the process of resolving names has evolved into a somewhat complicated procedure, consisting of internal cache checks, server lookups, broadcast queries, and host file lookups.

There are two types of names in an NT network:

- A NetBIOS or Windows Networking Name, which consists of 15 uppercase letters or numbers only.
- A DNS Host name, which is up to 256 characters long and consists of a host name and up to 63 hierarchical domain names separated by a period.

The complete name resolution process is shown in the following list. Note that the process stops as soon as the name can be resolved, so a step will only be reached if all previous attempts have met with resolution failure.

NOTE Windows Networking Name and NetBIOS Name are synonymous.

This is the Windows Networking Name lookup procedure:

1. If the name is longer than 15 characters or contains a period, go to step 6.
2. Check the internal NetBIOS name cache.
3. Check a WINS server.

4. Perform a local data-link broadcast query.

5. If the Enable LMHOSTS option is selected, perform a lookup in the LMHOSTS file.

6. If the Enable DNS for Windows Name Resolution option is not selected or if the transport is not TCP/IP, send an error message that the name could not be found on the network.

7. Perform a lookup in the HOSTS file.

8. Query a DNS server.

You can control somewhat how name resolution will occur for various clients by changing the NetBIOS node type, which is assigned either in the Registry or by DHCP. The previous list is the standard name lookup procedure for an H-Node NetBIOS client. A P-Node omits step 4. An M-Node swaps steps 3 and 4. A B-Node omits step 3. Some early NetBIOS clients, such as MS-DOS and earlier versions of Windows and OS/2, may be hard coded as B-Nodes.

> **NOTE**   DNS only works on a TCP/IP network. If you exclusively use IPX or Net-BEUI as your network transport, you cannot use DNS.

Browsing

NetBIOS browsing is built into all NetBIOS-based operating environments, including MS-DOS, all versions of Windows, and OS/2. Browsing facilitates the automatic discovery of named resources by using the broadcast mechanism of the network data link. Computers announce their name and address when they are booted and periodically thereafter. Network clients listen for these names and maintain a list of heard computers in a locally maintained name cache.

Browsing has two problems: It relies upon a broadcast mechanism, which does not usually pass through routed connections, and it relies upon broadcasting from every client, which can consume inordinate amounts of network time in large networks. This makes browsing unsuitable for networks of more than about 200 computers.

WINS

The Windows Internet Name Service (WINS) is Microsoft's attempt at fixing the problems that the name resolution broadcasts create. The WINS service maintains a database of found names permanently, and can be configured to replicate with other WINS servers on the network. Clients are configured to receive their name lists from a WINS server rather than relying upon the traditional broadcast mechanism. WINS is largely self-configuring and is not supposed to require maintenance once it is established.

However, WINS has its own problems. The WINS database can easily become corrupted and require manual intervention. WINS servers must either be physically attached to each segment of a LAN, or clients must have the address of the WINS server hard coded in their LMHOSTS file or receive it through their DHCP address assignment.

DNS

Because browsing and WINS do not completely solve the name resolution problem and for increased compatibility with other TCP/IP systems, Microsoft will use the DNS service for future versions of Windows. DNS can currently be configured to inter-operate with WINS for dynamic NetBIOS name lookup, but this is only necessary when you want NetBIOS-named resources to be available using DNS hierarchical domain names. Aside from interoperating with WINS, DNS requires manual configuration of the name database. Names are not added automatically. Windows 2000 will support Dynamic DNS, which features an automatic name registration feature.

File and Print Services

File and print services are the foundation upon which networks are built, and the most important services most servers will provide. Because of their importance, they're highly integrated with Windows NT's user interface and are managed through familiar tools like the Windows Explorer and the Printers Control Panel program. They are robustly stable and not likely to fail, even under a heavy load. For this reason, there's not much to talk about in this section other than to explain their purpose.

Server

The Server service implements the SMB file sharing protocol (now called CIFS, Common Internet File System) for Windows NT. This service allows clients (such as the Workstation service), called redirectors, to attach to the server and make file requests. The Server service supports the full functionality of a local file system (it is implemented as a file system), so users connecting over the network should notice little difference between a local hard disk and a network share.

The Server service is additionally controlled by the Server Control Panel, which shows file and IPC resources in use, logged on users, and other interesting information. The Control Panel allows you to close files and disconnect users, as well as transmit messages to users on the network.

If you do not use your NT Server as a file server (for instance, if it's a Web server or a firewall), you should disable the server service to increase security and free up memory on the machine.

Workstation

The Workstation service is a file system redirector for SMB. Redirectors intercept requests going to the local storage subsystem (hard disk) and transfer them over the network if they actually refer to a network share rather than a local disk. Workstation thus operates as the client to the Server service.

Directory Replication

The Directory Replication service is stupid. Don't bother using it. A lot of hoopla surrounded Microsoft's hype of this service before it actually appeared. Once it arrived, Microsoft's claims of usefulness came down to the fact that this service was only designed to replicate user logon scripts (also stupid) and profiles among machines. Microsoft soon stopped using replication as a bulleted item in their advertising for NT Server.

Directory replication allows you to automatically copy the contents of a single directory to a share on another server. The copy operation generally starts within five minutes of the file's appearance or a change in the source directory. The service is unidirectional—it cannot copy files back from the same directory. The service also cannot copy open files. These two restrictions make it all but useless for backup or high-availability services, which are what word replication means in the network industry and why everyone was so disappointed by the service (that should really be called a profile and logon script publishing service).

If you don't use directory replication, you can disable this service in the Service Control Manager and save some memory.

Services for Macintosh

Services for Macintosh provides AppleShare file and print services to Macintosh clients. The service actually simulates the functionality of the Server service, but it is entirely different. You can create Macintosh-compatible shared volumes using the Server Control Panel or the original File Manager from NT 3.5. Services for Macintosh is implemented by sfmsvr.exe. The AppleTalk network protocol driver is also installed when you install Services for Macintosh.

Services for Macintosh shares occasionally become corrupt under unusual circumstances. Correcting this problem is simple: In the Services for Macintosh panel of the Server Manager, delete the Macintosh shared volume and then recreate it. No data will be effected by this action.

Up and Running

PART 2

Spooler

The spooler receives print jobs from local and network print clients, spools them to disk and transmits them to the local print devices attached to the computer. Note that local print devices include network TCP/IP printers and printers attached directly to the LPT or COM ports on the computer.

The purpose of the spooler is to allow a single printer to be shared in a group by receiving multiple simultaneous print jobs from users and transmitting them serially to the printer. The print spooler is also capable of reordering print jobs based on priority settings.

Microsoft can't seem to figure out why the print spooler frequently hangs on print jobs. Rather than spending money improving the print spooler, their solution is to teach administrators to stop and start the spooler service whenever it seems that a print job is stuck in the print manager on the server. This seems to work most of the time, so I'll pass along the tip.

Sage Advice: Avoid Fancy Print Drivers

It seems like every printer sold these days comes with some fancy print driver that has to be installed by a custom installer program rather than simply providing a standard NT printer driver that you'd install using the Add Printers Control Panel. As if you really want some pseudo–back-lit–LCD window popping up in front of your working document just to tell you that you are printing something.

Case in point: Both of my printers at home, an OKIDATA laser printer and a Lexmark color printer have "high-performance" print drivers that do all sorts of silly things that don't work correctly over a network. In many cases, these print drivers can cause problems. My OKIDATA high-performance print driver steals so much CPU time that my cursor becomes jerky during printing on a 450MHz Pentium II with 512MB RAM. HP has a number of printers that only work in Windows 98, because they can't figure out how to port their silly driver to NT. Worse, some of their print drivers actually cause the Spooler service to hang.

Deep in the undocumented folders of the CD-ROMs that comes with these printers you'll usually find a standard NT driver. Manufacturers include these to appease those of us who don't need dancing clowns to announce every page we print. These drivers are standard, no-nonsense printer drivers that work correctly with the spooler, don't eat up gobs of CPU time or RAM, and work just as well or better on servers than the fancy driver included for desktop users.

> **Sage Advice: Avoid Fancy Print Drivers** *(continued)*
>
> If you can't find a printer driver like that on your CD-ROM, you'll find that most laser printers are actually compatible with some common model of HP printer like an HP LaserJet 4. This means that you can use the printer driver for that model of printer to drive your laser printer if it doesn't come with a standard printer driver. Some printers have to have these drivers to perform maintenance (like changing toner or ink cartridges), so you sometimes can't choose not to install them, but you may be able to install both and only use the silly driver when you need to change ink cartridges.

Internet Services

Internet services vary widely in their purpose and functionality. The two most popular Internet services, FTP and HTTP, are discussed here. Although these services can be stopped and started via the Service Control Manager, they have their own Internet Service Manager snap-in for the Microsoft Management Console. This Service Manager allows you to set all sorts of configuration information for the services to provide a truly useful and secure service environment. In addition to the MMC snap-in, HTML-based administration Web sites are available for performing remote administration, which attach to the IIS Admin Service.

> **TIP** For more information on using and configuring the HTTP and FTP services, see *MCSE: Internet Information Server 4 Study Guide*, by yours truly and Charles Perkins (published by Sybex). I hear there are some other good titles out there, too.

FTP

FTP provides the file transport protocol for legacy file transfers on the Internet or among Unix PCs. FTP is somewhat similar to the Server service except that it does not provide a rich enough API to allow for multi-user write access to a single file. Also, there are no redirectors like the Workstation service to provide seamless access to an FTP server (access to FTP is via a user-mode client application)—although, there's no technical reason why one couldn't be implemented. For these reasons, FTP is used exclusively for bulk file transfers.

World Wide Web (HTTP) Service

HTTP is similar to FTP in that it implements simple read/write data transfers of files over the network. The HTTP service provides a context (called a MIME type) to the receiving client to inform the client what type of data is contained in the file transfer and, therefore, how that data should be presented to the user. HTTP clients, called Web browsers, interpret the transmitted files according to the MIME type to present HTML, pictures, or any other data type for which a registered browser plug-in is available.

Troubleshooting Service Failures

A customer of mine called in a panic that their server was down. When he went to the server, he was astonished to find that it appeared from the console to be operating correctly, although it was reporting that a service or driver failed to start. I had him open the event log and read the stop messages to me. We determined that the root problem appeared to be that the Server service failed to start. I had him open the Services Control Panel and attempt to start the service manually. This produced an error message and another log entry. I then had him reboot the server. The server went down and came back up the same way, including the error message that server or driver failed to start. At this point, I could no longer troubleshoot over the phone so I came in.

I checked the event log and noted that the Server service was reporting strange errors. Since this machine was the Primary Domain Controller, I couldn't just remove the network services and reinstall them to see if that would fix the problem. I'd never seen the Server service error out before, so I was somewhat stumped; I could still ping all the other clients, and TCP services (such as FTP) worked just fine. Obviously, the lower-level network services were working correctly.

Faced with either long hours of digging through the technical support Web site trying to match error numbers or reinstalling Windows NT on a PDC, I asked the customer if he could remember anything that might have contributed to this problem. When I asked the customer what, if anything, had changed on the server since I was last there, he sheepishly mentioned that he'd installed the NetBEUI transport on the server so they could get some MS-DOS–based clients working on the network without using too much conventional memory. Although the installation went fine, nobody could log into the server afterwards.

Upon hearing that, I knew what was wrong: He used the original CD-ROM that came with the server, which contained Service Pack 0 (okay, there's no Service Pack 0, that's just how I refer to the original NT 4 with no service pack applied) source files. I reapplied Service Pack 3, rebooted the server, and everything came back up correctly.

24seven **CASE STUDY**

7

Securing Windows NT

Security in Windows NT is fundamentally simple—every securable resource (called an object) contains a list of permitted activities, each element of which indicates who is allowed to perform what action upon the resource. A user cannot perform an activity upon an object unless they are expressly permitted to by the object's permission list. That's all there is to it.

Of course, there are just a few details left to describe:

- How the system discerns who is attempting to access the resource
- How the system determines whether to allow or deny access
- How the system exchanges security information with other systems on the network

These details form the remainder of this chapter.

Windows NT also implements a sort of configurable customization scheme, called policies, that are related to security and are covered in this chapter.

The Windows NT Security Model

Windows NT network security is based on user accounts. Before you can use a Windows NT computer, you must supply a username and a password. The logon prompt identifies you to the computer, which then provides access to resources you are allowed to use and denies access to things you aren't.

TIP   Even when a group of people does the same job, each user should have an individual account so that when one user violates security, you can track the violation back to a specific user rather than a group of people who use the same account.

You can assign permissions for resources to groups of users. Every member of the group has the permissions granted to the group as if those permissions had been granted to the individual user account.

User and group accounts are only valid for the Windows NT computer on which they are created. These accounts are local to the computer. The only exception to this rule is computers that are members of a domain trust the users established on the domain controller.

When NT computers join domains, they trust the domain controller's account holders. Creating user accounts on a domain controller and joining all NT computers into a domain allows the use of a single account for all computers. These accounts are local to the domain controller but global to the domain. Trust relationships can be formed between domain controllers so that users of one domain can log into another.

User and group accounts are maintained by the computer for which they are valid; each Windows NT computer has its own list of local user and group accounts. The domain controller's local accounts are trusted by participants in the domain in the equivalent of a one-way–trust relationship between the domain members and the domain controller.

Windows NT computers use their own data structures to resolve security questions concerning local users and groups. Global user and group accounts are maintained by the Primary Domain Controller (PDC) and are backed up by the Backup Domain Controller (BDC). Domain security questions are resolved by referring to data maintained by the PDC or BDC.

Accesses involving domain accounts do not always require mediation by the PDC, because, as you will see in the following sections, Windows NT keeps track of security permissions.

Logging On to Windows NT

There are two ways to access a Windows NT account: directly from the Windows NT console or over the network from another computer. (Windows NT, Windows 95, Windows 98, OS/2, MacOS, or DOS can all be network clients to a Windows NT computer.) In either case, you'll provide a username and password. If you have logged on interactively from the Windows NT console, the Windows NT computer will perform object accesses directly.

If the user has logged on to the Windows NT server over a network from the client computer, the Windows NT server will perform the object accesses on behalf of the client computer. The Windows NT computer containing the resource (file, printer, or directory) will check to see if the user has permission to perform the operation and will disallow the operation if the user does not have permission to access the resource. Client operating systems, such as Windows 95, MacOS, or DOS, that don't have elaborate security mechanisms can still benefit from Windows NT security, because security is maintained by the resource-sharing computer.

When the WinLogon process (which logs you on and sets up your computing environment) needs to refer to the security database, it communicates with the Security Accounts Manager (SAM), which is the Windows NT operating system component that controls the account information. If the information is stored locally on the Windows NT computer, the SAM will refer to the database (stored in the Registry) and return the information to the WinLogon process. If the information is not stored locally (for example, it pertains to a domain account), SAM will query the PDC (or a BDC if the PDC is busy or down) and then return the information to the WinLogon process.

Security Identifiers

User accounts are represented as security identifiers. The SID uniquely identifies the user account to the operating system. When you create an account using the User Manager program, a new SID is always created, even if you use the same account name and password as a deleted account. The SID will remain with the account for as long as the account exists. You may change any other aspect of the account, including the username and password, but you cannot change the SID under normal circumstances—if you did, you would create a new account.

A group accounts also has a SID, which is a unique identifier that is created when the group is created. The same rules that apply to account SIDs also apply to group SIDs.

The WinLogon process checks your username and password to see if you should be allowed to access the network. If the account is valid and the password is correct, the WinLogon process will create an Access Token for you. The Access Token is composed of the account SID, the SIDs of the groups the account belongs to, and a Locally Unique Identifier (LUID), which indicates a specific logon session.

NOTE   An Access Token is created each time you log onto Windows NT. This is why you must log off and then log back on again after making changes to your user account—you need a new Access Token that will reflect the changes you have made.

Special SIDs exist. The System SID is reserved for system services; Access Tokens that contain the System SID can bypass all account-based security restrictions. This SID gives system services permission to do things that a regular user account (even the Administrator account) cannot do. Operating system services are started by the Windows NT Kernel, not the WinLogon process, and they receive the System SID from the Kernel when they are started.

The Authenticated Users SID, created as of NT 4 Service Pack 3, prevents unauthenticated (anonymous) users from accessing certain resources like Registry keys.

Resource Access

Processes must provide an Access Token at each attempt to access a resource. Processes receive their Access Token when they originate from the process that creates them. A user application, for example, usually receives its Access Token from the Desktop explorer. The Desktop explorer received its Access Token from the WinLogon process. The WinLogon process was started from a user-generated interrupt (The Ctrl+Alt+Del keyboard interrupt) and is specially able to create new Access Tokens by querying either the local Security Accounts Manager or the SAM of a domain controller.

Through this method, every process that is started after a user has logged on will have the Access Token that represents the user. By always providing that token to access resources, there is no way to circumvent NT resource security under normal circumstances.

Since the Access Token is passed to new processes upon creation, there is no further need to access the SAM database, either locally or on the domain controller, once a user has logged on.

Inheriting Access Tokens

When you log onto a Windows NT server over the network, the Access Token generated by the WinLogon process on the server is not sent back to your client computer.

Instead the Access Token is inherited by a session of the Server service on the Windows NT server, which maintains a connection to your client computer and performs the actions on the server (opening files, writing data, printing documents, and so on) for the client computer. Since the Access Token never leaves the Windows NT server, there is no chance it will be intercepted on your LAN, and it cannot be modified by a malicious program on an insecure operating system such as Windows 95.

Windows NT goes through the following steps when a user logs on directly:

- The user presses Ctl+Alt+Del, which causes a hardware interrupt that activates the WinLogon process.

- The WinLogon process presents the user with the account name and password logon prompt.

- The WinLogon process sends the account name and encrypted password to the Local Security Authority. If the user account is local to that Windows NT computer, the LSA queries the Security Accounts Manager of the local Windows NT computer. Otherwise the LSA establishes a secure channel via the NetLogon service and then queries the SAM of the Primary Domain Controller or Backup Domain Controller to authenticate the logon request.

- If the user has presented a valid username and password, the LSA creates an Access Token containing the user account SID and the group SIDs for the groups of which that user is a member. The Access Token also gets a Locally Unique Identifier (LUID), which will be described later in this chapter in the "Rights versus Permissions" section. The Access Token is then passed back to the WinLogon process.

- The WinLogon process passes the Access Token to the Win32 subsystem along with a request to create a logon process for the user.

- The logon process establishes the user environment, including starting the Desktop Explorer and displaying the backdrop and Desktop icons.

If you are logging on to a Windows NT computer (presumably a server) over the network, the following steps will occur:

- The user enters the username and password into the logon window of the network client software.

- The network client software opens a NetBIOS connection to the NetLogon service on the server.

- The network client software encrypts the password and sends the logon credentials to the WinLogon process on the server.

- The WinLogon process on the server sends the account name and encrypted password to the Local Security Authority. If the user account is local to that Windows NT computer, the LSA queries the Security Accounts Manager of the local Windows NT computer. Otherwise the LSA establishes a secure channel via the NetLogon service and then queries the SAM of the Primary Domain Controller or Backup Domain Controller (if it is a global account) to authenticate the logon request.

- If the user has presented a valid username and password, the LSA creates an Access Token containing the user account SID and the group SIDs for the groups of which that user is a member. The Access Token also gets a Locally Unique Identifier (LUID). The Access Token is then passed back to the WinLogon process.

- The WinLogon process passes the Access Token to the Server service of Windows NT, which associates the Access Token with the NetBIOS connection opened by the client computer. Any further actions (file reads, print requests, and so on) sent over that NetBIOS connection are performed on the server with the credentials established by that Access Token.

Objects and Permissions

Windows NT maintains security for various types of objects including (but not limited to) directories, printers, processes, network shares, ports, and files.

Each object exposes services that the objects allows to be performed upon it, for example: open, close, read, write, delete, start, stop, print, and so on.

The security information for an object is contained in the object's security descriptor. The security descriptor has four parts: owner, group, Discretionary Access Control List (DACL), and System Access Control List (SACL). Windows NT uses these parts of the security descriptor for the following purposes:

Owner   This part contains the SID of the user account that has ownership of the object. The object's owner may always change the settings in the DACL (the permissions) of the object.

Group   This part is used by the POSIX subsystem of Windows NT. Files and directories in Unix operating systems can belong to a group as well as to an individual user account. This part contains the SID of the group of this object for the purposes of POSIX compatibility. This field is not used by Windows NT for any other purpose.

Discretionary Access Control List   The DACL contains a list of user accounts and group accounts that have permission to access the object's services. The DACL has as many access control entries as there are user or group accounts that have specifically given access to the object.

System Access Control List   The SACL also contains access control entries (ACEs), but these ACEs are used for auditing rather than for permitting or denying access to the object's services. The SACL has as many ACEs as there are user or group accounts that are specifically being audited.

Each access control entry in the DACL and SACL consists of a security identifier followed by an access mask. The access mask in the DACL identifies those services of the object that the SID has permission to access. A special type of ACE, called a deny ACE, indicates that all access to the object will be denied to the account identified by the SID. A deny ACE overrides all other ACEs. Windows NT implements the No Access permission using the deny ACE.

Access will be allowed if an Access Token contains any SID that matches a permission in the DACL. For example, if an individual account is allowed read access, and the user account is a member of a group account that is allowed write access, then the Access Token for that logged-on user will contain both SIDs and the DACL will allow read and write access to the object. Deny ACEs still override any accumulation of permission.

The access control entries in the SACL are formed the same way as the ACEs in the DACL (they are composed of a SID and an access mask), but the access mask, in this case, identifies those services of the object for which the account will be audited.

Not every object has a DACL or a SACL. The FAT file system, for example, does not record security information, so file and directory objects stored on a FAT volume lack DACLs and SACLs. When a DACL is missing, any user account may access any of the object's services. This is not the same as when an object has an empty DACL. In that case, no account may access the object. When there is no SACL for an object, that object may not be audited.

The Security Reference Monitor

Processes do not directly access objects such as files, directories, or printers. The Windows NT operating system (specifically, the Win32 portion of it) accesses the objects on behalf of your processes. The primary reason for this is to make programs simpler—the program doesn't have to know how to directly manipulate every kind of object, it can just ask the operating system to do it. Another important benefit, especially from the security point of view, is that since the operating system is performing the operations for the process, the operating system can enforce object security.

When a process asks the Win32 subsystem to perform an operation on an object (such as reading a file), the Win32 subsystem checks with the Security Reference Monitor to make sure the process has permission to perform the operation on the object. The Security Reference Monitor compares the Access Token of the process with the DACL of the object by checking each SID in the Access Token against the SIDs in the DACL. If there is an ACE with a matching SID that contains an access mask that allows the operation and there is no ACE with a matching SID that denies all access to the object, then the Security Reference Monitor will allow the Win32 subsystem to perform the operation.

The Security Reference Monitor also checks to see if the object access is audited and should be reported in the Windows NT security and event log. It checks for auditing the same way it checks for permissions—by comparing each SID in the Access Token with each access control entry's SID. If it finds a match, it checks to see if the operation (or service) being performed is one of those services indicated in the access mask. If it is, and the result of the security check against the SACL matches the kind of auditing being performed (the access failed and failure is being audited or the access succeeded and the success is being audited, or both), then the audit event is written to the event log.

File and object accesses will only be audited if you enable file and object auditing in the User Manager or User Manager for Domains program.

Rights versus Permissions

There are activities that do not apply to any specific object, but instead apply to a group of objects or to the operating system as a whole. Shutting down the operating system, for example, affects every object in the system. Operations of this nature require the user to have user rights to perform the operation. User rights are enumerated in the Rights menu of the User Manager.

Earlier in this chapter, I mentioned the Local Security Authority includes a Locally Unique Identifier when it creates an Access Token. The LUID describes which of the user rights that particular user account has. The Local Security Authority creates the LUID from security information in the Security Accounts Manager database. The SAM database matches users with rights. The LUID is a combination of the rights of that specific user account along with the rights of all the groups of which that account is a member.

Rights take precedence over permissions. That's why the Administrator account can take ownership of a file to which the owner of the file has set the No Access to Everyone permission; the Administrator has the Take Ownership of Files or Other Objects right. The Windows NT operating system checks the user rights first, and then (if there is no user right specifically allowing the operation) the operating system checks the ACEs stored in the DACL against the SIDs in the Access Token.

User accounts have the right to read or write to an object the user account owns even in the case of a No Access permission. A user account may also change the permissions to an object owned by that user account.

User Accounts

One of the first things you'll do when you set up a new Windows NT network is to create user accounts. A user account is a combination of a username, password, and other identifying items for a particular user. As previously mentioned, user accounts serve several purposes:

- They are a first defense against network intrusion. Users who have not been assigned a password have no right to access the network.
- They uniquely identify each user. You can then assign file system and other rights to specific users or groups of users.
- They provide an audit trail. The username can be used in auditing and to stamp files created or modified by the user.

Creating new user accounts is a simple process, but there are many potential security problems you can inadvertently cause. In this chapter, we'll start with a review of the process of creating user accounts, then move on to specific policies you should use to avoid these pitfalls.

Mandatory Login

The foundation of Windows NT security is the mandatory login. Unlike some networking systems, there is no way to do anything in Windows NT without a user account name and password. The login screen is always displayed when a Windows NT machine boots, so even direct access to the server requires a password.

Although it's not the friendliest of keystrokes, there's a very good reason Windows NT requires this step to log in, and it's one of the reasons Windows NT is considered secure. Because the Ctrl+Alt+Del keystroke is handled by the BIOS as a hardware interrupt, there's literally no way to for a clever programmer to make the keystroke do something else without rewriting the operating system.

Without this feature, a hacker would be able to write a program that displayed a fake login screen and collect passwords from unsuspecting users. However, since the fake screen wouldn't be able to include the Ctrl+Alt+Del keystroke, users familiar with Windows NT would not be fooled.

Creating Accounts

When you create an account for a new user, you can specify a variety of options, many of which are related to security. We'll now take a close look at the process of creating user accounts. You create user accounts using the User Manager for Domains utility.

NOTE   Windows NT Workstation uses the User Manager to create user accounts, which is essentially the same program as the User Manager for Domains minus a few domain administration features.

When you create a new user, the following options are available:

User Must Change Password at Next Logon   Provides you with an easy way to allow users to choose their own passwords. You can create the account with no password or a default password; the user is forced to change the password when they log on.

User Cannot Change Password   Overrides the previous option and prevents the user from changing passwords at all. This is most useful for accounts used by more than one user.

Password Never Expires   Overrides the normal expiration of passwords, which you can configure with the Account Policy dialog box (explained later in this chapter). This option is a security compromise and should only be used with select accounts, such as guest accounts with few privileges.

Account Disabled   Disables the account entirely. This is useful for temporarily disabling the account of a user who is not currently allowed to access the network.

The buttons at the bottom of the New User dialog box are used to display related dialog boxes, which are discussed in the following sections.

Accounts created on domain controllers or member servers are, by default, global accounts. Accounts created on NT Workstations or stand-alone servers are, by default, local accounts, meaning they are not defined on the domain controller.

A special type of local account exists for domain controllers that can be used to provide a method for computers that cannot participate in domain security to attach to domain resources. This condition might exist if you're using older versions of Microsoft networking clients, OS/2, many Unix-based Windows network clients, or for specific users from untrusted domains. These local accounts are similar to standard local accounts, but they cannot be used to log on locally to a domain server. You can create local accounts on a domain controller by clicking the Accounts button in the New User dialog box and selecting Local Account.

Sage Advice: Local Accounts

Don't use local accounts, either on workstations or domain controllers anywhere in your network, except for those few times when you can't avoid it. Domain security is a much more manageable concept than local accounts, and I've yet to run into a situation where I actually needed to use local accounts to solve some specific problem. If your client software is old, upgrade it. If you work frequently with users from an untrusted domain, establish appropriate trust relationships. Using local accounts is a security hack that should be avoided, because it makes your account management more complex than necessary.

Group Memberships

The first thing you'll want to do when creating new users is to put each user into one or more groups. This is an easy way to give the user the rights they need. For example, if a user will be an administrator, adding them to the Administrators group assigns the necessary rights.

You can assign groups using the Group Memberships dialog box, which is accessed by clicking the Groups button in the New User dialog box. To keep the network secure, follow these guidelines when assigning groups to a user:

- Avoid assigning permissions to user accounts. Instead, create a new group, if necessary, and assign rights to it. Then make just a single user a member of that group. This helps prevent "orphan" ACL entries on resources when user accounts are deleted.

- Assign as few groups as possible. Never make a user a member of a group "just in case."

- It can be tempting to add a user to a group with too many rights. For example, in creating an account for an assistant network administrator, assigning the Administrators group seems like a simple task, but this may include many rights the user shouldn't really have. A more secure approach is to create a group with limited rights and assign the user to that group instead.

- Be sure you're familiar with the file system and administrative rights each group membership includes.

By default, a user is assigned to a single group, which is Domain Users in a domain or Users in a computer that is not a member of a domain. You may change the default group membership to any group, but you cannot eliminate the requirement that a default group membership exists.

Environment Settings

The User Environment Profile dialog box allows you to select a profile path that will be used to store preferences for the user. You can also choose a home directory for the user and specify a login script to be executed when the user logs on.

These settings have little effect on security. None of these settings grants any particular rights to the user. In fact, you'll need to give the user file system rights to access the home directory, profile, and login script.

Restricting Hours

You can limit the times a user is allowed to access the network. The Logon Hours dialog box is displayed when you press the Hours button in the New User dialog box. This dialog box displays a grid consisting of 24 columns representing the 24 hours in a day and 7 rows representing the days of the week. Highlight a time period and use the Allow or Disallow buttons to control whether login is allowed at that time.

While this feature can make life difficult for the administrator if it's overused, it greatly increases the security of user accounts. As an extreme example, if all employees worked during the typical hours of 8:00 A.M. to 6:00 P.M., you could restrict all user accounts except Administrator to this time period. This would make things difficult for a hacker—the only time to attack the network would be during business hours, when the administrator is on duty.

Of course, you probably don't need that level of security on your network, and the employees of the company probably don't work schedules that strict. Nevertheless, you can usually prevent intruders to some extent with this feature. For example, if the building is always locked between midnight and 6:00 A.M., it makes sense to disallow most employees access during this time.

TIP   By disallowing logons at least once per day and forcing disconnection during disallowed periods, you can prevent users from remaining logged on permanently. Forcing disconnection by disallowing logons during the period when your tape backup runs will also close all opened files to ensure a complete backup.

Restricting Workstations

When you select the User May Log Onto These Workstations option, you can specify up to eight workstation names that the user will be allowed access to. These are the Windows NT computer names shown in Network Neighborhood.

If your users frequently use the same workstations (or are required to), this option can greatly reduce the risk of an intruder gaining access.

Account Expiration

The most important security feature in the Account Information dialog box is the Account Expires option. This allows you to enter a date when the account will become disabled. You should specify an expiration date for any account you consider temporary (such as temporary employees, guests, and auditors).

If an account expires and you need to re-enable it, you can simply deselect the Account Disabled option in the User Properties dialog box and specify a later expiration date or choose the Never Expires option.

TIP   Don't confuse account expiration with password expiration, which we'll discuss later in this chapter. An expired account must be re-enabled by the administrator; an expired password simply means that the user is required to select a new password.

Controlling Dial-Up Access

The Dial-In Information dialog box allows you to grant the user permission to dial into the network remotely (using RAS). Unless the dial-in permission is set, NT will not allow that account to be logged on over a RAS session. You can also specify options for call-back. This is an increased security measure, because it calls the user back to establish a connection. This prevents use of that logon account from anywhere but the telephone number you assign.

TIP   When you're troubleshooting why a user can't log on over RAS, remember to set their dial-in permissions in the User Manager.

Account Policy

You should now have an idea of the sort of parameters you have control over for each individual user account. In addition, there are a number of features that apply collectively to all user accounts. These are listed in the Account Policy dialog box of the User Manager.

The following account policies are configurable through the account policy dialog box:

> **Maximum Password Age**   Specifies how long a user can use the same password. Shorter periods equal higher security.

Minimum Password Age   Specifies how long a user must keep the same password before changing it. This can help to prevent hackers from changing the passwords of accounts they manage to exploit.

Minimum Password Length   Specifies the length of an acceptable password. Longer passwords equal higher security. Consider eight characters an absolute minimum.

Password Uniqueness   Keeps users from switching back and forth between just two passwords. The higher the number of remembered passwords, the more passwords a user must rotate between.

Account Lockout   Specifies whether the account will prevent logons if presented with a number of incorrect passwords.

Account Lockout Count   Specifies the number of incorrect logons to allow before locking the account. Users should hit their correct password within five attempts at most.

Account Lockout Count Reset Time   Specifies the time frame in which to keep the same lockout count. A reasonable time frame, such as 30 minutes, is sufficient to keep automated logon attempts from succeeding without burdening users too greatly.

Account Lockout Duration   Is the period the account is locked out. Thirty minutes is sufficient to stymie automated hacking attempts. High-security installations may select Forever so the security administrator will know about every lockout incident.

Force Disconnection   Disconnects computers when their allowed logon times expire. Use force disconnection to prevent computers from being logged on permanently and to close all opened files for nightly backup.

Log Onto Change Password   Forces the user to log on before changing the password. If the password expires before it is changed, the account is locked out.

User Rights Policy

The User Rights Policy dialog box allows you to control how rights are matched to user accounts. Specific rights can be assigned to a number of users or groups.

Most rights are assigned to the Administrator account by default only, and have little effect on security. The Show Advanced User Rights option enables the display of a larger list of rights. While many of these are obscure and only useful to programmers, some deserve attention of network administrators.

As with other types of rights, it's a good idea to avoid directly assigning these rights to users unless they have a unique need. Otherwise, it's best to assign rights to a group.

> **WARNING** In some situations you may wish to assign rights to the Everyone group, a virtual group that automatically includes all users; be aware that this can be a security risk, since even the Guest account is a member of Everyone. A better choice is usually Domain Users or Authenticated Users or some equivalently large but still restricted group.

The following are some important rights, including those shown with the Show Advanced User Rights option, you should be aware of when securing the network:

Access This Computer from Network Is simply the right to log onto the domain (or the workstation in a nondomain setup) from a workstation other than the domain controller. By default, this right is granted to the Everyone group.

Add Workstations to the Domain Allows users to connect previously unknown workstations to the domain. Since the workstation gains access to the domain's list of users and global groups, this can be a security risk. By default, no groups appear in the list for this right; however, it is implicitly granted to members of the Administrators and Account Operators groups.

Back Up Files and Directories Gives users the ability to access files on the domain controllers for backup purposes. This is a dangerous right, because it grants read access to all files without regard to the file system rights you've assigned. By default, this right is granted to the Administrators, Backup Operators, and Server Operators groups.

Force Shutdown from a Remote System Allows a user to shut down the system remotely—at least in theory. In reality, this right isn't implemented in Windows NT 4 or previous versions. This dubious privilege is granted to the Administrators and Server Operators groups by default.

Log On as a Service Is an advanced right. This right allows a user to register with the operating system as a service. Obviously, normal users have no business doing this. This right is used by special-purpose accounts, such as those used by Internet Information Server or used for data replication. This right is not granted to anyone by default.

Log On Locally Allows users to log on at the domain controller itself or at a workstation in a workgroup system. You may need to grant this right in a small network where the domain controller can also be used by users. The right is normally granted to the Administrators group and all of the Operators groups.

Up and Running

PART 2

Manage Auditing and Security Log   Allows users to control auditing of file system objects. This right is normally granted to the Administrators group. Users with this right are *not* given access to the Audit Policy dialog box (described in the next section).

Restore Files and Directories   Is a complement to the Backup Files and Directories right and allows a user to restore files. Since this basically allows a user to overwrite any file on the system without the corresponding file system rights, it can be dangerous. It is granted to the Administrators, Backup Operators, and Server Operators groups by default.

Shut Down the System   Allows a user to access the Shut Down option on the Start menu. (In a domain system, this applies only to the domain controllers; users can shut down workstations without restrictions.) This right is granted by default to the Administrators group and all of the Operators groups.

Take Ownership of Files or Other Objects   Allows a user to become the listed owner of files and other objects. This is useful if the original owner of the files is a deleted or disabled user account. This right is granted to the Administrators group by default.

Auditing

The Audit Policy dialog box allows you to select events to include in auditing. You can audit events that succeed, fail, or both. For example, you may wish to audit failed logon attempts. The events you can audit include the following:

Logon and Logoff   Includes all attempts to log on or off of the network. This is useful to keep track of who was online when a problem occurred.

File and Object Access   Logs access to files and other objects. You can control the individual files that auditing applies to from the Security tab in the Properties dialog box for a drive, directory, or file.

Use of User Rights   Logs an entry whenever a user makes use of one of the privileges discussed in the previous section.

User and Group Management   Logs changes to users and groups, usually something only administrators are allowed to do.

Security Policy Changes   Logs changes to the three Policies options in User Manager, including the Audit Policy dialog box itself.

Restart, Shutdown, and System   Logs system events: shutdown, restart, and critical errors.

Process Tracking   Logs the individual processes involved in running a program (windows opening, thread execution, etc.) and is useful for debugging.

Account Security Problems

Now you should understand how Windows NT handles user accounts and passwords, and the many properties and policies you can set to improve user account and password security. In this final section, we'll look at some often-overlooked security holes relating to particular user accounts, such as Administrator, and groups, such as Everyone.

The Administrator Account

The Administrator account is the hacker's ultimate goal—and ironically, it is often the easiest account to break into. With most user accounts, the hacker must determine the username and then the password. With Administrator, the username is given—and is the same on almost every Windows NT system. Breaking in becomes a simple matter of finding the password.

There's one obvious solution to this problem: Use a long, complex, non-English word as the Administrator password. Don't write it down anywhere, and don't give the password to anyone under any circumstance. Change it frequently, just in case.

Less obvious, but more important, is to rename the account. A secret account name is just as difficult to guess as a password. If you rename the Administrator account with the intent of obscuring it, you've effectively created a longer password.

Another solution is to edit the Administrator account to limit its rights and create an account with a different name to use for most administrative purposes. Windows NT does not allow you to remove Administrator from the Administrators group or delete it entirely, but you can reduce the rights of the Administrators group and create an alternate group that has the real power. This also prevents the hacker from simply displaying the members of the Administrators group, as mentioned earlier in this chapter.

Regardless of which account you use for administration, never leave it logged on if you're not actively using it. For one thing, users could walk up to your workstation and obtain access. Also, the hacker can display a list of logged-on users to narrow down the list of potential administrators.

WARNING When you're using these or other methods to secure the Administrator account, be careful that you don't lock yourself out of the network. It's a good idea to assign an alternate administrator account and test it before modifying the main Administrator account.

The Everyone Group

The Everyone group is a built-in group that automatically includes all users on the network. This means that certain rights are given to all users, and it's easy to compromise security by assigning rights and privileges to this group.

One example of a default assignment to the Everyone group that you should definitely change lies in the file system. When you create and format an NTFS volume, the Everyone group is given Full Control privileges on the volume. This essentially means that any user can do anything to any file, basically rendering file system security invalid. This is the first thing you should change when creating a volume.

Guest and Anonymous Accounts

The final accounts you should be concerned with are Guest and Anonymous accounts. The Guest account is created automatically when Windows NT is installed. In Windows NT 4, this account is disabled by default; in previous versions, it was enabled by default. You may be required to enable the Guest account in certain situations, such as when running some Internet server products. Internet Information Server also creates an anonymous account when installed, and this account can be a security risk, as well.

While you can't always entirely delete these accounts, you can at least check to make sure they don't have significant file system rights or other rights. The best way to test this is to log onto the account and see what damage you can cause.

Network Security

So far I've described the local security mechanisms of a Windows NT computer—that is, those mechanisms it implements itself. When you connect NT computers together in a network, the security mechanisms are the same with one exception: NT machines can be configured to trust the account holders from other Windows NT machines.

There are three types of trust in Windows NT, all three of which are actually aspects of the same basic mechanism:

Workgroup   Membership to Workgroup basically means no trust. Users will have to log onto each machine with an account local to that machine.

Domain   Membership to Domain means that computers participating in the domain trust the account holders established on the Primary Domain Controller.

Trust Relationships   Interdomain trust relationships specify foreign domains that the Primary Domain Controller will trust accounts from.

A key aspect of network security is also the share object, which is required to present file resources on the network and which has its own access control list. Share security is separate from file and directory permissions, and both types of security can work in tandem to create a highly secure environment.

Share Security

Workgroups are peer-to-peer networks where workstations can share files and where no computer is dedicated as a server. Workgroups are most suitable for networks with 10 users or less and situations where high security is not a requirement. Workstations can be added to the workgroup without any security checks. Administration can be difficult, since you need to create user accounts for each user on each server with a share that the user needs to access.

Shares are directories or volumes made available from a workstation or server for access by other computers in the network. Shares can be publicly available or can be given a list of users or groups with permission to access them. Shares use share-level security, which allows you to control permissions for individual shared directories. File-level security is superior to share-level security but can only be used on NTFS volumes.

Although you can set up a reasonably secure small network with workgroups and shares, these techniques don't really scale well for larger networks and high-security applications because they are difficult to organize and keep secure.

As you probably know, there are two basic types of networks:

Server-Based Networks   Include a dedicated server and client workstations. The server is used for all file sharing, printer sharing, and other services.

Peer-to-Peer Networks   Consist only of workstations. Workstations can share files and printers and make them available to other workstations.

Microsoft's term for a peer-to-peer network is *workgroup*. A workgroup is comprised of a small group of computers (and users) that are related in some way—they're usually in the same department or the same building. It's possible to set up a network with several separate workgroups. A simple one-workgroup network is sufficient for many small companies.

Windows NT also supports peer-to-peer networking with workgroups and includes security features not found in Windows 3.1*x* or Windows 95 and 98. In the following sections, we'll look at the ins and outs of configuring and working with workgroups, beginning with a discussion of which networks should use this system and which should use the more complex domain system, Windows NT's server-based solution.

Up and Running

PART 2

Choosing Workgroups or Domains

The workgroup system is easy to set up and requires no dedicated server, but it's not for everyone. There are a variety of factors to consider in choosing whether to use the workgroup or domain model, but you can use a simple rule in most cases: The workgroup system works well with small networks with 10 users or less. If you have more users than that, or if your network spans multiple locations, you should seriously consider the domain system.

NOTE Windows NT Workstation's Server service is limited to 10 concurrent user sessions.

Even with a small network, the workgroup model can make life difficult for the administrator. As we'll see later in this section, you may need to create several user accounts for each user to arrange access to resources on various workstations in the workgroup.

Security is a final consideration. The workgroup model is really not meant for high-security applications, and so if you have critical data, you may wish to choose the domain system, even for a smaller network. We'll look at the security holes in the workgroup system later in this section.

There's no automatic way to convert a workgroup network into a domain network. If you change between the two, you'll need to move all of the shared resources to a server, create new domain accounts for each user, and set up a security system to match the original security of the workgroup. Since this is a major effort, you may wish to choose the domain model if you anticipate that the network will grow beyond 10 users in the near future.

Using and Securing Shares

The main reason to set up a workgroup—or most networks, for that matter—is to share files. Any directory on any workstation in the workgroup can be set up as a shared directory (*share*). Although shares don't have the same level of security as NTFS directories on a dedicated server, Windows NT does provide a simple set of security features for shared directories.

NOTE Although it's often associated with the workgroup model, you can also share files from workstations within a domain. In order to do this, the Server service must be running.

The basic share system in Windows NT is similar to the one found in Windows 95, although Windows NT adds a set of permissions for shares similar to the NTFS file permissions. In this section, we'll look at the process of creating and accessing shares, permissions for use with shares, and some security issues you should be aware of.

Creating a Share   You can create a share with any volume or any directory within a volume. You can create shares in either NTFS or FAT partitions, although shares in NTFS partitions can be made more secure. To create a share, right-click a drive or directory in an Explorer window and select the Sharing option. The Sharing Properties dialog box is displayed.

From this dialog box you can specify these options:

Not Shared/Shared As   Specify whether the volume or directory should be shared.

Share Name   Choose a name for the share. This name will appear as a directory name when users view a directory listing for the server. If the share will be accessed by users running Windows 3.*x* or if your users use DOS applications, be sure to use a DOS-compatible name for the share.

Comment   Enter a description of the share's purpose or other information. (This is optional.) The contents of this field are displayed in the Explorer window to the right of the share name if the user selects the Details view.

User Limit   If Maximum Allowed is selected, the number of users accessing the share is limited only by the Windows NT license. If a number is specified, only that specific number of concurrent users can access the share.

Permissions   Click this button to display a dialog box that allows you to change permissions for the share, as described later in this chapter.

When a directory or drive is shared, it is listed in the Explorer with a special icon that shows a hand underneath the drive or folder icon, as if to suggest an unseen hand reaching from across the network to steal items from the folder. (Microsoft probably didn't mean it this way, but this is a good way to picture just how secure shares are.)

Accessing Shares   Although a server might have several shares configured—some entire volumes, some directories several levels deep—they all appear to users as a single listing under the server's name. Users can navigate to the server name using the Network Neighborhood icon and then open it to display a list of shares.

As an example, suppose we created several shares, including VOL_F for an entire NTFS volume, and IE4 for the \Program Files\Plus!\Microsoft Internet directory. A user who navigated to the server through Network Neighborhood would see a flat list of shares.

To make access to shares more convenient for users in the workgroup, you can create Desktop shortcuts to particular directories. You can also map a drive letter on the workstation to the share. This method has the benefit of fooling not only users, but also DOS and Windows applications that otherwise might not support network access. To map a drive to a share, right-click the Network Neighborhood icon and then select Map Network Drive.

To use this dialog box, choose a local drive letter and then choose a server name and path to map the drive to. The window at the bottom of the dialog box displays a list of servers and shares. Select the Reconnect at Logon option to have the drive mapped each time the user logs on.

As an administrator, you have another option for displaying a list of shares on a server. The Server Manager utility includes a feature that allows you to list shares, add or remove shares, and monitor users who are currently accessing shares. To run this utility, go to the Start menu and select Administrative Tools ➤ Server Manager. Highlight a server and select Computer ➤ Shared Directories. A dialog box lists the server's available shares. From this dialog box you can add shares, edit the properties for an existing share, and remove (disconnect) existing shares.

You can also access a different set of features by double-clicking a server name within Server Manager or selecting Server from the Control Panel and then clicking the Shares button. The Shared Resources dialog box is displayed. From this dialog box you can view the number of users currently accessing a share, list the users accessing it, and disconnect individual users.

Default Shares   In the Server Manager dialog boxes, you may notice several shares with names ending in a dollar sign: D$, E$, ADMIN$, and so forth. These are *administrative shares*—shares automatically configured by Windows NT and accessible only to administrators and the operating system itself. These shares are used for remote administration and communication between systems.

Each drive is automatically given an administrative share, with the share name being the drive letter followed by a dollar sign. The ADMIN$ share is connected to the \WINNT directory on each server. There is also an IPC$ share that is used for interprocess communication between Windows NT servers, and there is a PRINT$ share, which shares printer information between servers.

As you've probably noticed, these shares don't appear in the browse lists that you can view from the Explorer. The only way to list them is with Server Manager, which was described in the previous section.

TIP   You can create your own "administrative" shares. Any share name ending with a dollar sign ($) will be hidden from browse lists. Users (administrators or not) can access the share if they know its exact name.

Administrative shares present a potential security risk. A hacker who has gained access to the Administrator account on a single workstation in the workgroup can access the system drives of other workstations, effectively allowing administrator-level access to the entire workgroup.

You can improve security by disabling the administrative shares. Disable these shares using the System Policy Editor as described in the policy section in Chapter 9. It's best to disable all of these and then add a share for any specific drives or directories that need to be available across the network.

Share versus File Security   Windows NT's file sharing system includes its own level of security, called *share-level security*. This type of security allows you to set permissions for a share, either for groups or individual users. This is similar to file system security, but not nearly as sophisticated (or as secure).

There is one significant advantage of share-level security: It works with any shared directory, whether it's on an NTFS or FAT volume. This is the only way to assign permissions to FAT directories. However, the share permissions you set only affect remote users. Users logged onto the machine locally can access anything on a FAT volume, shared or not.

If you're sharing files on a FAT volume, you can't use file-level security. Share-level security provides an alternative, but can be cumbersome. For example, suppose you wanted to share an entire volume but restrict users' access to certain directories. Using only share-level security, you would have to share the volume, then share each individual directory with restricted permissions. (The permissions of lower-level directories override those given to higher-level ones.)

On the other hand, if you have the luxury of using NTFS on the volume, you can simply add a single share for the volume with full access for Everyone, then use file-level security to restrict some directories.

TIP   File-level security is more sophisticated and more complex than share-level security. File-level security is explained in detail in Chapter 4, "Storage and Fault Tolerance."

Share Permissions   As mentioned above, share-level security uses a simple list of permissions. To set permissions for a share, click the Permissions button from the Sharing Properties dialog box. The Access Through Share Permissions dialog box will appear.

By default, the Everyone built-in group is given Full Control access to the share. In other words, share security is not implemented by default. The first thing you should do to secure a share is remove Everyone from the list. You can then add any number of users or groups and give them specific permissions. The following are the permissions available for shares:

    Read   Allows users to list contents of the directory, open and read files, and execute programs.

    Change   Allows all Read permissions. Change permissions also allow users to create, delete, or modify files.

    Full Control   Allows all Read and Change permissions. In addition, users can change permissions and change file ownerships.

    No Access   Disallows access entirely. This is useful in subdirectories, where it can be used to override access given at a parent directory.

NOTE   Since share permissions are not as powerful as file-level permissions for NTFS volumes, you should use file-level security for NTFS volumes. Share permissions are most useful for FAT volumes, which would otherwise have little security.

Domains and Trust Relationships

The domain model allows for greater security and easier administration than the workgroup model. In a domain, there is one list of user accounts. The domain can include a Primary Domain Controller (PDC), one or more Backup Domain Controllers (BDCs), and any number of member servers, which provide no authentication.

In a large network, multiple domains provide for greater security and convenience. By assigning trusts between domains, you can create a complex security model for access throughout the network. However, trusted domains don't allow you to administer the network as one giant domain; you must log onto each domain to assign trusts.

The domain model uses servers called *domain controllers* to manage a unified, shared security database. User accounts created on the domain controller are valid for all domain member computers. You can create a user account once for the domain, and the user can log on from any workstation to access data on the domain controller and other servers. A domain-based network can support fairly large networks—Microsoft claims 100,000 users, but 25,000 is a more reasonable number—and remain centrally manageable.

Domain Server Roles

In the domain model, workstations and servers have clearly defined roles. The domain model supports four basic server roles:

Primary Domain Controller (PDC)   This server acts as the main security checkpoint for the domain and stores the main copy of the security database.

Backup Domain Controllers (BDCs)   These servers serve two purposes: to store replicas of security information as a backup for the PDC and to authenticate users without slowing down the PDC. If the PDC goes down, one of the Backup Domain Controllers will automatically assume the primary role temporarily.

Member Servers   These are servers that are members of the domain. They may store shared data but don't act as domain controllers.

Stand-alone Servers   These servers are not members of any domain. They can be used as stand-alone machines or can participate in a workgroup.

> **NOTE**   Be sure you understand these server roles before installing any machines in the network, because you must choose the role a server will take when you install Windows NT. In most cases, you cannot change the server role after installation. The one exception to this rule is that PDCs can become BDCs and vice versa.

The Primary Domain Controller is the most important machine in the domain. There can be only one PDC per domain, although you can have multiple domains on the network. When a user attempts to log onto the domain, the PDC authenticates the username and password, providing an Access Token for future use.

The PDC should be the first server installed on the network. When you install it, you will be asked for a name for the domain. This can be changed later, but the server role can't. The security account database is created when the PDC is installed and is used from that point forward.

Up and Running

PART 2

The Backup Domain Controllers act, not surprisingly, as backups for the PDC. They periodically contact the PDC and obtain a copy of the security account database. This database can then be used to authenticate users just as the PDC can; however, the database on a BDC can't be changed. To make changes to user accounts, you must be able to reach the PDC.

Each domain controller in your network (primary or backup) can handle about 2,000 users if it's dedicated to the task of maintaining accounts. Servers used for multiple purposes will be less responsive. Plan for one domain controller per every 2,000 users or one domain controller at the end of every slower network connection in a wide area network. There is no practical limit to the number of domain controllers you can have.

If the PDC is unavailable for a period of time, the BDCs on the network contact each other and hold an election to determine which machine will assume the duties of the PDC. This machine can then act as primary controller and allow changes to user accounts. When the real PDC comes back online, it will take over again and update its database with changes made while it was down.

The Member servers are the simplest type of servers on a domain. These machines don't store a copy of the domain's security database at all and cannot authenticate users. You can use these servers to store shared data or as application servers. However, users will need to authenticate with a domain controller before they can access this server.

Stand-alone servers are not configured to join a domain at all. These can be used as stand-alone machines, requiring a local login to obtain access. You can also use them as members of a workgroup. Users at these servers can't authenticate with the domain without changing their configuration.

Securing Multiple Domains

The Domain security model used by Windows NT does not sufficiently address the needs of large organizations, especially those with many offices. Microsoft recognized this early on and implemented the concept of trusting domains to allow authorized users of one domain to access another. Domain administrators can establish trust relationships between domain controllers to give very specific access to members of other domains.

Multiple domain security is merely an extension of domain security. As such, at the time of this writing, there are no known bugs or security exploits that specifically target the trust relationship nature of domain security. Therefore, multiple domain security is deemed as reliable as domain security.

There are two participants in any trust relationship:

- The trusting party has faith that any users from the trusted party are authorized users and will allow them access to its resources contingent, of course, upon their presence in the access control lists of the objects.

- The trusted (the trustee or the recipient of trust) domain controls the account security of the users involved in the trust relationship and provides the user's credentials to the trusting domain.

Trust relationships simply provide a way to give users access to foreign domains without having to have a separate account in every domain. It is possible to create a user account for each user in every domain, and modern clients, such as Windows 95 and NT, will automatically log a user on when access is created. Trust relationships merely shortcut the domain account process by allowing users of one domain to access other domains that trust their domain. If you think of the trust relationship process this way, you'll have no problem keeping the intricacies of the process straight.

Trust Relationships   Trust relationships are established between domains using the User Manager for Domains utility. The establishment of a trust relationship involves two steps:

- On the domain controller of the trusted domain, you must add the new trusting domain to the list of trusting domains.

- On the domain controller of the trusting domain, you must add the new trusted domain to the list of trusted domains.

These steps can be performed in either order, but in this order the relationship is established immediately. If you do this in the reverse order, there is a delay of about 15 minutes while the domains are synchronized.

Trust relationships are unidirectional—that is, when one domain trusts another, the reciprocal relationship is not assumed. To initiate a bidirectional trust, you just establish two trust relationships. Add the foreign domain to both the trusting and the trusted domains lists at the same time and then perform the reciprocal operation on the other domain controller.

Groups and Accounts   Establishing trust between domains does very little to provide access to users, however. The only group membership that is automatically changed by trust relationships is membership in the Everyone group. Everyone automatically contains all interactive users and all network users, which implicitly includes members of trusted domains. Other than this, no automatic group memberships are assumed. If you've followed my advice so far, you've eliminated the presence of the Everyone group in all your shares and access permissions anyway, so this is of little help.

Up and Running

PART 2

Each global group can be considered to automatically contain the name of the domain from which the group comes—for instance, the Domain Admins group on the Finance domain should be thought of as Finance\Domain Admins rather than as Domain Admins. In this light, it's obvious that Finance\Domain Users is not the same thing as Manufacturing\Domain Users.

This means, of course, that you must now add the Finance\Domain Users global group to every share or NTFS folder that you want finance users to have access to inside the manufacturing domain. Since Windows NT doesn't allow global groups to contain global groups, the Finance\Domain Users global group cannot be added to the Manufacturing\Domain Users global group. The reasons for this are complex and have to do with the possibility of creating circular security lookups that would never resolve.

There is no easy or good way to automate the process of giving specific permission to users of other domains. You simply have to add the Domain\Global group permission to each resource to which those users should have access.

Centralized Multiple Domain Security　One of the fundamental security axioms is that of simplification: The simpler a security problem is, the easier it is to control. For instance, vaults have only one door. This means they need only one lock, which requires only one key, and the distribution of that key can be tightly controlled. More doors require more keys, which lead to more complex distribution problems and more opportunity for failure.

Microsoft's trust relationship model suffers from a lack of consideration for the large customer's need for centralized administration and authority. The original intent—single logon to domain resources—is a very solid idea. Trust relationships violate the original intent of the single logon to domain resources because they assume all domains are equal peers; there is no established authority over all domains the way a Primary Domain Controller is the established authority over all domain member servers. For this reason, a hierarchical group structure that can be noncircular is not available, so administration and security are made more complex.

Having a single authentication authority promotes security by simplifying the problem. The complexity allowed by numerous trust relationships makes it far more likely that you will, by accident, incorrectly implement security permissions. To contain the security problem effectively, there must be some way to centralize account management and trust relationships. Of course there is.

You can use the trust relationship model to implement your own central authentication authority, referred to as the *master domain*. In the master domain concept, all user accounts are created in one domain. That domain's Primary Domain Controller is dedicated to the task of domain control and logon authentication and should be used for no other purpose.

All other domains (referred to as resource domains) share resources and files as required by your organization. They do not implement user accounts of their own; rather, they trust the master domain for user account information. Now, because all of your users are members of a single domain, you can add share permissions for Master\Domain Users rather than simply Domain Users on each of your resource domains. Then, when you install the PDC for the various resource domains and set up security for the resources it provides, you can establish the trust relationship between the resource domain and the master domain and implement correct and simple permissions. Also you have the added benefit of being able to centrally administer all account management. It's simple and reasonably effective.

To make the process work correctly over wide area networks, simply establish a Backup Domain Controller for the master domain in each major location (those having more than 25 or so users). Smaller locations probably won't benefit much from a dedicated BDC.

Up and Running

PART 2

Domain Security for Remote Locations

A medium-sized semi-conductor firm has their management headquarters in the western U.S. They have a large manufacturing facility in Mexico and sales offices in the U.K., Germany, Japan, and Taiwan. In addition, the firm plans on opening a manufacturing plant in Malaysia next year and adding 15 sales offices in the next five years.

The network topology is as follows:

- The U.S. headquarters has a network with 50 users.

- The Mexico facility has a network with 200 users.

- Each sales office has a network with 25 users.

- Each office is connected via dedicated frame relay with a committed information rate of 256Kbps and a burst rate of 1.5Mbps.

What is the optimal network configuration for this network if the IS department is located entirely at the U.S. facility?

There are really only two good ways to set up security in a Windows NT network: Use either a single domain or a master domain. This network is not particularly large, but the slow network connections will make logging onto a single domain a chore. If the network goes down (a common problem with globe-spanning WANs), users may not be able to log onto the domain at all unless a Backup Domain Controller exists at every site.

A single domain with Backup Domain Controllers is optimal. This way, the Backup Domain Controllers at each site can respond to logon traffic, thus preventing its transmission over the network.

In this case, we opted not to go with the master domain model, because the total number of users is fairly small. We established a PDC at headquarters and established user accounts and profiles for each user. Then we attached each BDC directly to the PDC at headquarters in turn and logged on with the user accounts for users at the BDCs' ultimate destination. We copied the profiles to the BDCs, established shares, and created a secured directory structure on each machine. Then each BDC was packaged and shipped to its ultimate destination, where it was connected to the wide area network.

BDCs are difficult to get working over slower links, especially in areas where network outages are common. By installing them locally and moving profiles to them before we shipped them out, we could guarantee that they worked correctly and that any problems we had after that would be related to the data link.

8

The Internet and RAS

The Internet connects private networks together to make them more useful. It's highly likely that your own network either already is or will soon be connected to the Internet to share in this increased functionality. E-mail connects people far more efficiently than phone, fax, or letter, and Web documents distribute information and collect orders more easily than any manual method could hope to match. The Web's ubiquitous availability now means that remote users and branch offices can use it rather than high-cost long distance telephony or leased lines to connect to your corporate network. This obviates the expensive wide area networking equipment and services that made global networks the tools of only the largest businesses.

Windows NT works seamlessly with the Internet thanks to Microsoft's tireless efforts to conquer cyberspace. By deeply integrating Internet technologies (like TCP/IP) with Windows NT, working over the Internet can be as seamless as working over an in-house network (though fraught with peril unless you implement stringent security).

There are many different ways to connect a network physically to the Internet, but they all boil down to just two options:

- A direct routed network connection
- A dial-up connection using RAS

The first method is most appropriate for medium- to large-size companies or small businesses that make heavy use of the Internet already. The second method is appropriate for smaller businesses or businesses that neither need nor desire many Internet services but would like to use lower bandwidth services like e-mail.

TIP   Obtain and install the Routing and Remote Access Server update from Microsoft to improve your RAS server's routing performance and add demand dialing services. After you install the update, be sure to restore 128-bit security using the "Sage Advice: Restore 128-bit security" information in the trouble-shooting section of this chapter. Get the update from: `http://www.microsoft` `.com/ntserver/commserv/exec/feature/routing.asp`.

RAS in the Private Network

RAS solves three problems in private networks:

- Connecting the network to the Internet
- Connecting remote dial-up users to the network
- Connecting remote Internet users to the network

Of these three problems, connecting to the Internet is better done with direct routing. Connecting remote dial-up users is usually done better by ISPs. And connecting remote Internet users, while very effective, is often more easily and securely managed using tunneling software for your firewall.

The best RAS practice is not to use it. I make this recommendation having set up and supported numerous RAS networks for clients. RAS accounts for fully 50 percent of the administrative burden in smaller networks, and it allows for a number of different security attacks against your network. RAS is a complex administrative hassle, and its functionality for private networks is increasingly obsolete in the face of Internet access. The Internet is the only remote access technology you need. With encryption, its security can be better than that of direct dial or frame routed point-to-point options.

Using RAS with PPTP to establish encrypted tunnels over the Internet is still an excellent idea, but it is easy to do incorrectly. It also exposes your network that is secured only by a password to attack from the Internet. However, in combination with strong firewall policy, you can limit the range of hosts from which you will accept PPTP connections. Consider using an encryption key-based secure tunneling solution provided with your firewall rather than RAS and PPTP to support remote connections.

Connecting to the Internet with RAS

Remote Access Service (RAS) allows you to connect point-to-point dial-up networking devices like serial links, X.25 or frame relay connections, analog modems, and point-to-point tunnels to your Windows NT computer. A dial-up networking device is any device capable of establishing a real or virtual communication circuit on demand. This is inherently different than permanent circuits established over unchanging fixed circuits or network links because the software must be able to handle both the establishment of the connection and the possibility that it may suddenly disappear. Analog modems, ISDN, and X.25 devices all establish circuits on demand. Frame relay uses permanently established virtual circuits to create a constantly connected path, but since it's often done using X.25 links, it's frequently handled as a RAS device.

RAS integrates with networking software by acting as a virtual network adapter for the connection—it provides an NDIS compliant wrapper for point-to-point network devices that network lack drivers, such as a direct serial link or a modem. RAS also adds a layer of security and management for these connections to allow you to control how these connections are used. Finally, RAS handles the connection and disconnection inherent in demand-dialed devices such as modems, X.25, and ISDN.

Connecting to the Internet with a dial-up connection, such as ISDN or a modem, requires using the temporary connectivity features of RAS in either a permanently connected manner or with automatic session establishment (demand dialing) whenever connectivity is required.

Up and Running

PART 2

WARNING Windows NT Small Business Server has strong support for demand dialing to the Internet—so strong that you'll have to go through a number of steps to disable it if you use a direct routed connection. If you have a direct connection to the Internet, use the standard edition of Windows NT Server.

Problems with RAS Connections to the Net

Temporary Internet connections suffer from a number of problems that make them less than optimal for attaching an entire network. These problems are:

- Low speed
- Single IP address
- Dynamic IP address assignment
- Temporary connections

All RAS devices are fairly low speed. ISDN tops the pack at 128Kbps, which, although fast enough for a single computer, is far too slow to share among three or more simultaneous users. Higher speed devices are all permanently connected to the Internet.

Most ISPs provide only a single dynamic IP address for dial-up accounts, so you can only use a dial-up account to connect a single computer to the Internet. However, you can use a firewall to perform network address translation or a proxy to "reshare" protocols of this single server. This is the method used with Microsoft's Small Business Server, which includes demand-dialing software and MS-Proxy Server 2.

Most ISPs also provide a different IP address to dial-up accounts each time you connect to the Internet, which means that even private services like PPTP can't be shared easily over the Internet, because clients won't know which IP address to attach to.

Since a demand-dialed account is not constantly connected to the Internet, you cannot use it to provide services like HTTP or FTP; nor is it appropriate for SMTP, which assumes that mail servers are always available for e-mail delivery. Demand dialing is appropriate only for sharing Web connections in very small networks that do not handle Web or mail service.

Routing to the Internet

Routing to the Internet is, by far, the most common and efficient method to connect business networks. Routing to the Internet is generally installed and setup by your ISP—you usually don't need to do anything but attach your network to the Ethernet port on your ISP's Internet router located at your site.

The data-link technology used to connect to your ISP should be invisible to you, but the following technologies are commonly used for this purpose:

X.25/DS0/Frame Relay   Appropriate for slower connection speeds (56Kbps) in areas where other more advanced technologies are not available. Modems now approach the speed of frame relay connections and usually cost less, so consider using two bonded modem (or Multilink) connections instead of 56K frame relay.

ISDN   Integrated Services Digital Network is appropriate for slower connection speeds (128Kbps) in areas where ISDN is cheap and other more advanced technologies are not available. ISDN is a dial-up connectivity technology that is not especially well suited for permanent connections.

T1/DS1/Frame Relay   Appropriate for medium speed (1.5Mbps) connectivity and is the most common method used to connect business to the Internet. T1 connectivity is available everywhere, but special circuit lines and equipment make T1 fairly high in cost.

T3/DS3   Appropriate for high-speed networks (45Mbps) of very large companies, universities, and ISPs.

DSL   Digital Subscriber Line is appropriate for medium to high-speed access (1Mbps to 6Mbps) depending upon loop length and other local factors. DSL is the lowest cost medium-speed transport.

Alternative Access   Includes (currently) rare options like cable modem (asynchronous up to 10Mbps) and local proprietary high-speed optical fiber providers over transports such as FDDI (Fiber Distributed Data Interface), ATM (asynchronous transfer mode) and SONET (Synchronous Optical Network). These options vary too widely in their availability, speed, and cost to make general statements about, but they are generally priced to compete well against higher speed telephony options like T1 and T3.

In any case, a dedicated device will usually route your connection to Ethernet or Fast Ethernet for final connectivity to your network. Otherwise, you'll have to install a proprietary and rare network adapter in your server to connect directly to the ISP's network, which should be avoided.

WARNING   Rare devices suffer from poor driver support, problems with operating system upgrades, and migration problems when new technology emerges. Stay with common mass-market equipment as much as possible.

Firewalls and Remote Access

Whether your network is connected directly to the Internet or through RAS, a firewall should be used to manage Internet access and to keep the hacking millions at bay. Modern firewalls also support interoperation with encrypted tunnel software. In this case, the encrypted tunnel client software is installed on remote clients, and the firewall serves as the tunnel end-point in the network. This makes remote networking simple and easy (assuming the firewall software is easy to use) and fairly secure (depending on the specific package used). You should consider using the remote tunneling software built into your firewall rather than PPTP.

Windows NT supports fairly strong firewalling for RAS PPTP servers. When you select the Enable PPTP Filtering security feature for an adapter, only PPTP packets will be allowed in on that port. This feature will make your server very secure against Internet-based attacks using protocols other than PPTP. Since your server will not respond to Ping or other ICMP messages, it can be difficult to troubleshoot. Enable PPTP filtering only after you've gotten everything working exactly the way you want it to.

Remote Client Access with RAS

The primary purpose of RAS is to allow remote dial-up networking (DUN) clients to connect to an NT network. This was very important when RAS was released, because the Internet was not common or universally available. Now that it is, the importance of RAS is greatly diminished.

Many network administrators are reluctant to use Internet tunneling because they assume that RAS is more secure than encrypted tunnels over the Internet. This is not necessarily the case. With proper firewall policy, Internet-based remote access can be just as secure as dial-up remote access, which itself introduces a vector of attack into your network. As recently as 1997, dial-up networking still accounted for more than half of all network attacks.

RAS with X.25, ISDN, or Frame Relay

Don't use RAS to manage X.25, ISDN, or frame relay connections. These connectivity options are very rare, which means that there's not a lot of troubleshooting support out there, and even the technicians trained to set them up have problems getting them working.

Instead use dedicated routers designed to connect Ethernet to X.25, ISDN, or frame relay networks. By using a router to connect to these data links, the connection is constantly maintained, and you have just another Ethernet segment to attach to your server. You can eliminate the RAS service entirely in this case. The dedicated hardware to support these functions is fairly inexpensive—between $500 and $5,000 depending upon the data-link technology in use. You'll save far more than that by eliminating the hassle and downtime that you'll inevitably have if you manage these more esoteric connections with RAS.

Remember to put the resulting Ethernet segment on its own network adapter in the server though—you don't want to compete with other users on a network segment for bandwidth to your remote access devices.

Better yet, don't use X.25, ISDN, or frame relay at all except to connect directly to your higher level ISP—and in that case, let your ISP manage the connectivity equipment and connection. These days, DSL is a better option for that than any of the three previously mentioned options. It's higher speed, increasingly available, and costs less.

RAS with Modems

Whether you should use RAS with regular modems depends on your requirements. If you are an Internet service provider, consider using RAS with modems. If you aren't, avoid RAS with modems.

Why? Again, RAS is a difficult administrative problem. Even correctly operating RAS installations are subject to frequent failure. More importantly, you can easily use the Internet to solve the problem more easily and with less equipment.

Supporting even a few RAS connections on the RAS server requires considerable equipment: a modem to match each dial in modem, a serial port for each modem, and some method to connect the serial ports to the server (either additional serial port internal hardware cards, terminal servers, or Ethernet tunnels). This equipment costs an average of $200 per port. Figure 8.1 shows clients' connectivity using directly attached modems.

Figure 8.1   Direct Modem connectivity using RAS

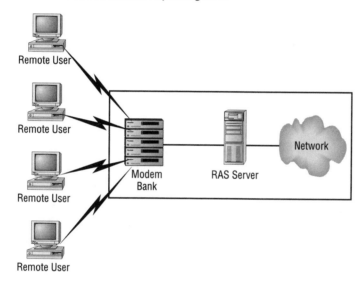

Using the Internet and PPTP, you can eliminate all of that hardware and use your existing routed connection to the Internet as an endpoint for all RAS communications. Remote users with modems simply need to dial into an ISP ($20/month) for connectivity on their end. This solution costs the same no matter what distance exists between the remote user and the server—no long distance or "local toll" charges will apply. See Figure 8.2.

The only case where this method doesn't make sense is when you have a small number (less than five) of users who will dial-in from within the telephone toll-free area around the server, because your users are too close to incur any toll charges, so the $20/month ISP access charge may be excessive. This use is actually fairly rare.

Figure 8.2 Pushing connectivity hardware out to the ISP

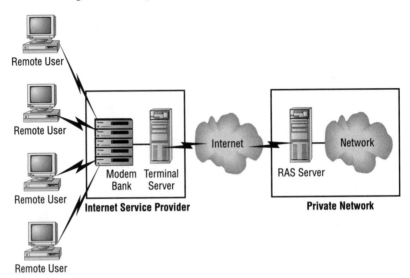

Finally, requiring PPTP makes your otherwise direct-dialed connections more secure. The information you send cannot be wiretapped or intercepted in the clear, since it's encrypted.

RAS for Virtual Private Networking

RAS is most appropriate for use with PPTP. Even though PPTP adds a layer of complexity to RAS, it eliminates one of the most common causes of failure: special connectivity hardware like modems, X.25 PADs, and ISDN routers. RAS with PPTP is a software-only solution to remote connectivity.

Since RAS with PPTP operates over your existing Internet connection, it requires no additional hardware to implement, which provides considerable cost savings. Although you must pay monthly for ISP connections for remote users, the cost is small and it provides other useful benefits, such as Web and e-mail access. Most remote users will already have these connections anyway.

Using PPTP with RAS rather than answering dial-up connections directly allows you to automatically support all types of client connectivity. For example, if you have one remote user with a modem and another remote user using ISDN, you'd have to have both types of equipment on your RAS server to support both customers. By using the Internet and PPTP, you push equipment support problems to the ISP, which simplifies your network. PPTP also future-proofs your network, because any new method of connecting to the Internet is automatically supported for connecting to your network without any additional equipment. For example, you'll be able to support Cellular Digital Packet Data (CDPD) connections from newer wireless ISP cards for roaming users.

Sage Advice: Joining a Domain over a Temporary RAS Link

You can join NT Workstations and Member servers to a domain over a RAS connection. Here's how:

Install networking, TCP/IP, and RAS on the workstation. Do not configure the workstation as a member of a domain—rather, configure it as a member of a workstation with the same name as the domain you want to attach to. Reboot the computer.

Connect to the network using RAS and a user account with RAS dial-in permissions. Change the network security group from a workstation to the domain name, using an account with administrative permission. When you receive the Welcome to X domain, the workstation has been successfully added. Restart the computer.

The workstation will still need to enumerate the domains on its next logon. Do this by logging on using a local workstation account, establishing a RAS connection to the remote domain, and logging off. The RAS connection will remain during the log off. Log back on using the normal process. A domain list will be created, and you'll be able to logon using a domain account. The domain list will be cached on the local workstation, so you won't have to perform this procedure again.

You can also use RAS and PPTP to connect two networks together over the Internet. By permanently connecting both servers to the Internet and using RAS to establish a connection using PPTP, both networks can be connected permanently.

Backup domain controllers can operate well over a remote link. In fact, if you have branch offices with their own server connected over RAS, that server should be a BDC to reduce logon traffic over the link. BDCs cannot be created over a remote link however, because a network link must be available during the installation. You'll have to set your BDC up locally and ship it to the remote site. Figure 8.3 shows a remote office connected via RAS.

Figure 8.3   Using RAS to connect networks

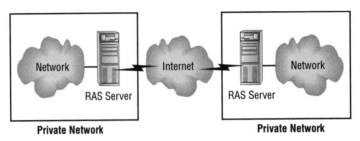

It is possible to create a Backup Domain Controller out of a domain controller from a foreign domain using tools like NewSID from System Internals, because domain controllers all have the same system SID. I've never done this though, and the consequences of doing it are not well documented, so I can't recommend it.

Sage Advice: Force 128-Bit Encryption

You should use only 128-bit encryption for PPTP RAS links because the 40-bit encryption is both weak and flawed in its implementation. You can force a RAS server to connect only at 128-bit encryption strength as follows:

1. Set the RAS service to require Microsoft Encrypted Authentication in the Networking Control Panel.

2. Open the Registry Editor to HKEY_LOCAL_MACHINE\SYSTEM\ CurrentControlSet\Services\RasMan\PPP\COMPCP.

3. Add the value ForceStrongEncryption (DWORD:"1").

4. Once completed, exit the Registry Editor and restart the computer.

Troubleshooting RAS

Because RAS is so complex, I decided to put its troubleshooting section in this chapter instead of in the more general troubleshooting chapter. RAS is easy to install, but it can be very difficult to get it working correctly.

Troubleshoot RAS from the bottom up, tackling simpler problems, such as connectivity, before more complex problems, such as protocol establishment. Use this same procedure whenever you have a problem with RAS, because higher-level problems can be caused by a number of different lower-level failures.

Separate the RAS client and server and determine which machine is actually having the problem. This is generally pretty easy—if only one remote client can't connect, it's a client problem. If no clients can connect, it's a server problem. If some clients can connect but others can't, find out what's different between the clients and troubleshoot that difference on the server.

To ensure a working RAS connection, verify the following:

1. The computer can communicate with the modem.
2. The modem can communicate with other modems.
3. RAS can communicate correctly with the modem.
4. RAS can communicate with RAS on a remote computer.
5. PPTP can establish a session with PPTP on a remote computer.
6. The transport protocols are communicating correctly.
7. RAS dial-in permissions are set correctly.
8. User account information is correct.
9. User permissions are set correctly.
10. Network browsing is operating correctly.
11. Network gating or routing is operating correctly.

These elements of RAS troubleshooting are detailed in the sections that follow.

Can the Computer Communicate with the Modem?

Although this seems rather basic, the inability of the computer to communicate with the modem is frequently the source of RAS problems—especially for a server that has worked with RAS before a hardware upgrade.

Check computer-to-modem connectivity by verifying that the serial port works correctly using the following method:

1. Stop the RAS service and any other service that might lock down the serial port (such as Microsoft FAX service for Windows NT).
2. Use HyperTerminal to establish a direct connection to the COM port.
3. Issue the ATZ command. If you don't get an OK response from the modem, one of the following problems has occurred:

    - The modem is not attached to the serial port.

- The modem is malfunctioning.
- The port is misconfigured or malfunctioning.

Assuming you're addressing the right serial port and don't have a cable problem, the most likely problem is that the serial port IRQ and port don't match the hardware settings in the BIOS for the port. Try deleting the ports in Windows NT's Ports Control Panel and then restarting the computer. Upon reboot, enter the BIOS and ensure that the port is enabled and set to the correct IRQ and port. Make sure no other peripherals are set to use the same IRQ. Sound cards and network adapters are frequently assigned to the same IRQs as serial ports. You may want to set your BIOS to reassign Plug-and-Play IRQ levels by moving a PCI adapter from one slot to another.

When the computer boots to NT, check the Ports applet in the Control Panel to make sure that the port appears and that its IRQ and port settings are correct. Try using the port again.

Can the Modem Communicate with Other Modems?

Once you've ensured that you can communicate with the modem, use HyperTerminal to ensure that you can establish communications with another modem. Use the ATDT 555-1212 command (replacing the phone number with the phone number of a modem known to you) to establish a connection. If the connection goes all the way through, the modem will report the connection speed, thus verifying that the modem is working correctly. You can hang up at this point, because the modem's ability to communicate with other modems is proven.

Can RAS Communicate Correctly with the Modem?

After verifying that the modem works, you'll need to verify that RAS is able to operate the modem correctly.

If you cannot get a RAS modem to dial out, use the following procedure to inspect the communication setup stream between RAS and the modem:

1. In the Registry Editor, browse to the `HKEY_LOCAL_MACHINE\SYSTEM\CurrentControlSet\Services\RasMan\Parameters` key.

2. Add or change the `logging: "1"` value.

3. Stop and restart the Remote Access Service in the Services Control Panel.

This will enable the creation of a `device.log` text file in the `%systemroot%\system32\ras` directory containing the text of the establishment session between RAS and the modem. If errors are apparent in the log file, you may have to replace the modem with one that is supported by NT (any Hayes command set-compatible modem should work).

There is another log file you can use to troubleshoot RAS: the ppp.log file. It can help when PPP users are not being authenticated. The ppp.log will appear in %systemroot%\ system32\ras and can be enabled similar to a device.log file.

1. In the Registry Editor, browse to the HKEY_LOCAL_MACHINE\SYSTEM\ CurrentControlSet\Services\RasMan\PPP\Logging key.

2. Add or change the logging: "1" value.

3. Stop and restart the Remote Access Service in the Services Control Panel.

Is the RAS Service Configured Correctly?

RAS must be configured to dial out on the machine establishing the connection and must be configured for dial in on the machine accepting the connection. If you use dial-back security, both machines must be configured correctly to support it.

Check the network settings for each computer and make sure that the computers are both properly set to support dial-in and dial-out sessions.

Each RAS dial-out port requires a separate memory pool, so you may find yourself running out of memory if you have too many RAS ports configured to dial out. Since there's usually no reason to have more than one dial-out RAS connection from a server, set all of your RAS ports to dial in except one. Dial-in RAS ports share a common memory pool.

Can RAS Communicate with RAS on a Remote Computer?

Establishing a RAS connection with a remote RAS computer is the next step. If you get an error message stating that a common protocol could not be established or that the user account or password was incorrect, then you've proven that RAS is communicating correctly between computers.

If you intend to support non-Microsoft PPP clients (such as Macintoshes or Unix computers) be sure to allow any authentication including clear-text. Third-party clients will not work with NT Challenge/Response Authentication.

If you get to this point but still get error messages that a connection could not be established, test the connection using the same model modem on both ends. In rare cases, modems by different manufacturers will not communicate correctly or at the highest possible speed.

Up and Running

PART 2

Are the Transport Protocols Communicating Correctly?

If you get an error message stating that no common protocol could be negotiated or that the protocol you want to use could not be negotiated, make sure the remote client and RAS server support the same transport protocols.

RAS does not automatically use installed protocols—you must use the RAS Manager to configure protocols and to specify the routing behavior of the protocol.

TCP/IP RAS ports require a method to assign IP addresses to remote hosts. DHCP is the most easily managed method to do this. Remember to create a scope in the DHCP manager specifically for RAS clients. You may also use a static address pool for client IP address assignment if you don't use DHCP on your RAS server. This is similar to DHCP. If you use static assignment, be sure to allow a pool that is one address larger than the number of RAS ports, because RAS always uses the first available address as the TCP/IP address of the RAS adapter.

DHCP only provides an IP address to RAS clients. All other networking information is either unnecessary, provided by the RAS host, or must be configured directly on the client.

If you can't get a more complex protocol such as TCP/IP working in RAS, try a simpler protocol like NetBEUI to make sure the data-link connectivity is working. Once you have NetBEUI connections established correctly, then tackle the additional configuration problems of TCP/IP.

Can PPTP Establish a Session with PPTP on a Remote Computer?

You may get an error message stating one of the following error messages if your server is set to only accept 128-bit encrypted connections and the client supports only 40-bit security:

- RAS could not negotiate a compatible set of protocols.
- The remote computer does not support the required encryption type.
- The PPP control protocol for this network protocol is not available on the server.

This error is also likely after the application of a service pack or the installation of the Routing and Remote Access Service update from Microsoft. Reapply the 128-bit version of the latest service pack on the client and the server to correct this problem.

Sage Advice: Restoring 128-Bit Security

You will need to restore your RAS server's ability to use 128-bit domestic grade security after installing RRAS or applying a 40-bit service pack. Use the following procedure to both determine and replace 40-bit security services with 128-bit security services:

1. Browse to the %Systemroot%\System32\Drivers directory.

2. Right-click on ndiswan.sys and select Properties.

3. The 40-bit security version contains *"export version"* in the description field; the 128-bit version contains "domestic use only."

4. If you have the 40-bit version, rename ndiswan.sys to ndiswan.off and copy ndiswan.sys from the installation directory of the latest service pack into the directory.

Up and Running

PART 2

Is the User Account Information Correct?

The user account provided when dialing into RAS is used only to check for dial-in permissions as set in the RAS Manager. The account provided must have specific dial-in permissions set in the User Manager for RAS to allow that account to dial-in. Make sure the correct user account exists on the RAS server and has dial-in permissions.

Domain security is a different matter. Once a connection has been established through RAS, the local logged on account information is used to check security permissions. This means that if you use different account information on the remote client, you may have network problems on the RAS server. There are two ways around this:

- Join the remote client to the domain and log in locally using a domain account. (See the Sage Advice on joining a remote computer to a domain.)

- Create a local account with the same name and password as the domain account. This name and password will be passed through the RAS server for security on the remote domain.

If using an account from a trusted domain, specify the trusted domain on the remote client rather than the domain you are connecting to.

These problems show up as typical user access or logon failures and should be fairly easy to troubleshoot.

User permissions through RAS connections are slightly more complex because it's not always obvious which account is being used to grant permissions on the domain—it could be a domain account or a user account on the remote client, depending upon how you logged on.

Is Routing or Gating Operating Correctly?

If you can connect directly to the RAS computer but cannot connect through it to other computers on the network, check the routing information for the protocol you're using in the RAS Manager. Make sure TCP/IP is set to forward data through the RAS server, and make sure that routing is enabled in the TCP/IP Control Panel.

Install the RRAS update if you can't route correctly through RAS servers. Although you can hack the Registry to enable proper routing through a RAS server, RRAS does this automatically and in a manner supported by Microsoft.

The NetBIOS gateway can also be used to connect through a RAS server, but its operation isn't nearly as efficient as true TCP/IP or IPX routing. However, since RAS blocks broadcasts by default to reduce traffic on remote links, you may have problems using IPX to find named resources through a RAS tunnel. Combine IPX with NetBEUI to solve this problem using the NetBIOS gateway, binding IPX before NetBEUI for maximum performance.

Is Network Browsing Operating Correctly?

If you can establish remote RAS connections but cannot browse the Network Neighborhood of the remote network, set the workstation and domain properties of the remote client to match the network. If this doesn't work, use the Find Computer option of the Start menu to search for the remote machine. Browsing often fails to function correctly over RAS connections. Consider setting important host names in the LMHOSTS file if finding named resources is a consistent problem—although I've seen cases where this doesn't work either.

The NetBIOS name of the connecting remote clients must be unique on the network—conflicting names can cause all sorts of bizarre connectivity problems. Make sure remote clients have unique NetBIOS names.

If you're using RAS to connect two distant offices on the same domain, make sure both RAS servers are also set up as WINS servers and are configured to replicate the WINS database correctly. This will make finding NetBIOS resources on the remote network quite a bit easier.

Connecting Telecommuters with RAS

A client of mine needed a method for scientists and engineers to work from home with company data. After trying the Zip disk shuffle for a few weeks, it became apparent that version control problems could not be solved unless remote workers were working online with the same data everyone else used. Because the company is based on proprietary scientific research, strong security was mandatory.

We first implemented a firewall based on CheckPoint's Firewall-1 engine running on Windows NT. This firewall puts low-level packet filters in the NDIS layer between the adapter driver and the TDI compliant TCP/IP protocol, so it leaves the server fully functional for additional purposes while providing strong security. Although Firewall-1 can be purchased with VPN software, the company wanted the ability to use shared secret authentication (passwords) and widely available client software, because some engineers worked in very remote locations and the company did not want to be license-limited. PPTP supports this functionality and doesn't cost extra.

We installed RAS and PPTP on the firewall and configured the Registry to support only 128-bit security. Firewall-1 was configured to pass PPTP packets to the system but to block all other inbound connection attempts. Furthermore, the firewall was configured to deny PPTP connections to all but the few known IP addresses of remote engineers.

A DSL connection to the Internet was established by our ISP using a constantly connected DSL-Ethernet router attached directly to the firewall.

Cable modems are available in this location, so remote engineers use them to connect to the Internet at high speed. Each remote computer has NetBIOS unbound from its TCP/IP stack and its Server service disabled to prevent exploitation from the Internet, so IPX is encapsulated in PPTP for access to domain resources. Remote computers are locked down to prevent users from installing services or viruses that might allow their exploitation from the Internet.

The connectivity path between clients and domain resources is shown below.

However, a few far-fetched security problems remain. Because PPTP does not use public key negotiation to authenticate session establishment, anyone who knows the account name and password of a network user could log in through PPTP, and password information can be secretly coaxed from Internet Explorer by an unscrupulous Web site. Although we set the firewall to allow only known IP addresses, it's fairly common for cable modem–using engineers to have more than one computer at home, which means they're likely to try to run a Windows proxy so other home computers can access the Net. This provides a vector for hackers to "launder" their IP address by connecting to the engineer's computer and then retransmitting (proxying) their PPTP requests from there so that it looks like the connection originates from the engineer's computer. Other programs, such as pcAny-

where, can cause similar problems, as can common Trojan horses, such as NetBus and BackOriface.

We used training about the dangers of home-proxy software and remote control software to combat this unlikely problem.

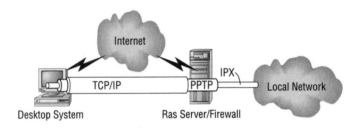

Part 3

NT Everyday

Topics Covered:

- Client support strategies
- Remote client support
- Develop user training
- User profiles
- System policy
- Remote server administration
- Planned maintenance
- Upgrading servers
- Migrating services to new servers
- Server monitoring
- IT departmental organization
- Help desk
- Budget IT expenditures
- Implementing complete, new systems

9

Supporting Clients

Client support, also known as desktop support, consumes more time than all other network administrative duties combined in a normal network. The reasons are simple: There are a lot more client computers than there are servers or dedicated network hardware, and the majority of people who use those computers are not computer experts, so they can accidentally cause malfunction.

Reducing the client support burden is the easiest way to reduce your overall administrative burden. Consider the following example: If you spend 40 percent of your resources supporting servers and 60 percent supporting clients, cutting your client support burden by 50 percent would yield a 30 percent savings in overall administration resources—that's your time and the company's money. Reducing administrative burden by 50 percent is fairly easy to do in companies where few measures have been taken to do this.

This chapter is divided into three sections. "Support Best Practices" covers the theory behind many client support techniques. "NT Client Support Tools" covers those resources already at your disposal to ease the client support burden. Finally, "Third-Party Tools" covers the invaluable tools you should acquire to make your support burden easier.

Support Best Practices

In the dawn of time, there were no networks. There were only large monolithic computers with hundreds of dumb terminals attached to them. The terminals performed no function of their own—they merely transmitted keystrokes and echoed responses on the screen over a simple directly connected serial cable. The central computer did everything.

Desktop management was easy. If a terminal broke, you replaced it. If a user didn't know what the F4 key did, you sent him to training. The administrator's most arduous duty was mounting the nine-inch tape for backup each night. Applications were not added to existing computers—rather, new computers were brought online to support any required additional functionality. Customization didn't exist. Order reigned supreme.

Times have changed. Desktop computers have moved computational power out to every individual user. Spacious local hard disks host a seemingly endless array of cryptically named operating system files, application files, and user files. Networks transmit volumes of data so sporadically that useful measurement can only be taken over large time periods. Servers are arranged in tiers, with myriad purposes and overlapping duties. Employees, forever freed from the bounds of a flashing green cursor, soared with new productivity. But alas, the administrator's job became so burdensome that the labor to fix this dizzying cosmos of equipment became far more costly than the equipment itself. They feared the day when failure occurred—simply determining what went wrong could take days. Chaos ruled.

Fear not. A middle ground between centralized computing and distributed processing exists. Employees can be free to innovate as networks allow while administrators retain control of network resources and are able to fix problems in a timely and controllable fashion. With planning and foresight—or money and hindsight—client administration can be controlled fairly easily.

The basic principle behind controlling the costs of client management is the concept of the replaceable desktop computer. If you can simply replace a broken computer, rather than fixing it, without burdening your user or taking too much time, then you can move all of your troubleshooting and repair efforts into your shop. By maintaining just a few "spare" computers that can immediately be swapped in place of a malfunctioning computer, you'll get your users back to work faster than any other method—and that, remember, is the goal. The broken computers can then be repaired when you have spare time and be turned into spares themselves.

Controlling client resources to reduce administrative burden doesn't mean stifling users. I've heard hundreds of users complain about "net nazis"—overzealous administrators who make policies where none are necessary and force their vision of control upon the unfortunate souls who use their network. This sort of administrative power struggle results in an adversarial relationship with users, who will then look for any reason at all to cast blame upon the IS group and will circumvent security and feel justified in doing so, and who will passively resist all future control mechanisms.

Effective control doesn't imply policy implementation based only on your desire to simplify your administrative problem. The network doesn't exist to give the IS staff a job to do, it exists for the users. Keep this fundamental principle in mind when you negotiate policies with your users. You'll find that the majority of your users don't want or need a free hand to customize their computers—they just want to get their work done. Those workers who desire more freedom from constraint should probably get it, depending upon their job function. But you can negotiate a tradeoff of administrative burden to them, meaning that if they break their computers it's up to them to fix it or to accept a more restricted desktop if they cannot. Most "knowledge workers" are experienced computer users who can be relied upon to make their own decisions about hardware platforms and software applications. Don't make policy decisions in a vacuum, because you must have the support of your users in order to implement sustainable control policies.

This section will go through the theoretical bases for reducing the administrative burden through centralization, reduction of the problem, replicated effort, and security.

Centralize Customization

Customization is the reason computers can't be replaced easily in typical environments. Every desktop in your environment is somewhat customized. It has its own set of files, its own applications, its own operating system, its own configuration, even its own set of hardware.

If client computers weren't customized at all, you could simply replace them when they broke. One desktop would be as good as any other. Employees could use any computer to access their resources, because whatever customized file they needed would be on a server.

Given that customization is the root of client support problems and that the only customized component in a computer is the hard disk, then controlling access to (or even the presence of) the local hard disk in a client computer is the key to reducing client administration throughout your entire organization.

Customization-restricted clients store all created data and user configuration on central servers. This makes the desktop computer completely replaceable. Users can log into any computer, not just the one they usually use. Broken machines can be replaced in minutes, and hard disk failure becomes just another replaceable component. New clients can be brought online quickly by cloning existing machines. The workstations do not need to be backed up, thus reducing the scope of your backup operations.

This line of reasoning explains the four major options that already exist for controlling clients:

- Windows terminals
- Diskless workstations

- Controlled access clients
- Standard workstations

These four desktop options represent four different levels of administrative control: from strictest, least useful, and most easily managed to relaxed, unfettered, and difficult to manage. Which method is most appropriate for your network depends mostly on the needs of your users. In most organizations, a mix of at least two types of desktops is usually appropriate across the strata of your organization.

Windows Terminals   Are functionally the same as terminals of old; they perform no processing on their own. Windows terminals merely display data sent from a central computer (a terminal server) and transmit keystrokes and mouse movements. Windows terminals share the compute power of a single terminal server. Unlike the terminals and mainframes of old, however, desktop applications are not designed for terminal servers—they're designed for complete computers. Modern desktop applications are extremely wasteful of compute resources, and for that reason, a single powerful server can only reasonably support about 50 computers (and even then response will be sluggish). Windows terminals are only appropriate for desktop applications that are not compute intensive (Web browsing or database entry). Graphical or mathematical applications are not suited to this environment.

Diskless Workstations   Are regular PC computers except that they lack a hard disk drive. They boot a special ROM embedded on the network adapter to connect to a remote-boot server, from which the operating system is loaded. This solves the problem of loading a single CPU with too many computing jobs, because each client has its own processor. Because diskless workstations do not have local storage, all file access must be transmitted over the network. Although a considerable amount of disk access is obviated using RAM-based caching, diskless workstations put about three times the load on the network that a normal PC does. However, with good network design, that's not really a problem. Diskless workstations also can take a bit of time to boot in the morning if all the computers are started at the same time. Diskless workstations are most suited to users who work with a well-defined set of lightweight desktop applications. Diskless workstations are not well suited to applications that involve heavy disk use, such as graphical, CAD, scientific modeling, or software development.

Controlled-Access Clients   Are normal PCs that use a combination of strict policy and security to prevent users from storing files on them or modifying their configuration. Controlled-access clients can be thought of as diskless workstations with disks. The local hard disk is used for booting, loading applications, storage of computer configuration information, and storage of temporary files. User configuration and storage of files created by the user are without exception stored on centralized servers. Because the configuration is locked down, the computer can still be swapped out with a replacement in a very short time. Users may or may not be restricted in their desktop activities—their personal configuration choices are simply stored on the server instead of the local client. Controlled-access clients are similar to diskless workstations in their application, but can be used for more disk intensive applications like graphical rendering.

Standard Workstations   Are simply normal PCs connected to a network using the traditional redirector method and with no specific control implemented. These computers are the traditional workhorses of the network environment, but these days, a standard PC is a lot more hardware than most office tasks actually require. Standard workstations are most appropriate for applications, such as graphics, rendering, scientific modeling, and programming. Fortunately, the users who work with these applications usually are expert computer users.

Your environment probably requires a mix of the above client technologies. The two most popular and easily implemented are the controlled-access client and standard workstations. The more esoteric costs of thin clients and remote boot workstations makes them about as expensive as a medium-power standard PC—a single hardware platform you could use to implement both controlled-access clients and standard workstations for those few users that really need them. Leaving standard workstations to all users with minimal controls in place means that you'll always have constant desktop-support hassles.

NT Everyday

PART 3

Sage Advice: Force Centralized File Storage

Do not allow users to store created files and documents on their local computers. This is anathema in a network environment because it makes it impossible to quickly swap out client machines. It also leads to disarray and confusion as to the location of files and makes it impossible to share files effectively in your group.

If users complain that working on files over the network is too slow, upgrade the network. 100MB Fast Ethernet is fast enough for the most demanding engineering applications. Although programmers can make heavy demands of a network, they spend most of their time editing, not compiling. The occasional extra minute to compile a large application is worth the collaborative environment that working directly from the server fosters.

Sage Advice: Force Centralized File Storage *(continued)*

If your company is in the removable cartridge hard disk habit, get out of it. It never ceases to amaze me that people would rather store their work files on a Zip disk than on the server, but I run into this insanity all the time. Files are lost to hot car seats, there is constant confusion about which poorly labeled cartridge a specific file resides on, and there is no way for two people to work on the same group of files at the same time.

If your users require the ability to work from home, set up virtual private networking. It's more consistent, reliable, and sustainable than removable cartridge hard disks. A modem can download a 1MB file in about five minutes, which isn't a big deal when performed at the beginning and end of a work session. The only time removable cartridge hard disks make sense is when a work-at-home requirement exists for truly huge files.

Reduce the Problem

Reduce the scope of your management problem by standardizing software and hardware. Although this sounds very obvious, most of my clients allow users to choose their own applications: The CEO uses WordPerfect, while most everyone else uses Word. Document-format issues abound, and data is lost because of it. Yet everyone blames the software rather than the silly notion that minor differences between applications are more important than standardization.

Hardware standardization is even more important. If you intend to be able to replace computers quickly, the new computer has to be able to boot the same operating system configuration as the old one. This doesn't mean that every computer must be of the same class or manufacture—it means that certain key components and platform choices should be standardized. For example, it's more important that your computers use Windows 98, boot IDE devices and all have the same network adapter than that they all be Dell Dimension P300s.

Larger companies typically purchase computers in larger batches, which makes standardizing a few classes of computer easy, but smaller companies may have difficulty enacting specific hardware standards, because computers are typically purchased on an as-needed basis. Companies that cannot purchase large numbers of the same model should enact strict standards for the following client computer components:

- Network adapters
- Video adapters
- Disk controller (if it's SCSI)

These computer components are not dependent upon specific drivers, so you have considerable flexibility in choosing them:

- Processor (assuming the same family)
- RAM
- Motherboard (assuming same number of processors)
- Hard disk (assuming same controller technology)
- Disk controller (if it's IDE)
- Keyboards, mice, and control devices
- CD-ROM (assuming same controller technology)

It's easy to maintain these standards if you select commonly available hardware for the standard components. You can either order computers to your exact specification, or you can order them without the two key driver devices: video adapters and network adapters. In those cases where you must order a computer with a video adapter, be prepared to replace it with the adapter you've specified. Nearly all computers can be ordered without network adapters these days.

Other more esoteric hardware (such as tape backup devices, removable media hard drives, sound cards, multimedia devices, and scanners) should not be part of your hardware specification. These peripherals are either not necessary in a network environment (for instance, desktop tape backup) or can be added to a desktop like an application (for example, desktop scanners). Choose connectivity technologies like USB or parallel port devices for external desktop peripherals, such as scanners, so they can be added to computers without opening them up.

NT Everyday

PART 3

Sage Advice: Client Hardware Standards

For the three important driver-controlled hardware devices, follow these practices:

- Network adapters should be selected based on a common manufacturer or a common chipset used by numerous manufacturers. For example, the DEC 21140 "Tulip" chipset is driver-compatible across more than twenty different manufacturers.

- Video controllers are more difficult to standardize, because video requirements vary widely among users. Video is not nearly as important for configuration, however, because all video adapters support the VGA lowest common denominator, which can be used until a new driver is installed.

> **Sage Advice: Client Hardware Standards** *(continued)*
>
> - Disk controller technology can be easy—use IDE. Though SCSI is still slightly faster in its fastest configurations, it isn't worth the minor increase in speed for clients considering the driver differences among controllers. A few off-brand UltraDMA chipsets are not compatible with Windows NT's built-in IDE driver, but these chipsets are rare and easily avoided. Use Intel's PIIX4 UltraDMA chipset for complete compatibility.

Work More, Walk Less

In a standard help desk environment, users submit a trouble report by phone or e-mail, and a request for help is logged. The user waits around for a support technician to arrive, who diagnoses the problem. Upon determining the problem, the technician returns to the IS department to get whatever hardware or software tools are required to fix the problem, goes back to the client, and performs the needed repairs. Technician time spent: about two hours. User time spent waiting: about six hours. This means that a support technician can handle about four incidents per day, and that, on average, those eight incidents result in 24 hours of lost user productivity.

Compare this to a just-in-time help desk that uses remote tools to solve these problems. The user calls the help desk, where a technician pulls up a real-time network map, selects their client, and opens a remote control session to that client. The technician can immediately see the specific error message the user is reporting and can initiate soft fixes remotely. The technician can perform software installation from server software sources, configuration, virus checks, or diagnosis over the remote link. In the event of a hardware problem or a computer that cannot be reset by the user to a booted state, the technician logs out a spare client that's been preconfigured with the OS and application package and brings it to the user, replacing the defective computer which he returns to the IS department for diagnosis and repair whenever time allows. Total average IS time spent: 15 minutes. Total user time spent waiting: 15 minutes. This means that the average support technician can perform 32 trouble calls per day, which results in eight hours of lost user productivity. The serious savings comes from the fact that a single support technician can perform the work of eight(!) support technicians from the previous model.

Remote control software can be used to perform routine maintenance (software installation or the application of service packs) and administration as well. Remote control interfaces like pcAnywhere or the remote agents for packages, such as NetWizard, Tivoli, or HP-OpenView, can increase the efficiency of an IS operation by an order of magnitude.

Train Users

User training is the other side of increasing efficiency. By training users to run their computers effectively, you can eliminate a significant portion of the trouble calls to your help desk. Proper training also allows users to respond to verbal direction from support technicians to fix or diagnose problems over the phone.

This discussion of training addresses only the benefit to network administration, but the improvement in user efficiency at their job is phenomenal. A typical $100 training class for an application is repaid in just a few hours of user efficiency, so it's a fairly easy business case to make.

Sage Advice: Train First

Train new employees to use their computers and applications before they begin working and have periodic training refreshers or more advanced courses for existing applications.

You may encounter resistance in upper management to training employees. I've heard ridiculous justifications like "trained employees have to be paid more," "I don't want to train people and have them leave the company," and "We can't afford (or don't have time to) train everyone." In extreme cases, management flat-out won't pay for professional training courses, and there's nothing a network administrator can do about it.

Or is there? You can personally develop training courses for the applications and systems you use in your network. Pass out network-specific user guides. Put up an intranet Web site with click-through training based on screen shots of applications and a frequently asked question guide. You can even put up a click-through troubleshooting guide that culminates in very specific e-mail trouble requests being posted to your support technicians.

Hold training seminars yourself. Keep them short and task-oriented, and, if necessary, hold them during lunch. Users will appreciate the training, and you'll see a serious reduction in trouble incidents.

Of course, these measures take time to put together up front, but proactive planning to avoid problems always does.

NT Everyday

PART 3

NT Client Support Tools

Windows NT comes with a few tools you can use to reduce your administrative burden and create a uniform environment for users. These tools are discussed in the following sections.

Profiles

User profiles allow more than one user to customize a Windows 95/98 or NT client. Start menu, Desktop, and Control Panel configurations, and a number of other user-specific data are stored in separate directories based on the logon name of the user. The Registry is customized upon logon with the configuration specific to that user, so the user's environment is unique for them.

Profiles also allow for customized user environment to be downloaded from a server at each logon, so the user's environment stays the same no matter what computer the user logs on to. For this reason, roaming profiles are an important part of the "replaceable client" philosophy of desktop management. Because even user configurations can be stored on a central server, desktop computers can be truly replaceable with minimal impact on users.

There are three types of user profiles:

Local Profiles   Stored on the client computer in the `%systemroot%\profiles` directory. Changes to local profiles are stored locally.

Roaming Profiles   Stored on a network share and downloaded when the user logs on. Changes to roaming profiles are transmitted back to the server when the user logs off.

Mandatory Profiles   Cannot be changed by the user and must be available in order for the user to log onto the client. Mandatory profiles can be used to make sure users cannot misconfigure or change their Desktop environment.

Roaming and mandatory profiles are stored on a central server's network share. Upon logging on, the user's profile Registry file is downloaded and applied to the Registry, and the profile directories are copied to the local machine. The location of the profile on the server is defined by the profile path in the User Manager for Domains for every individual account.

Profiles are implemented through a combination of configuration Registry settings and directories. Profile settings for the currently logged on user are applied to the HKEY_ CURRENTUSER Registry hive from the ntuser.dat file stored in the user's profile root directory. The following settings are applied to the Registry:

- Desktop Explorer settings
- Persistent network connections (drive mappings and network printer settings)
- Start menu settings
- Control Panel settings
- Standard accessories configuration

Profile directories are stored in the %systemroot%\profiles directory on the client. A profile directory is maintained for each user of the machine, for a default user that serves as a source when new user profiles are created, and for all users. The profile directory contains items that should remain consistent for all users.

The profile directory for every user contains the following:

Application Data   Stores anything an application needs to keep for each user

Cookies   Stores data from Web sites that apply to that user

Desktop   Stores the files, folders, and shortcuts that appear on the Desktop

Favorites   Stores shortcuts to the user's most often used directories

History   Stores URLs to recently browsed Web sites

NetHood   Stores persistent network connections

Personal   Stores that user's personal documents

PrintHood   Stores networked printer shortcuts

Recent   Stores shortcuts to recently used documents

SendTo   Stores shortcuts, batch files, and scripts that can be applied to files to perform various common tasks

Start Menu   Stores shortcuts to applications in a hierarchy that appears as the Start menu browse tree on the Desktop

Templates   Stores template documents for office applications

Temporary Internet Files   Caches Internet documents for quick retrieval

Ntuser.dat   Stores the Registry hive applied for this profile

> **WARNING**   Users should avoid storing large files on the Desktop when roaming profiles are implemented, because the files on the Desktop are copied between the server and client at every logon. Logon time is a direct function of the size of the profile, so keep it as small as possible.

Roaming profiles for Windows 95/98 are partially compatible with roaming profiles for Windows NT. The application directories are largely the same with the exception of the Application Data directory, which is not supported by Windows 95/98. Windows 95/98 supports creating shortcuts to Desktop files rather than downloading them as Windows NT does. The Registry files are different, because the Registry structures of the two operating systems are not compatible. Information contained in the Registry will not be the same between the two platforms.

> **TIP**   Complete information on creating and implementing roaming and mandatory profiles is available from the planning guide available from Microsoft at www.microsoft.com/ntserver/management/deployment/planguide.

DHCP

Dynamic Host Configuration Protocol is an important part of the replaceable-client philosophy—it removes yet another customization from the client to a centralized server. DHCP also reduces administrative burden considerably. Once it's implemented, no further TCP/IP configuration needs to be done for clients, and a number of possible problems caused by misconfiguration are obviated. Chapter 5 explains DCHP in detail.

System Policy

System Policies are specific user interface behaviors of Windows NT or Windows 95/98 computers that a network administrator can control via a System Policy file. A Policy is a named group of user restrictions that are implemented through Registry settings.

Policies are stored in policy files and applied by reading the appropriate policy file into the Registry when a user logs on. The Registry is a database of operating system settings in Windows 95, 98, and NT. For a complete discussion of the Registry, refer to Chapter 15 and Appendix A.

The System Policy Editor, found in the administrative tools section of the Start menu, is used to create policy files. You must use the Administrator account (or an account that is a part of the Administrators or Domain Admins group) to use the System Policy Editor to make changes in your system's Registry.

The System Policy Editor doesn't do anything for you that you can't do yourself (with a little more effort) using the Registry Editor of Windows NT or Windows 95/98. The System Policy Editor simply provides a more structured interface and gives you some guidelines for appropriate values to be placed in the Registry keys.

For example, if you wanted to set a Windows NT user's background pattern to `winnt256` `.bmp`, you could create a policy for that user in the System Policy Editor and then specify the `winnt256.bmp` wallpaper in the Desktop portion of that user's policy. You could also directly make the change in that user's profile in the Registry (identified by that user's SID in the HKEY_USERS key of the Registry.) Incidentally, if that user were to log on and change the Desktop background using the Display Control Panel, the Control Panel would just make the same change in the same place.

You should note that there are many more entries for each user in the Registry than are represented in the System Policy Editor or the Control Panel programs. You will find no reason to edit most of these settings (such as the WaitToKillAppTimeout setting), but they must be there for the operating system, and you should know about them.

System Policy Editor provides an easy to use interface to Registry settings by applying meaningful descriptions to Registry keys and their values and by automatically dereferencing user accounts from the SIDs that are stored in the Registry. The System Policy Editor draws its list of keys and valid choices from ADM text files. You can extend the System Policy Editor by extending these ADM files.

The System Policy Editor is capable of editing the Registry directly or editing system policy files. Editing the Registry directly is useful for one-time system-wide settings that you would like to change. Editing policy files is appropriate for defining user and group account-based policies that you want loaded when users log on. Registry changes occur immediately; policy files are applied when their respective user logs on.

A system policy takes effect the first time the user logs on and every time after that. For example, a system policy may set the background to `winnt256.bmp`. The user may change the background to something else using the Control Panel, but the background will be changed back to `winnt256.bmp` the next time the user logs on.

The policy file must be stored in the appropriate location in order for the computer to apply the policy, though. You can also have multiple policy files and copy the appropriate policy file to the proper location in order to change policies.

NT Everyday

PART 3

Policy Types

Once you have created or opened a policy file or connected to the Registry of a computer, you can edit two kinds of policies: computer policies and user or group policies. (A group policy is exactly the same as a user policy except that it applies to more than one user. The Registry keys that you can edit are identical.)

Computer policies affect all of the users of that computer, regardless of who the user is or which groups that user belongs to. User policies, on the other hand, control settings that affect only the user or group of users that the policy was created for.

> **WARNING** Don't edit the Default Computer or the Default User policies unless you are sure of what you are doing. Instead, create specific computer, user, or group policies for the computers and the users in your network. Once you make restrictive changes to the default policy accounts, you may find that you can't change the policies back. This is because these default policies are put in effect if there is not a more specific policy for the operating system to apply to that computer or user.

You can add, remove, and copy policies in a policy file using the Edit menu of the System Policy Editor.

Activating Policies

Policies must be saved in a location where the computer(s) will find them when a user logs on. The standard location for policy files is in the NetLogon share of the Primary Domain Controller. (The usual location of the NetLogon directory share is `winnt\system32\repl\import`.) You can always find the location of the NetLogon share by browsing through the Network Neighborhood rather than My Computer, or by using the Server Manager administrative tool to view the path of the NetLogon share.

You must also give the policy file the filename the operating system is looking for: `NTConfig.pol` in the case of Windows NT and `Config.pol` in the case of Windows 95.

You don't necessarily have to save the policies in the NetLogon share nor do you have to give the files those specific names (`NTConfig.pol` and `Config.pol`). Of course, you can change the location of the files or change the names that the operating systems will search for them under by editing the Registries of the computers.

The Registry key `HKEY_LOCAL_MACHINE\System\CurrentControlSet\Control\Update` may contain the entries NetworkPath and UpdateMode. If the UpdateMode entry contains the numeric value 1, then the operating system will check in the default location (the NetLogon share) for the policy file. If you change the value to 2, however, the operating system will instead look to the location you enter in the NetworkPath field. You must change this Registry key for every computer that will look for its policy file in a non-standard location. The NetworkPath field should contain a UNC path in the form of \\computername\sharename\filename.pol, because the policy file may reside on a remote computer (typically, the Primary Domain Controller.

You can make that Registry change using the Registry Editor (you may have to add the NetworkPath key), or you can use the System Policy Editor to do it for you. You can open the Registry on your computer using the File ➤ Open Registry option (or open the Registry of another computer on your network using the File ➤ Connect option.) Once you have opened a Registry you will find the settings you need to change in the Network section of the Local Computer icon. Follow these steps:

1. Open the Network book and then the System Policies Update book.

2. Select the Remote Update check box. The bottom of the window will show you your update options, including the update mode and the path for a manual update. (This is where you type your alternate location.)

3. Click the OK button in the Local Computer Properties window.

4. Select Close from the File menu and then click YES when it asks you if you want to save the changes to the Registry.

Windows 95 and 98 versus Windows NT Policies

The policies you create using the System Policy Editor take effect in the Registry of the computer that the individual uses to connect to the network. If the user connects from a Windows NT Workstation or logs on directly to a Windows NT Server console, then the changes take effect in the Windows NT Registry of that computer. However, if the user logs on from a Windows 95 or 98 computer, the Registry changes are made to the Registry of that Windows 95 or 98 computer, and the Windows 95 or 98 computer needs a different policy file than the Windows NT computer does.

NOTE   The distinction between Windows 95 or 98 and Windows NT policy files is important because the structure of the Windows 95 and 98 Registry differs from that of Windows NT. Many more security options can be modified in the Windows NT Registry, and some security options are implemented in a different way in Windows 95 and 98 than the way they are implemented in Windows NT.

You will find the Windows 95/98 Policy Editor on the Windows 95/98 installation CD-ROM in the ADMIN\APPTOOLS\POLEDIT directory. The file that contains the locations of Registry settings for Windows 95/98 is called Admin.adm. You can use the Admin.adm file with the Security Policy Editor that comes with Windows NT (select Options ➤ Policy

NT Everyday

PART 3

Templates and you can remove the two default templates and add Admin.adm). But it's easier just to use the Windows 95/98 POLEDIT program for your Windows 95/98 clients and the Windows NT System Policy Editor for Windows NT computers. Otherwise, you would have to switch the template files you are using every time you switch the platform you are configuring.

NOTE   You can run both the Windows NT System Policy Editor program and the Windows 95/98 POLEDIT program on your Windows NT Server computer.

Important Computer Policies

Before you begin on your tour through the possible policy settings, you should understand that you don't necessarily have to use all of the settings available to you. Many of the settings won't really make your network any more secure—some just make the administrator's job easier when there are a large number of computers and computer users. You should just select those policies that fit the specific circumstances of your network and leave the default settings for the rest.

When you create a new policy file there is one computer policy created by default for you—the Default Computer policy. You can create additional computer policies by selecting Edit ➤ Add Computer (you will be asked for a computer name for the new policy). Once you install the policy file on your Primary Domain Controller, any computer that logs on to the server will first look for a computer policy with a name that matches that of the connecting computer. If it finds a matching name, it applies that policy to the Registry of the computer. Otherwise, it applies the Default Computer policy.

The status of each policy setting is one of the following:

Checked   This policy option is in effect. You may have to enter data in information fields at the bottom of the Properties window.

Clear   This policy option is not in effect.

Gray   This policy option will not be changed from the state already stored in the Registry of the connecting computer.

The Default Computer and the Default User policies are created with all of the options in the third state (grayed out) so that none of the Registry settings will be changed when a client computer connects to your Windows NT Server computer. New computer and user or group policies are also created with all of the settings in the gray state.

Once you have made the changes for one computer policy, you can copy that policy as many times as you like. The copies will retain all of the same settings that you establish in the original policy. You can then customize the copies for the specific circumstances of a particular computer. Because Windows NT does not provide group accounts for computers (only users), you can't create a policy that will apply to a group of computers on the network.

The policy settings are organized in a tree structure, with the name of the policy at the top of the tree. Each section of the tree is represented by a book icon. By opening the book icon you see subsections (also represented by book icons) or the policy settings, each with a check box to indicate its state.

Network ➢ System Policies Update ➢ Remote Update   The Remote Update key governs where the Windows NT operating system will look for the Config.nt file. This is the setting you must change if you store the policy files in a nonstandard location. The settings for this key are as follows:

Update Mode   Automatically instructs the operating system to look in the default location for the policy files (the NetLogon share of the PDC). Manual instructs the operating system to look in the location indicated by the Path field.

Path for Manual Update   This is the manual location for the policy file. You enter a UNC path here (in the form \\server\share\file.pol).

Display Error Messages   Selecting this option instructs the operating system to report if there are errors accessing the policy file.

Load Balancing   Selecting this option allows the operating system to load the policy from a domain controller other than the Primary Domain Controller when the PDC is heavily loaded.

System ➢ Run ➢ Run   This key lists the programs that the computer will run when it starts up. The programs you add to the list can perform almost any security or administrative function, from scanning for viruses to resetting the contents of the hard drive to a preset state. Click the Items to Run at Startup button to edit the list of programs that will start automatically when the operating system starts.

TIP   When you can't figure out how to get rid of that annoying start-up feature that your latest application installed, look in the System ➢ Run ➢ Run policy setting for a list of tray icons and other user mode icons that start automatically.

Windows NT Network ➢ Sharing ➢ Create Hidden Drive Shares (Server)   Selecting this option instructs Windows NT Server computers to create the C$, D$, and other volume hidden shares, as well as the ADMIN$ hidden share. Clearing this option inhibits the creation of these shares.

NT Everyday

PART 3

> **WARNING** Clear the Create Hidden Drive Shares options for your computers unless you have a specific need for these shares, such as an administrative tool that relies on the existence of the shares. If you have such a tool, consider replacing it with another tool that doesn't rely on the existence of the shares, because these shares are often exploited by hackers.

Windows NT System ➢ Logon   Logon characteristics you can modify include the banner, the authentication dialog box, and how scripts are run, as follows:

Logon Banner   Informs users of the proper use of computers in your network when they log on. You can include legal warnings, computer use assignments, or organization identification in the logon banner text. The Caption field contains what will be shown in the banner title. The Text field is the body of the message that will be displayed to the user when they log on.

Enable Shutdown from Authentication Dialog Box   Allows users to shut the computer down without logging in. Since anyone can simply turn off the computer by unplugging it, you should generally enable this command. A methodical shutdown, even from the logon window, is much safer for the data stored on the computer than just turning the computer off.

Do Not Display Last Logged On User Name   Increases security in your network, because one objective of network intruders is to collect valid usernames. The convenience of not having to type your username in again, if you used the computer last, is not worth the security risk.

> **TIP**   Enable the Do Not Display Last Logged On User Name option so that valid account names won't be seen by unauthorized individuals.

Windows NT System ➢ File System   The three file system options primarily enhance the performance of your system at the expense of older programs that expect a file system to conform to the restrictions of older versions of MS-DOS. You should only enable these options if you are sure that your older programs will work properly in the new environment. You can modify the following Registry settings through this policy:

Do Not Create 8.3 File Names for Long File Names   Causes Windows NT to respond only to the longer filenames. Older programs often expect filenames to have no more than eight letters in the name with an extension of just three letters. Windows 95/98 and Windows NT both allow you to have filenames up to 254 characters in length. If this option is disabled, Windows NT must maintain two filenames—a longer one for new programs and a shorter one for older programs.

Allow Extended Characters in 8.3 File Names Enables the use of UNICODE characters in older, 8.3 filenames. Filenames in MS-DOS and Windows are limited to a subset of the ASCII characters. Windows NT supports a much wider range of characters that are encoded in UNICODE.

Do Not Update Last Access Time Gives you a great performance gain. By default, after every access, even a read access, NTFS will update the time of last access for the file. This update takes a considerable amount of time.

TIP Significantly increase the disk performance of your computer by enabling Do Not Update Last Access Time.

Important User and Group Policies

A computer policy affects a single computer or (in the case of the Default Computer policy) all computers that do not have a specific computer policy defined for them. User policies are similar to computer policies—if there is no specific user policy for a user who logs on, then the Default User policy is applied. But wait, there's more! If the user belongs to a group for which a policy is defined, then that policy is also applied.

Since a user can belong to more than one group, there may be more than one policy that may apply to that user. In the Options menu of the System Policy Editor you can establish priority among the groups; when policy settings conflict, the group policy with the highest priority will take precedence.

As with computer policies, you can create new user and group policies from the Edit menu of the System Policy Editor. The policies that are created will be blank—no options will be selected in the policy trees. However, once you have made policy changes in a policy file, you can copy that policy and those changes will be in effect in the new policy.

Control Panel ➤ Display ➤ Restrict Display The Control Panel policy options in Windows NT are primarily concerned with display settings. Since Windows NT adequately controls who may make changes to the display hardware without requiring the intervention of the System Policy Editor, these settings simply enforce a consistent environment and make administration easier. The following settings are available:

Deny Access to Display Icon Denies all access to the Display Control Panel item

Hide Background Tab Keeps the user from changing the background

Hide Screen Saver Tab Keeps the user from changing the screen saver

Hide Appearance Tab Keeps the user from modifying the appearance settings

Hide Settings Tab Keeps the user from accessing the hardware configuration settings

Shell ➤ Restrictions This section and the "System ➤ Restrictions" section contain the user policy settings that have the most impact on security. You should be careful when applying these options because you can quickly render a Windows NT computer unusable with them and then not be able to change the settings back. Shell restrictions are self explanatory and include:

- **Remove Run Command from Start Menu**
- **Remove Folders from Settings on Start Menu**
- **Remove Find Command from Start Menu**
- **Hide Drives in My Computer**
- **Hide Network Neighborhood**
- **No Workgroup Contents in Network Neighborhood**
- **Hide All Items on Desktop**
- **Disable Shutdown Command**
- **Don't Save Settings on Exit**

System ➤ Restrictions These two system restrictions can go a long way in securing a network against hacking from internal sources. Once a hacker has access to a computer on your network, he or she will need access to the Registry and to hacking tools in order to exploit the information stored on the computer. The System restrictions are:

- **Disable Registry Editing Tools**
- **Run Only Allowed Windows Applications**

Third-Party Tools

A confusing array of software and hardware tools exists to assist in the administration of networks. Most of them are worthless. This section will detail those tools that (in my experience) significantly improve your administrative efficiency.

There are four categories of network tools that I've found to be very helpful in the administration of networks:

- Common tools are regular applications applied to network administration and are appropriate for any size network environment.
- Remote control tools are appropriate for smaller networks (less than 50 clients).

- Desktop management software is appropriate for medium-sized networks (50–1,000 clients).

- Enterprise management software is appropriate for large networks (more than 1,000 clients).

Use Common Tools

Tools for diverse functions, such as network documentation tools, help desk support, network monitoring, and remote management, all purport to improve administrative efficiency. The chosen tools and the available budget varies widely and depends on the size of the organization. Some of these more esoteric tools do have a place in larger organizations, but for most organizations, most proprietary network management tools are a waste of money. Fortunately, more generic low-cost tools are available for the common functions required in smaller networks.

For network documentation, use HTML-generating word processors and graphical tools like Visio or SysDraw. These tools are cheap and commonly available. You can purchase Visio off the shelf at any software retailer.

For client configuration and equipment control, you can create a simple Microsoft Access database. No organization's configuration and control log is larger than a desktop database tool can handle.

Help desk software? Use e-mail. It's easy, it provides a tracking log, and it carries a complete history of the communication between the end user and the support technician. Keep the complete communiqué in a single e-mail message, which will serve as a cradle-to-grave log of the support session—including what actions the technician took to solve the problem. At the end of the troubleshooting session, have the technician forward the completed e-mail session to an e-mail account specifically created to store the sessions long term. You can use those e-mail messages as the basis of a troubleshooting database.

Do you want to centralize troubleshooting knowledge into a quick-access database? Use the Web. Each time a support technician solves a specific problem that hasn't been solved before, have them write up a quick document describing the problem, its symptoms, and its resolution. Link it into your troubleshooting "database" through a set of diagnostic click-through links based on the symptoms of the problem that get increasingly specific as the technician drills down. Use IIS's Index Server mechanism to provide a search interface, and you're done. You can even link it through to Microsoft's knowledge base on the Web if your network is constantly connected to the Internet.

NT Everyday

PART 3

Remote Control Software

In smaller networks, it doesn't make sense to pay $500 per client for a desktop management solution when you can use simpler, commonly available tools to perform the same function.

Use pcAnywhere, from Symantec, to remotely control client desktops. Other brands of remote control software come and go, but this one is consistently high-performing and widely available. Its current incarnations work over networks, the Internet, through PPTP tunnels, and over phone lines.

Don't leave pcAnywhere constantly running on client machines, because it's a security risk. Put a shortcut in all users' Start menus to launch it when a support problem arises. You can script its startup to automatically begin hosting a network session and then connect to it from your help desk. If the problem is serious enough to prevent the user from starting pcAnywhere, have them reboot their computer and try again. If that doesn't work, replace the desktop.

Desktop Installation and Rollout Software

Desktop management, such as Attachmate NetWizard or Tivoli Director, is the next step up from remote control software. In addition to support for remote control of desktop computers, it adds provisions for package-based rollouts of applications. Administrators can create application packages stored on central servers that can be automatically downloaded to client computers and installed without the intervention of the local user. Typically, installation packages can be downloaded on demand by the user, on demand by the network administrator, or based on a calendar schedule to spread the load of the software distribution. Desktop management software is fairly expensive, costing about $500 per supported desktop.

A lower price solution is to maintain a few "image classes" of software using networked image installation software, such as Ghost or DriveImage. Then, whenever a new version of software or an additional application is necessary, you could load the existing source image onto a prototype desktop machine, perform the installation, upgrade, or configuration change, and then recreate the source image. You can then reinstall affected desktop clients with the newly updated source image.

For example, you could have an office application's image consisting of the operating system and Microsoft office, e-mail, and other required basic applications. Another image could build on that but add programming environments for software developers. A third image might be based on the office application's image but add supported graphics design software. And a fourth image could include CAD/CAM applications for engineers.

Sage Advice: Restoration Made Easy

If you use image serving software to perform OS and application rollouts, tape to the side of each client computer an envelope containing a floppy that boots to MS-DOS, loads a network stack, and then executes your Image download software. This way, clients can update their own computers simply by inserting the MS-DOS boot floppy and choosing the appropriate image to install. After the image is installed, they reboot their computer and go back to work. You can talk inexperienced users through the steps over the phone and eliminate a trip to the desktop. You can even use this tactic to restore accidental mis-configuration or problems caused by software corruption or viruses.

Network Control Software

The final tier of network management software includes major management platforms like CA-UniCenter and HP-OpenView. These products create an entire network management software infrastructure that integrates SNMP device configuration management, visual network monitoring tools, remote control, archiving, and software rollouts all into one centrally controlled system. These systems are component-based. An entire industry of software add-ons to perform every imaginable network administration and management task exists.

Well-configured installations of these products are an amazing technical feat and a joy to behold (if this sort of thing excites you). They're also hideously expensive, costing anywhere from $25,000 on up for basic platform options and about $500 for every client depending on the options you install. Their cost is easy to justify for larger organizations, because they'll save you a tremendous amount of money in recurring support costs. However, they're exceedingly difficult to install correctly; have an experienced integrator perform the installation for you if you decide to go this route. It's also easy to go hog wild with feature options that cost extra and don't really reduce the administrative burden, so make sure you can justify all the expenses you'll incur with these products.

Penny Wise, Pound Foolish

A client of mine decided they were spending too much money on IS—with a staff of only 100 people, they had 10 IS technicians—10 percent of the company payroll was spent supporting computer systems, amounting to about $500,000 per year. They asked me to figure out how to reduce their IT costs (basically making me the IT hatchet man, but that's consulting).

I surveyed their current practices and determined the following:

- A Frankenstein network architecture existed. A few servers connected to a large switch, which was, in turn, connected to a sprawling Ethernet network of various grades and ages—some switched CAT5 Fast Ethernet, some 10Base-T over CAT3 wiring, and some 10Base-2 over coaxial wiring with media converters.

- Most clients were older 486-class computers, and, in some cases, workers made do with 386-class computers. Clients used a hodgepodge of operating systems: MS-DOS, Windows for Workgroups, Windows 95, and Windows NT. The really funny part was that the executive staff and IT staff all had brand new Pentium II computers running NT Workstation over Fast Ethernet, while all the task workers basically got along with whatever they had on their desks when they got their jobs. The IT staff had gotten into the habit of responding to the executive staff's problems while ignoring the problems of those people who had no authority over them.

- The staff spent most of their time replacing outdated Ethernet cards, reformatting hard disks, and reinstalling Windows 95 from floppy disks (because the computer didn't have a CD-ROM reader), and trying to track down faulty cable connections (because portions of the network ran over 10Base-2 thinnet coaxial cable). Needless to say, spending 8 hours of IT time troubleshooting a Thinnet Ethernet card is a complete waste.

I wrote up my findings and suggested the following:

- Replace every computer in the organization that hadn't been purchased in the last year with a machine conforming to at least a Pentium II 300MHz with 32MB RAM and a 2GB hard disk. These machines at the time cost about $1,500. Fifty computers needed to be replaced at a total cost of $75,000.

- Install a new category five cable plant throughout the organization to support a migration to Fast Ethernet. $150 per drop for 75 drops totaled about $11,000.

- Replace the network architecture with 100MB workgroup hubs having Gigabit Ethernet links to a central router. Seven 16-user hubs at $3,000 each totaled $21,000.

- Install Gigabit Ethernet adapters in the centrally located servers. Three servers at $500 per NIC totaled $1,500.

- Install a Gigabit Ethernet central router. A 12-port b/router cost $24,000.

- Purchase Tivoli's Director IT management suite, including application rollout, inventory management, and remote control software. The cost for this installation was $30,000.

- Use profiles and policies to make certain users store their files on servers so their computers could be easily replaced.

- Cut the IT staff (one director, three network administrators, and six technicians) to one administrator and two technicians (after we got the new network implemented, of course). Total Savings: $350,000 per year.

The bottom line is that the capital expenditures for my specification came to $165,000. The company saved that amount within six months of implementing my advice, and the remaining staff assured me that their jobs were far less hectic, affording them the time to set up a company intranet site. Lest the job cutting aspect of this case study seem overly drastic, the staff that were laid off took their new enterprise management implementation skills with them and quickly found new, better paying jobs.

24seven **CASE STUDY**

10

Supporting Servers

Supporting servers is considerably different than supporting clients, even if the hardware and operating system are very similar. The support tasks are different, because only one person is affected when a client goes down—when a server crashes nobody can work, so heads roll, starting with yours.

Server support encompasses three broad aspects:

- Administration
- Maintenance
- Monitoring

Because this entire book is about administration, I'll take this opportunity to focus on remote administration. Maintenance is the judicious application of preventative measures to forestall or eliminate many common failures. Monitoring is the continual process of measuring server activity in order to detect and respond to failures or potential failures as soon as possible.

Remote Administration

If you have servers in more than one location, remote administration is a necessity. The time you save just walking around is considerable. Windows NT's built-in support for remote administration is weak and incomplete. The remote administration functions that can be performed are crippled by the lack of tools to support such necessities as rebooting the server once you've made a change.

A number of third-party utilities exist to help solve this problem, including a free utility from Microsoft that's worth using. None of these tools implement any serious security, and they all add vectors through which hackers could take control of your servers. Don't even think about using remote administration software over the Internet without using an encrypted tunnel and a strong firewall. PPTP connections to a server that has PPTP filtering enabled should be considered the very least security you'll accept for remote administration. The following section discusses remote administration tools in detail.

Making Do with NT

The following Windows NT administrative tools support remote management by selecting another server or domain to manage in the File menu:

- Event Viewer
- License Manager
- Remote Access Admin
- Server Manager
- System Policy Editor
- User Manager for Domains
- Desktop Explorer (for NTFS file system permissions)
- Regedit and RegEdt32

Unfortunately, these tools do not provide enough flexibility to install software, reboot the server, or perform a number of other administrative tasks. No other NT administrative tools support remotely administering other servers. Functions that cannot be performed remotely using these tools require additional software for remote administration.

Web Administrator for NT

Microsoft seems to have noticed the need for remote server administration. They've responded with the Web Administrator for Windows NT, a versatile remote management application that is implemented as an ISAPI DLL for IIS 4 with a supporting Web site. To use it, you simply install Web Administrator on your server (a free download from `www.microsoft.com/ntserver`). When you need to manage the server, you can point nearly any modern Web browser to `http://yourserver.com/ntadmin` to view the management start page. The Web Administrator mimics the functionality of a number of NT administrative tools including:

> **User Manager for Domains**   Includes support for adding and modifying user and group accounts and setting dial-in permissions, but it is without support for account restrictions, policy, or user rights.

Remote Access Admin Support for displaying active users.

Server Manager Support includes adding Workstations or Backup Domain Controllers, managing shares, and sending messages.

Printers Control Panel Includes support to pause and resume printers and jobs and to flush the job queue.

Devices Control Panel Fully supported, which is odd considering the limited utility of this Control Panel.

Event Log Fully supported.

Desktop Explorer Supports setting NTFS file system permissions and rebooting the server.

Remote Console Supports the Resource Kit remote console utility.

Services Control Panel Fully supported.

Server Control Panel Supports user-session display and disconnection.

Windows NT Diagnostics Fully supported.

Performance Monitor Supports snapshot views of all counters.

Task Manager Mimics the performance quick view page.

Web Administrator's interface is necessarily somewhat goofy, and it's not organized the same way the NT administrative tools are. Actually, I would argue that it's organized more coherently.

The Web Administrator lacks support for administrative features like software installation. It doesn't do everything, but using a supported tool from Microsoft that you won't have to worry about will get you a long way down the path.

Security is something of a problem with any remote management tool. If you intend to perform management of a server over the Internet, remember that this tool doesn't implement any specific security of its own other than forcing an NT Challenge/Response authentication.

RemotelyAnywhere

RemotelyAnywhere is a third-party remote control application that works like Web Administrator on steroids. It provides low-level control of an NT server over a Web connection by installing a service application on port 2000 of your server and piping commands to the Service Manager and other executive components. Unlike Web Administrator, it does not require the installation of IIS or any other Web server software.

RemotelyAnywhere compliments the functionality of the Web Administrator, because it does not have support for administrative functions such as print control or remote access

NT Everyday

PART 3

permissions. Its File Manager is easier to browse, and it has a full Registry Editor (although the built in Registry Editor can be used for remote Registry editing).

RemotelyAnywhere includes a truly bizarre, full, remote control utility that gives you keyboard and mouse control of the remote computer through—of all things—screen shots of the remote computer, or, if you'd rather, a Java-based client doing something similar.

RemotelyAnywhere is a gnarly hack worth at least looking at just for the extreme oddity of its methodology and its obvious utility. Some administrators that I respect swear by it, but I've never used it in a production environment. Download it from www.bhs.com. Do not—I repeat—do not try to open a remote control session to the local host unless you want to see your computer crawl to a halt as an infinite number of remote control consoles open within each other, and you frantically try to find a way to end the process. Don't say I didn't warn you.

pcAnywhere

pcAnywhere is the granddaddy of remote control applications and the most popular. If you're going to use a simulated console remote control application, use this one. It's easy to use, has tons of features (such as screen resize and color interpolation when the resolution of the client doesn't match the server), and is inexpensive compared to most enterprise solutions.

Make absolutely certain you have strong firewall policy if you use applications like pcAnywhere over the Internet. As with all remote administration tools, you should also use encrypted tunneling so hackers can't discern that you even have remote administration software running on your servers. Although pcAnywhere has password blocking, it's not strong enough to keep hackers out, so don't rely upon it.

Enterprise Solutions

Most medium-sized enterprise management tools, such as Attachmate's NetWizard or Tivoli Director, include remote control software similar to pcAnywhere. Generally, these tools are reincarnations of formerly independent software products that were put out of business by Symantec's offering and then purchased by these enterprise management companies to add remote control functionality to their products. As such, they're (in my experience) generally inferior to pcAnywhere, but if you're going to use the Enterprise management tool anyway, you've already got their remote control software.

Enterprise solutions of this class typically include support for automated software installation to clients and hardware/software inventory keeping. You may or may not need these tools depending on the complexity of your problem. In my opinion, they aren't worth the cost when you consider the free alternatives. I've never had to deal with an inventory problem so large that a reasonably simple database and a good update policy couldn't deal with it effectively—even when I was in the military and had to track very nearly every electrical device and piece of software we used.

Likewise, software distribution is easiest if you teach users how to install the software they need to use, and then, when you've put something new on the network, e-mail links to the executable `startup.exe` file with any necessary explicit instructions to the candidate users. The user simply clicks on the link to begin the installation and can read through the steps you promulgate in the e-mail as the installation progresses.

You really don't have to worry much about "over installation" as long as you're using network license control applications that can tell you what your peak actual usage is. Casual users who install but then don't use applications will have very little effect on your license meters. When you use policies like these, even a massive software rollout is as easy as sending an e-mail message to a distribution list. For task-based workers who can't be trusted to figure out a setup program, use Windows terminals.

Maintenance

Server maintenance is a necessary evil. Servers that can be installed and forgotten about do not really exist because of the speed at which capacity is used up in our rapidly growing movement to an information society. Hard disks fill up, servers are outgrown and overloaded, and hardware fails.

The key to good administration is not to be surprised by these events when they happen. A methodical routine for maintenance ensures that you'll find problems before they get out of hand. This means that you can plan for downtime around *your* schedule, instead of putting your company on a work stoppage while you try to troubleshoot a crashed server in the middle of a workday. You'll spend more cumulative time on preventative maintenance than you would have spent on corrective maintenance, but you'll save everyone else's time, and that's what network administration is all about.

Planned Maintenance

You can avoid a lot of unexpected troubleshooting and server crashes by performing routine planned preventative maintenance on your servers. Scan the operations manual for each component that is included in your server (both hardware and software) to find planned maintenance items. Make complete lists of every periodic task listed, and add them to a more general list.

Weekly maintenance should include the following:

- Check hard disk capacity for each volume. Record the weekly usage and keep a trend calendar of disk usage so you can plan for disk upgrades.
- Check the peak memory and page file usage statistics in performance monitor logs for cases of large or unexpected increases in memory use.
- Check the system, security, and application logs for unexpected entries.
- Review any application logs for services, such as IIS, that do not make use of the event viewer.

Monthly maintenance should include the following:

- Clean tape backup mechanism if required.
- Review the permission structure of the disk using the CACLS command-line utility.
- Review share permissions.
- Review TCP/IP security settings.
- Delete any leftover temporary files manually.
- Create a new Emergency Repair Disk.
- Reboot the server if possible.

Yearly maintenance should include tasks that require planned downtime:

- Evaluate the server for a complete upgrade. Is it keeping up with current demand, or has it become and increasing maintenance hassle?
- Open the machine and vacuum dust the interior of the case, paying special attention to the power supply and exposed slots.
- Test the floppy disk drive by formatting a disk and copying files to it.
- Run a complete hardware diagnostic program, such as PC-Check or PC Doctor, from a DOS boot floppy.
- Perform a complete read and rewrite test for all disks after a complete system backup. Grown defects appear most often during write operations, so this test should get them all at one time.
- Perform a hard test of your RAID system by pulling a hard disk out during operation (after a complete backup, of course). Make sure your RAID system still performs as it did when it was originally installed.
- Upgrade the CPU to the highest performing model that will work in the same socket.

- Double the amount of installed RAM until the motherboard can hold no more. You may want to move lower-capacity memory modules to clients and replace them with fewer modules of the highest available capacity.

Scheduling Maintenance

When you plan to take a server down for maintenance, you obviously need to do it when the server isn't needed for any service purposes. If you have a fault-tolerance or load balancing software, this isn't an issue; you can simply choose a time during the day when the load is reasonably low and take down one of the servers, confident that the other server(s) will take up the slack.

But if you're like most network administrators, you'll have to wait for evening or the weekend to take servers down. This can cause some strain—most network professionals are salaried, and working during the nights or weekends means working without compensation.

Install new software and service applications during the day, but do not allow rebooting until the end of the day. After normal user traffic has dropped off, simply reboot the server, verify that everything is running correctly, and go home. You don't have to reboot a server immediately after installing new software, you just have to reboot it before the new software will work correctly.

Schedule the IS workweek from Sunday through Thursday or Tuesday through Saturday for at least one person. That person can handle all necessary server maintenance during their normal workweek.

Schedule the IS staff to work "core" hours from 10:00 A.M. to 2:00 P.M., but allow flexibility for coming in early or staying late to manage the network around peak usage times. Schedule any staff meetings to occur during the core hours when all staff must be at work. This also allows your staff to manage their commute times around rush hour.

Use the comp time concept to allow workers to accrue the extra hours they've worked and then take that time off later on. This allows workers the greatest personal freedom while ensuring (if properly managed) that time spent and compensation are fair.

Upgrading Servers

Server upgrades are never easy or convenient because you must take a server offline to upgrade it. Even rather simple software installations can require a reboot, because most of NT's operating system components only read Registry information when they're booted.

NT Everyday

PART 3

TIP You often don't need to reboot a server after installing or modifying an existing service even if the setup program says you need to. You can usually just stop and restart the service. There's no way to tell whether this will work except to try it, but it's safe to try. If it doesn't work, just go ahead and reboot.

Server upgrades take two forms: hardware and software. Hardware upgrades, such as upgrading a microprocessor or adding RAM, can be quick and painless. Other hardware upgrades, such as changing out a motherboard that requires a different HAL, can require you to perform a repair reinstallation.

Software upgrades are usually fairly simple, even when they require an OS reinstallation, because companies know that their reputation for quality generally rests on how easy it is to install their software.

Adding Storage

Adding hard disk space to a server is generally pretty easy. In fact, if your system partition is in a different partition than your shared directories, you can simply create a spanning volume set across drives using the Disk Administrator.

If you need to migrate to a different storage subsystem altogether (for example, if you're moving to a RAID pack), you can do it the hard way or the easy way.

The hard way is to install the new storage subsystem as the bootable disk, install a fresh version of Windows NT, reinstall all your application software, copy user files back from the old drive, and re-establish shares. If the computer was the Primary Domain Controller, you have to promote Backup Domain Controller to Primary Domain Controller, install the upgrade server as a BDC, and then promote it again.

The easy way is to leave the original storage bootable and then install the new storage. Next, install the disk driver for the new storage controller, if necessary, expand the boot.ini file to be able to load the operating system from the new storage, and then use NT's mirroring software to sector copy the entire disk from the old to the new. Once the mirror is finished, shut the server down and remove the old storage system.

If for some reason you can't use mirroring, use a disk-cloning utility, such as DriveImage.

Most RAID controllers have their own BIOS setup programs that allow you to define how the disks attached to the controller are used. The entire RAID pack then appears to the operating system as a single, normal hard disk. You'll be able to use the mirroring technique or a disk cloning utility to migrate from your older storage system.

Migrating to a New Version of NT

Upgrading an existing server to a new version of Windows NT is easy—all versions of Windows NT can automatically handle any necessary migration through the setup program's upgrade option.

A simple migration isn't usually the best option, though. First, there's no reason to upgrade a server just because a new version of NT has been released. Unless you have a specific reason to upgrade a working server, don't waste the time or the money. Compelling reasons to upgrade include significant performance improvements, security fixes or enhancements, or new features that you need. Although it has a new interface, Windows NT 4 is substantially the same operating system as Windows NT 3.51. Microsoft does not continue upgrading operating systems with service pack releases much past the time a new version is released, but if your server is inside a firewalled network, security and performance improvements aren't all that important.

I'm not suggesting that you never upgrade a server, but by the time an operating system is actually obsolete, the hardware it's installed on usually is obsolete, too. Rather than upgrading an existing server to a new OS, consider migrating your server to an entirely new hardware and software platform. And if you do this, you can continue to use your old server for some less-demanding task, such as print service, domain control, a router, or RAS server.

Changing Basic Logic

Changing the motherboard of an existing server is usually not a problem because most motherboards work with the standard PC HAL. If you change your motherboard and find you can't reboot, you can perform a repair installation to install the correct HAL for the machine. You may have to replace the system key in the Registry to make sure the correct settings are maintained after the installation.

Upgrading a single processor is no issue at all as long as your motherboard supports both the old and the new processor. However, if you add a processor to a single-processor computer, you'll have to upgrade the HAL using either a repair installation or the Resource Kit utility uptomp.exe, located under Performance and System Monitoring Tools.

Adding RAM to a server is also no problem as long as your motherboard supports the extra RAM. Be wary of mismatched RAM however. Using SIMMs from different manufacturers can cause random crashing on NT machines. Even DIMMs, which only need be installed one at a time, are very sensitive to differences between manufacturers. Also be aware of the differences between EDO, PC100, and other types of memory. Make absolutely certain that all the memory in your server is compatible with your motherboard, that the motherboard is configured correctly for the ram, and that all the memory is from the same manufacturer. If after installing new memory your server begins crashing, even at long intervals, suspect the newly installed memory first.

NT Everyday

PART 3

Adding Servers

When you add servers, don't just add a server to shore up some needed capacity in file or application service without examining the service structure among your current servers. For example, if you're adding a new file server because your primary server has run out of disk space, don't just add another file server and leave your original server handling Exchange, IIS, the original file service, and print sharing. Use the Performance Monitor to determine how the services load your original server and split them among the two machines. You may find that the best way to correctly share the load is to use both machines for file and print service, and then have one machine run Exchange and the other run IIS for intranet service. Or you may find that one machine should share files, and all the other services should run on the other machine. Adding servers without examining your network load will create a Frankenstein network that is a patchwork of services with nonoptimal network loading.

Larger networks usually concentrate specific service applications on their own servers and then have numerous identically configured servers for groups of users. For example, a medium-sized enterprise might have a central Exchange server, a central intranet server, and then a file and print server for each workgroup.

Moving Services to a New Server

Replacing a server with an entirely new server is a task that will probably take at least a day to complete. There are a few land mines in service migration that can make your job difficult though: Windows Names migration and permission migration.

Migrating Windows Names   Migrating Windows Names is important when you want to move file or print services to another machine. By migrating the name of the server and its shares, you can keep using the access paths that are already installed on your client machines. Windows Names migration has to be done according to a fairly strict process in order to work with the least possible hassle.

Name migration can be a serious problem, because both servers can't operate on the same network at the same time. You have two options: Rename the old server or the new one. If you rename the new server, you'll have to change the Universal Naming Convention (UNC) path name to access services on every client. Assuming you don't want to do that, the only remaining option is to rename the old server. Once you rename the old server, no client will be able to access it, so you should perform the entire migration during a reasonably long time period when client access isn't necessary (i.e. the weekend).

> **Sage Advice: Migrating a Server's Windows Names to a New Server**
>
> The process for name migration is fairly easy. Install the new server on a network that is physically detached from the old network using the same name as the existing server. At a convenient time, detach the old server from the network and rename it. Once it's renamed, attach it directly to the new server and move all necessary files from the old server to the new server. Recreate shared files and printers using the same name as on the old server. Remove unnecessary services from the old server and introduce both to the network again.

Migrating Domain Control   Migrating domain control is easy. Simply add the new server to the domain as a Backup Domain Controller and then use the Server Manager to change the new server's role to Primary Domain Controller. The old server will automatically downgrade itself to Backup Domain Controller and can then be taken offline, if necessary.

Migrating File and Print Services   Migrating File and Print services is somewhat more difficult. The problem is that simply copying files from one machine to another will result in the loss of any established file permissions for all files. If your NTFS security architecture is simple, you can simply reapply your security settings through the Desktop Explorer. If your NTFS security architecture is complex or unknown, use the scopy.exe utility contained in Windows NT Server 4 Resource Kit to copy the files. scopy.exe copies each file's Access Control List along with the file so its permissions remain the same on the new volume. You can then simply reestablish share names using the same Windows Names as the old server used.

Migrating Print service is very simple. Simply attach your old printers to the new server (if necessary), install any necessary drivers or service software, and create new shared printers with the same Windows Names as the printers had on the old server.

Migrating TCP/IP Services   Migrating TCP/IP services, such as DNS, WINS, FTP, Web service, mail, or news, require the migration of the old server's IP address and host name. Both migrations are easy. Simply change the TCP/IP address and host name of the old server before the migration and install the new server with the necessary IP address and host name of the new service. Install the requisite services on the new server and migrate the hosted Web, FTP, news, or mail files. You will have to reestablish Web sites and security, but that's not particularly difficult to do manually on all but the most complex Web servers. Moving DNS and WINS services is best performed by replicating the WINS or DNS databases on the network with another WINS or DNS server before the old server goes offline and then synchronizing the name services with the new server when it comes back online.

NT Everyday

PART 3

Monitoring

Monitoring has two purposes: to measure load in order to predict impending problems and to monitor attempted misuse. Windows NT has a number of very strong utilities to support both of these monitoring goals. It amazes me how many NT administrators never use them.

Third-party monitoring tools exist, but few do anything you can't get done with NT's built-in utilities. Most are hideously expensive and not worth the money. Beyond a good firewall (which you can't pay too much for), most security tools are a waste of time. It's easy to get caught up in security hysteria and spend a boatload of money on expensive monitoring tools that really don't improve your security posture more than a simple investment in a good security book does. I shamelessly recommend mine, *NT 4 Network Security,* published by Sybex, 1998.

Security monitoring is not an optional component of server management—it's a necessity. At the very least, use Windows NT's tools to monitor your machine. Don't let anyone have free rein on a network you depend on and are responsible for.

Windows NT Utilities

Windows NT comes with a number of utilities that can be used to monitor security in addition to their usual purpose. A description of each of these tools follows.

Event Viewer and Audit Policy   Can be used as a strong security monitor. By setting up the security events you wish to monitor using the Audit Policy panel of the User Manager for Domains and then monitoring the contents of the security log in the Event Viewer, you can keep track of every successful and attempted logon and logoff, access to critical files, changes to security policy, and server restarts. With this information, attempts to breach the security of your server become quite clear.

The Network Monitor   A complex application that decodes and displays the low-level contents of network traffic. It is primarily useful as a troubleshooting tool—with it, you can determine exactly what information is being transmitted between your servers and clients.

The Performance Monitor   Can be used to monitor a number of security-related events, such as failed logon attempts and logons per second. The Performance Monitor is able to immediately alert you to a threat condition by running a program whenever monitored counters have passed a certain threshold. Use this alerting feature to snoop for events that indicate an attack in progress, such as an extremely high number of failed logons.

Netstat   Shows the current status of all TCP/IP connections on your server. When you type Netstat at the command-line prompt, you're presented with a scrolling list of all the TCP connections current on your computer. This is somewhat useful for security monitoring, but the most useful way to use Netstat is to set a frequent interval by issuing the number of seconds you want Netstat to automatically rerun, as in `netstat 5`, which will pause the program for five seconds after each display. A more convenient real-time Netstat viewer is the TCPView program (discussed later in this chapter).

Resource Kit Tools

The Resource Kit contains a bunch of little tools that are extremely useful for server and network administration. Each of these tools is somewhat supported by Microsoft, though many were written by third-party vendors and purchased by Microsoft for inclusion in the Resource Kit.

Network Watch   A clever little utility that shows shared resources and their connections. The application is easy to figure out. Its most useful mode for monitoring is the Show in Use Shares Only option, which makes it easy to monitor shared-resource usage at a glance. The Network Watch will show you which users are logged onto which share and using which files in what manner. It's basically an at-a-glance monitor of your file service and an indispensable monitoring tool.

Third-Party Utilities

Although Windows NT has the strongest support for network and security monitoring of any network operating system I've seen, you'll need some third-party utilities on occasion. I've found the following tools to be very useful.

SysInternals

SysInternals is the public-service side of Winternals LLC, a company composed of two Doctors of Computer Science who have a highly developed sense of charity to go along with their brilliant programming minds. Although they charge for some of their more useful tools, they give a number away for free, including the source code, simply to advance the art of programming for Windows NT. Their tools are written primarily for programmers, but some of them have very definite troubleshooting and monitoring purposes in normal networks. Check out Systems Internals at `www.sysinternals.com`.

Filemon   Filemon shows all file activity on your server in real time. Filemon is useful for those times when you cannot figure out a cryptic "file not found" message from a program; Filemon will show you what file the application was looking for when it failed out. It can also be used to glean information about a new service or to get an idea of which applications are repeatedly using the disk.

> **WARNING**   Filemon puts a tremendous CPU load on your server. Don't use it during production uptime unless you have a problem you can't debug any other way.

Regmon   Regmon shows you all the Registry activity that occurs on your server in real time. When you start Regmon it begins logging all Registry accesses to the screen. It's wonderful for fixing problems with Registry corruption and for decoding how a specific application uses its Registry settings.

> **WARNING**   Like Filemon, Regmon puts a tremendous CPU load on your server. Only use it during times when extreme CPU load is not going to interfere with the normal services the computer provides.

Because so much Registry activity occurs on a normal machine, you will quickly get lost in the quagmire of Registry activity unless you use filters. Filters allow you to specify exactly which processes you are interested in monitoring and which types of Registry access you are interested in.

> **TIP**   Launch Regmon before you install new software, and then keep a filtered log of all the new keys that the setup program created during the installation and that the application created the first time it was run. Save this info as a text file so you can manually remove the Registry keys created by the application in the event that it doesn't uninstall completely.

TCPView   TCPView is a "must-have" security-monitoring utility. It shows the real-time status of TCP connections. Every connection established to the server is shown by its port number and the IP address and port of the remotely connected host. It basically has the same functionality that is provided by the Netstat program that ships with Windows NT, but it has a prettier interface.

It would be great, for security purposes, if this program had a facility to log all new TCP connections to a file with their resolved names and ports. (Are you reading this Mark?)

Other Tools

A number of other small tools are very useful for security and network administration.

Servers Alive?   A shareware application that pings, at a specified interval, a list of TCP hosts. Should a server fail to report, you can specify how you want to be alerted. Servers

Alive? can also probe specified TCP services so that you can be alerted when a certain service (for example, Exchange) freezes on a server. Servers Alive? includes strong support for alerting and alert escalation; in combination with a paging gateway, you can be immediately alerted to any change in your network's status. Servers Alive? belongs in the toolbox of all serious network administrators. Get it at `www.woodstone.nu/salive`.

Suck Server   A small Java-based security utility for Windows NT (or any other platform) that establishes listening TCP services on specified ports and then logs the results of connection attempts without responding. I know it sound pretty useless, but it's great for catching attempts to hack into your server.

By establishing services on frequently attacked ports on your external servers (such as Telnet:23, FTP:21, or NetBIOS Session:139), your computer will appear to hackers to be providing these services when they use a port scanner to determine your server's vulnerabilities. When they attempt to "log on" or otherwise attack these ports, the information they provide, along with their TCP/IP address, will be logged by the program. The program will also run any command-line program you specify, so you can be paged, e-mailed, or alerted over the network of hacking attempts as they occur. It's a must-have for the security-conscious network administrator.

Suck Server comes free with a copy of *NT 4 Network Security*, by Matthew Strebe, Charles Perkins, and Michael Moncur (published by Sybex). You really should read that book to fully appreciate its application, but Suck Server is also available for download at the 24seven Web site.

NT Everyday

PART 3

A Hacker in the Midst

While reviewing a customer's security event log, I came across a small series of failed logon attempts against an account—not enough to warrant much attention, but more than a user would normally make against their own account. I looked at the account and noted that it was the company president, known to be a fairly poor typist.

I nearly dismissed it, except that the company president generally blamed his occasional inability to type his password correctly on the network. Usually I would have received a call about it if he'd been unable to log on and had the account lockout policy gone into effect as the security log showed. The person using his account simply waited patiently and tried again—the next day.

I could see his normal pattern of logging on in the morning and logging out at night occurring in the log, and then was struck by the fact that the failed logon attempts were occurring while he was already logged on. Knowing his disdain for computers, I knew for a fact that he would not be logged onto two machines at the same time. More log analysis revealed that the attack was coming through a PPTP channel that he occasionally logged on through at night, but these attempts were happening during the day while he was at work.

Someone other than the president of the company was in possession of his valid account name, knew which private network it pertained to, knew that the only way into the network would be through PPTP, and was simply running a password guessing attack against the firewall to gain access to the network using a PPTP client from somewhere on the Internet. Rather than hitting the network at full speed, they were presenting just a few logon attempts per day at reasonable intervals—an obvious attempt to outsmart any logon lockout delays that might be set up and to prevent the activity from pegging the Performance Monitor.

I pulled up the User Monitor and restricted the account's ability to log on from any computer other than the ones the president actually used at work and at home. I also got a list of people who logged on from home and what their IP addresses or address ranges were so that I could tighten up the firewall's policy for allowing PPTP connections to only specific addresses.

After restricting the firewall's PPTP policy, the attacks ceased showing up in the event log. The hacker probably noticed the change in firewall policy, and with no way around it, the hacker had to simply give up.

The unfortunate side effect of shoring up the network protection is that we were unable to then discover the identity of the hacker. The company made the decision that protecting their proprietary secrets was more important than determining the identity of the culprit. I personally would have rather restricted the account permissions, made the password fairly obvious, and assigned a new account to the president in an attempt to see what the hacker was after.

11

Information Technology Management

Contrary to popular opinion, IT management is far from black magic or controlled chaos. In fact, it's one of the most deterministic business fields I've ever dealt with. This chapter will show you how to select technologies appropriate for the size of your business, how to organize an IT division, and how to implement new systems.

Often—especially in small- or medium-sized businesses—the roles of IT manager and network administrator are both performed by the same person. That person probably hasn't worked in a larger IT environment and may not have experience managing large systems. Growth environments can be intimidating, especially for isolated administrators who have little contact with the industry beyond catalogs and Web sites. This chapter will present the basic facets of large-scale IT management toned down for the small- or medium-scale business where management and administration are one in the same.

This chapter may not seem immediately appropriate for every reader of this book. Those who work for small businesses will find it more immediately beneficial than those in the trenches at a large business. But most IT directors and chief information officers of tomorrow will come from the ranks of network administrators today, so if you don't need the information presented here right now, chances are you will need it sooner than you think.

Management Scales

Approaches to Information Technology (IT) vary widely depending upon the size of the organization implementing it. Because sophisticated solutions are expensive, they're usually out of the range of small- and medium-sized businesses. Other solutions are targeted towards these smaller scales. IT management solutions are traditionally divided into three scales based on the size of the business:

Small-Business Solutions   Defined by a small number of users (typically up to 25) using a single server at a single site.

Medium-Business Solutions   Bounded by a somewhat fuzzier top end, although most network analysts would consider the boundary to be between 1,000 and 2,000 clients, with up to 25 or so servers. The business may exist at a single site or might have a headquarters and a number of satellite offices.

Large-Business Solutions   Support thousands of users and multiple sites or large campuses that operate as autonomous interconnected networks.

Oddly enough, networks seem to cost about $3,000 per desktop initially—no matter how large your company is or what you try to do to contain costs.

If you've ever toured the IT department at a company larger than yours and seen an HP-OpenView–based network operation center with real-time updated network maps showing the immediate status of every client in the network, you may have come away thinking that if you don't use those tools, your managing IT incorrectly. That is not the case. Small businesses have different requirements and different measures of success. The goal of all IT management is to make the appropriate information tools available all the time to everyone who needs them in the company at the lowest possible cost. Techniques vary. The chapter sections delineate the scales that most software vendors create solutions for. Read the descriptions of the businesses carefully, because you may find that although your business does not fit directly into the seat count for a certain scale, its management practices will fit perfectly.

Small-Sized Businesses

Small businesses are traditionally construction contractors, medical offices, law and other professional consulting firms, contract manufacturers, and other firms that operate with a tight binding between specific customers and jobs. Small businesses do not advertise beyond their geographical region and are usually privately held. Small business managers generally spend their time searching for strategic partners or large companies to buy them out.

In most small businesses, network administration is usually a corollary duty for someone in business administration or who has shown a propensity for figuring out computers. Many small businesses outsource IT support to consultants who stop in on a regular or as-needed basis.

Two types of products target small businesses:

- Limited versions of larger scale product suites are generally discounted in the hope that the customer will not switch to a competitor when the business grows.

- Specific-purpose utilities are written by smaller publishing houses or individuals to address a particular need. These small-scale tools are not integrated, so the small business IT manager typically has a "toolbox" of unrelated tools used for specific purposes rather than a monolithic, integrated management suite. This set of small tools is entirely normal and appropriate for this scale.

Because of the limited scope of the small-business IT management problem, most management tools generally are not necessary. That's convenient because many management tools are priced outside the budget of small businesses anyway.

Most small businesses do not have dedicated IT staff. IT management in small businesses tends to be very routine. A single server supports standard PCs in a single Ethernet collision domain. The network either has an Internet server/firewall and a dedicated frame-relay or DSL connection (if the business is really hip) or relies on dial-up networking to connect to the Internet. Security is usually ignored beyond the logon password, and the server runs for years without assistance. It just sits under the Xerox machine, humming away. Most service calls are to fix user caused misconfiguration, and the most demanding IT problem might be to get Mathematica to work with the latest service pack on NT workstations.

Medium-Sized Businesses

Typically, medium-sized businesses still have a centralized IT management philosophy, because the companies, in general, retain a very centralized corporate management philosophy—one site is the headquarters, and if other sites exist, they are satellite or branch offices. Businesses that typify this structure include banks, military units, insurance companies, component manufacturers, and other operations that produce services or products independent of a specific customer. Medium-sized businesses advertise in very targeted channels, such as trade magazines to specific customers, if at all. Managers of medium-sized businesses chase the goal of going public, getting ISO9000 certified, and trying to differentiate their mission statement from everyone else's.

NT Everyday

PART 3

High-end management tools such as CA-UniCenter and HP-OpenView are still outside the range of what these businesses need or can afford. A large selection of medium-scale management tools exist for functions such as remote administration and software rollout. Tivoli Director, NetWizard by Attachmate, and Microsoft's Systems Management Server are good examples of these tools. Medium-sized businesses generally have an IT director, a number of technicians, and usually at least one network technician at each site.

Check out medium-sized business management tools at the following Web sites:

www.tivoli.com

www.attachmate.com/netwizard

www.microsoft.com/smsmgmt

Large-Sized Businesses

Large-sized businesses typically have distributed IT management to match the distributed nature of the business. These businesses never have the effort of the entire company dedicated to a single product, contract, or customer, and they are usually involved in the mass production of consumer goods. Most government agencies operate in the same manner as large businesses. Large businesses advertise in the mass media and are usually publicly traded. These companies spend their time fending off lawsuits from their customers and stockholders, publicizing meaningless strategic partnerships to manipulate their stock price, and buying every interesting business they can find in the hopes that they might accidentally acquire the next Internet Solutions.

For large businesses, sophisticated directory services are required to manage access to resources, and a large IT is nearly always required. Large businesses usually have a chief information officer (CIO) or chief technology officer (CTO)—which one depends on the market focus of the company—and an IT director and network staff at each site. Large businesses may be highly integrated, or because of acquisition or politics, they may have vastly different networked systems between sites. Often, integrating existing IT resources is the biggest challenge for large business managers. Check out large business management tools at the following Web sites:

www.cai.com/products/uctr.htm

www.openview.hp.com

www.tivoli.com

Organization

IT is a unique function within any business. Most business functions are compartmentalized into their discreet arenas with very little informal contact between divisions—the Accounting department accounts, Marketing markets, Manufacturing makes, Sales sells, and Human Resources does whatever the heck it is they get paid to do. IT is a different beast. IT staff works closely with all operations in the business.

It's easy to let all that power and access go to the collective head of the IT staff. But IT doesn't exist to make the lives of typical workers hell by refusing to support them without the proper forms filled out in triplicate, nor does it exist to give the IT director a fiefdom over which to reign; IT exists to keep business processes flowing as quickly and efficiently as possible. IT management exists to solve problems, not create them.

Fearful of the power of an IT division, many businesses don't have centralized IT management. Rather, every business division has its own cadre of network administrators and technicians. These administrators typically have their own offices, their own desks, their own coffee mugs, and rarely carry pagers. Even large businesses should not squander their resources on the duplicity and inefficiency created by attaching IT staff to every division specifically. Centralization of all IT resources, including staff, is the only way to create a coherent, unified network.

It's easy for IT directors to direct—it's quite difficult for them to accept feedback from mere users. This generally results in an environment where IT management makes technology decisions independent of user requirements and then self-righteously declares that anyone who doesn't like that state of affairs is unqualified to proffer an opinion and doesn't really understand the problem. In environments like this, everyone winds up with a Windows terminal on their desk that runs pathetically slow because the IT department got all their usage metrics out of some book (okay, some other book) rather than rolling out a proper load-testing network first.

Run your IT organization like an independent consulting firm. Treat every user on the network like they are your customers, because they are. Respect their opinions—they are the ones who will have to live with the decisions the IT staff makes. Act like your entire organization could be fired if enough people were dissatisfied with the way the network ran. Above all, teach technicians to be friendly and courteous to users. Remember—it's their network. You just run it.

Effective IT organization is usually structured in four tiers:

Help Desk   The first line of support. Via telephone, remote control software, or e-mail, these technicians receive and immediately respond to user problems in the network. Most organizations can centralize help desk support, even when offices are remote. If a help desk technician cannot solve a problem, the issue is escalated to desktop support.

Desktop Support Dispatched by the help desk whenever an issue cannot be resolved remotely. These technicians examine the client computer for hardware failures and software misconfiguration. There is usually one desktop support technician per site or per 100 or so client stations (depending on the support requirements of the desktop technology). In smaller sites, multiple support tiers may be collapsed into an individual who covers any or all roles. They can fix the problem, replace the malfunctioning machine, or escalate to the next level of support.

Network Administrators Dispatched either by desktop technicians or by the help desk during problem deluges. Network administrators examine the health of the whole network entity, including servers, data-link devices, and the physical layer to map the extent of the problem and then solve it. Short-term problems never escalate beyond the level of network administration. Pandemic network problems are escalated to management for permanent architectural solutions.

IT Management Makes strategic core-technology decisions, evaluates and selects applications, and creates the architecture of the network. IT Management decides when and how to bring in outsourced consulting staff. IT problems don't normally escalate past IT management to business management except when a management deficiency exists.

Staffing

Hiring IT staff is something like picking good watermelons—except that you have less information to go by, because you aren't allowed to thump people to see how they sound. Resumes, especially among the brighter applicants of the IT world, only discern which applicants know how to write the best resumes.

There is only one qualification a junior (help desk or desktop support) IT applicant must have—a nimble mind. Computer technology moves too quickly to assume that you can learn a specific skill and be done with learning forever. Information technologists must be able to adapt to an environment that changes completely every two years.

I don't want to decry specific experience. It's important, especially in troubleshooting situations, and when you can get both experience and intelligence in an applicant, good for you. When choosing between the two, go with the more intelligent, less experienced applicant.

But when experience becomes too specific, like hiring someone based entirely on their AS/400 experience for example, you should consider simply outsourcing those portions of your network's problem that require that specific experience to a firm that handles more than one customer. I've never seen a mainframe or a mini that needs the constant attention of a dedicated employee.

Beware of substituting certifications or degrees for either experience or aptitude. A certification or degree alone merely says that an applicant has the persistence to achieve a long-term goal. Certifications are a useful discriminator to narrow the field of applicants if you have some overwhelming response to an opening. But once an applicant is in the door, consider their certifications and diplomas meaningless and look strictly at aptitude and experience.

Higher-level staff (i.e., network administrators and IT management) should be stolen from your competition if they can't be raised within your organization. Good network administrators and IT managers are in constant demand, so the odds of finding a good one by placing ads in the paper are pretty slim.

Institute a policy of hiring candidates—even your IT upper management—only after a short-term contract with the company, say six months long, has been fulfilled. IT management has recently become the job of choice for former middle managers who were laid off in the early 90s following a particularly severe storm of management consultants. Some are excellent; others merely have excellent resumes. Let them show you their talents before you permanently hire them. Better yet, hire your employees from a technical staffing company. Quality is worth the extra cost.

Don't fall into the trap of letting your staff's qualifications choose your network technology. I have clients who are reluctant to upgrade their Novel NetWare networks solely because their staff (who already know Windows 95 inside and out) are reluctant to learn NT or Unix. That's ridiculous. Staff training follows technology, not the other way around.

I'm a fan of training IT staff through the ranks rather than hiring people into upper-level IT management. This works especially well if the business is growing, because IT staff can grow along with the business. Unfortunately, IT staff tend to have a rather myopic view of the world outside their network, so it's easy to get a feed-back loop in your technology path, where familiar technology is preferred over more optimal solutions. For this reason, it's imperative that your IT staff participate in the IT community at large through magazines, Web sites, and trade shows.

NT Everyday

PART 3

TIP I know trade shows have a bad reputation as a boondoggle, but IT trade shows, especially NetWorld+Interop, really do a lot to broaden the horizons of IT staffers. I go to them regularly and so should you. (And, hey, you can get this book signed!)

The four levels of IT support staff match the four tiers of IT organization:

IT Managers Should be well versed in all aspects of information technology, including mainframes, client/server applications, database management, and client technologies. The idea that any MBA can read "IT Management for Dummies" and become a CIO is silly. The IT Manager should be the most experienced technician in your company, not the executive who first purchased a Palm V Organizer. Good CIOs don't have time for golf. Select IT managers with experience implementing specific systems and those who've worked first hand with database management systems.

Network Administrators Should be subject matter experts in the server operating systems they support. They should be certified in the network operating systems they support, and they should be able to completely rebuild a server from scratch. Network administrators should understand how to measure a network's performance in the critical areas of network load and server responsiveness and should know the architecture of your network inside and out.

Desktop Support Technicians should understand the operation of computers and operating systems. They should be able to build and troubleshoot computers using typical components, and they should be able to install operating system and application software without assistance. They should know how to troubleshoot the various levels of network connectivity and what to do when a client can ping a server but can't log in.

Help Desk Staff/Trainers Should understand the use and function of the desktop operating system and all of the installed applications. They should be able to troubleshoot basic problems (such as saving files in various formats and printing) and should be able to discern the difference between a training deficiency and an actual computer problem.

Outsourcing

Consulting in many business arenas has been reduced nearly to the point of a joke—nobody is actually ever unemployed anymore, they just consult. Carpetbaggers abound in the area of management consulting, and they've given a bad connotation to the word.

In computer and network services, however, consulting is a vibrant and important sector of the industry. It does not make sense to hire people for a number of installation- and configuration-related problems that your company will never again have once your systems are in place. Consultants are especially appropriate in the following areas:

GroupWare   GroupWare integration, includes developing Lotus Notes and Exchange applications, establishing e-mail services, and setting up help desk and newsgroup software. If you can, avoid it.

Web and E-Commerce   Development for both your Internet and intranet sites. Don't hire Web developers unless you sell Web services. And don't make the mistake of thinking that because you can write XML by hand in emacs that you're a qualified user interface expert and a graphic designer. Hire professionals.

Enterprise/Manufacturing Requirements Planning (ERP/MRP)   Software to run the production side of manufacturing businesses. All of these packages require subject matter experts to install and configure correctly.

Database   Development at all scales, from simple Access or Filemaker applications all the way up to Oracle enterprise solutions. (Run in fear from PeopleSoft though—both of the installations I've been peripherally involved with have been cost-overrun disasters.)

Office Software   Training can be important for businesses that deal with documents as a matter of course (such as law and professional firms) and for small businesses that are able to use Office applications to drive their business processes. Although these applications run perfectly well out of the box, getting a good trainer/consultant to teach everyone to use these tools to their potential is more than worth the investment.

Software Development   Should be outsourced if it can't be avoided—unless your firm is a software development company. And you shouldn't consider developing software, even then, unless the software falls specifically in the realm of your company's expertise.

The idea behind all these consulting suggestions is to determine what you and your staff can do well and what isn't worth the time it takes to learn. If you're only going to do it once, outsource the effort. You'll get a better product in less time for less money and without the headaches.

Small- and medium-sized businesses should strongly consider outsourcing all their IT requirements, having just one or two employees to manage the outsourced companies, control security directly, and act as an liaison between users and the outsourced companies.

NT Everyday

PART 3

Outsourcing all of your IT has a number of advantages:

- You can concentrate on your business, not IT.
- IT resources and costs grow or contract linearly with the company. When you need more support, buy more. There's no hire/fire cycle to worry about.
- You get real experts without being stuck with anyone less than competent. If you don't like an outsourced company for any reason, don't use them again.
- You can save serious money if you have a smaller business that doesn't need full time staff.
- You know you're getting the best value because you can always hire competing companies.
- You can hire more than one company to do network designs and then choose the one matching your needs closest.

However, outsourcing also has some problems:

- Responsiveness may suffer, since technicians will usually have to be dispatched from a distance.
- IT people are never around when anything breaks, so more troubleshooting is generally required.
- Some companies may have significant turnover, so you may find some companies have no memory of your network.
- Costs can spiral out of control if you pay on a time-spent basis.

Most of these problems can be contained simply by finding the right support provider and negotiating a firm, fixed-price retainer based on the size of your network rather than the amount of time the company spends at your site. I run my consulting firm based only on fixed-price monthly retainers and contracts. My customers love the controlled and budgetable cost, and I get paid whether I show up or not, so the better their network runs, the more I can make. It's a win-win situation.

Budget

IT budgeting is something of a black art. Determining the costs of a network (or surveying the value of an existing network) is a fairly simple exercise, but determining how much money it's going to take to keep that network running is less clear.

Most large businesses plan for six times the price of the initial investment per year to support their network. However, I have small business customers who spend only 25 percent of their initial capital investment in support every year. That's quite a wide variance and testament to the difficulty in determining the recurring costs of network maintenance.

I've always found it easiest to compare networks based on how many clients are supported. (Supported clients are called "seats" in the industry, because presumably everyone has to sit down in front of whatever device they use. Bizarre, but that's how jargon in the computer industry works.) Planning for support costs then is most easily performed by thinking about the hard costs of supporting each individual client on a yearly basis—a unit I call the seat-year.

You can presume a few things about network maintenance:

- Every computer will be obsolete in three years. This means that you need to plug in $\frac{1}{3}$ the cost of a new business-grade computer ($1,000) per seat-year.

- Every operating system will be upgraded at least once every three years. This totals, on average, $50 per seat-year.

- Software applications should be upgraded every two years or so. Figure that it should cost $200 per seat-year for application upgrades.

- Desktop/Helpdesk/training support costs will run about $40 per computer per month. That's about $480 per seat-year.

This totals about $1,750 per seat-year to support one client.

There are two major components remaining: the network infrastructure and the service computers. Most data-link layer and network layer hardware (bridges, routers, hubs, and switches) have a useful lifetime of about 10 years. Divide the total cost of your network hardware by 10 and apply that as a yearly replacement/upgrade budget item. For a typical network, connectivity costs about $50, which translates (assuming a 10-year useful life) to just $5 per seat-year, which is really lost in the noise of these other calculations anyway.

Servers are another matter: They're expensive. Networks generally require a server for every fifty or so clients. The service life of a server can be stretched to three years, but that's pushing it harder than pushing clients out to a three-year replacement cycle. Assuming you pay an average of $10,000 per server (including hardware, software, and client access licenses), and you replace them every three years, you'll need to spread $3,333 among 50 clients, which leaves a mere $66.66 per seat-year.

All these calculations make a number of presumptions, so we wind up with numbers that seem a lot more precise than they really are. But they are useful for getting us into the budgetary ballpark, which is right around $2,000 per seat-year, just to maintain the status quo, which is 66 percent of the initial installation cost.

NT Everyday

PART 3

TIP   Plan on spending $2,000 per seat-year to maintain your network.

This budgetary figure doesn't include the extra burden ERP/MRP or custom databases put on your budget. These support costs vary too wildly for me to attempt to put a real cost on, but you should be able to get a very solid idea from the consultants that you use to put these systems in.

Selecting Core Technologies

The core technologies you build your network around will define the character of your network, the nature of your support operation, and the capacity of your business to perform its work. For these reasons, selecting core technology is the most important network decision you'll make.

You probably already have a network, but that doesn't mean you can't reengineer it, often using the same hardware you already own.

The most important core technology that you'll choose is your majority client, based largely on these basic types:

- Standard PCs are most appropriate for scientific, engineering, design, development, or CAD work.
- Remote-boot PCs are most appropriate for a wide array of standard business functions like word processing, finance, communications, and presentation.
- Windows terminals are most appropriate for light task-based work (database access or data entry).

Flexibility is the antithesis of ease of use; standard PCs are both the most flexible and the most difficult to support. Windows terminals are the least flexible and the easiest to support. Remote-boot PCs strike a middle ground between the two.

With Standard PCs, you are free to run any client operating system you want. With remote-boot PCs, you are limited to MS-DOS or Windows 95—Windows 3.11 for Workgroups, Windows 98, and Windows NT cannot be reliably remote booted. Windows terminals are even more limited; they run on the terminal server only, providing an execution environment most similar to Windows NT Workstation.

TIP Some Windows terminals can remote boot either Windows NT Terminal Server Edition for a Windows execution environment or X-Windows for a Unix-execution environment.

Standard PCs place the lowest overall demand on network servers. Remote-boot workstations place a substantial load on servers and the network while booting but behave pretty much as normal computers once booted. Windows terminals do not place much of a load on the network, but they seriously burden the CPU and memory resources of the terminal server.

Evaluating Total Cost of Ownership

Total cost of ownership for the various client technologies is remarkably similar. If we break down each of the major client types by cost, we find something like Table 11.1.

Table 11.1   Comparative Costs of Client Technologies

Component	PC	Windows Terminal	Remote Boot
Monitor, keyboard, mouse	$500	$500	$500
Box	$1,500	$800	$1,300
OS license	$100	$150	$100
Client-access license	$40	$40	$40
Total	$2,200	$1,500	$2,000

By client cost alone, Windows terminals would seem to make the most sense. But that's not the whole story. Remote-boot PCs require a boot server that can serve about 35 clients, assuming it has no other duties. Windows terminals require a terminal server for every 20 machines. Since these machines are in addition to normal file servers, there is no associated cost of this nature for standard PCs. So to level the TCO playing field among the various client types, we must add $\frac{1}{35}$ the price of a $7,000 server to remote boot PCs, which equals $200. Similarly, $\frac{1}{20}$ the price of a $7,000 server must be added to the price of a Windows terminal ($350). Adding these costs to the price of each client type levels the playing field considerably.

NT Everyday

PART 3

The total cost of ownership for all client types is roughly the same. With client licenses for office software and applications, they all cost about $3,000 per seat for typical business purposes. The real difference between the client technologies lies in the recurring cost of administering the different technologies.

Small-sized businesses usually prefer standard PCs because of their flexibility and availability—they work when the network is down, and they can be purchased from any computer retailer.

Medium-sized businesses can make good use of any of the technologies and should select their technology based primarily on the needs of the users—PCs for heavy-duty use, remote-boot computers for typical functions, and Windows terminals for task-based workers.

Large-sized businesses should make their client decisions based mostly on the needs of users. Because of the size of the management problem, easily supported technologies like remote-boot computers and Windows terminals will play a larger role, and because they can be purchased in bulk, their cost advantage can become significant.

Implementing Systems

Implementing any new system, or upgrading existing systems, doesn't have to be a chaotic morass. With a little planning and foresight, you can re-engineer your entire network without so much as a hiccup in the daily operation of the company. The following are the phases of system installation:

- IT evaluation
- Test installation
- Training
- Back-end rollout
- Client rollout
- Cutover
- User support

Each of these distinct phases is important to the process in the order it's presented. Short-cutting these phases will make a system implementation more difficult.

IT Evaluation Phase

The entire IT organization becomes familiar with the new system during installations of the IT evaluation phase test, during test configurations, and with technical support from the manufacturer. The purpose of the IT evaluation phase is to make sure the entire IT organization is prepared to support the new product and is familiar enough with it to troubleshoot even unexpected problems.

Take as much time as you need during the IT evaluation phase to become comfortable with the product. Rushing new technologies into production environments is asking for trouble and serious delays. Your rollout will go smoothest when your IT staff is comfortable with the new products.

The IT evaluation phase should include at least one complete simulation. The simulation should mimic the function of your entire network, with multiple clients, routed connectivity between machines, and anything else your network includes.

Test Installations

Never, ever, ever install new technologies directly in your network without first performing a test installation. Test installations are limited-scope rollouts to more sophisticated users in order to determine how the product functions in a production environment. Your test installation may, in many cases, be entirely within the IT department, but it can also include small groups in other divisions if these groups are technically oriented and can work through configuration problems. Candidate groups would be software developers, scientists, and engineers.

Besides building a database of technical support problems, you'll be able to use this phase to monitor the performance of the product in an environment that more closely matches the environment of your whole network, yielding far more accurate usage statistics than any synthetic loads could provide. The usage characteristics you determine during this phase will determine the exact server-to-client ratios that you'll use in your full-scale rollout.

Don't finish your test installation phase until you have determined the precise performance characteristics of the new technology in your environment, compiled a support database that is extensive enough to handle most user problems during and after the rollout, and completed a training course and materials for standard users. Once these functions are complete, you're ready to move on to the training phase.

Wide-Scale User Training

Wide-scale user training is the next step in an organized implementation. By training users before the technology arrives at their desk, you've made them comfortable with the coming change, and you seduce them into anticipating the new system. Thus, when the new product arrives, users are prepared to use it, excited to have it, and ready to begin working immediately. You'll preempt passive resistance to the new methods, and you'll

NT Everyday

PART 3

avoid users who try to blame the IT division for whatever problems they have with the new system. By simply preparing users in advance, you can avoid the appearance that the IT division simply makes policy without user feedback—even if you do.

During the training session, be prepared for millions of silly questions aimed squarely at debunking the new system from people who'd rather not change, or amazingly detailed questions from those who fear that they won't be able to adapt to the new system. ("Yes, but after I've created my monthly usage reports, what will the hotkey for sorting them by SKU number be?") Don't be sidelined by these questions during mass training sessions; tell everyone they can schedule one-on-one training with an IT staff person, if they need, when the product is installed for them. Most people will be able to figure out how to integrate the new product into their work without help. Remember that the purpose of the wide-scale user training is less to actually train than it is to elicit support for the new system among users by eliminating their fear, uncertainty, and doubt.

Back-End Rollout

If your system is client/server, there will be two phases to the rollout: first the servers and then the clients. Rolling out servers is easy because there's no demand on the new systems. You can move the back-end servers into production using only the test rollout group or the IT division for system validation. Once the back-end servers are in place, tested, and online, you can begin the client rollout.

Client Rollout

Now you're ready for the full-scale rollout. Depending on the type of system you're implementing, you may either replace an existing system, upgrade a system, or add a system alongside a legacy system that will be removed when the rollout is completed. In any case, the rollout is the period where client stations are individually updated to the new system.

Hardware rollouts will always take far more time than software rollouts, because every client station must be visited. Software rollouts can often be completed in a day if you have the right infrastructure for it. If you don't, they're much like hardware rollouts, because you'll be visiting every desktop.

Rollouts do not have to be a frenzied IT activity where nerves are worn thin by late workdays and a rushed pace. The rollout doesn't have to occur any faster than the IT evaluation phase—take it easy and save your energy for the support phase after the cutover.

Cutover

Cutover is the moment when all users simultaneously stop using the old system and begin using the new system. Cutover is necessary whenever the new system is not compatible with the old system—it creates a demarcation that prevents some information from going to the old system while other information is processed by the new system.

If the new system was used with testing information prior to the cutover, that test information must be deleted immediately prior to the cutover. Cutover is usually performed over a weekend to give the IT staff time to test the production system before work starts on Monday. The apparent difference to typical users is that they used the old system on Friday and the new system on Monday.

The old system should be taken offline during the cutover to prevent users from reverting to it in the mistaken belief that that's what they should do if they have problems with the new system. After the old system is offline, there may be a data migration to the new system or an archival process depending on how the information processed by the old system should be managed in the future.

Once the old system is offline, any legacy client hardware or software can be removed from users at the leisure of the IT department.

Help Desk/Desktop Support

The period directly following the cutover is always the most frenetic period of a system implementation. It is during this period that the IT staff finds out that it really was necessary to sort monthly usage reports by SKU number and has to have the consultant add that functionality to the system. User-training problems will abound.

If you're consulting a system integrator for the installation, consider paying for supplemental support from their staff, because you'll find your staff is probably less prepared for the onslaught then you thought.

The key to handling the support phase after cutover is good preparation. Have your help desk in place with procedures that don't rely on the newly installed system to get help. For example, don't implement an e-mail system and then stipulate that users should send e-mail to the help desk to get support.

Don't immediately dispatch desktop support staff for every call. Assign priorities to each support incident and have your staff handle them in priority order. They key here is not to waste your time helping the facilities manager while the production line sits idle awaiting support. Base your support priorities on the criteria of minimizing work stoppage. Is it a work stoppage issue, or can the user work around it? If it's not a work stoppage, prioritize it below problems that are.

How many other people depend on this specific user's work to continue theirs? Obviously those who cause a bottleneck in the workflow for others are the highest priority. Note that this isn't the same question as how many people work for the affected user—management above a working group typically doesn't interfere with daily operations, so don't waste your time getting executives online until you've knocked down all the bottleneck users in your organization.

A Study in IT Management Techniques

These miniature case studies highlight various approaches to IT management and their effects.

"Healthy Competition"

I once had a customer that had two separate IT directors—both with equal power and the same set of responsibilities. The idea was that they were supposed to compete with one another so the company would always have the best implementation at the lowest cost. A management consultant came up with this glimmer of brilliance.

The net effect was that the two IT directors hated each other. They had to have consultants (like me) come in to make even the most mundane decisions because they could not agree on how the department should operate. The network became schismatic, with each director taking control of the portions they installed or supported. They'd deny documentation to each other, foment dissent within the ranks, and work to make the other look bad. It was by far the most dysfunctional IT organization I've ever seen. Don't be tempted to do this.

"Not without My Budget"

A major public university (which shall remain nameless) does not have a dedicated IS staff. Rather, each college funds its own networking operation and staff. A good friend of mine was the director of one of these college network operations. Being distributed as they were, his staff was small and so was the problem: He supported about 500 clients and perhaps 10 servers. His staff regularly attended meetings and he had his own desk and coffee mug. He was paid a miserable wage ("not much money for the network this year") but he had just finished college, so he didn't need much money. The net effect of this structure was that no college had a truly professional staff. No central point of operations existed—even for controlled access to the Internet; effectively, every server in the university is a public host on the Internet, and even today they routinely suffer major hacking breaches. There isn't even a common e-mail standard or basic platform—some colleges use Unix, some NetWare, and some NT. Many have PC clients, others have Macintoshes, and still others use Windows or X terminals. The university as a whole pays for more IT staff than any organization I've seen, but some colleges languish with too little support while others pay people to drink coffee and write e-mail systems from scratch. Worst of all, nobody involved thinks there's anything wrong with this.

"The Occupation Army"

A major pharmaceutical company has a lovely IT department. They supposedly operate as an independent organization, but each site pays directly for the staff they support. The site has no power to compel the IT staff to do anything, but they are compelled to pay them. The support procedure works like this: Requisitions for equipment are made through the local divisions who will have to pay for it, but all equipment purchases are actually

24seven **CASE STUDY**

24_seven_ **CASE STUDY**

made through the central IT division that has veto authority over all in a vain attempt to control the proliferation of platforms in the company. Support requests also go through the central office for dispatch; even though an on-site technician is always dispatched to look at the problem, local employees cannot request assistance directly.

It became easier for a group of programmers at one site to outsource their department's IT problems to me than it was to get support from the on-site staff. Because they had control of their own budget, the IT staff couldn't stop them from doing it, but they still had to pay the on-site staff. They decided to retain me and pay them, because at least that way the problems that they had been living with for months on end while the local staff sat on their butts and awaited the proper authorization from the east coast office were solved.

Part 4

When Things Go Wrong

Topics Covered:

- Bottlenecks
- Architecture optimization
- Network optimization
- Server optimization
- Performance optimization
- Troubleshooting techniques
- Troubleshooting networks
- Troubleshoot computer hardware
- Troubleshooting resources
- The Registry

12

Performance Optimization

Performance optimization is the process of finding the resource that slows your network the most, speeding it up until something else has the most impact on speed, and then starting over by finding the new slowest resource. This cycle of finding the speed-limiting factor, eliminating it, and starting over will allow you to reach the natural performance limit of your network in a simple, methodical way.

Windows NT provides low-level support for performance monitoring by including counters in every object that can be meaningfully measured. Windows NT uses the performance information to automatically tune itself for the tasks it's used for by changing various thread priorities, caching characteristics, network timings, and many other factors.

Windows NT also provides the Performance Monitor, a tool that enables you to measure system performance through object counters. You can use the Performance Monitor to find bottlenecks (performance-limited resources) in your server. The Performance Monitor enables you to inspect the value of the object counters in real time so you can see how various activities affect the resources of your server.

To effectively find bottlenecks, you must look at the overall performance of your computer under a typical load. Using more general counters and averages will give a good indication of where to look for specific bottlenecks. Processor performance, memory performance, and disk performance are the three major capacities that you should check.

The Network Monitor is used to capture packets, broadcasts, or multicast frames that are being sent to or from the server it's installed on. The Network Monitor is a limited version of the same tool that ships with Systems Management Server (SMS, a Microsoft BackOffice application that can be purchased separately). The SMS version can capture network packets from the entire network, not just those involving the server. You can filter captured data based on the protocol used, the computer address, and the protocol properties. Filtering allows you to take a large amount of information and display only the frames that match your criteria.

Tuning a network's performance is the perpetual cycle of finding performance bottlenecks, eliminating them, and starting over with the next most limiting factor. When a system can no longer be tuned for greater performance, it is at its natural performance limit.

By using the Performance Monitor to tune the performance of individual servers and the Network Monitor to tune the performance of your network, you can increase the speed of your network and stave off major hardware upgrades until the system reaches its natural limit.

This chapter first covers performance theory, then the practical aspects of architecture, network, and server optimization, and ends with a section on optimization shortcuts and best practices.

Performance Theory

There are only two ways to improve the performance of a single component in any system:

- Reduce the load placed upon the component.
- Increase the capacity of the component.

Reducing the load placed upon the component could require changing how the component is used, adding other components to share the burden, or removing functionality. Increasing capacity generally requires upgrading to hardware that can perform more work, but it might also require tuning the component to work more efficiently with available resources.

In a system, the complex interactions between components can make ferreting out which components are the cause of undesirable effects somewhat difficult. However, systematic measurement of the load across all the components of a system will make it obvious which components are responsible for performance limitations.

Bottlenecks are factors that limit performance in a computer. For instance, slow memory limits the speed at which a processor can manipulate data—thus limiting the computer's processing performance to the speed that the processor can access memory. If the memory can respond faster than the processor, the processor is the bottleneck.

A slow hardware resource, such as a hard disk drive, causes the microprocessor and system RAM (both fast) to wait for the resource to complete I/O requests. Thus, during disk I/O, the speed of the hard disk is the speed of the computer.

Although you cannot make your hard disk faster (except by replacing it with a faster one), you may be able to reduce the number of times the computer needs to access it, or you can limit the amount of information that is transferred. You may also be able to spread the load across many hard disk drives, thus dividing the time you spend waiting for drive access by the number of drives available.

Users of client computers in your network should be the bottleneck in your network. To achieve performance nirvana, their computers must be more responsive than the users need, the network data link must be more responsive than the clients attached, and the servers must be more responsive than the networks to which they are attached.

Eventually, you will find a limitation that you cannot overcome. This point is the natural limit of your system, and finding it is the ultimate goal of performance tuning. If you need speed beyond the natural limit of your system, you will need to upgrade the hardware resource causing the limitation.

Ferreting out bottlenecks involves a little understanding of how computers and networks work, and it requires some software. Even the best system engineers can only guess at what causes a complex system to run slowly unless they have proper monitoring tools. Windows NT provides a comprehensive set of tools for finding and eliminating bottlenecks in both servers and networks.

To find a bottleneck, you must be able to measure the speed of the different resources in your system. Measurements enable you to find the one resource that is performing at its peak and, therefore, causing the bottleneck.

When Things Go Wrong

PART 4

TIP Hardware resources operating at their maximum performance level are the bottlenecks.

Different resources require different measurements. For example:

- Network traffic is measured as a percentage of utilization.
- Disk throughput is measured in megabytes per seconds.
- Interrupt activity is measured in interrupts per second.

To compare resources, you must use measurements that are equal. In most cases, Windows NT provides a basic "percentage of processor time spent doing this" that you can use to compare dissimilar resources.

To find a bottleneck in a network, you use the Network Monitor to determine whether your data-link layer is sufficient for the number of computers on it. With an Ethernet or Fast Ethernet network, a sustained network utilization of 30 percent or more is an indication that you need to consider splitting that network into two or more subnetworks or moving to a faster data-link technology. If your network is not experiencing excessive utilization, servers that are too loaded to quickly respond to client requests may be causing slow performance. Perhaps the servers are not optimized for their tasks, or perhaps they simply aren't powerful enough to handle their duties for the number of clients attached.

To find a bottleneck in a server, you first run the Performance Monitor that is discussed later in this chapter. You then need to put your server under the load that causes it to perform more slowly than you want, attach multiple clients to your network file server, and start copying files. Then you should run SQL Server and put it under a load by generating complex queries or do whatever normally makes your server slow.

The Performance and Network Monitors will suggest a few broad measures that will show you where to search more deeply to find the exact bottleneck. For example, if after showing processor time and disk time, you see that the disk is running at its peak, you know to concentrate on disk-related measurements. Or if the Network Monitor shows that the network is under excessive load, try to find the clients that are transmitting excessively and determine if their traffic is appropriate. If it is, you should try splitting your subnetworks further or upgrade to a faster data-link technology.

> **TIP** Make certain you've found the bottleneck before concentrating on detailed performance monitoring. Since performance-limited resources hide behind other, slower resources, you won't be able to see the difference if you make changes to objects that are not the true bottleneck.

Finding a bottleneck is only half the battle. Eliminating it (making it fast enough that something else is now the primary bottleneck) may involve changing a Control Panel setting, or it may involve replacing every cable in your network and the devices that connect to them. You will have to determine how to relieve the load placed on the resource.

Usually, you will be able to look at more detailed measurements to determine the specific activity that is loading down your network. For instance, if you determine that your network utilization is high, you should then use the Network Monitor to determine which computers are generating that load and why. You may find that you have a malfunctioning device on your network that is generating spurious traffic or that your replication or backup scheme is generating far more network traffic than you suspected. These problems can be easily corrected. Sometimes, however, you'll find that your network simply isn't fast enough, and major architectural changes are in order.

> **TIP** When troubleshooting, make only one change at a time. Otherwise, you will not be able to tell which change fixed the problem.

Achieving maximum performance from your network is a continuing process. Once you have eliminated the major bottleneck in your system, you start over and eliminate the next new bottleneck. Your system will always have a bottleneck, because one resource will always cause other resources to wait for it.

You want to eliminate bottlenecks until

- You make your computer so fast that you never need to wait for it.
- You find the component to replace or upgrade.
- You realize that you can't afford to buy any more new components and settle for what you have, knowing that it is as fast as it will get.

When Things Go Wrong

PART 4

Architecture Optimization

Architecture optimization is the group of optimizations that affect every aspect of your network system—not just physical data-link speed, server performance, or application speed. Architecture optimization is the process of making the entire system as efficient as possible.

An analogy to separate the processes of architecture and network optimization can be made to freeways: A network optimization approach would be to build more, whereas an architecture approach would be to change the environment to effect working at home or living close to work.

Architecture optimization will produce the greatest overall benefit. Network optimization will produce the next best benefit to performance, and server optimization the least beneficial. Oddly, these three components of system optimization become increasingly complex and difficult even as their returns decrease.

Redesigning an existing network is considerably more difficult than putting an effective architecture in place to begin with, but even that is not particularly difficult in most cases, because the optimization usually involves only the connections between workgroup collision domains. Therefore, only networking equipment and servers are involved.

Architecture optimization involves these key components:

- Create the least amount of network traffic possible by selecting the client hardware and application software that generates the lowest amount of network traffic while performing the necessary work. For task-based work, this may require using terminal servers or highly controlled workstations, or it may require loading applications on the local hard disk rather than over the network.

- Make network traffic travel the shortest possible distance by placing file or terminal servers in workgroups on the same collision domain as their supported clients.

- Use content-efficient protocols for data that must, by its nature, travel long distances to centralized network resources. Do this by selecting data dense protocols, such as e-mail and client/server databases, rather than less efficient word processors and file-based databases.

- Make effective use of caching and data replication to push frequently accessed non-changing data as close to the data subscribers as possible. For example, use HTTP proxy servers on workgroup file servers to cache the corporate intranet site, and make them BDCs so they can perform logons locally. Put user profiles on the server closest to them.

Network Optimization

Because the speed at which network clients can work is usually tied to the speed at which they can access the network, the speed of the network limits the speed of every computer attached to it. Many factors affect the responsiveness of a network from the point of view of client computers, but the two that have the most impact are the availability of network bandwidth and the responsiveness of network servers.

Measure your network performance before you measure the performance of individual servers. The network performance measurement will first tell you whether your network is a bottleneck, and if not, it will tell you which network resources are the bottlenecks.

If too many computers are competing for a single, shared media subnetwork, if the computers are able to process data faster than the data rate (or bandwidth) supported by the network data link, or if the network servers are too loaded down to respond quickly, then the speed of network clients will be limited by the network. This problem is most apparent when you run network-limited clients, such as Windows Terminals or diskless workstations. Standard workstations are less limited, because they do not rely on the network for their system and application files.

Conversely, if the network is immediately available in most cases, if the data-link bandwidth is greater than the amount of data that the client can process, and if the servers are able to quickly respond to client requests, then the clients will not be limited by the speed of the network. Therefore, a fast network requires that the data rate of the data-link technology exceeds the ability of the clients to process data, that competition to access shared media networks is not excessive, and that servers be fast enough to respond to all simultaneous client requests.

Improving network performance is rarely easy. When networks begin to run slowly, speeding them up can be very difficult. There are two ways to improve network performance:

> **Reduce Traffic**   This option is best when circumstances permit it, because it works regardless of your current network architecture and does not require any physical changes. Reducing traffic may involve localizing servers inside departmental subnetworks or migrating network applications to lower-bandwidth Internet client/server protocols. You can also reduce traffic by splitting subnetworks.

> **Increase Speed**   This option works very well, but it is also very expensive; it requires the replacement of every data-link device on the network. This option should be regarded as a major network architectural change and should be implemented gradually.

Reducing Traffic

There is no systematic way to reduce network traffic. You must monitor your network using the tools discussed later in this chapter and decide whether you can relieve the traffic load on your network. However, you can look for the following problem areas:

- Users that generate excessive traffic (in excess of their peers). Find out why. If they don't have a valid work-related reason, encourage them to stop.

- Diskless workstations running Windows. These stations generate an enormous load on networks. Hard disks are very inexpensive compared to the cost of a network upgrade, so consider adding hard disks to these machines and booting the operating system locally.

- Network loading of applications that could be stored locally. Although I recommend the central installation of applications for ease of administration, decreasing the load on your network may be a higher priority for you. This trade-off is typical of the many cost, performance, and ease-of-use compromises you will make.

- Replace inefficient client applications that rely on data stored on the network with true client/server application. An example would be to migrate an Access database that is stored on a server to a client/server database using an Access front end and an SQL server back end.

- Stop the wasteful practice of using Office applications (for example, Word and Excel) to store or transmit data in your environment. The documents created by these applications are huge compared to their information content. E-mailing them as attachments around your network causes an unnecessary burden on every resource involved. Encourage people to use bandwidth-conserving technologies, such as e-mail text, databases, and HTML (Web pages), rather than Word, Excel, and PowerPoint for internal communications.

Identifying Top Talkers

Reducing your network load usually involves identifying which computers generate the most load, determining why, and reducing the load generated by that specific computer if possible. Repeating this process until you cannot relieve the load any further will reduce traffic to the extent possible.

Routers, bridges, and servers normally generate the most apparent load on the network. Servers usually respond to each client request, so they normally generate about 50 percent of the load on a network. Bridges and routers are actually forwarding data from other networks, but their Media Access Control (MAC) addresses will appear in the Network Monitor as the source of the traffic.

If you see multiple IP addresses coming from single MAC address when you are using a packet sniffer (such as the Network Monitor) to monitor network traffic, you are looking at traffic coming through a bridge or router. Inspect source IP addresses to determine which devices are truly using the most bandwidth.

Splitting Networks

Unless your network is far behind your traffic requirements, you will be able to get a lot of mileage out of simply splitting your shared media networks into multiple subnetworks joined by bridges, routers, or servers that are performing the routing service.

Splitting networks is analogous to building more highways. In theory, doubling the number of collision domains cuts the traffic on each network in half. However, that method works only when you can guarantee that both sides of the conversation are on the same subnetwork. For instance, if you split your network but two computers that spend most of their time communicating on the network are on different subnetworks, you haven't solved the problem. Their traffic will simply be retransmitted on both subnetworks.

You have to make sure you've isolated on the same subnetworks computers that spend time talking to each other, which is why basing subnetworks on some real grouping of individuals, such as by department, usually works well. These users, and by extension, their computers, will spend most of their time communicating internally.

The vast majority of all network traffic in client/server local area networks is between clients and servers. Peer-to-peer networks may be communicating with other computers on the network, making splitting subnetworks difficult. However, because most clients spend the majority of their time communicating with a single server, you can usually make the server a part of each subnetwork. Figure 12.1 shows a network that puts a single server on each subnetwork, thus efficiently multiplying the total bandwidth to the server without upgrading to a higher-speed network.

This solution isn't quite as easy when you have more than one server, but you can still identify the server that each client usually talks to and put that client on the same subnetwork as that server. Then, by attaching all your servers to a single high-speed subnetwork, you can route any traffic for other servers over a higher-speed link rather than upgrading the link technology of your entire network. The configuration in Figure 12.2 shows a high-speed backbone between servers localized to subdomains.

When Things Go Wrong

PART 4

Figure 12.1   A central server on multiple subnetworks

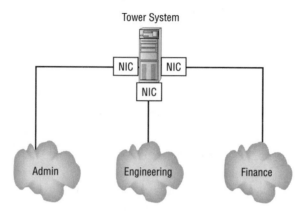

Figure 12.2   Many departmental servers on a high-speed backbone

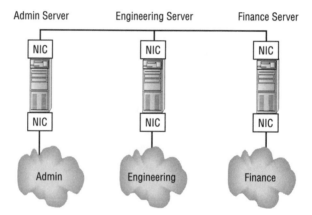

When clients must access many different servers without preference (this is rare), you may need to implement servers on a high-speed backbone, using dedicated routers to attach client subnetworks. This architecture has the disadvantage of requiring expensive routers to attach to the backbone. It also requires every packet transmitted to a server to traverse the backbone, which forces the backbone to deal with the vast majority of all the traffic on the network. Figure 12.3 shows servers on a high-speed backbone.

Figure 12.3   Many servers on a high-speed backbone

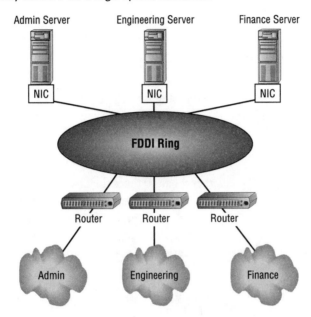

In some situations, clients must access not only their departmental server but also many other servers (for example, an intranet server, a messaging server, and an Internet gateway). An obvious solution would be to simply put all the servers on a backbone and route to them, but that configuration might not be the best solution. Even if the clients spend only 25 percent of their network time communicating with their departmental server, you are better off directly attaching them to it and using it to route to a backbone that contains the other servers. Remember that every packet you keep off the backbone makes the backbone faster. For instance, a network with four departmental servers that are able to deal with 25 percent of their clients' requests without forwarding them to the backbone will cut backbone traffic in half. That load reduction can stave off migrating to a higher-speed network technology for years.

However, routing can be a significant performance hit for servers. Whenever you configure servers to perform a routing function, you should monitor them periodically to ensure that they are not causing a significant network bottleneck. If they are, you should move the server inside the department and use a dedicated bridge or router to perform the routing function.

When Things Go Wrong

PART 4

Increasing Speed

If you can no longer reduce traffic or efficiently divide subnetworks, you will have to upgrade the physical data-link network protocol. Usually, this upgrade involves moving from Ethernet or Token Ring to Fast Ethernet or Fiber Distributed Data Interface (FDDI).

Remember that you may not have to upgrade your entire network. You may be able to simply upgrade your backbone technology, the links between servers, or certain subnetworks or users to higher-speed networks. Use the Network Monitor to identify top talkers on your network and migrate those users to faster protocols first.

Fast Ethernet

Fast Ethernet is simply regular Ethernet at 10 times the raw throughput. Fast Ethernet runs at 100Mb rather than 10Mb. The two major varieties of Fast Ethernet are 100Base-X, which is a regular Ethernet at a higher speed, and 100Base-VG (AnyLAN), which uses a similar but incompatible access method that can guarantee throughput even in heavily loaded networks, making such applications as real-time voice or video over the network reliable.

Three varieties of 100Base-X fast Ethernet exist:

- 100Base-TX runs over standard category 5 twisted pair wiring on two pairs.
- 100Base-T4 runs over Category 3, 4, or 5 twisted pair wiring on all four pairs.
- 100Base-FX runs over one pair of multi-mode optical fiber.

You must use special media converters to adapt from any one type of cable to another. Some hubs include media converters or transceivers that do the job for you. Most 100Base-FX adapters and some 100Base-TX adapters can operate in a special mode called Full Duplex, which allows them to simultaneously transmit and receive data and eliminates collisions on the wire (however, collisions still occur inside hubs). This technology not only doubles the capacity of Fast Ethernet to 200Mbps, it extends the distance limitation of 100Base-FX from 400 meters to 2,000 meters.

Fiber Distributed Data Interface (FDDI)

FDDI is essentially 100-megabit Token Ring over fiber-optic cable with a second counter-rotating (the data flows in the opposite direction) ring that provides a measure of fault tolerance in case of cable faults. A copper variant called CDDI runs over the same category 5 twisted-pair wiring that fast Ethernet runs over.

FDDI is the oldest high-speed network technology in common use. Early problems with fault tolerance features were solved long ago, and although it remains expensive, FDDI is very stable and can support operations at metropolitan-area distances.

Asynchronous Transfer Mode (ATM)

ATM is the new telephony standard for wide area telecommunications links. Because it supports different guaranteed levels of service for voice, video, and data networking at very high data rates, ATM has become a compelling new option for campus area transports. ATM standards using the same frame technology have been defined for the following data rates:

- ATM-25 runs at 25Mbps and is intended as a competitor to Fast Ethernet in local area networks.

- STS-3 runs at 155Mbps over fiber or category 5 twisted-pair wiring as an alternative to Fast Ethernet or FDDI in high-speed workstations or network backbones.

- STS-12 runs at 622Mbps over fiber as a campus area transport.

- STS-48 runs at 2.2Gbps over fiber as a metropolitan area transport. Few computer networks will implement this speed, but they may be attached to telephone networks operating at this speed.

- STS-192 runs at 8.8Gbps over fiber as a long-distance intercity transport. Only telephone companies will install this grade of ATM.

The compelling factor in ATM is that the same frame technology can be switched among any of the data rates listed above by relatively simple switches. Unfortunately, the ATM standards are still not completely defined, and you may have trouble getting devices from different manufacturers to operate properly. Be certain to choose equipment that the manufacturers guarantee to be compatible before purchasing any ATM equipment.

TIP   OC (Optical Carrier) grades are equivalent to STS (Synchronous Transmission Signal) speeds. STS refers to the digital bit rate, whereas OC refers to a specific STS rate over optical fiber carriers. STS-N rates are multiplied by 51.84Mbps to determine the aggregate bit rate.

When Things Go Wrong

PART 4

FiberChannel

FiberChannel was developed as a high-speed peripheral interconnection bus for disk arrays and mainframe computers, but it's very high data rate (256Mbps or 1Gbps) make it compelling as a point-to-point, full-duplex, server-to-server connection.

Gigabit Ethernet

Gigabit Ethernet encapsulates regular Ethernet frames inside the data payload of FiberChannel frames, which makes the endpoints of a FiberChannel network work similar to an Ethernet bridge. Gigabit Ethernet will probably be the least expensive high-speed backbone technology available for quite some time, especially for networks using Ethernet or Fast Ethernet.

The Network Monitor

The Network Monitor monitors data sent over the network. Data is sent through the network in frames or packets, each containing header information that identifies the protocols being used to send the frame, a destination address, a source address, and the data. Each package must contain a source and destination address to be delivered correctly.

Most people don't make a habit of opening packages not addressed to them. The network is the same way. By default, a network card will ignore any packet that is not addressed to its computer. On the other hand, network monitors really don't care whom a packet is sent to. They are able to capture all packets on the network.

Network monitors use a special mode, called *promiscuous mode*, that is supported by most modern network cards. Promiscuous mode allows the network adapter to capture all the data packets on the network. Special promiscuous mode drivers work by capturing the data of every packet, as opposed to capturing only packets that are addressed to the computer network card.

The Network Monitor that ships with NT Server 4 is not a fully functional network monitor. It is a limited version of the Network Monitor that ships with SMS. Instead of being able to capture all of the network packets, this version of Network Monitor can capture only the following:

- Frames sent from the server
- Frames sent to the server
- Broadcast frames
- Multicast frames

Because the Network Monitor that ships with NT Server 4 is not fully functional and does not capture every network packet, the server's network card driver does not have to run in promiscuous mode. Network Monitor is able to use the network driver interface specification that your network card uses. The frames that are detected are then copied to the server's memory in a capture buffer. Using the NDIS standard instead of promiscuous mode reduces the CPU load up to 30 percent.

In contrast, the Network Monitor that ships with the SMS product is able to capture all packets on the network, regardless of the source or destination computer address. The SMS Server must use a promiscuous mode network driver.

Server Optimization

You may never have to deal with manual performance tuning, because Windows NT tunes itself very well for most users and most situations. Unlike many operating systems, you will not have to manually adjust arcane environment variables to improve Windows NT performance. Windows NT takes care of that for you. The tuning you will need to do to optimize Windows NT performance involves determining which hardware resources are under the greatest load and then relieving that load. Windows NT comes with some very powerful tools to assist you, but because of the self-tuning nature of Windows NT, you may never have to use them.

Multiprocessing

Multiprocessing divides the processing load across several microprocessors. Windows NT uses *symmetric multiprocessing*, a technique in which the total processor load is split evenly between processors. Simpler operating systems use *asymmetric processing,* which splits the processing load according to some criterion other than load. Usually, those operating systems put all system tasks on one processor and all user tasks on the remaining processors. Support for multiprocessing varies by product:

- Windows NT Workstation ships with support for two processors.
- Windows NT Server ships with support for four microprocessors.
- Windows NT Server Enterprise Edition ships with support for eight processors.

Scheduling and resource assignment between processors takes computing time. Because of this load, two processors are not twice as fast as one. A Windows NT system with two processors generally runs at about 150 percent of the speed of a one-processor system, depending on the type of programs run. An application that has only one thread cannot be run on more than one processor.

In many computing problems, threads depend on results provided by other threads. This circumstance is like a relay race in which a runner (thread) must wait for the baton (results) before starting. Obviously, splitting these threads among processors doesn't make the application run any faster. Multiprocessing works best with large computing data sets that can be broken into chunks and solved independently of one another.

You can use multiprocessing to improve the performance of CPU-limited applications, such as Windows NT Server Terminal Server Edition, which puts a heavy demand on terminal servers. Other applications (for example, databases) or Internet application servers can also soak up a lot of compute time. It is probable that you will have to upgrade your motherboard in order to add more processors. That's usually not a problem, because motherboards generally cost less than the processors you put in them.

When Things Go Wrong

PART 4

One modern processor is more than enough for more mundane server operations (such as file and print services)—these functions demand more from disk and network resources.

If you determine that your processor is the bottleneck, you will need to upgrade to a newer microprocessor or computer or upgrade to multiple processors. If you can't get a microprocessor that is twice as fast to work in your computer, don't bother upgrading the microprocessor. Upgrade the entire computer.

Memory Optimizations

Page swapping, while useful to at least keep a server running, is a good indicator that you should add memory. In fact, with RAM as cheap as it is these days, you should add enough memory to your servers so that they do not swap to disk under normal operating conditions. This will provide optimal memory performance.

The more memory you have, the less time the system spends on page swapping. Windows NT systems with less than 32MB of memory will spend a significant amount of time swapping pages to the virtual memory page file, especially if they are running more than one application at a time. This swapping activity slows the computer dramatically, because hard disks are very slow (but also very cheap) compared to physical RAM.

The faster page swapping happens, the lower its impact on system responsiveness. To speed this process, Windows NT supports simultaneous writing to more than one hard disk for its virtual memory paging file. Since physical drives can operate simultaneously, splitting the virtual memory swap file among different disks allows Windows NT to divide the time spent processing virtual memory swaps by the number of physical disks. You can use the System Control Panel to assign a portion of the page file to each disk in your server.

Windows NT allows you to split your swap file among volumes on the same physical disk, but there is no performance-related reason to do so. In fact, this configuration increases swap time by forcing the drive head to move much more than normal during swapping. You should set only one swap file per physical disk and avoid putting the page file in fault tolerance volumes, such as mirrored partitions or stripe sets with parity. You should also consider setting the initial and final sizes for the swap file to the same number (physical RAM plus 12MB unless you have a reason to do otherwise) to prevent your page file from becoming fragmented if NT increases its size automatically.

Caching Disk Requests

Windows NT uses disk caching to reduce the amount of input/output traffic to the hard disk drive. Caching works by reserving a portion of memory as a staging area for hard disk reads and writes. When data is read from the disk, it is stored in the cache. If the same data needs to be read again, it is retrieved from the very fast memory cache, rather than from the slower disk.

> **NOTE**   In this book, the term *memory* is synonymous with *random access memory* (RAM), not with hard disk space.

Actually, disk read operations don't just bring in the data requested. Entire clusters are transferred from the hard disk to the memory cache, because read and write operations are most efficient at the cluster size. Consequently, a good portion of the data located on the hard disk immediately after the data that is requested also comes into the memory cache. Because read accesses tend to be sequential, the next read request is likely to be in the cache.

The disk cache is also used for write operations. The Windows NT file system (NTFS) doesn't write data to the hard disk immediately. It waits for system idle time so that it will not affect the responsiveness of the system. Data writes are stored in the memory cache until they are written to disk. Often, especially in transaction-oriented systems such as databases, new changes supersede data written in the cache even before it is written from the cache to the hard disk. Consequently, the write cache has completely eliminated the need to write that data to the disk.

Data writes waiting in the cache can also be read back if they are subsequently requested, which allows yet another cache-related optimization. The type of caching used in Windows NT is called *write-back caching,* as opposed to *write-through caching,* which immediately writes data to the disk while preserving it in the cache for subsequent rereads. Write-through caching is used in operating systems that cannot otherwise guarantee the integrity of data on the disk if power is lost while data is in the cache waiting to be written to disk.

> **TIP**   The caching schemes used in hardware to make your microprocessor run faster operate on exactly the same cache theory as presented here.

Windows NT uses all the memory that remains free after the running processes have the memory they need as a disk cache. Windows NT dynamically changes the amount of memory assigned to the disk cache as new processes are started to ensure the optimal performance boost from caching. Windows NT balances the amount of disk cache and the amount of virtual memory page swapping to optimize the use of physical memory.

Performance Monitoring

The Windows NT Performance Monitor is an amazing tool—unique to the Windows NT operating system—that provides the ability to inspect the performance of just about every process and resource that occurs in your computer. The Performance Monitor allows you to determine the exact cause of every performance-related problem your computer experiences.

Performance and the Performance Monitor are broad topics. An entire book could be dedicated to the various features and the work flow theory used to discern where and why bottlenecks occur. Windows NT automatically makes most adjustments for you though, so that level of detail is not required to make your computer run well for most tasks. So this section explains how the Performance Monitor works and tells you which indicators to watch in order to quickly narrow down performance problems. You cannot harm your system by experimenting with the Performance Monitor, so feel free to see the effect of the different low-level indicators.

Heisenberg's uncertainty principle states that to measure quantum phenomena is to change it. This principle is also true of performance monitoring. Running the Performance Monitor takes a small amount of CPU time, and enabling disk monitoring also slows input/output requests slightly. Therefore, you cannot measure system performance without causing the performance to change slightly. In almost every case, this change in performance is slight and will have no undesirable effect on your measurements or the validity of your conclusions, but you should be aware that it is happening.

Object Counters

Each Windows NT software object is associated with counters that are incremented each time that object performs a function. For instance, each time a network device driver reads a packet, the device driver increments the packet's read counter by one and the byte's read counter by the size of the packet. Also, each time the processor switches threads, it updates the time spent in that thread in a counter used for that purpose.

Counters permeate all Windows NT objects, and they allow meaningful measurement to occur by accounting for everything that happens. Windows NT uses many of these counters to measure performance for its own automatic optimizations. It is the first PC operating system to include this level of support for performance monitoring. Table 12.1 shows the objects that you can monitor with the Performance Monitor.

Table 12.1   Windows NT Object Counters

Object	Purpose
Cache	Microprocessor level 2 cache performance
Logical disk	Mass storage performance, including network storage
Memory	Memory performance and usage
Objects	Process and thread counts
Paging file	Virtual memory usage
Physical disk	Hard disk drive performance
Process	Executing process performance
Processor	Microprocessor performance
System	Windows NT performance
Thread	Individual thread performance

You will also see objects for each network service you have installed. Actually, any software can be written to register performance monitoring counters with the system, so you may see even more counters than are shown here.

Processor Performance

The microprocessor is generally the fastest component in a computer. In Pentium class and higher computers, the microprocessor is rarely the cause of a bottleneck unless you are running scientific, mathematical, or graphical software that puts a heavy load on the floating-point unit of the microprocessor.

Processor ➤ % Processor Time

The Processor ➤ % Processor Time shows the current utilization of the microprocessor(s). The microprocessor does not become a bottleneck until you see a sustained 80 percent or better level of utilization when watching the Processor ➤ % Processor Time counter in the Performance Monitor. If after tuning your computer to eliminate processor

When Things Go Wrong

PART 4

bottlenecks, it still runs in this zone, you need to upgrade to a faster (or just another) microprocessor. This counter shows how busy the microprocessor is. The processor will spike to 100 percent at times—this spike is normal and does not indicate a bottleneck. As long as the processor normally runs somewhere between 0–80 percent, your processor is sufficient for the workload. After adding this counter, let the computer idle for a moment. Then move your mouse around on the screen and notice the effect on the Processor ➤ % Processor Time measure. Dramatic, isn't it?

Processor ➤ Interrupts/Sec

Processor ➤ Interrupt/Sec measures the rate of service requests from peripheral devices. An unusual amount of activity on this counter without a corresponding increase in activity in the computer indicates that a hardware component is malfunctioning and is sending spurious interrupts. This counter should operate continuously between 100 and 1,000, but spikes up to 2,000 are acceptable.

System ➤ Processor Queue Length

System ➤ Processor Queue Length counts the number of threads waiting for attention from the processor. Each thread requires a portion of microprocessor time. Many threads running simultaneously may exceed the supply of processor time, causing the microprocessor to become a bottleneck. A sustained thread queue that is greater than two indicates a processor bottleneck; too many threads are standing in line awaiting execution, which bogs down the processes that rely upon those threads.

If you try to watch the processor queue length indicator only, you will notice that it always sits at zero. This reading occurs because the Performance Monitor must be monitoring a thread-related counter in order to determine how many threads are awaiting execution. To see the true value of the processor queue length counter, monitor a thread counter of some sort. A good one to try is the Context Switches/Sec, which shows how many thread switches occur each second.

Disk Performance

Disks affect computer speed more than any other component. Booting, application loading, storing and retrieving data, and virtual memory swapping performance are all tied to the speed of your disk, because disks are so much slower than the processor or memory. For these reasons, the speed of your disk(s) affects the overall speed of your computer.

As with all performance monitoring in Windows NT Server, you can use the disk monitor to profile your disk activity. However, your computer also comes with a performance indicator that works in any operating system: the hard disk drive light. If your disk light is on most of the time under normal working conditions, you need to add RAM to decrease paging. If paging is already not a problem, you need to move to RAID. If you've already got fast RAID in place, you need to split the function of this computer across two or more machines. You can't avoid these solutions, and all the performance monitoring on the planet isn't going to uncover a different answer.

RAID works on the same theory as stripe sets. The difference is that a RAID controller replaces your regular SCSI controller and makes the stripe set look like one physical disk to Windows NT.

RAID controllers include a microprocessor that handles breaking up and recombining the disk data so that the computer's microprocessor doesn't have to. Most RAID controllers also use some RAM as a cache to increase the speed of transfers to and from the controller. This cache works the same way as the Windows NT cache described in the memory optimization section.

RAID controllers essentially perform the same service as stripe sets, but because they relieve the computing burden of stripe sets from the processor and add a memory cache dedicated to disk transfers, they can help relieve processor bottlenecks. Unfortunately, RAID controllers can be very expensive, so they are generally used only in servers.

A new breed of less expensive processorless RAID-0 and RAID-1 controllers exist. These controllers are actually just hard disk controllers with BIOSes that implement a disk striping or mirroring function and come with drivers that support that striping or mirroring for Windows NT. Because no computation is required for either of these functions, they are both fast and effective.

Physical versus Logical Disk Performance

In Table 12.1 you may have noticed two disk-related objects: a logical disk and a physical disk. The logical disk is used to measure performance at a higher level than physical disk.

The logical disk object can measure the performance of network connections that are mapped as drives and the performance of volume sets and stripe sets that cross physical disks. You will use the logical disk object to uncover bottlenecks initially and then move to the physical disk object to uncover the reasons why that bottleneck is occurring.

Physical disk measures only real transfers to and from actual hard disk drives or a RAID sets. These measures isolate performance differences between disks in your system and provide detailed information about the specific performance of a certain disk.

Disk counters cause measurable performance degradation by distracting the processor at critical input/output periods. These counters are disabled by default. If you attempt to monitor physical or logical disk performance without enabling these counters, you will

When Things Go Wrong

PART 4

not see any disk data. When you have finished monitoring disk performance, remember to disable the disk performance monitors. Leaving them enabled serves no purpose and slows your machine down.

Monitoring Disk Performance

You can enable disk performance counters using the diskperf.exe command-line utility. Issue the command at the command prompt for instructions. The following are important counters you'll want to watch:

Memory ➤ Pages/Sec   Indicates how many page swaps are written to the disk. Leave this counter showing in the Performance Monitor while watching the % Disk Time to see how dramatically page file performance affects your overall performance.

% Disk Time   Shows how much processor time is spent servicing disk requests. It is a good broad indicator for determining whether your hard disk drive is a bottleneck during activities when you would not normally expect to wait for your hard disk drive. Note that this counter is a processor metric, not a physical disk metric. Measure this counter against Processor ➤ % Processor Time to see if disk requests are eating up all your processor time.

Disk Bytes per Second   Shows how fast your hard disks are transferring data. Turn this counter on and then copy a large directory of files between disks to get a good baseline of the speed at which your disk or disks run.

Average Disk Bytes per Transfer   Shows the size of the average transfer. Average transfers that are larger make more efficient use of disk hardware and execute faster; smaller transfers cause the computer to work too hard to write them to disk.

Current Disk Queue Length   Shows how much data is waiting to be transferred to the disk. Many processes must wait for disk requests to be serviced before they can continue. A long disk queue indicates that many processes are being delayed by disk speed.

When you interpret performance data, keep the following information in mind. Pages/Sec should be consistently less than 20, or excessive paging is taking place, and you need to add RAM. All counters that have the word *Queue* in them have an acceptable threshold value of 2 or less. (Queue is 2.) Also, disk counters are not turned on by default, you must type **DISKPERF –Y** at a command prompt and restart the computer.

You need to upgrade your processor (or add another one) under the following circumstances:

- % Processor time exceeds 75%
- Processor Queue length exceeds 2

You need to add RAM under the following circumstances:

- Pages/Sec exceeds 20
- Available Bytes is less than 4MB
- Committed Bytes exceeds physical RAM

You need to upgrade your disk subsystem under the following circumstances:

- % Disk Time exceeds 50%
- Disk Queue Length exceeds 2

When Things Go Wrong

PART 4

Compute Bound Problems

A customer of mine used a Windows NT workstation to run heat-stress analysis on modeled components using a technique called finite element analysis. The process involved designing three-dimensional software models of their product and then running an application designed to perform the analysis on the models. Using a Pentium-II 450Mhz computer with 128MB RAM and a 12GB UltraDMA IDE hard disk, a single analysis took about 10 hours. This, unfortunately, meant they could run only a single analysis per day without investing a significant amount of money in additional software.

They asked me to determine how they could use their existing resources to perform more analyses. The scientist performing the analysis was considering installing a RAID array in the machine to improve its performance.

Using the Task Manager for a quick look at processor load and RAM usage, I determined that their software put a 100 percent CPU load on the microprocessor and allocated all the remaining physical RAM in the computer (but not virtual memory, which it seemed to avoid using). About five hours into the process, the hard disk would begin heavy activity for quite some time.

These numbers meant basically that the problem was bound by the speed of the processor. The heavy disk activity was likely the result of the process writing out its first batch of results to free up memory for the next batch.

We were already using the fastest processor available at reasonable cost (the Pentium III hadn't yet been released, and it wasn't significantly faster anyway), so we had no where to go for raw speed improvement, but we could add more processors to the computer. Using the performance monitor, I determined that their software ran in just a single thread. The heat-stress analysis software was not multithreaded, so it would not be able to make effective use of another processor.

These problems made it seem that there was nothing we could do to improve the computing performance of the problem: The software was limited to using a single processor and we already had the fastest processor available.

So I looked next at the disk-swapping problem. Obviously, the analysis my customer wanted to solve didn't fit entirely into memory, because the software would begin writing results out to disk before it had finished. This meant that if we could eliminate disk writing, we might be able to speed the analysis.

We borrowed a 128MB DIMM from a sister machine, installed it in the analysis machine, and ran the analysis again. This time, the analysis completed in half the time! The program was designed to use as much physical memory as was available before it began swapping to disk, so by doubling the amount of RAM in the machine we were able to forestall the slower disk process. Further increasing the amount of RAM in the computer lowered the analysis time even further, so they are now able to perform many times more analyses per day than they had been originally even though we couldn't increase the processor speed.

Best Optimization Techniques

In my networking practice, I've found the following optimizations to be the most useful. They're specific in nature, but they solve a wide variety of problems and are fairly easy to implement.

- Buy and use dual processor servers. Although a second processor only improves CPU performance by about 50 percent, it guarantees that no single thread can utilize 100 percent of your available computing power. This will make any heavily loaded server more responsive.

- Upgrade your servers to the latest processor technology. Because you can upgrade processors, motherboards, and RAM without many hassles, you should stay in the habit of upgrading your servers about once every two years.

- Add RAM to your servers. 256MB of RAM is common for servers these days. The more memory your servers have, the faster they'll respond on your network.

- Add servers. You should probably have one multipurpose server for each group of approximately 25 to 50 clients depending on how much traffic your users generate. That server should be the location of the user's home and profile directories, the BDC from which they log in on, the router between them and the rest of the network, and a proxy for Web and intranet sites. If this means you would have a large number of servers, just treat them as a higher-level client—make them all the same and use workstation rollout techniques to manage them.

- Use Gigabit Ethernet on your backbone. A single 100MB network connection for a modern server is okay for file servers, but is usually a bottleneck for application servers. Use Gigabit Ethernet for the central database, the Web, and the domain controllers on your backbone. Connect your backbone to multi-homed workgroup servers with a gigabit adapter up to the backbone and Fast Ethernet out to a maximum of four workgroups per server.

- Upgrade your network to Fast Ethernet. If you don't have category five cabling installed, either install category five wiring or use 100Base-T4 to operate over category three or four wiring.

- Migrate from a switched Ethernet architecture to a routed TCP/IP architecture. Routing gives you a lot more flexibility once you take the time to implement it. You can create multiple data paths to support redundancy in the face of failure, too.

- Switch from diskless workstations to policy-controlled normal workstations. This will allow you to remove the operating system and application load from your network and put it where it belongs—in the computer. Don't use centrally stored applications either—it's a waste of bandwidth. Remember the ideal: Push data

24seven **CASE STUDY**

CASE STUDY 24*seven*

out as close as you can to its ultimate point of use.

- Prefer central shared printers to desktop printers. For example, don't put a $300 laser page printer on every desktop when you can put a central $3,000 network printer in place that prints wide-format 11"x17", legal, and letter and can hold reams of paper in multiple paper trays. Don't put a $200 ink jet printer on 50 desktops when you can put a $5,000 color laser printer on your network. You'll have far fewer support problems, your users will get faster and better printers, and that short walk to the printer provides a refreshing break from staring at a monitor. Use scanners like the HP 6200 series that can be shared in the workgroup, too.

- Spend money on servers rather than clients. Clients don't need voluminous hard disks, they only need enough to load the operating system and applications— approximately a gigabyte these days. Clients rarely need top-of-the-line processors or a lot of RAM. Any Pentium MMX with 32MB of RAM is sufficient for running office applications. Put that money into server RAM and hardware RAID for servers instead. You'll be ahead with both money and performance.

13

Troubleshooting Theory

Networks are incredibly complex. Network software is even more complex than network hardware and computers, and network operating systems are the most sophisticated pieces of software that programmers can create. Making such complex and sophisticated things foolproof is virtually impossible, so although Windows NT is as robust as any operating system you will encounter, you will occasionally need to fix problems with your servers. Often, network problems can seem like server problems, so you need to develop the skills to quickly determine what components are likely to be at fault whenever a fault condition occurs.

Troubleshooting is a skill like any other. You can apply certain general principles to any troubleshooting situation, but you must know how the specific system you are troubleshooting works if you want to be able to diagnose faults. As with any other skill, you get better at troubleshooting with practice.

This chapter introduces you to some general computer troubleshooting principles and then shows you how to troubleshoot computer hardware, Windows NT operating system software, and network connections.

The Troubleshooting Process

Troubleshooting is the methodical process of eliminating faults from a system. Although troubleshooting a computer is difficult, you can quickly isolate the culprit following a few basic rules that allow you to focus your troubleshooting efforts on components more likely at fault.

Troubleshooting a network involves determining the component that is at fault, changing the hardware or software configuration of suspect components, and then testing to see whether the configuration change has eliminated the problem.

If a hardware failure caused the fault, you will have to find and replace (or repair, but that's rare these days) the failed component. If a software configuration caused the fault, you will have to reconfigure your system to eliminate the fault. In some cases, you may not be able to reconfigure your system, because the configuration problem involves the denial of some service that is required to reconfigure the faulty component. If you run into this catch-22, you may have to reinstall the operating system on the server or client that is faulty.

> **WARNING** Working on electronic devices, including computers, can be dangerous. You should only attempt to troubleshoot a computer if you are very familiar with electrical safety, electronic equipment, and computer hardware.

Windows NT software has been thoroughly debugged by Microsoft. However, bugs exist in all nontrivial software, especially in the less frequently used areas. Nonetheless, Windows NT runs, and it runs well. All of its services operate properly. If you have a persistent problem with a Windows NT server, it is likely caused by less-than-compatible hardware or improperly configured software.

> **TIP** Bugs are most likely to exist in rarely executed code.

Windows NT is very specific about which hardware it will work with. Early in NT's design cycle, Microsoft chose not to support all hardware devices that can be added to a PC because of the security holes DOS-mode drivers allow—and because Microsoft could not possibly write drivers for all the PC-compatible hardware that exists. If you are having a problem with a new Windows NT installation, chances are good that you are using hardware that does not appear on the Windows NT hardware compatibility list (HCL).

> *TIP*   Bugs are more likely the fault of a third-party driver than of Windows NT standard components. Consider these drivers as primary suspects when troubleshooting.

Focus is important in troubleshooting. Making random changes in a system, just hoping something will work, is a good way to waste a lot of time and to create more problems, especially with untracked changes. Focus on a specific component, and test it thoroughly. If you are not able to correct the fault, restore the original configuration before moving on to another component.

Troubleshooting is relatively easy when you are dealing with only one fault, as is generally the case with a hardware failure. Software failures, however, are usually a lot more complicated. You may be faced with a situation in which two or more simultaneous problems are causing a fault. Correcting only one fault at a time will change the symptoms but will not correct the problem. For instance, suppose your modem doesn't work. You have a hardware conflict because your modem is set to the same IRQ as your LAN adapter, which caused your modem software to automatically detect the wrong modem. You will have two problems (a hardware setting and a software configuration) to fix before you can operate your modem. Correcting one or the other problem will not allow you to use your modem.

> *TIP*   Rotating between symptoms is usually a sign that there is more than one problem.

Troubleshooting is either quick and easy, as in the case of a simple failure when you are pretty certain what is wrong, or long and complex, for example, when you return to work to find a computer that went down during the night and refuses to reboot. Often you will come upon more than one fault that has to be resolved to progress to the fault. This sequence is the natural cycle of troubleshooting.

> *TIP*   Partial success usually indicates a complex failure involving two or more faults.

The rest of this section covers the general principles of troubleshooting that apply to any system. Following these guidelines will help you quickly determine what is at fault in your system. However, no book or set of rules will really help you find a problem unless you understand the system you are troubleshooting.

A Needle in the OSI Stack

Complex systems, such as computers, operating systems, and networks, are designed and constructed in layers. In a layered system, simpler constructions provide a foundation upon which more complex constructions can rely. Layers of these interdependent constructions provide, at their top, the amazingly complex functionality that you experience when you use the system.

Layers arise in system design partly because it's too difficult to create the ultimate functionality of the system from scratch and partly because systems evolve over time. As a system is used, new functionality becomes available, which is layer atop the existing functionality, to provide new utility.

Imagine trying to conceive of and implement Windows NT as a single unified program. Such a task would be far too difficult for even a software giant like Microsoft to accomplish, and the resulting program would be unmodifiable. It would take far longer to implement and would be impossible to add new functionality to it without rewriting it.

Monolithic (nonlayered) system design is part of the reason NetWare's functionality lags so far behind Windows NT and Unix, why far less third-party software is available for the operating system, and why Novell takes far longer to release significant operating system upgrades than their competition. Novell designed the original version of NetWare as a single program and has basically rewritten every significant upgrade from scratch rather than building upon an existing platform. NetWare 2.*x* was scrapped and rewritten for 3.*x*, which was basically rewritten for 4.*x*, which represented Novell's first attempt at layered design.

Windows NT, on the other hand, has merely evolved from the original NT 3.1 source code. NT 3.5 was an evolution of NT 3.1. It fixed a number of bugs, changed the functionality of some basic components, and added TCP/IP support. NT 3.51 fixed more bugs, added more comprehensive TCP/IP support, and extended file system features. NT 4.0 added the user interface from Windows 95, and Windows 2000 will merge usability components (for instance, USB), better PC-card support, and the user interface of Windows 98 (which is an evolution from Windows 95), as well as enterprise network features. The layered design philosophy on which NT is based is why Microsoft's operating system is far more nimble.

The price for layered design is speed and efficiency. NetWare remains faster than NT for basic services (such as file and print), because service requests don't have to "drill down" through layers of APIs and through security checks. On the other hand, it's far less secure and lacks support for many less common services, because they're more difficult to develop since the operating system doesn't provide many services to applications.

Design layers make troubleshooting far easier because you can start the troubleshooting process at the bottom layer of the system and work up to the top. By validating the proper operation of each layer, you've eliminated components that could be at fault.

When you troubleshoot, start at the beginning of these lists and verify that the symptoms of correct operation occur. Because of the complexity of these systems and the fact that many elements of a layer may be tolerant of faults, a faulty component in a layer may not be obvious if the layer seems to operate correctly. These sorts of problems require more rigorous testing but can still be approached on a layer-by-layer basis.

Computers can be divided into the following layers (in this order) for troubleshooting purposes:

Processor, Motherboard, Video   These components must operate correctly for the computer to turn on.

RAM, Caches   These components must operate correctly for the computer to execute software.

Hard Disk Controller   These components must operate correctly to load software.

Hard Disk Drive(s)   These components must operate correctly to reliably store and retrieve software and data.

Peripheral Hardware   These components must be in place to provide their service, such as attachment to the network, printing, or access to CD-ROMs.

POST   The Power On Self-Test must correctly complete before the computer will relinquish control to the BIOS.

BIOS   The Basic Input/Output System must be in place to identify and load the operating system from a mass storage device.

Boot Sector   The bootstrap routing must load and execute properly to bring the operating system in from disk.

Operating System   The operating system must operate to provide its services.

Operating systems in general can be divided into the following layers (in this order) for troubleshooting:

Boot Loader   This software must be able to find the operating system files to load the operating system.

OS Load   The operating system must load and start correctly to provide service to higher layers.

Drivers Load   Most peripheral components require drivers, whether those drivers are built into the system or provided separately.

Services Load   Executable files that provide wide ranging operating system services and act as part of the system load next.

User Interface Start   Once system files are loaded, connections from the local console and/or the network can be made to establish user sessions.

Failure usually occurs in the startup phase of the failed component. For example, if your system crashes during the services load phase, it's because a service has failed. The service may fail because it or the data upon which it relies is damaged or because a previously loaded component has failed, but the failure was not critical until a dependent service started.

Network connectivity can be divided into the following layers (in this order) for troubleshooting:

Physical Layer   The cable infrastructure must be able to reliably transport data for communication to exist. Test the physical layer with cable test devices.

Data Link   The network interfaces, hubs, repeaters, and bridges must be functioning correctly for data to be transmitted between machines.

Network Protocol   The transport protocol software on the end systems and routing, gating, and firewalling functions of intermediate systems must be functional and correctly configured for reliable communication to occur. Test the network and data-link layers using the IP Ping utility.

Session Management   The operating system's session establishment, logon, and higher-level transportation software must be operational and configured correctly for network services to operate.

The remaining portions of this section detail these troubleshooting layers.

New Networks

New networks can create a number of troubleshooting problems: Bad routing tables abound, cabling may not be completely tested or working, bad connectors can keep links from working, and even power sources can be problematic.

Troubleshoot network problems from the physical layer up. Always insist on a full cable test report for newly installed cable, including a category five network scan. Don't let a cabling contractor tell you that cable scans aren't necessary, or they already did a continuity test. Full 100MHz cable scans with a wire map showing that all pairs are properly wired will keep you from wasting days of your time troubleshooting intermittent network failures. Insist on cable scans.

Test workgroup and enterprise hubs and switches as you bring them online one at a time. Don't wait until you've got an entire network set up before you start testing end-to-end connectivity, because any malfunctioning component can make the entire system seem bad. Test as you install using laptops.

Routing can be a real bear, especially in new networks. Make sure you understand TCP/IP routing before you start installing equipment, and make a complete network map on paper showing how everything connects together along with assigned network numbers, subnet masks, and gateways. Build your router tables for each device on paper before bringing them online.

Once you have your network equipment online, perform end-to-end throughput testing using laptops before you put servers in. Be sure you know your network is operating before you complicate your troubleshooting problem with additional hardware.

New Computers

Brand new computers from any major manufacturer will work correctly with Windows NT—right out of the box. If you have serious problems installing Windows NT on a new computer, you should suspect a hardware failure, because all new computers are designed to work smoothly with NT.

The exception to this rule is computers that you specify the components of or build yourself. You may find you have considerably more trouble installing NT on these machines. At fault is usually the disk controller technology—some RAID and SCSI controllers can be very difficult to work with under NT even when they come with drivers.

If you are building a computer from scratch, save yourself a lot of time by getting it working correctly under MS-DOS or Windows 95 before trying to install Windows NT. Better yet, save yourself even more time by buying a complete computer with Windows NT factory-installed. If you can't buy Windows NT pre-installed, check the Microsoft Web site (www .microsoft.com/ntserver) for computers listed on the Windows NT hardware compatibility list. Microsoft has certified that these computers will run Windows NT properly.

Microsoft will not certify individual components for use with Windows NT—it certifies only complete computers. Therefore, you can't be sure that all your hardware will work correctly under Windows NT if you have your computer custom built. For these reasons, even the most experienced PC technician should think twice before building a Windows NT machine from components.

If you are determined to build your own computer, study the Windows NT knowledge base on the Microsoft Web site so you can avoid buying hardware that is known to cause problems under Windows NT. Pay special attention to the specific type of SCSI adapter and motherboard you purchase.

When Things Go Wrong

PART 4

New Windows NT Installations

Be certain that you don't have any interrupt, DMA channel, or memory port conflicts before attempting a Windows NT installation. Windows NT does not allow interrupt sharing, which is used in DOS serial ports and can be set up under many PCI motherboard BIOS settings. Modems and sound cards are especially likely to share interrupts under less sophisticated operating systems like MS-DOS or Windows 95.

If you have a hardware conflict, turn off PCI Plug-and-Play compatibility if it is allowed in your BIOS and manually assign interrupt settings to hardware. Record these settings so you know what they are. Remove any hardware that is not necessary for the operation of the computer, such as modems, sound cards, and (if possible) your network adapter. This step reduces possible sources of conflict when you install Windows NT. Once the operating system is running, you can add these components one at a time to be certain they are configured correctly.

If you are using SCSI devices, be aware that many common SCSI adapters have compatibility issues running under Windows NT. Check the Windows NT knowledge base using the search key "SCSI Adapters" for a run down of the compatibility issues of certain controllers. Also, with some SCSI controllers, the NT loader can have a hard time finding your boot drive if you have an active IDE bus and SCSI devices set on ID 0.

Axioms of Troubleshooting

Finding the component at fault is the primary purpose of troubleshooting. Once you know exactly what is wrong, fixing the problem is usually trivial. Following is a list of axioms for general troubleshooting that will help you quickly isolate and repair hardware and software faults in Windows NT:

- Be patient.
- Know the system.
- Isolate the fault.
- Check the most recent change.
- Check the most common failure point.
- Check things that have failed before.
- Perform easy tests first.
- Make assumptions to guide your troubleshooting.
- Use what you know.
- Change only one setting at a time.

- Track the changes you make.
- Try to make transient failures repeatable.
- Try to isolate individual faults in multiple fault malfunctions.
- Resort to permanent changes last.

Be Patient

Patience is not just a virtue when troubleshooting, it's an absolute necessity. If you are under time pressure to get a system working, if possible, you are better off using another computer. If you can't, you will just have to forget about your deadline because rushing through the troubleshooting process usually doesn't work. You will save yourself more time in the long run by taking your time to troubleshoot than by frustrating yourself with rushed efforts that don't work and may introduce additional faults. Most troubleshooting efforts will take hours.

Know the System

You can't troubleshoot unless you know your system. Troubleshooting is the process of diagnosing symptoms, postulating causes, and testing your hunch by making configuration changes. If you don't understand the symptoms you see, the rest of the troubleshooting process breaks down, and you will be unable to make a reasonable diagnosis.

If you are reading this chapter first, because you have a Windows NT computer that isn't working, you should turn back to page one and start reading there. The knowledge you gain about the inner workings of NT from the rest of this book will help you diagnose your problem.

Isolate the Fault

The fastest way to determine fault in a malfunctioning computer is to remove what you know works from the list of suspect components. Narrowing your search will help you focus on components that could be at fault and keep you from making changes in other working portions of the system. For instance, if you can reliably see information on the screen, most of the hardware in your computer is working properly. You can eliminate the processor, motherboard, RAM, video card, and monitor from your list of suspect components.

In many cases, you will be able to quickly isolate a component by validating many components at a time. For instance, a computer that boots completely probably does not have any failed hardware components.

Check the Most Recent Change

If you've just changed something and your computer no longer works properly, it doesn't take a rocket scientist to figure out that the most recent change caused the problem (or exacerbated an existing unexpressed problem). This logic would normally go without saying, but when a malfunctioning computer frustrates you, it's easy to forget.

In addition, a fault might not show up immediately, and you may have to think about what you changed last. Or someone else might have changed something on the computer that you are not aware of.

Often users accidentally break something when they try to make a change to their system and then pretend not to know what is wrong to avoid embarrassment or liability. You should try to foster an environment where users will not be afraid to come clean with this information, because ultimately it will cost you a lot more time to try to get to the bottom of a fault if you don't know about recent changes.

Here are some suggestions to facilitate troubleshooting in a corporate environment:

- Implement security on workstations to prevent users from being able to incorrectly configure a system.
- Try to change policies that hold your coworkers liable in some way for accidental damage to a computer, or they will never help you troubleshoot anything.
- Make sure your clients understand that your ability to work quickly will save them money.

Check the Most Common Failure Point

This is another rather obvious point, but it is an important axiom of troubleshooting. Hard disks have become very reliable lately, but they are still the third most likely-to-fail component in a computer, after the monitor and the floppy disk drive. Unlike monitors and floppy disk drives, a crashed hard disk will quite probably make your computer useless. Hard disks are also complicated enough that the failure might not be obvious. Hard disk faults can also be a software problem that looks like a hardware problem.

Connectors and cables are also common failure points. Cables inside computers can become loose if a computer is moved or subject to vibration. PCI bus card edge connectors are very sensitive to movement compared to ISA bus cards, and single inline memory modules can also come loose easily. Check all these components when you have a mysterious hardware failure that keeps your computer from booting.

Peripherals that rely on jumpers for option settings are susceptible to loose jumpers. Check to make sure no jumpers are missing and that they are firmly seated in their correct positions if you suspect a component is faulty.

Check Things That Have Failed Before

If you have a component that has failed or disconnected in the past, chances are that it will do so again. If you are experiencing the same sort of failure symptoms as you have in the past, the first thing to check is the component that failed before.

If you find that a recently replaced component has failed again, some other component may be causing that component to fail.

Perform Easy Tests First

If you don't have any idea what might be wrong, you should start by checking components that are easy to test. This process is most easily accomplished if you have a computer that you know is working and is configured similarly. You can swap easily removable components between the two computers to see if the fault moves with a component.

TIP   Check BIOS settings if you have a problem with any hardware embedded on the motherboard.

Quick software reconfigurations should be performed before more lengthy or sweeping changes (for example, reinstalling the operating system or swapping out a hard disk).

Make Assumptions to Lead Your Troubleshooting

When troubleshooting, you will refine or redefine your initial diagnosis as you work. This diagnosis will lead in the direction of failed components. For instance, if your computer boots but does not come up on the network, you can assume one of the following:

- The network software is configured incorrectly.
- Another piece of hardware conflicts with that network adapter.
- The network adapter has failed.
- The network adapter cannot reach the network because of a cable fault.
- The server is down and not responding.

You can test each of these hypothesis to determine the true cause of the problem.

Use What You Know

You might know the events that precipitated a failure without realizing it. For example, in the network scenario previously described, you can use your knowledge of the computer's environment to guide your troubleshooting.

When Things Go Wrong

PART 4

For instance, if the computer used to work fine on the LAN but stopped networking after a new sound card was installed, the LAN adapter and the sound card are conflicting. If the computer stopped networking after a recent remodel, there's a good chance that a cable was broken or unplugged during the construction. Or if a network administrator has been reading this book and playing with the Registry, there's a chance the networking software is no longer configured correctly for your network.

Change Only One Setting at a Time

This axiom is very important. Often, especially with software configuration trouble-shooting, you are tempted to try something, see if it works, try something else, and see if that works. Unfortunately, this haphazard process causes you to unwittingly change configuration information that may, in turn, produce another fault. You can easily fix the original fault but introduce another without even realizing it.

Each time you make a change, restore the original settings if the change didn't correct your problem—*before* continuing on to your next test.

Track the Changes You Make

Write down each change you make. You need a way to keep track of the multiple changes you implement simultaneously in an effort to solve a complex problem. A change log also allows you to update the computer configuration report you keep on all your computers.

Try to Make Transient Failures Repeatable

Transient failures indicate either an environmental variable failure (such as a loose connection) or conflicting software that causes the faulty condition when in certain states.

If you suspect an environmental fault, try to exacerbate the condition to make the fault stable. If you suspect a software fault, try stopping services and unload running applications until the fault disappears. Then begin restarting services until you can get the fault to reappear.

Try to Isolate Individual Faults in Multiple Fault Malfunctions

Unusual symptoms (those you don't see in this chapter) usually occur because more than one fault is present. To get a computer up in a multiple-fault malfunction, you may have to correct each fault simultaneously if the faulty components are dependent upon one another. This makes troubleshooting exponentially more difficult. If you can isolate a fault by removing a hardware component or stopping a software service that allows you to determine one of the factors in the malfunction, you will be able to concentrate on that factor until it works correctly.

If you cannot isolate an individual fault in a multiple fault situation, you should start with the basic troubleshooting procedures of validating the proper performance of your hardware and then reducing the complexity of your software by stopping unnecessary services and unloading running software. This reduces the complexity of the environment and narrows down the list of suspect components. When you have reduced running software environment to the minimum level required to operate, reintroduce components until the fault appears again.

Resort to Permanent Changes Last

Permanent changes, such as replacing hard disk drives, reinstalling the operating system, or deleting files should be your last resort. All of these repairs will take a long time to implement and will reset your security permissions, shares, and network names. Be certain you are replacing the component at fault before making these drastic repairs.

Reality Check: When Debugging Goes Awry

This case study is going to take a somewhat different tack than the other case studies in this book by presenting an example of a time when I ignored my own advice and let an incorrect presumption lead me into a three-month struggle with a crashing server.

In this case (thankfully) the server was mine, and it's one I had built by a manufacturer to my specifications. It was to replace my current office server, an aging dual Pentium 200 with a 10GB IDE RAID-0 disk pack based on a Promise Technology FastTRAK controller. I bought the new machine without disks, because I intended to migrate the RAID pack from the old machine—that was the point behind buying a custom configuration rather than an off-the-shelf computer.

To perform the migration, I backed up the computer to tape, shut the old server down, extracted the disks, RAID Controller, Tape, CD-R, network adapters, and all the other high-value equipment, and I installed it in the new machine. I was prepared to re-install Windows NT Server, because the new machine had a single processor and the old machine had two, so the HALs would be different.

I booted the machine and, sure enough, got an error message about the HALs. So I set it to boot the CD-ROM and went through an upgrade. Everything seemed fine.

When I rebooted, the machine crashed (blue screen: IRQL not less than or equal) indicating a problem in ntfs.sys or ntoskrnl.exe each time I tried to get it up.

I tried to reinstall again, but could not get all the way through the CD-ROM installation without crashing.

The fact that the machine crashed in ntfs.sys lead me to believe the problem was caused by the RAID controller—perhaps it was not tested to function in a PC100 (100MHz RAM bus) machine. The controller was not listed on the hardware compatibility list, but it had worked well in the other machine.

The volume on the RAID pack had become increasingly corrupt through these failed installs—leading to actual volume structure damage that, in my mind, further vilified the RAID controller or its driver.

So I called the RAID controller manufacturer and got a number of things to check on the pack. I deleted the pack, low-level formatted each of the drives, recreated the pack, and performed a fresh installation. The installation crashed part way through—just as it had earlier.

By this point, I decided it had to be the RAID controller, so I purchased a single large disk big enough to hold the contents of the RAID pack and installed it. I set the BIOS to boot from that disk, and installed the operating system. It worked fine. So I restored the backup tape and that worked, too. I left the RAID controller installed with disks running, just to test it, and put the server back online.

It seemed to work fine when being used as a server, but it would blue-screen crash randomly whenever I launched applications on

it—same thing in `ntfs.sys` or `ntoskrnl`
`.exe`. I presumed the problem was the RAID
controller still extant in the system, so I removed it and unloaded the driver.

The problem continued unabated, if not
more frequently. I was stumped. The controller was out of the picture completely,
yet the problem didn't go away. So I pulled
out the Performance Monitor and began
profiling the use of the server when I
launched applications on it. I found that the
server crashed whenever an application
caused the allocation of more memory
than physically existed on the machine—
whenever the swap file came into heavy
use. So I disabled large caches in the Registry, and voilà! The problem went away.

Except that the applications still crashed—
it just didn't show a blue-screen. Access violations abounded. I remained perplexed.

So I stepped back, took a deep breath, and
thought about the system. The errors I
now saw clearly indicted the memory subsystem, so I replaced the RAM with high-
er-quality memory, at a cost of about
$200. The machine hasn't had a problem
since, even after putting the RAID controller back in and moving the OS to it. It had
been the RAM the entire time.

What did I do wrong?

- I assumed that the machine from the
  manufacturer was built correctly, even
  though I know that incomplete computers can't really be tested.

- I jumped to a conclusion about a portion of the system that was very
  difficult to troubleshoot and test without first checking the easy things. I had
  memory in another computer I could
  have swapped in at the beginning in
  five minutes—just to see what would
  happen—or I could have moved the
  RAID pack and disk set into anther
  computer to test it, especially since I
  ignored the fact that it had been working correctly in an older machine.

- I know that new unproven components
  are far more likely to be failure components than older proven components,
  but I failed to test the new components
  in another machine. Had I moved the
  RAM into another computer, the crashing problem would have moved with it.

- I didn't resort to permanent changes
  last—I tackled them first. This caused a
  serious delay.

- Finally, I knew from earlier experience
  that NT is highly sensitive to proper
  RAM timings and compatibility between the motherboard and the
  memory. I ignored this in my untested
  certainty that the RAID controller might
  have a problem operating in a newer
  computer.

Had I followed these basic tenets of troubleshooting, I would have solved this problem
in a day rather than a few weeks.

24seven **CASE STUDY**

14

Practical Troubleshooting

Practical troubleshooting is a skill born of practice—and lots of it. Although you can learn and adopt a troubleshooting methodology by reading a book, you won't find the answer to every problem specifically delineated in any single work. It's simply not possible for me to explain enough explicit errors to cover everything you might run into. What I can do is explain those things you are most likely to see and teach you how to search for answers to the problems I can't cover.

This chapter is broken down into three general categories: network troubleshooting, computer hardware troubleshooting, and software troubleshooting specific to Windows NT.

Troubleshooting Networks

Networks never completely fail unless acted upon by an external factor, such as power loss or flooding. This means that usually only a single component of a network has failed in any fault situation. When external factors that cause multiple faults occur it's usually quite obvious (by the darkness or the damp carpet) what happened, so that factor can lead your troubleshooting. Because networks tend to fail one piece at a time, and because the voltages transmitted on normal network cables are so low that even a malfunctioning device won't damage other devices attached to the cable, you can usually be certain that once you've found the problem, you'll be able to fix it. Lightning strikes can cause power surges on network cables, thus causing all the equipment attached to the affected cable to fail—but, again, that's usually fairly obvious.

So, the trick to troubleshooting networks is to quickly isolate the failed component and then troubleshoot that component. Network failures can be broken down into the following four categories:

Client Problems   Affect only a single client. Other computers will work normally on the network.

Server Problems   May deny access to the server to everyone on the network and can, therefore, be confused with data-link problems. Try to connect one peer to another without involving the server to validate the cable plant and data-link equipment.

Data-Link Faults   Occur with hubs, bridges, routers, switches, and network interface adapters. They fall into common categories such as addressing problems, incompatible frame types, and outright component failures.

Cable Faults   Include breaks, shorts, grounds, or loose connections that cause spurious faults. Most difficult network faults that involve random numbers of computers, partial or temporary loss of server, or other non-deterministic faults are cable faults.

Client Problems

Client problems are easy. If the problem affects only a single station on your network, it's a client problem. Use the following steps to find the fault in a client-based problem:

1. Validate the cable running to that client by attaching another known-good client to the same outlet and jumper cable.

2. Make sure the network interface adapter is installed correctly and is not conflicting with another device in the computer.

3. Make sure the correct driver is installed and configured to work with the hardware resource settings of the network interface adapter.

4. Check to make sure the proper transport protocols are installed and that any addresses, frame types, or network numbers are set correctly.

5. Use the Ping tool in TCP/IP networks, or the IPXPING tool in NWLink networks to see if the server is reachable from the client.

6. Make sure the client software is properly installed and configured and that the client computer has been properly named and identified as a member of the correct domain or workgroup.

7. Try adding the NetBEUI protocol to two computers on the same subnetwork to see if you can share resources over that protocol if you are having problems with NWLink or TCP/IP, since NetBEUI is automatically configured correctly.

TIP If more than one workgroup shows up in your domain browser, at least one of your computers is on the other workgroup. If you only have a single workgroup in your organization, that computer won't be accessible.

Server Problems

Server problems are just like client problems, but since they affect the one computer everyone is trying to talk to, nothing happens on your network. For this reason, they may look like data-link problems. When running through server problems, first check all the steps shown in the client troubleshooting steps. Then try these steps:

1. Change two client computers to the same workgroup and share a resource from one to the other. If it doesn't work, move to data-link troubleshooting.

2. If you have another server available, verify that clients can attach to it. If they can't, move to data-link troubleshooting.

3. Troubleshoot the computer hardware to validate that the server is operating correctly.

4. Replace the network adapter with an adapter from a different manufacturer using a different driver.

5. Use RDISK to create an emergency repair disk, and reinstall Windows NT Server using the Repair option. Remove any third-party drivers and services except those absolutely necessary to operate the server.

When Things Go Wrong

PART 4

NOTE Duplicate Windows names on your network can cause some serious and bizarre problems. For example, if a newly installed client has the same name as your server, other clients on that network will lose their ability to communicate with the server's higher-level services (Server services) but will still be able to ping the server and access lower-level network services. Check for name conflicts whenever you have problems with file or print sharing. A similar set of problems can be caused by duplicate TCP/IP addresses.

Data-Link Problems

Data-link problems occur when a device that connects the network together physically or logically fails. These faults are relatively common, especially in larger networks having many data-link devices. Data-link faults usually affect entire subnetworks, generally denying the network access or access to other subnetworks, depending upon the function of the specific device. Use the following steps to validate your data-link equipment:

1. Put a client right next to your server and attach it via a single cable to the server (it must be a crossover cable for UTP or fiber networks) and try to log in from there.

2. Take each hub in the affected areas of your system and verify with your colocated client and server that you can attach to the server through each port of each hub. This will quickly validate the proper operation of your hubs.

3. If you have two subnetworks that cannot connect to each other, replace the bridge between them.

4. If you suspect a router may be at fault, reboot it. Some routers will allow you to use the Telnet tool to check the configuration of the router.

Cable Faults

Cable faults are rather common in network environments. Jumper cables that attach computers to wall outlets are always underfoot, so they often get run over by office chairs or pulled out of their sockets. Contractors working in ceiling areas may accidentally cut or kink network cables, and cables that are under stress may eventually break under the strain. Unfortunately, most installations have no way to fix damaged cable, so all you can do is determine that the problem is in fact a bad cable and call in a cabling contractor to fix it. That's why this section is last—you should exhaust all the possibilities that you can correct before assuming that you have a cable fault. Use the following steps to identify cable faults:

1. Determine how many computers are affected and in what areas. Since cable faults generally affect only a single cable, check the one cable that the affected computers rely upon.

2. Try using another computer at the failed station location to determine if it's really a cable fault. If a known-good computer doesn't work at that location, it's probably a cable fault.

3. Validate the data-link devices between the failed station and the server using the steps for client problems and data-link problems.

4. Disconnect the cable on both ends of the link. Use a cable tester to check for continuity, shorts, or grounds.

5. Run a temporary long jumper between the computer and the closest hub or other data-link device. If the computer starts working with the long jumper, you have a cable fault.

6. Have a cabling contractor come in to repair the damaged cable.

Troubleshooting Computer Hardware

In order for your software to run correctly, the hardware in your computer must be operating correctly. Whenever a hardware component is possibly at fault in a malfunctioning computer, you should validate it is operating correctly before you attempt to correct software faults.

The few simple troubleshooting techniques presented here help you isolate common hardware problems quickly. These techniques are not all inclusive, nor do they in any way replace the general techniques presented in the previous section. These techniques are simply the culmination of a great deal of troubleshooting experience.

DOS as a Troubleshooting Tool

Windows NT requires a completely functional hardware and software environment from a computer just to boot. Windows NT probes hardware and exercises the entire system as it comes online. Consequently, any number of faults will prevent Windows NT from starting at all. Simpler operating systems, like MS-DOS, can operate on a computer that is significantly degraded. A floppy disk that boots a simple operating system can be an invaluable troubleshooting tool.

In addition, quite a few DOS-based hardware validation tools are available. You can use these tools to inspect hardware, check for hardware conflicts, and validate the proper operation of a number of computer components. These tools can be run from a floppy disk on a system that doesn't boot Windows NT at all.

Remember, however, that MS-DOS will not have access to NTFS file system partitions. The DOS partition and format tools will not be able to modify an NTFS partition. Because NTFS creates partitions in larger boundaries than the FAT file system, you are likely to find 1 or 2 megabytes of free space after the end of an NTFS partition that can be partitioned and formatted for MS-DOS. You can use this area to verify the physical operation of a hard disk drive by checking to see if you can read and write to it. You can also store MS-DOS utilities and Plug-and-Play software configuration tools for the hardware in your computer.

When Things Go Wrong

PART 4

Finding Hardware Faults

The following is a short list of components to consider suspect under a range of trouble-shooting issues. Check these in order to progressively narrow your search. Remember that complex faults (those involving more than one specific failure) may not fit into any one category. Also, many software problems can look like hardware faults until you test the component under a different operating system, such as MS-DOS.

Power

If nothing happens when you turn the computer on, check the power cords and switches. Even in the worst failure situation, you should at least hear the fan spinning in the power supply. If you hear the fan in the power supply, check to see if the microprocessor fan is spinning. If it is, you probably don't have a power supply problem. See if you can hear hard disks spinning.

WARNING   Never install or remove anything while the power to your computer is on. Dropping a screw onto a powered motherboard will probably destroy it and some of your peripheral cards.

Motherboard, Processor, RAM, and Video

The computer's motherboard, processor, RAM, and video adapter must all be operating correctly for the computer to complete the power on self-test (POST) performed by the BIOS each time you turn the computer on. If you see the normal boot screen after turning on your computer, these components are probably all working correctly. If they are not, you may hear a few beeps (POST codes) or there may be no activity at all. Some computers can operate with a bit of failed RAM. These computers will either give an error message while testing RAM or will not count up to the entire compliment of memory.

If you suspect a problem with any of these components, remove and reseat the video card and memory modules. Processor failures are very rare. The only way to test for a processor failure is to swap in a known-good processor of the same brand, model, and speed rating. Motherboard failures are also rare and very difficult to validate. Verifying the processor, RAM, and video adapter in another computer of exactly the same make is usually easier than swapping out the motherboard.

TIP   Problems with mismatched RAM show up in Windows NT as blue screens (IRQL not greater than or equal is the most common error), or they show up as access violations in applications that you know work correctly. Replace your RAM with matched high-quality memory and you'll see your problems go away.

BIOS Configuration Problems

With many computers, it is possible to set BIOS information incorrectly. The BIOS determines such critical parameters as how fast RAM memory is accessed, what type of hard disk drive is attached, and how interrupts are assigned to PCI slots. Incorrectly configuring your BIOS can very likely degrade its performance or keep it from working at all.

> **WARNING** If you don't understand a BIOS setting's purpose, don't change it without recording its present value so you can change it back.

When you suspect a hardware conflict or a problem with the video, memory, processor, or the motherboard, check your BIOS parameter settings before you replace anything. The manual that came with your computer or motherboard should show the proper settings for your computer. If it does not, check with the manufacturer's technical support.

Failing all else, you can usually use a BIOS Default Settings option to get your computer working, although generally at a lower-than-optimal speed. Use this setting to verify whether you are having a BIOS configuration problem and then tune parameters to increase the speed.

Hardware Conflicts

Hardware conflicts are by far the most common problem in PCs running any operating system. Hardware conflicts occur when two peripherals are configured to use the same interrupt, DMA channel, port address, or buffer memory. Windows NT is especially sensitive to hardware conflicts, because it does not allow devices to share resources, as MS-DOS and Windows 95 do. For this reason, a computer that worked fine under MS-DOS or Windows 95 operating systems may malfunction under Windows NT.

You troubleshoot these problems by removing all peripheral cards that are not absolutely essential to boot the computer. These peripheral cards include modems, LAN adapters, sound cards, I/O controllers, secondary hard disk controllers, CD-ROM controllers, and any other peripheral cards except video and your primary (boot) hard disk controller.

If your computer goes through a normal start-up process, reintroduce each peripheral card, starting with the secondary hard disk controller and adding each additional card in order of its importance to you. Turn the power to the computer off, install the card, and then check for a normal boot. If you have a diagnostic tool that will show you interrupt, DMA channel, and port assignments, use it to make sure a hardware conflict has not occurred. Repeat this process with each card until the problem reappears. When the problem reappears, the most recent card installed is either conflicting with an installed device, incorrectly configured, or has failed.

When Things Go Wrong

PART 4

Hard Disk Controllers and Drives

Hard disk failures are the most damaging of all computer component failures. All hardware components can simply be replaced. But because hard disks contain the most recent set of all the data you store on your computer, their loss means the loss of irreplaceable data. Every component in your computer can fail without causing significant data loss—except the hard disk. Hard disk problems fall into just a few categories:

- Power or connection problems
- Hardware configuration problems
- Failed mechanisms
- Failed hard disk controllers
- Bad sectors
- Corrupted boot sectors
- Corrupted partition tables
- Corrupted file systems

Following are symptoms and solutions for each of these problems.

TIP   Backing up your data to other media, usually tape or magneto-optical disk, is the only way to recover completely from a total hard disk failure. If your data is important, you need to back it up daily.

Power or Connection Problems   Power or connection problems are easy to find. Check to make sure each hard disk drive is receiving power. If the hard disk is spinning, it is powered up correctly. On IDE drives, check to make sure the cables are securely and correctly installed. If you can't tell which way the cable should fit and the connector isn't keyed to prevent incorrect insertion, remember that the side of the connector with two notches mates to the side of the hard disk port that has a notch in the center. Make sure the cable is correctly attached to the motherboard/hard disk controller by matching the red striped side of the cable to the pin labeled *1* on the circuit board.

SCSI is slightly more difficult. A SCSI bus must be properly terminated and the total cable length should be as short as possible. Proper SCSI termination is set when the devices at each end of the SCSI bus have termination enabled or a physical terminator is installed at the end of the bus. No device, including the controller card, should have termination enabled if it is not at the end of the SCSI bus. Often, one SCSI bus will have some internal components and some external components. In this case the last drive attached to the internal bus should be terminated, the SCSI controller should not be terminated, and the last device on the external bus should be terminated. Refer to your SCSI adapter manual for more information on SCSI termination.

Hardware Configuration Problems   Drives can be incorrectly configured in ways that will prevent them from operating. Make sure that you don't have two devices on a SCSI bus with the same SCSI identification number. Also make sure that you don't have two IDE devices both set to master or slave. If you have only one IDE device, it should be set to master. If you have an IDE CD-ROM and an IDE hard disk on the same bus, the CD-ROM should be set to slave.

Some SCSI drives must be set to have the SCSI controller issue a start-up command before the disk will spin up. Make sure the controller is set to issue a start-up command to these disks. If your controller can't issue start-up commands, jumper the drive to start up at power on.

Incorrect BIOS Information   In the past, you had to set the specific drive parameters for each hard disk in the BIOS so that operating systems knew how to partition and format the disk. Most modern controllers and motherboards are capable of automatically detecting hard disk geometry. But some computers have BIOS programs that are too old to recognize new large disks. In these cases, you should upgrade to a hard disk controller that can recognize the full capacity of your disk.

> **TIP** Use the automatic hard disk geometry detection setting if it is available.

Sector translation is provided in many IDE and SCSI disks to allow operating systems that have a 1,024-cylinder limit to access an entire large disk. You may need to turn on this feature to complete the MS-DOS portion of the Windows NT installation if your primary disk has more than 1,024 cylinders. Once you have turned on sector translation, it must remain enabled for that drive.

Failed Mechanisms   Failed mechanisms are the worst hard disk problem you can have. This problem is caused when the hard disk spindle or head assembly physically breaks. Unfortunately, you cannot recover from this situation, and you will lose the data on that hard disk.

> **TIP** Because you cannot prevent hard disk failures, back up regularly to another mass storage device to prevent losing your data.

This fault is signaled by strange noises coming from your hard disk. If your disk is "knocking" when you try to access it or you hear strange grinding or scraping noises, it is usually too late. Sometimes the disk will bind and fail to spin at all. This symptom can make a physical disk failure seem like a power problem.

Failed Hard Disk Controllers   Hard disk controllers rarely fail, but they can conflict with other devices in your computer. Check these cards the same way you would check any other hardware conflict. If you seem to have no access whatsoever to your hard disk or if during the BIOS phase of the boot process your computer tells you that you have a hard disk controller failure, check the seating and settings of your hard disk controller. Swap it with another hard disk of the same type if necessary. If your hard disk controller is embedded on your motherboard, disable it and install a peripheral card hard disk controller set to the same interrupt, port, and DMA channel.

Bad Sectors   Bad sectors are a fact of life in hard disks. As hard disks age, they gradually lose their ability to store information. This gradual loss shows up as bad sectors, also known as "grown defects" in the hard disk industry. Hard disks typically ship from the factory with bad sectors, so all operating systems are capable of marking sectors bad. Sectors will usually fail on a write operation rather than a read operation, so the NTFS hot-fixing feature will usually keep you from having to worry about them.

When you have many sectors fail suddenly, you are about to experience a failed hard disk mechanism. This failure is signaled by unexplained loss of hard disk space during the normal operation of Windows NT as NTFS marks more and more sectors out of use. You may also experience unrecoverable read errors. Transfer data off the disk as soon as possible and replace it with another hard disk.

Corrupted Boot Sectors   Corrupted boot sectors can occur when a file system installation is taking place and the computer is interrupted by a power fluctuation. Sometimes boot sector corruption is caused by installing another operating system over Windows NT. This problem can be corrected using the MS-DOS fdisk utility and issuing the following command at the C:\> prompt:

```
fdisk /mbr
```

The /mbr switch tells fdisk to write a new master boot record to the hard disk. You may also see this problem if you turn off sector translation in the BIOS of your hard disk controller. Try changing the sector translation setting before issuing the fdisk command. If you are unable to correct the problem by changing sector translation, change the translation setting back to its original setting and issue the fdisk /mbr command.

Unless you have the sector translation in a different state than when the disk was originally formatted, the fdisk /mbr command will have no adverse effect on your system—even if it doesn't correct the problem.

Corrupted File Systems   NTFS has a number of built-in mechanisms to keep it from becoming corrupt. However, some problems, especially hardware configuration, can cause NTFS to become corrupted. NTFS will check for hard disk corruption each time you reboot your computer.

FAT file system volumes are very likely to become corrupt over time with normal usage. You should use the Microsoft Scandisk utility frequently, at lease once a month, to detect and correct file system corruption.

Troubleshooting Windows NT

Windows NT is a complex environment with myriad software components. But it does work correctly out of the box on systems with completely supported hardware that is correctly configured. If you have one of those systems, a fresh Windows NT system will always work.

This provides a good baseline for the operation of all further services. As a machine is further customized with applications, user configurations, upgrades, and so forth, opportunities for misconfiguration multiply exponentially. It is usually the complex interactions between software components that cause problems in servers.

You may run into situations where two pieces of software are mutually exclusive— because of their differing requirements, they cannot run on the same machine. For example, a firewall may not work correctly with Service Pack 3 because of the numerous security changes and API differences that Microsoft introduced in that service pack. But Microsoft requires Service Pack 3 to install the Option Pack that includes Internet Information Server 4, so these two functions cannot exist simultaneously. This unfortunate situation is fairly common in server applications, because many of them are written to the very specific network APIs that tend to change frequently between service packs.

The following sections detail troubleshooting information for the NT boot process, general environment, and networking services.

Boot Process

After you have determined that the computer hardware is operating properly, you must be sure that Windows NT is being loaded correctly. This section will first show you some of the boot sequence errors and what they mean, teach you how to diagnose boot.ini problems, and then explain how to use Windows NT boot disks and emergency repair disks to repair the Windows NT boot process.

When Things Go Wrong

PART 4

Boot Sequence Errors

The boot sequence, is a complicated process. If one of the boot components is damaged or removed or your boot.ini file is incorrectly configured, you may see one of the following messages (in which case you need to use a boot disk or an emergency repair disk to fix the boot sequence). The following message indicates that the NTLDR file is missing or corrupt:

```
BOOT: Couldn't find NTLDR
Please insert another disk
```

If this message repeats after you have selected the Windows NT operating system on the boot menu, then ntdetect.com is damaged or missing:

```
NTDETECT V1.0 Checking Hardware …
NTDETECT V1.0 Checking Hardware …
```

This message indicates that the Windows NT operating system is damaged or missing or that the boot.ini file is missing and that Windows NT was installed in a directory other than \WINNT or that boot.ini directs the operating system loader to a location that does not contain a valid ntoskrnl.exe:

```
Windows NT could not start because the following file is missing or
corrupt:
\<winnt root>\system32\ntoskrnl.exe
Please reinstall a copy of the above file.
```

This problem can occur when you partition free space on your hard disk if the partition number that contains the Windows NT changes. Edit the boot.ini file to reflect the new partition number for the partition that contains Windows NT.

The following message indicates that the boot sector is missing or corrupt:

```
I/O Error accessing boot sector file
multi(0)disk(0)rdisk(0)partition(1):\bootsect.dos
```

This indicates that the Windows NT entry in boot.ini points to a missing or malfunctioning device or to a disk partition that does not contain a file system recognized by the Windows NT boot loader:

```
OS Loader V4.00
Windows NT could not start because of a computer disk hardware
configuration problem.
Could not read from the selected boot disk. Check boot path and disk
hardware.
```

```
Please check the Windows NT™ documentation about hardware disk
configuration and your hardware reference manuals for additional
information.
```

This error occurs when the NT loader cannot access the hard disk upon which your Windows NT partition is stored or when NT loader is confused about which hard disk controller to consider the primary device:

```
STOP: 0x000007E: Inaccessible Boot Device
```

Because a number of SCSI adapters do not conform to the complete SCSI standard, they may cause this problem.

STOP messages are also heralded by the infamous "blue screen" of Windows NT–crash fame. Due to circumstances Microsoft does not report until the problem has been corrected in a downloadable service pack, these screens very rarely indicate a serious failure from which Windows NT was not able to recover. These problems are usually related to I/O, and the bug that crashed the computer probably resides in a driver. If you have a problem with a STOP message blue screen, log onto the Windows NT Knowledge Base and use search key "STOP:" to find the bugs Microsoft knows how to correct.

If you have just added a SCSI controller to a Windows NT computer that boots from an IDE hard disk, make sure that no SCSI device is set to ID 0 (or otherwise disable bootable SCSI hard disks). This setting will prevent the SCSI controller from attempting to boot the disk and will prevent the NT DETECT portion of the boot loader from assigning the SCSI adapter a bus number of zero, thereby causing `boot.ini` to refer to the wrong partition.

The Windows NT Boot Disk

Your Windows NT Server will normally boot from its hard disk drive. You may have installed NT into the boot partition of your hard drive, in which case the boot files and the operating system all reside in the same volume, or you may have installed Windows NT on another partition, in which case the boot files will reside in the boot partition, separate from the operating system.

A third boot configuration is possible for Windows NT. You can create a floppy boot disk that contains the boot files that are necessary to start the Windows NT operating system. Booting from a floppy is slower than booting from a hard disk, but a floppy boot disk can be very useful when your computer is not booting properly.

To create a boot floppy, format the floppy disk in Windows NT. This will write an NT specific boot sector to the floppy. Then copy the following files to the disk:

- `boot.ini`
- `ntldr`
- `ntdetect.com`
- `ntbootdd.sys` (if it exists)

If the problem you are experiencing booting NT is because one of the boot files (boot.ini, ntldr, ntdetect.com or ntbootdd.sys) is missing or corrupt, you can boot NT with the boot floppy disk you have just created. Then you need to copy the files from the floppy disk to your boot drive (C: drive). This process will restore the missing or corrupted files and allow the boot process to proceed normally.

The Emergency Repair Disk

The trouble you are experiencing may be more severe than simply missing or corrupted boot files. If any of the files that contain Windows NT Registry information become corrupt, Windows NT itself can become unstable, even to the point of making it impossible to fix the problem from within NT.

You can create an emergency repair disk to restore the Registry from the last time you performed an emergency repair disk update. The emergency repair disk includes the security account manager (SAM) database, disk configuration, and numerous other system parameters. The RDISK utility will only back up the SAM if it is run with the /s switch. If you do not do this and use the emergency repair disk to restore your settings, all your accounts will be lost.

Emergency repair disks are created or updated with the rdisk.exe utility included with Windows NT. This utility has two options—update the repair information or create a new repair disk.

When you choose to update the repair information, rdisk.exe copies the system hive, the security accounts manager, the security hive, the software hive, the default hive, and copies of the config.nt and autoexec.nt files used when initializing a Windows NT virtual DOS machine into a directory off the Windows NT root directory called \repair. The utility then asks if you want to create an emergency repair disk containing this information.

WARNING   The emergency repair disk is not a replacement for regular backups. The emergency repair disk stores only Registry configuration information, not your data.

The Create Emergency Repair Disk option simply formats a floppy disk and copies the contents of the repair directory onto it.

Restoring Windows NT

The process of restoring a Windows NT installation that has somehow become damaged or corrupt is similar to reinstalling the operating system. In fact, you are reinstalling the operating system, but rather than using default information, you are restoring security and account information in the Registry from the emergency repair disk.

The restoration process checks the hard disk for errors and can verify the Windows NT system files. It restores some or all of the Registry information if you want it to.

You will need your Windows NT Setup boot disks, Server 4 CD-ROM, and the emergency repair disk for the computer. The repair process will reinstall the security database from the last time you updated your repair disk. If your repair disk is very old or you don't think you can remember the administrator password from the time the disk was made, you will be better off not reinstalling the Registry from the emergency repair disk.

General Windows Environment

If you are sure that you have no hardware problems and your Windows NT Server boots properly but are still experiencing difficulties, you will need to troubleshoot the running operating system. Windows NT provides an excellent environment for troubleshooting—you can view almost any aspect of the operating system with tools provided by Microsoft. The tools you will most often use are the Event Viewer, which records problems detected by Windows NT, and the Windows NT diagnostic tool, which shows you how Windows NT is configured. You can also use the Performance Monitor to find programs that are using more resources than you might expect and degrading the performance of your machine. Use of the Performance Monitor is covered in Chapter 12, "Performance Optimization."

Troubleshooting with the Event Viewer

Rather than reporting nonfatal error messages on screen during operation, Windows NT adds a record to the event log. This technique keeps users from being bothered by annoying messages that they may not have the permissions to fix and, more importantly, keeps a written log of all error messages for you to review. If you've ever had a user call you to fix an error and then not remember what the error was, you'll appreciate the event log. You review the event log with the Event Viewer.

You should begin all troubleshooting sessions by reviewing the event log with the Event Viewer. Quite often, the event log will tell you exactly what is wrong. Three separate logs are managed by the Event Viewer:

- System events are recorded by the Windows NT Services.
- Security events are recorded when they occur. Security events are designated by your audit and user policies.
- Application events are recorded by applications other than the operating system.

When Things Go Wrong

PART 4

The log that an application uses is entirely up to the application, so you'll find lots of annoying thematic overlap. Just get in the habit of checking both the system and application logs, because it's not always clear where error messages will show up.

Events in the event log are recorded with three priorities:

- Informative messages are marked with a blue icon containing the letter *i*. these events are supposed to be for your information only and should not affect the operation of your server.
- Alerts are recorded with a yellow icon containing an exclamation mark (!). These events indicate that your computer is operating in a degraded condition or that some noncritical resource is not operating correctly.
- A red stop sign indicates a critical warning. Something serious is wrong with your computer or configuration, and it will cause denial of a service.

The Security section of the event log has two event icons:

- A key shows passed audit policy events.
- A padlock shows blocked audit policy events.

You should check your event log any time you suspect something isn't working correctly in your system. You should check it periodically (at least once a month) even when things are working fine.

Because many services fail due to underlying problems, a single problem might have four or five associated error messages from various portions of the system. Network adapter failures would typically show a Service Control Manager error and various other service errors, because services that rely upon that adapter will also fail.

Note that drivers and the Kernel cannot log messages to the event log because the Event Log service runs outside the Kernel. All Kernel and driver problems that don't cause a blue-screen crash will show up as Service Control Manager errors because higher-level services that use the functionality of failed devices also will not start.

The Windows NT Diagnostic Tool

WinMSD is also called the Windows NT diagnostic tool. Through this tool, you can inspect everything Windows NT knows about your computer to verify that it works correctly. WinMSD is split into sections accessed by the tabs near the top of the WinMSD window. These sections are the following:

Version   Tells you what version of Windows NT you are running, what build of the operating system you have, how many processors are installed, and who this copy is registered to. This information is not of much value when troubleshooting.

System   Identifies what sort of motherboard and microprocessor you are using and shows you the BIOS date and manufacturer. This information is not of much value when troubleshooting.

Display   Shows the BIOS date and revision for your video adapter, as well as the current settings. You should see the manufacturer of your video adapter and the type of digital-to-analog converter used. This information is not of much value when troubleshooting.

Drives   Shows all of the currently installed volumes, grouped by type (such as removable drives, hard drives, CD-ROM, and network drives). Clicking on individual drives will give you information about that drive, such as the file system time and how much data is stored on it. This tab is not available when viewing diagnostic information on a remote computer.

Memory   Shows how memory is being used in the system. In addition to showing the amount of physical RAM, this tab shows how much memory is being used by the Kernel and how much is being used by the page file. At the bottom of this screen, you can see how the page file is distributed across your physical disks. The Memory tab also shows the number of heap handles allocated, how many threads are running, and how many processes are currently executing. This tab is not available when viewing diagnostic information on a remote computer.

Services   Shows the state of all loaded services and drivers. Services are shown when you click the Services button at the bottom of the screen, and devices are shown when you click the Devices button. When you double-click a service or device driver, a window will appear showing the start type of the service or device driver and some other less-useful information. You can click the Dependencies tab to show what services must be running for this service or device driver to operate.

Resources   Shows the state of all hardware in the computer that Windows NT knows about. This is the most important part of the Windows NT Diagnostic screen. This tab will help you iron out hardware conflicts by showing the resource use for all devices installed in Windows NT.

You select the resource type you want to see by clicking the IRQ, I/O port, DMA, Memory, or Devices buttons located at the bottom of the Resource pane. When you double-click a resource item in the display drop-down box, a window will display information about that resource line item. For the most part, useful information is shown only when viewing devices. For example, the window will show all the resources used for that device.

When Things Go Wrong

PART 4

Before installing a new device in your computer, review the Resources tab of the Windows NT diagnostic tool to be certain other devices aren't already using the interrupt, DMA channel, and I/O port settings you intend to use for the new device. This step will prevent hardware conflicts and keep you from having to troubleshoot new hardware installations.

Environment   Shows the environment variables that Windows NT uses to communicate simple information to applications about the Windows NT environment. Environment variables in Windows NT appear to applications the same way DOS-environment variables do, so older applications can use them to find information or change their state based on the current system settings. You will probably not need to change or inspect any of these settings.

Network   Shows information about the current network session. Use this tab to determine which workgroup or domain you are logged onto and under which account. This tab also shows the name of the logon domain and server.

Troubleshooting Security Problems

If a user cannot access a program or some data on a computer that he or she knows is there or can see the file, chances are that the user does not have sufficient permissions to perform the action in question. To troubleshoot security problems, log on as the administrator and attempt the same operation. If you can perform the operation, the problem is a security problem. You can either assign the user permissions to use the resource, or you can move the resource to an area where the user has sufficient permissions.

Sometimes even the administrator can't use or delete a resource that is visible. The reason is that the resource was created and assigned permissions under a previous installation of Windows NT that has been overwritten. Now the old administrator account that no longer exists is the owner. Because Windows NT assigns a new security ID to the new administrator during the new installation, no current user has permission to use or delete the resource.

Fortunately, Windows NT has a way around this problem. For any resource, the administrator can take ownership of the resource and then reassign permissions as necessary.

Network Services

Troubleshooting network services can be rather difficult, because the complex interactions between all the modules often cause problems themselves. In fact, it's usually the bindings between services and drivers that are the cause of networking problems.

These interactions are controlled by the Registry, and it is Registry "corruption"—or misconfigured or missing Registry keys—that cause the vast majority of Windows NT service problems. This is such a large topic that Registry troubleshooting is covered separately in the next chapter.

This section contains a common, quick methodology for restoring network services between computers. Generally, most networking problems can be solved by removing the networking service components and transport protocols, rebooting, reinstalling them, reapplying the latest service pack, and rebooting again. This restores Registry settings to their default values.

Make sure the computer is communicating on the network by pinging another computer. If you can't ping another machine on your network, you've either got a problem with your adapter, driver, cabling, or TCP/IP stack. Validate the cable by connecting a working computer to it and logging it. Validate the adapter and driver by removing and reinstalling the driver. Validate the TCP/IP stack by removing and reinstalling it. Remember to reapply the latest service pack after you do so. If you still can't ping another computer at this point, try replacing the adapter with one of another model.

Once you can ping another machine, try to connect from the client or server in question to a resource on the other end system that uses a low-level service, such as FTP or HTTP. For example, try pointing a Web browser on the client to a Web site on the server, or a telnet client to the echo simple TCP/IP service on the machine. Proving out a connected TCP/IP path is a very good reason to use simple TCP/IP services on a server.

Once you've validated a complete round-trip path between the end-systems, try again to use the higher-level network services. If you cannot log in, try an administrative account. Make sure all the normal networking services are running on both machines and that the event logs show no errors. Determine which of the end systems is actually having the problem by using a known-good third system to connect to each.

Once you've identified the problem machine, try removing and reinstalling all network services. This quite frequently solves bizarre service problems because it recreates the dependency settings in the Registry.

If you cannot manually remove a network adapter, protocol stack, or service, the computer's Registry is definitely corrupted. You'll have to manually remove the service or driver from the Registry, as explained in Chapter 15.

In extreme cases where you've definitely ruled out hardware failure, you may need to reinstall Windows NT in its repair mode. This can be done without too many hassles as long as you don't replace the software or the security accounts' hives in the Registry. However, you should replace the system hive—it's the hive that is preventing the computer from operating correctly. Remember to reapply the latest service pack when you're finished unless you suspect the service pack is actually causing the problem.

When Things Go Wrong

PART 4

Troubleshooting Resources

Once you have exhausted your own knowledge and skills and the diagnostic utilities provided by Microsoft give you no more useful information, you will need to turn to other resources for help.

The TechNET CD and the Microsoft Knowledge Base Library are invaluable for NT troubleshooting. Beg, borrow, or steal access to these resources if you must, because you won't get far without them. You can also ask others for help on the Internet or on online services, or you can search the Usenet news archives at Dejanews on the World Wide Web.

Windows NT Help Files   A good first-line troubleshooting resource. These Help files are based on Microsoft's experience with customer support, so they include specific troubleshooting help for the problems that are most often reported to Microsoft. You stand a good chance of finding a help file that can walk you through the steps for fixing software configuration problems.

TechNET   The CD-ROM Microsoft distributes to technical support professionals who subscribe, contains much of the same information that you can find on the Microsoft Web site, but it is far faster because your searches are not limited by the speed of your modem. You can subscribe to the TechNET CD-ROM service by calling (800) 344-2121. MCSEs get a free subscription to TechNET for one year after obtaining their certification.

The Internet   By far the best troubleshooting resource for any computer problem. The cumulative experience of thousands of Windows NT experts is available through both Microsoft-sanctioned and private resources. Unless you are working with an experimental release of Windows NT, you can presume that someone else has had the same problem you are having. There's a good chance they posted a question on a news group that was answered by someone who knew what to do about it.

Most hardware manufacturers also maintain Web sites that contain current versions of their Windows NT drivers. If you are having a problem with a third-party driver, check the vendor's Web site for an updated driver. If you can't find the site, use AltaVista to search for it.

The Microsoft Knowledge Base is the official repository for support information about all Microsoft products including Windows NT. The Knowledge Base is an accumulation of answers to technical support questions received by Microsoft since Windows NT was first released. You can access this database at `www.microsoft.com`.

Web search engines provide a very fast method to find information about Windows NT and troubleshooting. Frequently, you can find answers from people who have had the same problems you are having. These search engines are provided free of charge by corporations who are interested in furthering the development of the Internet and the World Wide Web. The largest index provider and the largest search engine provider are presented here. Many others exist, and you will find links to them through these providers:

- www.yahoo.com
- www.altavista.com
- www.excite.com
- www.dejanews.com

Solving Problems Quickly

A customer of mine needed to connect their network to the Internet and asked me for assistance. I recommended a good firewall (Checkpoint Firewall-1) and Windows NT Server. I recommended Windows NT Server, because RAS connectivity was part of the package—otherwise, most firewalls work perfectly well on Windows NT Workstation.

I installed the operating system and firewall software without a hitch, but I was connecting to a type of service I'd never used before: Digital Subscriber Line (DSL), which is a megabit service that operates over standard telephone wiring.

After connecting everything and attaching the DSL adapter to the Ethernet port of the firewall, I called the ISP to have them program the DSL adapter (I assumed at that time that it was a router) with the routing tables to reach our internal network. The support technician waffled a bit, claiming he'd never heard of a thing called a routing table, so I asked for his supervisor. His supervisor explained that the DSL adapter wasn't actually a router, it acted more like a bridge. There was no way for it to forward IP packets into our network; rather, all clients would have to be connected to the same Ethernet hub to receive their IP information. This configuration is impossible to secure so it was not acceptable.

I needed to have the firewall server respond to all network IP addresses itself—a method known in the Unix world as proxy arp. The idea is that a single computer will "answer" address-resolution protocol requests for an entire range of IP addresses so that it looks like a bunch of different computers. I wouldn't be able to add IP addresses to the adapter using NT's multiple IP functionality, because I needed those addresses for internal clients. Assigning them to the firewall through its TCP/IP address stack would mess up the firewall's routing, because it would think those addresses were local to it and wouldn't forward them. What I needed was true Unix-style proxy arp functionality, which I'd never dealt with in NT before.

I fired up Windows NT's arp command-line utility and added proxy arp addresses to its arp tables. Data began to flow, and everything worked fine. I declared the problem solved and began to pack up. About an hour later, the newly surfing Web users noticed that all the Internet connections suddenly failed. I went back to the firewall, viewed the arp tables, and noted that my additions were gone. I re-added them, but to no avail; the Internet connection would work for about an hour and then stop.

My first call was to Checkpoint's tech support line. They wouldn't talk to me without a $400 per-incident tech support charge, and they would not guarantee to fix the problem for that. I so detest their model of providing broken software and then charging for support that I declined and went hunting on my own.

A visit to Microsoft's Web site and Knowledge Base yielded no answers—apparently, nobody uses proxy arp in the NT world. So I pulled up a search engine and went hunting. Within just a few pages, I came across a technician who had the exact same problem. His page pointed to a support link inside Checkpoint's internal support Web site that posted a note about an undocumented problem with Windows NT and a fix for it.

Windows NT does not really support proxy arp, even though its arp command will let you install proxy arp addresses. It seems the arp addresses just disappear after about an hour, and they don't persist through reboots—exactly the problem I had.

Firewall-1 supported proxy arp to correct this problem through an undocumented feature. By simply creating a text file called config.arp that contains the IP addresses to arp for and the Ethernet MAC address to arp to, the firewall itself would perform the proxy arp feature missing in Windows NT.

By searching the Web, I was able to quickly find exactly the support information I needed for a bizarre, low-occurrence problem that neither vendor involved was willing to actually support.

15

The Registry

Don't fear the Registry. It's big, it's Byzantine, and it's fragile—it's understandable that many NT administrators avoid it, but sooner or later you'll have to get comfortable with its structure and use if you're going to maintain a Windows NT system. This chapter will cover why and how the Registry is organized, how you should work with it, and some general troubleshooting procedures that are fairly common. Appendix A is a detailed encyclopedia of Registry settings you can use as a reference when you have a specific problem or when you're rooting around looking for some specific configuration.

WARNING Standard Registry warning and disclaimer: Changes in the Registry settings can cause your computer to become misconfigured and the computer will no longer behave as expected. It may require a reinstallation of Windows NT. Proceed with caution and at your own risk. And don't run with scissors.

The Registry is a unified database of program configuration settings. All programs installed on a Windows NT machine and written to the Win32 programming specification (including the operating system) store their configuration information in the Registry. Using Registry editors you can customize, correct, or even misconfigure Windows NT or any installed applications.

The Registry is also the biggest design flaw of Windows NT in my opinion. (The other contestant in the major design flaw race is the dynamic link library architecture.) The centralized nature of the Registry and the fact that it does not work with standard file handling tools causes the following problems:

- Applications cannot be reliably copied between machines, because there's no uniform way to tell which Registry keys are associated with which applications.

- Applications usually cannot be moved because Registry keys store their fixed location for internal reference. Moving an application will usually cause it to work incorrectly.

- Applications must be specifically installed and de-installed, which would not be necessary if Registry data and DLLs were located in the same directory as the application. If applications did not require installation, network clients could simply begin using network-stored applications, rather than requiring a network technician to install them. Application roll-out tools and many enterprise management tools would not be necessary.

- Backup and restore operations cannot be simple file-copy operations—special API calls must be used to backup and restore the Registry.

- You cannot completely delete an application by simply deleting its file system directory. If the application's Registry data is corrupt, you can't use its de-installation tool either, which means you may never be able to completely remove a malfunctioning application.

- Damage to the Registry files can cause widespread application failure—the Registry is a single point of failure.

Microsoft originally used the Registry architecture because they wanted applications to be able to modify the configuration of other applications and so that read/write access to the Registry could be speed-optimized easily. While this sounds like a good idea, it makes it possible for poorly written software to mess up perfectly good software, a problem that happens all the time. And the speed optimization could easily be handled by simply reading the configuration settings of running software into memory and then letting the virtual memory manager page the settings back out to disk. In fact, Registry access isn't fast enough to support many applications—IIS4 was reengineered to use its own high-speed Registry, called a metabase, because NT's Registry slowed down its ability to respond to numerous client requests. My point that applications should have their own Registries is basically proven by Microsoft's own example of spinning off application specific Registries when the centralized Registry failed to meet their requirements. Unfortunately, we're stuck with the Registry and all its flaws for quite some time. Sadly, it's better than the maze of text settings files used in earlier versions of Windows and in UNIX.

WARNING Don't mess with the Registry on a production server. Do all of your testing of Registry effects on a test computer before making any changes in the field.

The Registry Structure

The Registry is a simple hierarchical database, which means that elements of the database can themselves contain elements, thus creating a tree-structure hierarchy. The elements in this case are called Registry keys. Keys are named entities that may contain named data elements (called values), much the way that folders contain files in a hierarchical file system such as NTFS or FAT. The values contained in the Registry keys have a reference name, a data type, and a value associated with them. Figure 15.1 shows the structure of the Registry.

Figure 15.1 A Registry structure

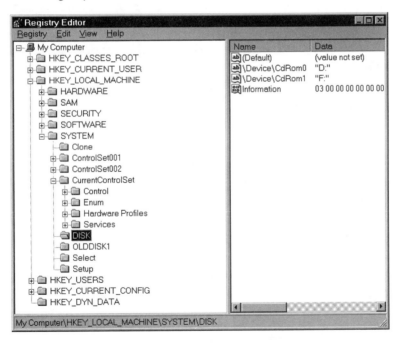

Windows NT and the applications that run on it use the Registry to store configuration information. This is data that must persist from one running session to another, because the data is used to provide operating parameters for the software that depends upon it.

Any Win32 application can create, store, change, and retrieve values from the Registry. Registry keys are secured objects, so they have an access control list and can be locked to prevent modification. However, most are not locked, and administrators have wide access to the Registry to make changes.

Specific Registry keys and values only have context for the applications that use them. They mean nothing to other applications, and although most keys have fairly obvious human readable names, their purpose is inscrutable if you don't understand which applications use them and what the values they contain do. For this reason, you will usually need a guide to the Registry settings to explain them or at least specific directions on how to add, change, or delete keys to perform a specific change. Changing or deleting keys without understanding their purpose is a recipe for disaster—Windows NT cannot completely boot if a combination of specific keys are missing or changed, and applications will not behave normally if keys they rely on are missing or changed. Never delete or modify a Registry key unless you understand its purpose and you know what the effects of the change will be (or you're willing to live with the unknown consequences).

Top-level Registry keys are called hives. The hives store various types of Registry keys as described below:

> **HKEY_LOCAL_MACHINE**   Stores the Registry keys that are created by applications (including Windows NT's services and Explorer). As such, this hive stores very nearly every useful troubleshooting key that you'll work with.
>
> **HKEY_CLASSES_ROOT**   Stores application dependency data (for example, Explorer extension associations and OLE class registrations).
>
> **HKEY_CURRENT_CONFIG**   Stores changes to the CURRENT_CONFIG key contained in the HKEY_LOCAL_MACHINE\Software and HKEY_LOCAL_MACHINE\System keys.
>
> **HKEY_CURRENT_USER**   Points to the logged on user's user profile in the HKEY_USERS key. This key contains desktop settings, Control Panel configurations, and other settings that are specific to the current user.
>
> **HKEY_USERS**   Stores user profiles and all the information they contain as above.

Hives are either automatically created at boot time or when a user logs in, or they are stored in one of the hive files located in the %systemroot%\system32\config directory.

Some Registry keys are merely pointers to other locations in the Registry. For example, the HKEY_CURRENT_USER key isn't a copy of the current user's profile from HKEY_USERS, it's a pointer to it. When you change a value in HKEY_CURRENT_USER, that value actually changes in HKEY_USERS. You can think of HKEY_CURRENT_USER as shorthand notation for the specific key of the logged on user. Other keys, like HKEY_CURRENT_CONFIG and HKEY_LOCAL_MACHINE\SYSTEM\CurrentControlSet work this way as well.

Control Sets

Windows NT stores the system configuration (Registry settings that control how drivers and services run) in keys called control sets. There are usually at least two control set keys that have a numerical enumeration suffix, as in the following:

    ControlSet001

    ControlSet002

Two "meta" keys also exist:

- CurrentControlSet is a pointer to the control set used to boot.
- Clone is a copy of the CurrentControlSet that the system actually operates from.

The SYSTEM\Select key contains values that show which control sets are used for what purpose:

Value	Description
Current	The current control set
Default	The default control set used at startup
Failed	Any control set that cannot be booted
LastKnownGood	The control set used if the Last Known Good option is used at start-up

You should usually manipulate the CurrentControlSet Registry key to ensure that you are manipulating the correct control set.

Registry Tools

Every program that modifies a configuration setting for any pieces of software, system or otherwise, is a Registry tool. Registry tools make use of the Registry as a named value store by using special function calls built into Windows NT to create, change, and delete Registry values.

The Control Panel is the primary Registry configuration tool that you should use to configure your Windows NT machine. Aside from being easier to use than the manual Registry editing tools, different versions of Windows NT may store Registry values in different places. Using the Control Panel ensures that you always change the values you intended to change.

Unfortunately, there are a number of configuration settings that have no associated Control Panel, and there are some Registry corruption problems that higher-level Registry editors (for example, the Control Panel or a piece of applications software) would not be able to solve.

RegEdt32 and Regedit

To handle cases where no alternative to changing a Registry setting exists or when a Registry corruption problem prevents the standard tools from working with the Registry, Windows NT comes with two general-purpose Registry editors. Each of the following Registry editors has features that the other does not have, so you'll probably use both on occasion, although most people favor one or the other for routine editing:

RegEdt32   The original Windows NT Registry editor. It opens five different windows for the various hives rather than presenting them all in a hierarchy. For security reasons, `regedt32.exe` can be used to modify access control lists for Registry keys or to load and unload hives from other installed copies of Windows NT. The text export function of RegEdt32 creates files that can be read by system administrators but cannot be reimported.

Regedit   The Windows 95 Registry editor that is included with Windows NT 4. It opens the entire Registry as a single hierarchy, so it's easier to browse. It allows you to import and export text files of Registry settings for program installation or for changing Registry settings in batches. Regedit cannot modify Registry security, nor can it load or unload hives. This tool works the same way in all 32-bit versions of Windows.

Some claim that Regedit should not be used for editing the NT Registry, citing the fact that you cannot modify Registry security with it. That argument is silly. Regedit would not be included with NT if it didn't have a purpose, and you'll rarely if ever change the security setting of Registry keys. I personally prefer Regedit, because I can easily browse the entire Registry hierarchy and I can use the same interface on all versions of Windows. Regedit also allows me to save the keys that I'm about to edit to a text file so that if I realize that I made a mistake, I can simply reimport the text file to revert to the original settings. RegEdt32, on the other hand, has a read-only mode that will prevent you from accidentally changing anything while you browse.

Neither Registry editor has a Start Menu item associated with them. You can either create a shortcut to the editor or use the Start ➤ Run facility to run them by name.

Loading and Unloading Hives

It is possible to directly load Registry hive files—not textual representations of Registry files. For instance, you may need to do this if you have to repair a non-booting Windows NT machine using another installed copy of Windows NT. In the newly installed copy of Windows NT, you can directly import the Registry hives from the directory containing the misconfigured NT system. Then you can correct the Registry settings in the old Registry hive and resave the hive to reboot the crashed machine.

You can't load a Registry hive with the same key name as an existing hive in your Registry, because the configuration settings for the other installation will not be the same as the settings that are required for the running operating system.

Registry hives can only be loaded using `regedt32.exe`. Select the key under which you wish to load the hive. This should usually be the key where the hive would be loaded anyway. From the File menu, select Load Hive. Select the path to the hive file. NT system hives are stored in `%WINNTROOT%\System32\config`. Enter a new name for the hive, such as "othersystem." The hive will be added to the Registry editor. You can now make any changes you need to the Registry settings in this hive. When you are finished, select the hive and then select File ➤ Unload Hive. This will remove the hive from the Registry and save it back to the disk.

Saving and Restoring Registry Keys

For individual keys and settings, the Registry editor supports reading and writing textual representations of Registry keys. You can use this functionality to automatically create and maintain groups of Registry settings. This functionality would be required when distributing new applications. The text files created by the Registry editor have the extension `.reg` and are automatically associated with the Registry editor in the Desktop Explorer. When you click on a REG file, its keys are automatically loaded into the Registry. The structure of a REG file is something like the INI files used in earlier versions of windows. The following text is an example of a Registry key exported to a REG file:

```
REGEDIT4

[HKEY_LOCAL_MACHINE\SYSTEM\CurrentControlSet\Services\Tcpip]

"Type"=dword:00000001

"Start"=dword:00000002

"ErrorControl"=dword:00000001
```

When Things Go Wrong

PART 4

```
"ImagePath"=hex(2):5c,53,79,73,74,65,6d,52,6f,6f,74,5c,53,79,73,74,65
,6d,33,32,\

  5c,64,72,69,76,65,72,73,5c,74,63,70,69,70,2e,73,79,73,00

"DisplayName"="TCP/IP Service"

"Group"="PNP_TDI"


[HKEY_LOCAL_MACHINE\SYSTEM\CurrentControlSet\Services\Tcpip\
Parameters]

"DataBasePath"=hex(2):25,53,79,73,74,65,6d,52,6f,6f,74,25,5c,53,79,73
,74,65,6d,\

  33,32,5c,64,72,69,76,65,72,73,5c,65,74,63,00

"Domain"=""

"Hostname"="xxxxxxx-a"

"NameServer"=""

"ForwardBroadcasts"=dword:00000000

"IPEnableRouter"=dword:00000001

"SearchList"=""

"DhcpDomain"="nowhere.com"

"DhcpNameServer"="10.0.3.33 10.0.3.34"

"EnableSecurityFilters"=dword:00000000

"PPTPTcpMaxDataRetransmissions"=dword:00000009
```

As you can see, the file starts with a text tag identifying the version of the Registry editor, and then contains one or more Registry key entries. Each key is enclosed in square brackets. Values are enclosed in parenthesis, and value data is defined with an equal sign and then the data.

WARNING   Never double-click on a *.reg file in the Desktop Explorer unless you intend to add its contents to the Registry. There's no warning or confirmation process. Do not import *.reg files from anyone you do not know.

Emergency Repair Disks

The Emergency Repair Disk program (rdisk.exe) is a utility that backs up critical portions of the Registry to a floppy disk or to backup files in the %systemroot%\system32\config directory. Emergency repair disks provide a specific Registry backup mechanism that can be used from the Windows NT Setup program. To restore a failed NT Server, you use the most recently created emergency repair disk during a Windows NT reinstall. The NT setup program will import the Registry settings contained on the emergency repair disk so that your machine will have the configuration settings to operate properly.

Emergency repair disks are not required for Registry restoration if you are restoring from tape and your tape software is configured to backup the Registry. When you restore from a backup tape, the Registry is restored along with all the other files in the system.

The System Policy Editor

The System Policy Editor is a close cousin to the Registry editors. In fact, it's a more sophisticated Registry editor that provides a purpose-oriented (system control, in the case of the policy editor) hierarchy for browsing Registry keys.

The keys displayed and configurable in the policy editor are loaded from the `%systemroot%\inf\common.adm` text file.

This file contains a script that defines the settings available in the policy editor and which Registry keys they modify. You can create your own ADM files if you want to use the policy editor to edit other Registry keys.

Third-Party Tools

Microsoft provides two tools, `regback.exe` and `regrest.exe` in the NT resource kit to backup and restore the Windows NT Registry from within a running NT environment. These tools are similar to the functionality provided by the `rdisk.exe` Emergency Repair Disk utility.

A number of high-speed Registry search tools exist. The only time I've ever needed to use a tool of this nature was when I installed Windows NT on the D: drive and later decided to change it to the C: drive using the Disk Administrator. Suddenly no settings files could be found, so I used a high-speed search-and-replace Registry editor to change every instance of D: in the Registry to C:, which fixed the problem. I can't really recommend doing this sort of thing regularly, though. I actually had no way to tell if some setting that was not related to drive management but that matched the search criteria might be changed. Check out www.download.com if you're interested in third-party Registry search utilities.

Hacking the Registry

I've discussed Registry editors, but I haven't really mentioned why you would need them. In a perfect world, you wouldn't need them, but NT is far from operating system utopia.

There are innumerable reasons why the Registry becomes corrupted. Common reasons include failed software installations, a crash in the midst of a batch of Registry setting changes, and the failure of software de-installers to remove all the necessary Registry keys.

TIP   Instead of deleting Registry keys, export them to a text file first, then delete them. That way you can reimport them if you've made a mistake.

In any case, there are a number of reasons why you might have to directly modify Registry settings. Although the Registry is huge and in many cases oddly structured, you can quickly develop a feel for which portions of the Registry are relevant to the trouble-shooting and configuration processes. Once you're comfortable with the Registry, the chances that you will cause Registry corruption by incorrectly deleting keys is signifi-cantly reduced.

Sage Advice: Creating Registry "Scripts"

I frequently move my diagnostic laptop computers between the networks of many different customers. Some customers use DHCP, others (despite my constant pro-tests) prefer to use manually assigned IP addresses. Reconfiguring each machine for the different network environments used to be a major pain, until I hit upon the idea of using Registry files to make all the necessary Registry changes with one double-click and a reboot.

The best part of this method is that you don't have to hack the Registry files. You can setup the computer to work in a certain environment using the network Control Panel and then just use the Registry editor to export all necessary keys. Using a text editor, merge the different REG files into one file and give it the name of the environment for which it was created (such as "DHCPclient.reg" or "192.168.1.234.reg").

Then all you have to do is click the REG file to import all the necessary Registry keys and reboot the computer.

The only issue with using this method is making certain you've changed all relevant Registry settings. The easiest way to be sure is to export the entire TCP/IP key and the appropriate adapter driver key. You can split these into two files if you frequently change network adapters, but that's usually not necessary. This method creates more Registry entries than you actually need, but it's guaranteed to change every-thing properly.

Fixing NT Machines That Can't Boot

Installing new services (or forgetting to apply the latest service pack) on NT machines occasionally can cause the machine to crash before it is entirely booted. Since the computer crashes during the boot problem, you cannot fix the problem from that version of Windows NT. There are three solutions to this problem:

1. Reinstall Windows NT. This is the longest and most intrusive method.

2. Install another copy of NT onto the same disk and use that copy to repair the originally installed version.

3. Move the computer's hard disk into a working NT machine and make the necessary changes to fix the problem.

Assuming you're going to use the second or third method, you can then use the procedure for editing the failed computer's Registry that is described in the previous section on loading and unloading hives. The system hive file contains all driver and adapter information that might need to be changed.

To change the startup value for a service or driver in a non-operational system, use the Registry editor to browse to the `ControlSet001\services` (or the current control set as defined by the value *Current* in the system hive). Browse to the service or driver you suspect is causing the problem, and change the *Start* value to *0x4* (Disabled).

An easier method to deal with newly installed drivers or adapters is simply to rename the driver or service executable or DLL. This will prevent the service from attempting to start (and subsequently crash) NT. You'll then be able to use the system's own Registry editing tools to remove the corrupted driver information.

Repairing Higher-Level Applications

Applications installed in Windows NT seem to suffer Registry corruption far more often than they should. The usual method for dealing with this problem is removing and reinstalling the application, which works fine most of the time.

However, there are times when it doesn't work. If the de-installation program doesn't remove all the corrupted Registry keys, the second installation will be just as corrupt as the first. The solution here is to manually find and remove those keys after de-installing.

Then there are those times when de-installing an application would cause a lot of work or when an application simply can't be removed. In those cases, you will probably need to get technical information from the publisher of the application about its Registry settings so you can add or change them manually.

Sage Advice: Repairing the Desktop Explorer

Desktop Explorer is an application that is frequently corrupted but which can't be de-installed and reinstalled like most software. Certain keys in HKEY_CLASSES_ROOT hive are necessary for the proper operation of the Desktop Explorer. Absence of these keys can cause unusual Explorer behavior, such as unexplained failure to launch an application (clicking the icon does nothing) or various error messages. These keys are listed below in a format that can be used to create a REG file for direct importation into the Registry:

```
[HKEY_CLASSES_ROOT\.exe]
@="exefile"
"Content Type"="application/x-msdownload"

[HKEY_CLASSES_ROOT\exefile]
@="Application"
"EditFlags"=hex:d8,07,00,00

[HKEY_CLASSES_ROOT\exefile\CLSID]
@="{08c524e0-89b0-11cf-88a1-00aa004b9986}"

[HKEY_CLASSES_ROOT\exefile\DefaultIcon]
@="%1"

[HKEY_CLASSES_ROOT\exefile\shell]

[HKEY_CLASSES_ROOT\exefile\shell\open]
"EditFlags"=hex:00,00,00,00

[HKEY_CLASSES_ROOT\exefile\shell\open\command]
@="\"%1\" %*"

[HKEY_CLASSES_ROOT\exefile\shellex]

[HKEY_CLASSES_ROOT\exefile\shellex\PropertySheetHandlers]

[HKEY_CLASSES_
ROOT\exefile\shellex\PropertySheetHandlers\PifProps]
@="{86F19A00-42A0-1069-A2E9-08002B30309D}"

[HKEY_CLASSES_ROOT\.lnk]
@="lnkfile"

[HKEY_CLASSES_ROOT\.lnk\ShellEx]
```

Sage Advice: Repairing the Desktop Explorer *(continued)*

```
[HKEY_CLASSES_ROOT\.lnk\ShellEx\{BB2E617C-0920-11d1-9A0B-
00C04FC2D6C1}]
@="{500202A0-731E-11d0-B829-00C04FD706EC}"

[HKEY_CLASSES_ROOT\.lnk\ShellNew]
"Command"="RunDLL32 AppWiz.Cpl,NewLinkHere %1"
```

Adding Functionality

Windows NT has a number of features that aren't associated with the Control Panel, but can be really useful. Some of these features are associated with Windows NT Resource Kit programs, but most of them are just hanging out in the Registry waiting to be enabled by an intrepid Registry guru. You'll come across these little nuggets of functionality in Tips and Tricks books and Web sites, in Microsoft's technical databases, and on occasion by simply playing with the Registry.

Cool Trick: Explorer BMP icons

You can force Explorer to display the contents of a BMP file as the icon rather than using the default MS Paint icon by changing the following Registry key:

HKEY_CLASSES_ROOT\Paint.Picture\DefaultIcon

Change the (default value) entry to %1 in place of the mspaint.exe,1 entry. The change will take effect immediately.

When Things Go Wrong

PART 4

Manually Removing Software

You will often find that software developers don't spend much time getting their de-installation software working correctly, so you'll frequently have to remove software manually.

Application

For the vast majority of applications, you can remove all their Registry settings by deleting the HKEY_LOCAL_MACHINE\SOFTWARE\<*Vendor Name*>\<*Product Name*>key.

You usually shouldn't delete the vendor name key because vendors use that single key for all their software. Delete the key associated with the product name instead.

If the program has created an association to a file type, you should have to delete that association in the HKEY_CLASSES_ROOT hive. If the software has installed any drivers or services, treat them as shown in the next section.

Services and Drivers

Services and drivers are located in the same place in the Registry and handled the same way. To disable a service or driver (less permanent and more stable than removing the key), browse to the following Registry key and change the Start value to 4 (disabled):

HKEY_LOCAL_MACHINE\SYSTEM\CurrentControlSet\Services\<Service or Driver Name>

This is equivalent to using the Drivers or Services Control Panel to set the start-up type to disabled.

Network Adapter

You can manually remove a network adapter by deleting the following key:

HKEY_LOCAL_MACHINE\SYSTEM\CurrentControlSet\Services\

<Adapter Name>

Network Transports

Manually removing network transports can be somewhat involved, especially in the case of TCP/IP because of the number of peripherally related services.

TCP/IP If you receive a Registry Subkey Already Exists error message while trying to install TCP/IP or a TCP/IP service, an existing TCP/IP service has not been completely de-installed and has left the Registry in a corrupt state.

You can remove the TCP/IP transport by deleting the following Registry keys and then rebooting:

HKEY_LOCAL_MACHINE\Software\Microsoft\

DhcpMibAgent

DhcpServer

FTPSVC

LPDSVC

NetBT

RFC1156Agent

SNMP

SimpTcp

Tcpip

TcpipCU

TcpPrint

Wins

WinsMibAgent

HKEY_LOCAL_MACHINE\SYSTEM\CurrentControlSet\Services\

DHCP

DhcpServer

FTPSVC

Lmhosts

LPDSVC

NetBT

SimpTcp

SNMP

Tcpip

Wins

WinSock

WinSock2

<Adapter Driver>\Parameters\Tcpip

HKEY_LOCAL_MACHINE\System\CurrentControlSet\Enum\Root\

Legacy_DHCP

Legacy_Lmhosts

Legacy_LPDSVC

Legacy_NetBT

Legacy_TCPIP

LanManServer\Linkage\Bind

LanManWorkstation\Linkage\Bind

IPX/SPX   To manually remove the IPX/SPX transport, delete the following keys from the Registry:

```
HKEY_LOCAL_MACHINE\SOFTWARE\Microsoft\
   NwlnkIpx
   NwlnkNb
   NwlnkSpx


HKEY_LOCAL_MACHINE\SYSTEM\CCS\Services\
   NwlnkIpx
   NwlnkNb
   NwlnkSpx
```

The following values must be removed from this key:

```
HKEY_LOCAL_MACHINE\SYSTEM\CurrentControlSet\Services\
WinSock\Parameters\
   NwlnkIpx
   NwlnkSpx
```

Printers

It's sometimes necessary to manually remove and reinstall printers.

To delete a local (My Computer) printer, stop the spooler service using the Services Control Panel, delete the following Registry keys, and then restart the spooler:

```
HKEY_LOCAL_MACHINE\SYSTEM\CurrentControlSet\Control
\Print\Environments\Windows NT x86\Drivers
\Version-2\<Printer Name>


HKEY_LOCAL_MACHINE\SYSTEM\CurrentControlSet\Control
\Print\Printers\<Printer Name>
```

To delete a network printer, stop the spooler service using the Services Control Panel, delete the following Registry keys, and then restart the spooler:

```
HKEY_CURRENT_USER\Printers\Connections\<Server Name>
HKEY_LOCAL_MACHINE\SYSTEM\CurrentControlSet\Control\Print
```

```
\Providers \LanMan Print Services\Servers
\<Server Name>\Printers\<Printer Name>
```

Important Registry Keys

Only a few portions of the Registry are extremely useful for troubleshooting. Following is a list of important Registry keys and their uses. You should study the function of these keys in Appendix A.

HKEY_CURRENT_USER   This key stores environment settings that apply to the current user. You can edit these keys more conveniently using the Control Panel or the System Policy Editor than using the traditional Registry editors, but there are keys that don't appear in either of those tools.

HKEY_LOCAL_MACHINE\SOFTWARE   This key contains keys for installed software applications. Subkeys identify the software publisher, and each publisher's subkeys identify individual products. Deleting the keys for products will usually eliminate most of the Registry settings for the product unless there are document extensions located in HKEY_CLASSES_ROOT.

HKEY_LOCAL_MACHINE\SOFTWARE\Microsoft   This key contains keys for software published by Microsoft—including Windows NT itself. I think it's silly to establish important system keys inside a key used for more pedestrian purpose, but that's the way Microsoft decided to do it.

HKEY_LOCAL_MACHINE\SOFTWARE\Microsoft\Windows\CurrentVersion   This key contains keys that apply to all 32-bit versions of Windows, including Windows 95 and Windows 98. Most of these keys address user-interface options and options related to the Desktop Explorer.

HKEY_LOCAL_MACHINE\SOFTWARE\Microsoft\Windows\CurrentVersion\Run
This key contains a list of programs that should be executed by the Desktop Explorer after it launches. This is the place to look for those annoying auto-start programs that you can't find in the start-up folder.

HKEY_LOCAL_MACHINE\SOFTWARE\Microsoft\Windows NT\CurrentVersion   This key contains keys that apply only to Windows NT. Most of these keys apply to executive services, subsystems, and network settings.

When Things Go Wrong

PART 4

**HKEY_LOCAL_MACHINE\SOFTWARE\Microsoft\Windows NT\CurrentVersion\
Winlogon**   This key contains values that control how the logon process is controlled.
Check it out in Appendix A.

HKEY_LOCAL_MACHINE\SYSTEM\CurrentControlSet\Control   This key contains
control values for Kernel and executive services of Windows NT.

HKEY_LOCAL_MACHINE\SYSTEM\CurrentControlSet\Services   This key contains
keys for every installed service and driver. You'll edit this key to control errant services
and drivers, so make sure you're familiar with it.

Stream of Consciousness Registry Hacking

For some strange reason, the Internet Explorer desktop icon on my workstation changed from the orbital blue *e* to a regular folder icon. Obviously, some minor form of Registry corruption was to blame, but how was I going to figure out what and where the specific Registry keys to fix were located? A quick search of TechNet yielded no useful results.

Thinking about the problem for a moment, I decided the culprit must be located in the Desktop Explorer's Registry key area, which should be in the HKEY_LOCAL_MACHINE\SOFTWARE\MICROSOFT\WINDOWS key. I opened Regedit and went browsing. I browsed down through the \EXPLORER subkey, then the \DESKTOP subkey, and then the \NAMESPACE subkey. Sure enough, this key contained two CSLIDs (COM component class identifiers), one with a default value of "Recycle Bin" and the other with a default value of "the Internet."

But these keys were merely references to the identifiers that actually define the components. Knowing that CSLIDs are the unique identifiers for COM components, I figured that I would probably find the Icon file in the HKEY_CLASSES_ROOT\CLSID key. So I copied the text of the CSLID into the clipboard and did a Registry search for it.

Since Internet Explorer has multiple COM entries in the Registry, the CLSID cropped up a number of times. But only once did it appear as a key directly under the CLSID key, so I figured that key must the CSLID for Internet Explorer desktop component itself rather than just a reference to it.

Unlike some of the other CSLIDs I'd just seen, the Internet Explorer entry didn't have a DefaultIcon key. I did another search through the Registry on IE's CLSID to view the other four or five references and to examine their DefaultIcon entries. In one reference, I found the DefaultIcon value had the following data: "%SystemRoot%\system32\mshtml.dll,0". I interpreted this system file's name to mean "Microsoft HTML" and figured that it was probably the right resource file to contain the correct icon. I copied the data to the Clipboard and continued the CSLID search until I came back to the Internet Explorer entry that I had found earlier. I created a new DefaultIcon key and gave it the default value from the other entry. I then pulled up the Task Manager and ended and restarted the Explorer process. Sure enough, the familiar blue *e* was restored on the Desktop.

24seven **CASE STUDY**

Appendix

Useful Registry Keys

The Registry is a massive collection of individual values for hundreds of autonomous or semi-autonomous programs. Microsoft has not completely documented it in one place since the release of Windows NT 3.1, which is now six years obsolete—so I thought I'd do it for them.

The impetus for writing this appendix was simple—searching Microsoft's archives and the Web for the purpose of a Registry key is tedious and often difficult to do unless your machine is working correctly. And if that was the case, you likely wouldn't be hunting down the value of a Registry key.

I compiled this appendix from three sources: the Registry of my primary server with all of the default services installed, Microsoft TechNet, and the rest of the World Wide Web. To write this material, I went through my Registry, key by key, and searched on the key names and value names in TechNet and on the Web. In some cases, the purpose of certain keys was either obvious, irrelevant, or inscrutable, so I've left those keys out of this appendix in the interest of saving space...and wear on my fingers. Wherever possible, I documented the changes caused by manipulating Control Panels and other configuration tools, such as the System Policy Editor. I also included the keys I came across that were documented but not extant in my Registry. This method means that there are certainly keys I've missed—those both undocumented and not present in my machines. Unfortunately, I can think of no method for anyone but Microsoft to complete the task of documenting those keys. Each Registry key is included as an entry in this list. Where specific important values are present, a table of values and their associated description (or in some cases the data they contain) is included. Values in parentheses are the default value for the key.

Keys often have a default or unnamed value that is associated with the key. This value is expressed using the @ symbol in Registry export files and, by default, in this text.

Much of the information in this chapter is of little value to most people—but some of it is highly valuable to nearly everyone. If you want to see the inner workings of Windows NT for yourself, you can read through the entire appendix. If you just want to jump ahead to the good parts, skip to those entries denoted by the star symbol (★).

HKEY_CLASSES_ROOT
Maintains Explorer file associations for document extensions and file types.

Each document extension type is represented by a key of the same name; this key contains a value that associates the extension with an abstract file type. Each file type contains keys and values that associate activities with icons, such as Open or New. (The remaining glossary entries for this key are representative rather than exhaustive, as most keys for this hive do not vary.)

Some document extensions contain ShellEx or ShellNew keys. These keys describe the functionality of the right-click context menu. For example, the presence of a ShellNew key with a NullFile value and an empty string data will cause Explorer to list the document type in the New context menu and to create a new blank file in the current Explorer location.

HKEY_CLASSES_ROOT\<.ext>
Identifies the abstract file type that handles the extension. May also include a MIME type identifier called Content Type.

HKEY_CLASSES_ROOT\<.ext>\ShellEx\<CLSID>
The CLSID (OLE Class Identifier) of the application that handles this extension.

HKEY_CLASSES_ROOT\<.ext>\Shell\<selection>\command
Command line text that executes when this context menu item is selected.

HKEY_CLASSES_ROOT\<Abstract File Type>
Descriptive name of this file type.

HKEY_CLASSES_ROOT\<Abstract File Type>\CLSID
The CLSID (OLE Class Identifier) for this file type.

HKEY_CLASSES_ROOT\<Abstract File Type>DefaultIcon
Path to the default icon for this file type.

HKEY_CLASSES_ROOT\<Abstract File Type>\Shell
Default context menu selection from the subkey types.

HKEY_CLASSES_ROOT\<Abstract File Type>\Shell\<Selection>
String containing the context menu text.

HKEY_CLASSES_ROOT\<Abstract File Type>\Shell\<Selection>\command
Command-line text that performs the menu action.

HKEY_CLASSES_ROOT\<Abstract File Type>\Shell\<Selection>\ddeexec
DDE (Dynamic Data Exchange) parameter text that performs the action specified.

HKEY_CLASSES_ROOT\<Abstract File Type>\Shell\<Selection>\ddeexec\application
The OLE registered application that handles the DDE action.

HKEY_CLASSES_ROOT\CLSID
Contains the class identifiers (CLSIDs) of registered Component Object Model (COM) (formerly OLE) types. CLSIDs refer to a number of COM components of the Explorer interface, such as the Control Panel, permanent Explorer desktop components, and any other display object that is not handled in the same manner as a standard folder or file.

HKEY_CLASSES_ROOT\.hlp
File type association for the .hlp extension. The values for help files are shown in these keys as an example of how extensions are handled, not because these keys are especially important.

Value	Description
(default)	Abstract file type key ("hlpfile")

HKEY_CLASSES_ROOT\hlpfile
Executable file activity association for the hlpfile abstract file type.

Value	Data
(default)	Plaintext description of the abstract file type ("Help File")

HKEY_CLASSES_ROOT\hlpfile\DefaultIcon
Defines the displayed icon for the hlpfile extension.

Value	Data
(default)	Resource file containing the icon image and the image index ("%SystemRoot%\System32\shell32.dll,23")

Appendix

HKEY_CLASSES_ROOT\hlpfile\shell\open\command

Defines the shell action to perform when the Open command is applied to a hlpfile (.hlp). The %1 environmental variable contained in the string refers to the first parameter, which Explorer sets to the path and filename of the activated help file.

Value	Data
(default)	Shell command that launches the executable file that performs the open command for the hlpfile file type ("%SystemRoot%\System32\winhlp32.exe %1")

HKEY_CLASSES_ROOT\Interfaces

Contains interface descriptions for Registry COM components.

HKEY_CURRENT_CONFIG

This key contains information about the loaded hardware profile.

HKEY_CURRENT_USER

This key contains policy settings that apply to the current user. It is a pointer to the profile key located in HKEY_USERS of the person logged in.

HKEY_CURRENT_USER\Console

Contains values defining the visual layout of the command prompt. These values can be changed using the Console Control Panel.

HKEY_CURRENT_USER\Control Panel\Accessibility

Contains values defining the settings of the accessibility Control Panel. The values correspond directly to their counterparts in the Control Panel.

HKEY_CURRENT_USER\Control Panel\Appearance\Schemes

Defines the color schemes available in the Display Control Panel. Each value is the name of the scheme, and its corresponding data is a record containing the color and size settings for that scheme.

HKEY_CURRENT_USER\Control Panel\Colors

Defines the colors used by the various elements of the Windows Desktop as set by the current scheme and modified by the user in the Appearance panel of the Display Control Panel.

HKEY_CURRENT_USER\Control Panel\Current

Defines the currently selected color scheme.

HKEY_CURRENT_USER\Control Panel\Cursors

Defines the paths to the cursor bitmap paths for each cursor context as set in the Mouse Control Panel.

HKEY_CURRENT_USER\Control Panel\Cursors\Schemes

Defines the available cursor schemes. The value is the scheme name and the data is a comma-separated list of cursor bitmap paths that define the scheme.

★ ### HKEY_CURRENT_USER\Control Panel\Desktop

This key contains values that control how Windows Explorer operates.

Value	Data
AutoEndTasks	1 = Kill apps at shutdown without asking. (0)
CoolSwitch	(1) = Enables Alt+Tab switching.
CoolSwitchColumns	Number of icon columns in the switch panel. (7)
CoolSwitchRows	Number of icon rows in the switch panel. (3)
CursorBlinkRate	Cursor blink rate in milliseconds.
DragFullWindows	(1) = Drag windows with contents. (0) = Drag outline.
FontSmoothing	Amount of anti-aliasing to perform on fonts. (2)
GridGranularity	Defines the size, in units of 8 pixels, of an imaginary grid in which to position windows on the screen. (0) = No grid.
HungAppTimeout	Milliseconds to wait for response from hung application. (5,000)
IconSpacing	Horizontal pixels between icons. (75)
IconTitleFaceName	Font to use for icon titles. (MS Sans Serif)
IconTitleSize	Font size for icon titles. (9)
IconTitleWrap	(1) = Wrap long icon names.
IconVerticalSpacing	Vertical Pixels between icons. (75)
MenuShowDelay	Milliseconds to delay automatic menu dropdown. (308)
Pattern	Selected background pattern.
ScreenSaveActive	1 = Screen saver enabled.
ScreenSaverIsSecure	1 = Require password to clear screen saver.
ScreenSaveTimeOut	Seconds until screensaver activation.

Appendix

Value	Data
TileWallpaper	1 = Tile wallpaper. 0 = Center wallpaper.
WaitToKillAppTimeout	Milliseconds to wait before option to end hung application. (20,000)
Wallpaper	Path to selected wallpaper.
WheelScrollLines	Intellimouse wheel lines to scroll. (3)

HKEY_CURRENT_USER\Control Panel\International
Constants associated with internationalization variables as set in the Regional settings Control Panel.

HKEY_CURRENT_USER\Control Panel\Keyboard
Keyboard settings defined in the keyboard Control Panel.

HKEY_CURRENT_USER\Control Panel\Mouse
Mouse settings defined in the Mouse Control Panel.

HKEY_CURRENT_USER\Control Panel\Patterns
Color masks to create the various patterns that are available in the Display Control Panel.

HKEY_CURRENT_USER\Control Panel\Screen Saver.<screen saver>
Settings specific to various Control Panels.

HKEY_CURRENT_USER\Environment
Contents of the user environment variables such as TEMP and PATH.

HKEY_CURRENT_USER\Network\<drive letter>
Contains information about mapped drive shares and printers.

Value	Data
ConnectionType	1 = mapped drive. 2 = shared printer.
ProviderName	Network provider for this drive. ("Microsoft Windows Network")
RemotePath	UNC path to the shared directory.
UserName	Connect as username.

HKEY_CURRENT_USER\Printers
Contains user settings for installed printers. These values should be changed using the Printers Control Panel

HKEY_CURRENT_USER\RemoteAccess

Contains a list of defined Dial-Up Networking connections established for this user along with the settings required to establish the connection.

HKEY_CURRENT_USER\Software

This key contains all user-mode application software settings that are specific to users. Most of these keys are maintained by third-party applications. Each vendor creates a key named after their company the first time a product of theirs is installed. Each installed product creates a key named after the product to maintain its Registry keys and values.

HKEY_CURRENT_USER\Software\Microsoft\Windows\CurrentVersion\Explorer

This key contains values affecting the operation of the Desktop Explorer.

Value	Data
DirectoryCols	Contains a list of column widths for the default directory view in the Explorer. Delete this key to re-establish standard column widths.
IconUnderline	Controls the underlining of icons based on the cursor position.
ShellState	Affects how Internet Explorer interacts with the Desktop Explorer.

HKEY_CURRENT_USER\Software\Microsoft\Windows\CurrentVersion\Explorer\ AutoComplete

Controls the functionality of the IntelliSense AutoComplete feature.

Value	Data
Use AutoComplete	Autocomplete enabled. ("yes")

HKEY_CURRENT_ USER\Software\Microsoft\Windows\CurrentVersion\Explorer\BrowseNewProcess

Controls whether the explore functionality of the Explorer is run in a new process or the same process.

Value	Data
BrowseNewProcess	Explore in new process. ("no")

HKEY_CURRENT_USER\Software\Microsoft\Windows\CurrentVersion\Explorer\ RecentDocs

Contains keys that define the menu of recent documents in the Start menu.

Appendix

**HKEY_CURRENT_USER\Software\Microsoft\Windows\CurrentVersion\Explorer\
Shell Folders**

Defines the physical paths to the various shell folders for the current user. Standard values when logged in as the administrator are the following:

Value	Data
AppData	("C:\\WINNT\\Profiles\\Administrator\\Application Data")
Cache	("C:\\WINNT\\Profiles\\Administrator\\Temporary Internet Files")
Cookies	("C:\\WINNT\\Profiles\\Administrator\\Cookies")
Desktop	("C:\\WINNT\\Profiles\\Administrator\\Desktop")
Favorites	("C:\\WINNT\\Profiles\\Administrator\\Favorites")
Fonts	("C:\\WINNT\\Fonts")
History	("C:\\WINNT\\Profiles\\Administrator\\History")
NetHood	("C:\\WINNT\\Profiles\\Administrator\\NetHood")
Personal	("C:\\WINNT\\Profiles\\Administrator\\Personal")
PrintHood	("C:\\WINNT\\Profiles\\Administrator\\PrintHood")
Programs	("C:\\WINNT\\Profiles\\Administrator\\Start Menu\\Programs")
Recent	("C:\\WINNT\\Profiles\\Administrator\\Recent")
SendTo	("C:\\WINNT\\Profiles\\Administrator\\SendTo")
Start Menu	("C:\\WINNT\\Profiles\\Administrator\\Start Menu")
Startup	("C:\\WINNT\\Profiles\\Administrator\\Start Menu\\Programs\\Startup")
Templates	("C:\\WINNT\\ShellNew")

**HKEY_CURRENT_USER\Software\Microsoft\Windows\CurrentVersion\Explorer\
SmallIcons**

Controls whether to use small or large icons.

Value	Data
SmallIcons	Use small icons. ("yes")

HKEY_CURRENT_USER\Software\Microsoft\Windows\CurrentVersion
Explorer\Tips
Controls the start-up tips program (`tips.exe`). Change these values for the default user
to eliminate tip window start-up for new users.

Value	Data
DisplayInitialTip Window	(1) = Displays tips at start-up.
Next	Value of next tip.
ShowIE4	Shows IE4 tip window when starting Explorer.

HKEY_CURRENT_USER\Software\Microsoft\Windows\CurrentVersion\Explorer
User Shell Folders
Controls the path to various directories associated with the user shell. You can set these
values to a shared UNC path to use a common folder for all users.

Value	Data
AppData	Location of the Application Data folder
Cache	Location of the Cache folder
Cookies	Location of the Cookies folder
Desktop	Location of the Desktop folder
Favorites	Location of the Favorites folder
History	Location of the History folder
NetHood	Location of the Network Neighborhood folder
Personal	Location of the Personal folder
PrintHood	Location of the Printers folder
Programs	Location of the Programs folder
Recent	Location of the Recent Documents folder
SendTo	Location of the Send To folder
Start Menu	Location of the Start Menu folder
Startup	Location of the Startup folder

HKEY_CURRENT_USER\Software\Microsoft\Windows\CurrentVersion\Extensions
This key associates various Microsoft Office file type extensions with the location of the
Office program that edits them.

Appendix

Value	Data
doc	("C:\\Program Files\\Microsoft Office\\Office\\Winword.exe ^.doc")
dot	("C:\\Program Files\\Microsoft Office\\Office\\Winword.exe ^.dot")
mda	("C:\\Program Files\\Microsoft Office\\Office\\msaccess.exe ^.mda")
mdb	("C:\\Program Files\\Microsoft Office\\Office\\msaccess.exe ^.mdb")
qry	("C:\\Program Files\\Microsoft Office\\Office\\msqry32.exe ^.qry")
rtf	("C:\\Program Files\\Microsoft Office\\Office\\Winword.exe ^.rtf")
xls	("C:\\Program Files\\Microsoft Office\\Office\\excel.exe ^.xls")

HKEY_CURRENT_USER\Software\Microsoft\Windows\CurrentVersion\Internet Settings

This key controls various Internet Control Panel settings.

Value	Data
@	("1")
AllowCookies	(1) = Allows Web browsers to post informational cookies to the local machine.
AutoConfigProxy	Name of the proxy auto configuration DLL. ("wininet.dll")
DisableCachingOfSSL Pages	1 = Does not cache secure socket layer pages. (0)
DisconnectIdleTime	Time before Auto Disconnect.
EmailName	("IE40user@")
EnableAutodial	1 = Automatically dial a dial-up networking entry when establishing a TCP/IP connection.
EnableAutodisconnect	1 = Enables Auto disconnect.
EnableHttp1_1	(1) = Enables HTTP 1.1 extensions.
EnableSecurityCheck	1 = Enables security warnings.

Value	Data
FtpDefaultExpiryTime Secs	Undocumented. Probably: Default time to expire FTP cache.
GlobalUserOffline	Controls whether IE4 starts in online (0) or offline (1) mode. Set this value to 0 (on-line) if you cannot change IE4 to online mode manually.
GopherDefaultExpiry TimeSecs	Undocumented. Probably: Default time to expire Gopher cache. (obsolete in IIS 4)
HttpDefaultExpiry TimeSecs	Undocumented. Probably: Default time to expire HTTP cached pages.
MimeExclusionListFor Cache	List of MIME types that should not be cached. ("multipart/mixed multipart/x-mixed-replace multipart/x-byteranges ")
ProxyEnable	1 = Use Proxy to connect to Internet.
ProxyHttp1.1	(1) = Proxy HTTP 1.1 requests.
SecureProtocols	Defines the security protocols in use.
SyncMode	Determines how often Internet Explorer checks for new versions of Web pages. (3) = Every time you visit a page 2 = Once per day 0 = Never
Trust Warning Level	Controls the trust warning level. ("High")
User Agent	Controls the text that IE4 uses to negotiate compatibility with remote Web servers. You can change this text to individually identify Web browsers in your organization. ("Mozilla/4.0 (compatible; MSIE 4.01; Windows NT) ")
WarnonBadCert-Recving	(1) = Warns when invalid or expired certificates are received.
WarnOnPostRedirect	(1) = Warns when posting.
WarnOnZoneCrossing	(1) = Warns when moving between internet zones.

Appendix

HKEY_CURRENT_USER\Software\Microsoft\Windows\CurrentVersion\Internet Settings\Cache
Controls the type and amount of content Internet Explorer will cache.

HKEY_CURRENT_USER\Software\Microsoft\Windows\CurrentVersion\Internet Settings\Cache\Content
Controls the number of HTML pages Internet Explorer will cache.

Value	Data
CacheLimit	Maximum number of Web pages to cache.
CachePrefix	("")Text prefixed to stored Web pages.

HKEY_CURRENT_USER\Software\Microsoft\Windows\CurrentVersion\Internet Settings\Cache\Cookies
Controls the number of cookies IE4 will cache and how they will be identified.

Value	Data
CacheLimit	(0×2000) Maximum number of cookies to store.
CachePrefix	("Cookie:") Text prefixed to stored cookies.

HKEY_CURRENT_USER\Software\Microsoft\Windows\CurrentVersion\Internet Settings\Cache\History
Controls the number of visited sites IE4 will cache.

Value	Data
CacheLimit	(0×2000) Maximum number of history files to cache.
CachePrefix	("Visited:") Text prefixed to history files.

HKEY_CURRENT_USER\Software\Microsoft\Windows\CurrentVersion\Internet Settings\Url History
Controls the number of URLs IE4 will cache for the purpose of displaying visited links in an alternate color.

Value	Data
DaysToKeep	(1) Days to maintain clicked links.

HKEY_CURRENT_USER\Software\Microsoft\Windows\CurrentVersion\Policies\Explorer
This key controls policy settings for the Desktop Explorer. These settings are configurable using the System Policy Editor.

Value	Data
DisableTaskMgr	1 = Prevents user from running the Task Manager.
NoDriveTypeAutoRun	Controls the CD-ROM AutoRun feature. (0xe19dfae8)
NoNetConnectDisconnect	1 = Removes "Map Network Drive" and "Disconnect Network Drive."
NoSaveSettings	1 = Does not save changes to Explorer settings.
NoStartBanner	1 = Disables start banner.
NoTrayContextMenu	1 = Disables right-click contact context menu in the tray, Start button, and Application buttons.
NoViewContextMenu	1 = Disables all context menus in Explorer.

HKEY_CURRENT_USER\Software\Microsoft\Windows NT\CurrentVersion

Controls software settings specific to Windows NT and the logged on user.

HKEY_CURRENT_USER\Software\Microsoft\Windows NT\CurrentVersion\Extensions

Contains a list of file name extensions and the commands used to launch the programs associated with those extensions. The extension is the key name and the command is the data.

HKEY_CURRENT_USER\Software\Microsoft\Windows NT\CurrentVersion\Network\Event Viewer

Controls user settings for the Event Viewer.

HKEY_CURRENT_USER\Software\Microsoft\Windows NT\CurrentVersion\Network\Persistent Connections

Contains persistent network connections for the current user.

Value	Data
a	UNC path of the first persistent connection. Subsequent connections are b, c, d, etc.
Order	Order in which connections should be restored, by key name.
SaveConnections	("Yes") = Keeps persistent network connections.

HKEY_CURRENT_USER\Software\Microsoft\Windows NT\CurrentVersion\Network\Remote Access Admin

User settings for the Remote Access Administrator.

Appendix

HKEY_CURRENT_USER\Software\Microsoft\Windows NT\CurrentVersion\Network\User Manager for Domains

Contains such user settings for the User Manager for Domains as font names, window sizes, etc.

HKEY_CURRENT_USER\Software\Microsoft\Windows NT\CurrentVersion\PrinterPorts

Contains port information for this user's installed printers.

Value	Data
<Printer>	<Parameters to send to the printer at startup>("winspool,LPT1:,15,45")

HKEY_LOCAL_MACHINE

Contains keys pertaining to the configuration of the computer. Most useful troubleshooting and configuration keys are found under this key.

HKEY_LOCAL_MACHINE\HARDWARE

This key contains the hardware resources detected by the BIOS and the NTDETECT.COM boot loader. The values in this key are dynamically created each time the computer boots.

HKEY_LOCAL_MACHINE\SAM\SAM

This key contains a pointer to the HKEY_LOCAL_MACHINE\SECURITY key that contains the Security Accounts Manager database. Each user and group entry is identified by the account's security identifier. You should only edit this key with the User Manager for Domains unless you're following specific instructions.

HKEY_LOCAL_MACHINE\SECURITY

The security key contains the Security Accounts Manager database of users and groups, as well as data required for domain security and policies. The structure of the security key is undocumented, and the internal structure of the key is protected by an ACL. You can change permissions using RegEdt32 to view the internal structure of this key, but you should only make changes to this key using the User Manager and other Windows NT tools.

HKEY_LOCAL_MACHINE\SOFTWARE

Contains a key for the manufacturer of every installed application. Under that key, each manufacturer's installed products are enumerated. These keys are used to store configuration data specific to each application.

This key also contains the Microsoft\Windows and Microsoft\Windows NT keys, which contain numerous keys and settings critical to the operation of the system. Since these elements are not applications and cannot be un-installed, it is interesting that Microsoft chose to enumerate them under the Software key rather than in a key of their own.

HKEY_LOCAL_MACHINE\SOFTWARE\Microsoft\Windows\Help
Contains an entry for every installed help file, which associates the file with a physical file path.

HKEY_LOCAL_MACHINE\SOFTWARE\Microsoft\Windows\CurrentVersion
This key stores data used by the Win32 environment.

Value	Description
CommonFilesDir	Location of the Common File directory.
DevicePath	Location of the .inf files used for device driver installation.
MediaPath	Location of the media directory.
MediaPathUnexpanded	Location of the media directory using the %SystemRoot% environment variable.
PF_AccessoriesName	Name of the Program Files Accessories directory.
ProgramFilesDir	Location of the Program Files directory.
ProgramFilesPath	Program Files directory location using the %SystemDrive% environment variable.
SM_AccessoriesName	Name of the Accessories Start menu item.

HKEY_LOCAL_MACHINE\SOFTWARE\Microsoft\Windows\CurrentVersion\Explorer\Desktop\NameSpace
Contains a list of CSLIDs that define the icons permanently installed on the Desktop (Recycle Bin, The Internet, InBox, etc.). Deleting these keys will remove Desktop icons

HKEY_LOCAL_MACHINE\SOFTWARE\Microsoft\Windows\CurrentVersion\Explorer\FindExtensions
Defines the entries that appear in the Start ➤ Find menu.

HKEY_LOCAL_MACHINE\SOFTWARE\Microsoft\Windows\CurrentVersion\Explorer\MyComputer\NameSpace
Contains a list of CSLIDs that define the icons permanently installed in My Computer (Printers, Control Panel, Dial-Up Networking). Deleting these keys will remove My Computer icons.

Appendix

HKEY_LOCAL_MACHINE\SOFTWARE\Microsoft\Windows\CurrentVersion\Explorer
RemoteComputer\NameSpace
Contains a list of CSLIDs that define the icons available to remote users of this machine
(the Add Printer icon is the only default).

HKEY_LOCAL_MACHINE\SOFTWARE\Microsoft\Windows\CurrentVersion\Explorer
Shell Folders
This key contains values that identify the file paths of the Desktop, Start menu, Programs,
and Startup directories for all users.

Value	Description
Common Desktop	Path to the desktop for all users, usually `C:\WINNT\Profiles\All Users\Desktop`.
Common Programs	As above.
Common Start Menu	As above.
Common Startup	As above. If this value is missing, Explorer will open all folders in the root directory by default. Correct this problem by recreating the value with this data: %SYSTEMROOT%\Profiles\All Users\Start Menu\Programs\Startup.

HKEY_LOCAL_MACHINE\SOFTWARE\Microsoft\Windows\CurrentVersion
Explorer\Tips
Contains a series of values that define the Windows NT Tip text that appears in the Tip
of the Day dialog box at start-up.

HKEY_LOCAL_MACHINE\SOFTWARE\Microsoft\Windows\CurrentVersion\Explorer
User Shell Folders
Specifies the UNC path for Start ➤ Programs entries in the common groups division. This
value can be configured using the System Policy Editor.

Value	Description
Common Desktop	Path to the desktop for all users, usually `C:\WINNT\Profiles\All Users\Desktop`.
Common Programs	As above.
Common Start Menu	As above.
Common Startup	As above. If this value is missing, Explorer will open all folders in the root directory by default. Correct this problem by recreating the value with this data: %SYSTEMROOT%\Profiles\All Users\Start Menu\Programs\Startup.

HKEY_LOCAL_MACHINE\SOFTWARE\Microsoft\Windows\CurrentVersion\Policies

Stores keys and values created by the System Policy Editor to restrict access to the local machine.

**HKEY_LOCAL_MACHINE\SOFTWARE\Microsoft\Windows\CurrentVersion\
Reliability**

NT 4 SP 4 writes a time stamp to this key every five minutes (or as otherwise defined by the TimeStampInterval value) that is used to log the time the server crashed in the event of an abnormal shutdown.

Value	Description
LastAliveStamp	0 = Disables time stamp logging, otherwise date and time of last valid time stamp.
TimeStampInterval	Time stamp interval.

★ **HKEY_LOCAL_MACHINE\SOFTWARE\Microsoft\Windows\CurrentVersion\Run**

Contains the paths to Explorer extensions, such as tray items, that run each time Explorer is started. Of these values, only SystemTray (with a value of "SysTray.exe") is required for Windows to start properly. This value is configurable using the System Policy Editor Default Computer profile.

HKEY_LOCAL_MACHINE\SOFTWARE\Microsoft\Windows\CurrentVersion\RunOnce

Contains the paths to programs that should run the next time that Explorer starts. Generally used to complete installations after a reboot, this key should normally be empty.

HKEY_LOCAL_MACHINE\SOFTWARE\Microsoft\Windows\CurrentVersion\Setup

Contains information about the current setup of Windows NT. Used by the Add\Remove programs Control Panel to determine which Windows components are currently installed.

**HKEY_LOCAL_MACHINE\SOFTWARE\Microsoft\Windows\CurrentVersion\
SharedDlls**

Contains a list of shared DLLs, each with a counter datum enumerating the number of installed applications that use the DLL. Upon de-installation, an application decrements the counters of each DLL it uses. When a DLLs counter reaches zero, the user is prompted to delete shared DLLs no longer in use.

Appendix

★ **HKEY_LOCAL_MACHINE\SOFTWARE\Microsoft\Windows\CurrentVersion\ Uninstall**

Contains an entry for each application that can be uninstalled using the Add\Remove programs Control Panel. If you have manually deleted an application, remove its entry under this key to eliminate its presence in the Add\Remove Control Panel list.

★ **HKEY_LOCAL_MACHINE\SOFTWARE\Microsoft\Windows NT\CurrentVersion**

This key contains values entered or identified during the original operating system installation.

Value	Description
CSDVersion	Identifies the current service pack level as a string.
CurrentBuild	Identifies internal build versions (obsolete).
CurrentBuildNumber	The OS build number ("1381" for NT 4).
CurrentType	Identifies the HAL in use.
CurrentVersion	Operating system version number ("4" for NT 4).
InstallDate	Installation date (dword).
PathName	OS Installation Path.
ProductID	Product unique number.
RegisteredOrganization	Organization name entered by the user during setup.
RegisteredOwner	Owner's name entered during setup.
SoftwareType	Identifies type of software ("SYSTEM" for NT 4).
SourcePath	Path to the installation i386 source directory. Change this value if you copy the i386 to your hard disk.
SystemRoot	Path to the Windows NT System directory.

HKEY_LOCAL_MACHINE\SOFTWARE\Microsoft\Windows NT\CurrentVersion\Fonts
Contains an entry for every installed font that associates the font name with a physical file path.

HKEY_LOCAL_MACHINE\SOFTWARE\Microsoft\Windows NT\CurrentVersion\Fonts
Contains entries describing acceptable replacement installed fonts for fonts that are not installed (usually, Macintosh fonts).

HKEY_LOCAL_MACHINE\SOFTWARE\Microsoft\Windows NT\CurrentVersion\Hotfix
Contains keys identifying installed hot-fixes by their KnowledgeBase unique ID.

★ **HKEY_LOCAL_MACHINE\SOFTWARE\Microsoft\Windows NT\CurrentVersion\ NetworkCards\<Adapter #>**

Contains keys enumerating the installed network adapters. Each key is named for the bind order of the network adapter (1...*n*). Values for each adapter are as follows.

Value	Description
Description	Text description of the adapter.
Hidden	1 = Adapter does not appear in the Network Control Panel.
InstallDate	Date of Installation. (dword)
Manufacturer	Text identifying the manufacturer.
ProductName	Text identifying the product.
ServiceName	Text identifying the name of the driver\service that controls this adapter.
Title	As Description value above but prefixed with the bind number in brackets.

HKEY_LOCAL_MACHINE\SOFTWARE\Microsoft\Windows NT\CurrentVersion\ Perflib\009

The ACL for this key controls which users have permission to remotely monitor this computer's performance using the Performance Monitor. 009 is the language identifier for English—internationalized versions will be different.

HKEY_LOCAL_MACHINE\SOFTWARE\Microsoft\Windows NT\CurrentVersion\ Ports

Port setting information as defined in the Ports Control Panel.

HKEY_LOCAL_MACHINE\SOFTWARE\Microsoft\Windows NT\CurrentVersion\ProfileList\<User SID>

Contains an entry for each profile stored on the local machine. Keys are identified by the SID of the user. Profiles only exist for users who have logged on locally or whose profiles have been moved to this machine. Use these keys to identify the SID of a user by account name. Values for each profile are as follows.

Value	Description
ProfileImagePath	Path to the location where this profile is stored. Change this entry to move the profile to another location.
Sid	SID of the user account. Key name provides a human readable SID.

Appendix

★ **HKEY_LOCAL_MACHINE\SOFTWARE\Microsoft\Windows NT\Current Version\ Winlogon**

This key is used to set configuration data related to interactive logons.

Value	Description
AllocateCDRoms	1 = Restrict CD-ROM access to interactively logged on user.
AllocateFloppies	1 = Restrict Floppy access to interactively logged on user.
AutoAdminLogon	1 = Perform auto logon using DefaultUser and DefaultPassword entries.
AutoRestartShell	1 = Restart shell process (`explorer.exe`) if it is closed.
CachedLogonsCount	0 = Disable caching of domain logon credentials on local machine.
DebugServerCommand	"Yes" or "no."
DefaultDomainName	Domain in which DefaultUserName is defined.
DefaultPassword	Text password for auto-logon user.
DefaultUserName	Name of user to automatically log on, if any.
DeleteRoamingCache	1 = Delete cached copies of roaming profiles.
DontDisplayLastUserName	1 = User Name field cleared in logon dialog.
LegalNoticeCaption	Title for the legal notice dialog box, if any.
LegalNoticeText	Text of the legal notice dialog box, if any.
PowerdownAfterShutdown	Send API command to power machine off after shutdown.
ReportBootOk	0 = Disable the automatic (default) start-up acceptance, which happens after the first successful logon. Do not change values in the BootVerificationProgram key unless you need a custom verification program to satisfy specific start-up criteria at your site.
RunLogonScryptSync	1 = Run logon scripts synchronously (logon scripts must complete before the shell will be loaded).
Shell	Filename of shell executable.
Show	0 = off or time in seconds to wait for user profile information before the default is accepted.
ShutdownWithoutLogon	1 = Enables shutdown button in logon screen.

Value	Description
SlowLinkDetectEnabled	1 = Automatically detect slow network connections.
SlowNetworkTimeout	0 = Off, or time in milliseconds to wait before slow network is determined.
System	Undocumented.
Userinit	(USERINIT, nddeagnt.exe) Specifies executables to be run by WinLogon when a user logs on. These executables are run in the user context. The first entry (USERINIT) is responsible for executing the shell program. nddeagnt.exe is needed to run NetDDE.

HKEY_LOCAL_MACHINE\SYSTEM

The System key contains values that pertain to the operation of the Kernel, the executive, services, and drivers. These keys are usually critical to Windows NT's ability to boot, so you should be especially cautious when changing them.

HKEY_LOCAL_MACHINE\SYSTEM\Clone

This key contains the working copy of the current control set. It is locked and unchangeable as it is in use by the operating system.

HKEY_LOCAL_MACHINE\SYSTEM\ControlSet00x

Each of the control sets is a different system configuration. 001 is usually the originally installed control set. 002 is usually the "LastKnownGood" control set. You may have additional control sets, especially if you've had boot problems with your machine in the past.

★ HKEY_LOCAL_MACHINE\SYSTEM\CurrentControlSet

CurrentControlSet is a pointer to the ControlSet00x that is current. Make changes in this key to guarantee that they'll be used the next time you boot your system.

HKEY_LOCAL_MACHINE\SYSTEM\CurrentControlSet\Control

The control key contains settings for the kernel, executive services, and drivers that are required for the proper operation of Windows NT.

Value	Description
CurrentUser	This key is supposed to contain the name of the logged on user, but it actually contains the default value: "USERNAME".
RegistrySizeLimit	Maximum size the Registry can grow to (25 percent of the PagedPoolSize).

Value	Description
SystemStartOptions	Options specified on the boot.ini command line.
WaitToKillService-Timeout	Allows you to specify a length of time that the Service Control Manager must wait for services to complete the shut-down request.

HKEY_LOCAL_MACHINE\SYSTEM\CurrentControlSet\Control\BootVerification-Program

This key contains the filename for programs that establish a last known good configuration upon successful boot. The default of no entry should not be changed except by software specifically designed to perform this function.

HKEY_LOCAL_MACHINE\SYSTEM\CurrentControlSet\Control\ComputerName\ActiveComputerName

The contained value ComputerName is the active name of the computer. Do not set this key directly—use the Network Control Panel to change the computer's name.

HKEY_LOCAL_MACHINE\SYSTEM\CurrentControlSet\Control\ComputerName\ComputerName

The contained value ComputerName is the name that the ActiveComputerName key will receive upon next boot.

HKEY_LOCAL_MACHINE\SYSTEM\CurrentControlSet\Control\ContentIndex

Registry settings pertaining to the Content Index service of Internet Information Server. Microsoft does not specifically document these values, but their use is generally obvious from the value name if you understand the function of the Content Index.

HKEY_LOCAL_MACHINE\SYSTEM\CurrentControlSet\Control\CrashControl

Settings that determine how to handle kernel dumps (blue screens). These values are set in the System Control Panel.

Value	Data
AutoReboot	1 = Reboot automatically.
CrashDumpEnabled	1 = Write memory dump file.
DumpFile	Path to the memory dump file. ("%SystemRoot%\MEMORY.DMP")
LogEvent	1 = Send event to system log.
Overwrite	1 = Overwrite the memory dump file automatically.
SendAlert	1 = Send alert on network.

HKEY_LOCAL_MACHINE\SYSTEM\CurrentControlSet\Control\FileSystem

Value	Data
NtfsAllowExtended CharacterIn8dot3Name	1 = Allow extended characters in 8.3 filenames. This can cause problems on computers that do not use the same code page. This value can be set in the Windows NT System ➤ File system ➤ Allow Extended Characters in 8.3 Filenames section of the System Policy Editor.
NtfsDisable8dot3Name-Creation	1 = Do not create 8.3 filename hashes for long file names. This value can be set in the Windows NT System ➤ File system ➤ Do Not Create 8.3 Filenames section of the System Policy Editor. Disabling short name generation on an NTFS partition will improve the performance of directory enumeration, but may cause problems for 16-bit applications.
NtfsDisableLastAccessUpdate	1 = Disable updating last access time. This can speed file system performance on disk bound systems. This value can be set in the Windows NT System ➤ File System ➤ Do Not Update Last Access Time section of the System Policy Editor.
Win31FileSystem	1 = disable long filename support on FAT volumes. (0)
Win95TruncatedExtensions	1 = Truncate extensions longer than three characters in the NT command prompt. File operations specifying a three character extension will be applied to files containing longer extensions (for example, `dir *.htm` will list both `*.htm` and `*.html` files). This may cause unexpected application of commands to files. (1)

HKEY_LOCAL_MACHINE\SYSTEM\CurrentControlSet\Control\GroupOrderList

Defines the load groups that drivers and services may be members of, and sets the order in which those groups are loaded. The Group value of a driver or service defines which of the groups listed in this key that driver or service belongs to.

Appendix

HKEY_LOCAL_MACHINE\SYSTEM\CurrentControlSet\Control\hivelist
Defines the disk location of the various Registry hives. One value per hive is listed.
Default entries are listed in the following table.

Value	Data
\REGISTRY \MACHINE \HARDWARE	("") This key contains a null entry because the hardware list is built dynamically rather than read from a file.
\REGISTRY \MACHINE \SAM	("\Device\Harddisk0\Partition1\ WINNT\system32\config\SAM")
\REGISTRY \MACHINE \SECURITY	("\Device\Harddisk0\Partition1\ WINNT\system32\config\SECURITY")
\REGISTRY \MACHINE \SOFTWARE	("\Device\Harddisk0\Partition1\ WINNT\system32\config\software")
\REGISTRY \MACHINE \SYSTEM	("\Device\Harddisk0\Partition1\ WINNT\system32\config\system")
\REGISTRY \USER \.DEFAULT	("\Device\Harddisk0\Partition1\ WINNT\system32\config\default")
\REGISTRY \USER \<Admin Account SID>	("\Device\Harddisk0\Partition1\ WINNT\Profiles\Administrator\NTUSER.DAT")

HKEY_LOCAL_MACHINE\SYSTEM\CurrentControlSet\Control\Keyboard Layout
Contains selections for DOS international keyboard layouts. Use the keyboard Control
Panel to modify the information in this key.

HKEY_LOCAL_MACHINE\SYSTEM\CurrentControlSet\Control\Keyboard Layouts
Contains paths to various keyboard control libraries for various languages. Use the keyboard Control Panel to modify the information in this key.

★ **HKEY_LOCAL_MACHINE\SYSTEM\CurrentControlSet\Control\Lsa**

The Local Security Authority manages authentication and auditing functions for the local computer. Most of these values have serious implications and should not be implemented without a solid understanding of their use. Search the TechNet CD for more information regarding their proper use.

Value	Data
AuditBaseObjects	1 = Enables auditing of base objects. Also enables auditing of system objects in the User Manager to begin tracking base object use.
Authentication	Name of the authentication package library.
CrashOnAuditFail	1 = Forces NT machine to shutdown when the audit log is full. Only administrators can log on, and they must clear the log or reset this value to allow other users to log on.
FullPrivilegeAuditing	Enables auditing of all user privileges, especially use of backup and restore.
LMCompatibilityLevel	0 = Send both NT and LM password hashes. 1 = Send LM only if server requests. 2 = Do not send LM hash. LanManager hashes are far less secure than NT hashes.
Notification Packages	Contains a null separated string of password filter DLLs. Default value is FPNWCLNT (null) (null), you can add PASSFILT (null) (null) to enable stronger password filtering.
RestrictAnonymous	1 = Prevents anonymous users from enumerating shares or viewing account information.
Submit Control	1 = Allows system operators to schedule AT service commands.

HKEY_LOCAL_MACHINE\SYSTEM\CurrentControlSet\Control\NetworkProvider\Order

Provides the order in which networks should be accessed.

Value	Data
ProviderOrder	A string containing the order in which network providers should be accessed. ("LanmanWorkstation")

HKEY_LOCAL_MACHINE\SYSTEM\CurrentControlSet\Control\Nls

Contains values for code pages and internationalization language files for the system.

Appendix

HKEY_LOCAL_MACHINE\System\CurrentControlSet\Control\Print

Contains print spooler control values and subkeys identifying installed printers, drivers, and print monitors. Some settings under this key can be made by opening the Printers Control Panel, selecting the Add New Printer icon, and selecting Server Properties in the File menu.

Value	Data
BeepEnabled	1 = Beeps every 10 seconds when a remote job error occurs on a print server. This value can be set in the Windows NT Printers ➤ Sharing ➤ Error Beep Scheduler section of the System Policy Editor.
DisableServerThread	1 = Print spooler does not transmit shared printer information to other print servers. This value can be set in the Windows NT Printers ➤ Sharing ➤ Disable browse thread on this computer section of the System Policy Editor.
SchedulerThreadPriority	1 = Higher than normal. 0 = Normal. FFFFFFFF = Lower than normal. This value can be set in the Windows NT Printers ➤ Sharing ➤ Scheduler priority section of the System Policy Editor.

HKEY_LOCAL_MACHINE\System\CurrentControlSet\Control\Print\Environments

Defines file locations and names for driver DLLs and help files for various NT platforms.

HKEY_LOCAL_MACHINE\SYSTEM\CurrentControlSet\Control\Print\Environments\\<Platform>\Drivers\\<Print System Version>\\<Printer Name>

Value	Data
Configuration File	Filename of the print driver configuration DLL.
Data File	Filename of the print driver data file DLL.
Datatype	Undocumented.
Dependent Files	Null separated list of files upon which this printer driver depends.
Driver	Filename of the print driver.
Help File	Filename of the printer HLP file.
Monitor	Name of the print monitor (if not default).
Version	Print system version.

HKEY_LOCAL_MACHINE\System\CurrentControlSet\Control\Print\Forms

Contains a list of values defining various paper sizes.

HKEY_LOCAL_MACHINE\System\CurrentControlSet\Control\Print\Monitors\ <Monitor Name>

Associates a monitor name with a monitor driver DLL.

Value	Data
Driver	A string containing the filename of the print monitor driver.

HKEY_LOCAL_MACHINE\System\CurrentControlSet\Control\Print\Printers

Contains a key for each installed printer. Key names differ based on the printer, but values below each key are relatively static.

Value	Data
DefaultSpoolDirectory	Location of the default spool directory (`"C:\WINNT\System32\spool\PRINTERS"`)

HKEY_LOCAL_MACHINE\System\CurrentControlSet\Control\Print\Printers\<Printer Name>

Control values for each specific printer. These values are the same for all printers.

Value	Data
Attributes	Printer attributes. Values for the bitmask are undocumented. (8)
Datatype	Spooler data type. ("RAW")
DefaultDevMode	A character string send to the printer to identify its operating mode.
DefaultPriority	Default priority. (0)
Description	Contents of the Printer Description Field.
Location	Contents of the printer Location Field.
Name	Name of the printer in the Printer Control Panel.
Parameters	Printer specific parameters.
Port	Port to which print requests are directed.
Print Processor	Print processor for this printer.
Printer Driver	Identifies the printer driver for this printer.
Priority	Printer priority.
Security	Printer security data as set in the Printer Control Panel.
Separator File	Path to the file containing a page to be printed to separate print jobs.

Appendix

Value	Data
Share Name	Printer's shared NetBIOS name.
SpoolDirectory	Spool directory if other than the default.
StartTime	Printer accepts jobs starting at this time. (0) = Always available.
Status	Printer status.
TotalBytes	Bytes transmitted to printer since installation.
TotalJobs	Print jobs handled since printer installation.
TotalPages	Pages printed since installation.
TxTimeout	Seconds to wait before sending timeout error message.
UntilTime	Printer rejects jobs after this time of day. (0) = Always available.

HKEY_LOCAL_MACHINE\System\CurrentControlSet\Control\Print\Printers\<Printer Name>\PrinterDriverData
Values unique to a specific printer driver are stored here.

★ **HKEY_LOCAL_MACHINE\System\CurrentControlSet\Control\Print\Providers**
Contains control values for the LanMan print provider and a key defining that provider. Other network providers install their own print providers here.

Value	Data
EventLog	A bit flag indicating what classes of error messages should be logged in the event log. Sum values to combine. 0 = No event logging. 1 = Errors only. 2 = Warnings only. 4 = Information only.
NetPopup	1 = Enable that annoying pop-up dialog box whenever anyone prints through the local print server.
Order	A string containing the order in which print providers are checked for service fulfillment.
RetryPopup	1 = Retry pop-up on fail.

HKEY_LOCAL_MACHINE\SYSTEM\CurrentControlSet\Control\PriorityControl
This key contains the value that controls the priority boost given to the foreground application. This value is normally set in the Performance tab of the System Control Panel.

Value	Data
Win32PrioritySeparation	0 = Foreground and background applications are equally responsive (for file servers).
	1 = Foreground is more responsive than background (for mixed-use machines).
	2 = Best Foreground responsiveness (for workstations).

HKEY_LOCAL_MACHINE\SYSTEM\CurrentControlSet\Control\ProductOptions

The value in this key identifies which version of the operating system is running on the machine, and the information is used by a number of services to determine optimizations and limitations. Changing this value is a violation of your End User License Agreement with Microsoft.

Value	Data
ProductType	"LanmanNT" = Windows NT Server
	"WinNT" = Windows NT Workstation

HKEY_LOCAL_MACHINE\SYSTEM\CurrentControlSet\Control\SecurePipeServers\ winreg

The permissions set on this key in RegEdt32 define the remote access permissions to the Registry. To restrict Registry access from the network, set permissions on this key. This key contains only one value, which must be present for the Registry server to handle permissions properly.

Value	Data
Description	("Registry Server")

HKEY_LOCAL_MACHINE\SYSTEM\CurrentControlSet\Control\SecurePipeServers\ winreg\AllowedPaths

This key contains a value defining the Registry paths available to remote users or services irrespective of the security settings on the winreg key. This allows you to define specific Registry paths available to remote users who would normally be restricted by the permission settings on the winreg key.

Value	Data
Machine	Allowed Registry paths, null separated

Appendix

HKEY_LOCAL_MACHINE\SYSTEM\CurrentControlSet\Control\SecurityProviders
Contains a value that defines the security provider DLLs installed in the system. Security providers may have unique data that is defined below this key and identified by the name of the security provider service.

Value	Data
Security Providers	List of security provider DLLs, comma-separated string

HKEY_LOCAL_MACHINE\SYSTEM\CurrentControlSet\Control\ServiceGroupOrder
This key contains a null-separated byte array that defines the order in which drivers are loaded into memory.

Value	Data
List	Null-separated byte array that lists the names of services and drivers in their load order

HKEY_LOCAL_MACHINE\SYSTEM\CurrentControlSet\Control\ServiceProvider\ Order
This key defines the way the Win32 API will use name service providers when resolving a network name.

Value	Data
Excluded Providers	(0) List of identifiers of name services that should not be used when resolving names.
ProviderOrder	Order in which major protocols will be used for name resolution.

HKEY_LOCAL_MACHINE\SYSTEM\CurrentControlSet\Control\Session Manager
This key defines values used by the Kernel during its operation and during the boot process.

Value	Data
AutoChkTimeOut	Seconds to delay running BootExecute program, thus allowing user to bypass by pressing any key. Default (10) if non-existent.
BootExecute	Specifies programs to run after the Kernel load phase of the boot process. ("autocheck autochk *")
CriticalSectionTimeout	A debugging parameter for timing-out deadlocked thread conditions in the Kernel. Deadlock timeout is not normally used.
GlobalFlag	Global flags are used by the executive for purposes such as debugging and disabling subsystems.

Value	Data
LicensedProcessors	Number of processors the NT product is licensed to use. Changing this value can cause a Kernel mode exception at boot time. (4)
ObjectDirectories	Specifies object directories to create during start up. (`"\Windows\RPC Control"`)
PendingFileRename Operations	NT will copy files specified in this key before booting the operating system, so files constantly in use can be replaced. See KnowledgeBase article Q181345.
ProtectionMode	1 = Base OS objects should be secured at C2 level. See NT Resource Kit.
RegisteredProcessors	Number of processors this NT product will use at most. (4) Defaults are 2 for NT Workstation, 4 for NT Server, and 8 for Enterprise Server.(Four is default for this product.)
ResourceTimeoutCount	Specifies four second ticks until resources time-out. Retail versions of NT never time-out.

HKEY_LOCAL_MACHINE\SYSTEM\CurrentControlSet\Control\Session Manager\ AppPatches\<Application Name>

Defines code segments used to patch commercial applications for proper operation under Windows NT.

HKEY_LOCAL_MACHINE\SYSTEM\CurrentControlSet\Control\Session Manager\ DOS Devices

This key contains symbolic links created during start-up as an interface for MS-DOS devices.

Value	Data
AUX	("\DosDevices\COM1")
MAILSLOT	("\Device\MailSlot")
NUL	("\Device\Null")
PIPE	("\Device\NamedPipe")
PRN	("\DosDevices\LPT1")
UNC	("\Device\Mup")

Appendix

HKEY_LOCAL_MACHINE\SYSTEM\CurrentControlSet\Control\Session Manager\Environment

This key contains a list of environment system variables available to all users. These values can be modified in the System Control Panel's Environment tab.

Value	Data
<Environment Variable>	<Environment Variable Data>

HKEY_LOCAL_MACHINE\SYSTEM\CurrentControlSet\Control\Session Manager\Executive

This key is undocumented. It appears to contain values relating to the way the executive allocates its own threads and their priorities.

HKEY_LOCAL_MACHINE\SYSTEM\CurrentControlSet\Control\Session Manager\FileRenameOperations

This key is used by the system to perform file-rename and delete operations during the boot process before the files are locked for use. Little additional documentation exists, and Microsoft recommends that the system maintain these entries.

HKEY_LOCAL_MACHINE\SYSTEM\CurrentControlSet\Control\Session Manager\KnownDLLs

This key associates library short names with the actual file names of the DLL

Value	Data
<Driver Name>	<Corresponding DLL file name>

HKEY_LOCAL_MACHINE\SYSTEM\CurrentControlSet\Control\Session Manager\Memory Management

Value	Data
ClearPageFileAtShutdown	1 = Zero-fill page file at shutdown.
DisablePagingExecutive	1 = Kernel and drivers cannot be paged to disk.
IoPageLockLimit	Specifies the maximum number of bytes that can be locked for I/O. 0 = use default of 512K. I/O-intensive machines may benefit by increasing this value in increments of 512K.
LargeSystemCache	1 = Prefer file caching and page applications to disk. On non-file servers, this causes excessive paging activity. Set to 0 for higher application performance and reduced paging activity.

NonPagedPoolSize	Size of the non-paged memory pool in bytes. 0 = Automatic. Changing this value can cause wide-ranging failure due to inability to automatically allocate memory.
PagedPoolSize	Size of the paged pool. 0 = Automatic. Changing this value can cause wide-ranging failure due to inability to automatically allocate memory.
PagingFiles	String containing the path to the page file, the current size, and the maximum size. For example, "C:\pagefile.sys 27 140"
SecondLevelDataCache	Amount of processor's 2nd level cache to use. 0 = 256K. Change this value to the actual size of your 2nd level data cache to increase performance. (Pentium II = 512.)
SystemPages	Number of page table entries for PCI cards. 0 = Automatic.

HKEY_LOCAL_MACHINE\SYSTEM\CurrentControlSet\Control\Session Manager\ SubSystems

This key maintains a list of application subsystems and their locations.

Value	Data
Debug	Location of the Debug driver if installed. ("")
Kmode	Location of the Win32 subsystem driver. (`"%SystemRoot%\system32\win32k.sys"`)
Optional	Null separated list of optional subsystems. ("Os2 Posix")
Os2	Location of the OS2 subsystem executable. (`"%SystemRoot%\system32\os2ss.exe"`)
Posix	Location of the POSIX subsystem executable. (`"%SystemRoot%\system32\psxss.exe"`)
Required	Null-separated list of mandatory subsystems. ("debug windows")
Windows	Location of the Win32 subsystem. Includes some named parameters. (`"%SystemRoot%\system32\csrss.exe` ObjectDirectory = \Windows SharedSection = 1024,3072,512 Windows = On SubSystemType = Windows ServerDll = basesrv,1 ServerDll = winsrv:UserServerDllInitialization,3 ServerDll = winsrv: ConServerDllInitialization,2 ProfileControl = Off MaxRequestThreads = 16`"`)

Appendix

HKEY_LOCAL_MACHINE\SYSTEM\CurrentControlSet\Control\SessionManager
This key contains keys that identify executables that are known not to work properly with Windows NT.

HKEY_LOCAL_MACHINE\SYSTEM\CurrentControlSet\Control\Setup
This key contains values established by the Windows NT setup program relating to the console video type, keyboard type, and pointer type.

HKEY_LOCAL_MACHINE\SYSTEM\CurrentControlSet\Control\TimeZoneInformation
This key contains values that define the computer's relation to Greenwich mean time (GMT).

Value	Data
ActiveTimeBias	Current offset from GMT in minutes.
Bias	Standard offset from GMT in minutes.
DaylightBias	Offset from GMT during daylight savings time.
DaylightName	Text name of the daylight savings time zone.
DaylightStart	Daylight savings start date.
StandardBias	Offset from GMT during standard time.
StandardName	Text name of the standard time zone.
StandardStart	Start date of the daylight savings time zone.

★ **HKEY_LOCAL_MACHINE\SYSTEM\CurrentControlSet\Control\Update**
Changes the policy file update mode.

Value	Data
UpdateMode	0 = Policies will not be applied. 1 = Policies are applied automatically from the validating domain controller. 2 = Policies are applied manually from a specific UNC share. This Registry key can be set in the Default Computer ➤ Network ➤ System Policies Update ➤ Remote Update section of the System Policy Editor.

HKEY_LOCAL_MACHINE\SYSTEM\CurrentControlSet\Control\VirtualDevice-Drivers
This key contains all Virtual DOS Machine (VDM) virtual device drivers from vendors who wish to provide virtual drivers for their NT-native drivers. Very few venders actually do this, and the key contains no useful data by default.

HKEY_LOCAL_MACHINE\SYSTEM\CurrentControlSet\Control\Windows

This key contains values that control the operation of the 32-bit Windows subsystem.

Value	Data
CSDVersion	Undocumented. May display the current service pack version in the second byte.
Directory	Defines the system variable that points to the system directory. ("%SystemRoot%")
ErrorMode	Controls how Windows NT handles a class of internal errors called hard system errors. 0 = Errors are display in series, and dialog boxes wait for a response from the interactive user. 1 = Nonsystem errors are handled as usual. System errors are written to the event log. No user intervention is required, and no dialog box is displayed. 2 = Errors are written to the system log, no dialogs are displayed.
NoInteractiveServices	Nonzero value will prevent services from interacting with the logged on user irrespective of service's interactive flag. (0)
ShutdownTime	Contains the date and time of the last shutdown. (New in SP4.)
SystemDirectory	Defines the location of the Win32 system directory. ("%SystemRoot%\System32")

HKEY_LOCAL_MACHINE\SYSTEM\CurrentControlSet\Control\WOW

This key contains values that control the operation of the 16-bit windows subsystem (Windows-On-Windows or WoW) that runs in the Virtual DOS Machine (VDM).

Value	Data
Cmdline	Path to the executable used to create VDMs. ("%SystemRoot%\system32\ntvdm.exe")
DefaultSeparateVDM	Specifies whether to run each 16-bit executable in a persistent shared memory environment ("no") or in a separate VDM for each 16-bit application. Speed your machine when not running VDMs and protect them from one another by setting this value to "yes."

Appendix

Value	Data
KnownDLLs	List of known 16-bit DLLs installed in NT, which replace DLLs of the same name that have been provided by vendors.
LPT_timeout	Printer timeout in seconds. If no printing activity from the VDM occurs within this period, the print handle is closed and spooling can begin.
Size	Size of VDMs in MB. 0 = Automatic.
Wowcmdline	Path to the executable used to create WoW VDMs. (`"%SystemRoot%\system32\ntvdm.exe -a %SystemRoot%\system32\krnl386"`)
Wowsize	Size in MB of the WoW VDM.

HKEY_LOCAL_MACHINE\SYSTEM\CurrentControlSet\Enum

Contains hardware configuration data for devices and drivers. This key was added to NT 4 to allow support for unified Windows 9x/NT Plug-and-Play device drivers. Do not change the information below this key.

HKEY_LOCAL_MACHINE\SYSTEM\CurrentControlSet\Hardware Profiles

Contains hardware configuration data specific to a certain profile. Also appears in HKEY_CURRENT_CONFIG.

HKEY_LOCAL_MACHINE\System\CurrentControlSet\Services\<Adapter>\ Parameters\Tcpip

These keys contain TCP/IP protocol entries specific to a network adapter. Although adapters are simply drivers, these keys can only be added to adapter drivers and so are categorized separately.

Value	Data
DontAddDefaultGateway	1 = Disables the creation of a default route for LAN adapters when PPTP is installed.
PPTPFiltering	1 = Enables PPTP filtering for this adapter.
PPTPTcpMaxDataRetransmissions	The number of times a PPTP packet will be retransmitted without acknowledgement. Value should be set higher than the default TCPMaxDataRetransmissions value to prevent dead gateway detection on congested links.

★ **HKEY_LOCAL_MACHINE\System\CurrentControlSet\Services\<Driver>**
The Services key contains keys specific to loaded services and drivers in Windows NT. Contains start-up and control information for the drivers and services loaded by Windows NT.

Value	Data
Autorun	(1) = Automatically run the autorun CD-ROM file. (CD-ROM only)
DependOnGroup	Driver groups that must be started before this driver or service can run.
DependOnService	Name of any services that must be loaded before this service.
DisplayName	Display name of the driver or service.
DriverVersion	Revision number of the driver.
ErrorControl	Determines what will happen if a driver fails to load during startup. Options are: 0 = Ignore and continue booting. 1 = Normal. Continue booting, but display a message indicating the failure. 2 = Severe. Switch to LastKnownGood, or if already in the LastKnownGood, continue. 3 = Critical. Fail the attempt to start up.
Group	Identifies the driver group to which this driver or service belongs.
ImagePath	Path to the driver.
ObjectName	Logon name of the account that runs the service when Type = 0×10 or the driver object that is used to load the driver if Type = 0×01 or 0×02.
RequestedSystem-Resources	Contains memory, IRQ, and DMA resources requested by the device.
Start	This value controls if and when the service or driver will be loaded during the boot process. 0 = Boot 1 = System 2 = Automatic 3 = Manual 4 = Disabled

Value	Data
Tag	Load order within the service or driver group. This tag is equal to the driver's position in the GroupOrderList.
Type	Service or driver type.
	0x1 = Kernel device driver.
	0x2 = File system Kernel device driver
	0x4 = Adapter arguments
	0x10 = Win32 service
	0x20 = Process sharing Win32 service

HKEY_LOCAL_MACHINE\System\CurrentControlSet\Services\<Driver>\Enum

The purpose of this key is not documented. It probably has to do with the Plug-and-Play assignment of the hardware adapter that is bound to the driver.

HKEY_LOCAL_MACHINE\System\CurrentControlSet\Services\<Driver>\Linkage

These keys determine how services and drivers interact. They are detailed more fully in the Windows NT Resource Kit. Generally, you should not modify these values.

Value	Data
Bind	Names of system objects created by the driver.
Export	Exported object interfaces.
Route	Path through the binding protocol.

HKEY_LOCAL_MACHINE\System\CurrentControlSet\Services\<Driver>\Linkage\ Disabled

This key contains information about disabled service interactions just as the previous key.

HKEY_LOCAL_MACHINE\System\CurrentControlSet\Services\<Driver>\ Parameters

This key contains keys and values specific to the service or driver.

HKEY_LOCAL_MACHINE\SYSTEM\CurrentControlSet\Services\Afd\Parameters

This key contains values specific to the Windows Sockets (WinSock) interface. Default values of some parameters are expressed in three units (small, medium, and large) that are based on the amount of RAM in the machine. All modern machines use only the last value.

Value	Data
BufferMultiplier	Priority boost for threads that AFD sets when I/O is completed.

Value	Data
DefaultReceiveWindow	Bytes to buffer before imposing flow control. Bursty large-packet applications may benefit by increasing this value, but the value can be negotiated per socket using the SO_RCVBUF option so that modifying this value is not usually necessary. (8192)
FastSendDatagramThreshold	Size below which packets are buffered on send.
IgnorePushBitOnReceives	1 = Completes all Receive operations whether or not the Push bit is set. (0)
InitialLargeBufferCount	Number of large buffers to allocate at start-up. (0/2/10)
InitialMediumBufferCount	Number of medium buffers to allocate at start-up. (2/10/30)
InitialSmallBufferCount	Number of small AFD buffers to allocated at start-up. (5/20/50)
IrpStackSize	Default IRP stack size. (4)
LargeBufferSize	Bytes to use for AFD large buffers. (4096)
MediumBufferSize	Bytes to use for medium AFD buffers. This number should match the largest MAC frame length. (1504)
SmallBuferSize	Bytes to use for small AFD buffers. This number should match the smallest MAC frame length. (64)
StandardAddressLength	Typical TDI address length. (24)
TransmitIOLength	Default chunk size for TransmitFile operations. Defaults to page size. (4K/8K/64K)

HKEY_LOCAL_MACHINE\System\CurrentControlSet\Services\Alerter\Parameters
This key contains values specific to the alerter service.

Value	Data
AlertNames	Specifies the usernames of those to whom administrative alerts should be sent as set in the Server Manager.

**HKEY_LOCAL_MACHINE\System\CurrentControlSet\Services\AppleTalk\Adapters\
<Adapter>**
This key contains values specific to AppleTalk compatible network interfaces on the computer.

Value	Data
ArpRetries	Number of address resolution tries.
DdpCheckSums	1 = Use DDP checksums.
DefaultZone	Default zone if this adapter seeds the network zone information.
NetworkRangeLowerEnd	Low end of the network number range if this adapter seeds the network.
NetworkRangeUpperEnd	High end of the network number range if this adapter seeds the network.
PortName	AppleTalk protocol name specific to this adapter.
SeedingNetwork	1 = This adapter seeds the network.
ZoneList	Zone list to seed the network with.

**HKEY_LOCAL_MACHINE\System\CurrentControlSet\Services\AppleTalk\
Parameters**
This key contains values specific to the AppleTalk service.

Value	Data
DefaultPort	The network on which Services for Macintosh names are registered. This is, by default, the first network adapter found. Change this to the network adapter attached to the Macintosh network if SFM stops working after a network adapter installation.
DesiredZone	Specifies the AppleTalk zone of the server. Default zone for the network is used if this value is not present.
EnableRouter	1 = Route AppleTalk to all interfaces. Microsoft recommends not using this feature unless absolutely necessary.

HKEY_LOCAL_MACHINE\SYSTEM\CurrentControlSet\Services\bh\Parameters
Values specific to the Network Monitor Tools and Agent.

★ **HKEY_LOCAL_MACHINE\SYSTEM\CurrentControlSet\Services\Browser\
Parameters**
Values specific to the Browser service.

Value	Data
IsDomainMaster	"TRUE" = This computer is the domain master browser.
MaintainServerList	"Yes" = Maintain server list.

**HKEY_LOCAL_MACHINE\SYSTEM\CurrentControlSet\Services\DHCP\Parameters\
Options**
Contains keys identifying the Registry locations of DHCP service parameters.

**HKEY_LOCAL_MACHINE\SYSTEM\CurrentControlSet\Services\EventLog\<Event
Log>**
Contains values identifying and controlling the Application, Security, and System event
logs.

Value	Data
File	Path to the application event log. ("%SystemRoot%\system32\config\AppEvent.Evt")
MaxSize	Maximum file size of the event log. (0x80000)
Retention	Specifies that records that are newer than this value will not be overwritten. This is what causes a log full event. This value can be set using the Event Viewer. (604800) (7 days)
Sources	List of applications that send messages to the application event log.

**HKEY_LOCAL_MACHINE\SYSTEM\CurrentControlSet\Services\EventLog\<Event
Log>\<Source>**
Contains keys identifying and controlling the sources of event log messages.

**HKEY_LOCAL_MACHINE\SYSTEM\CurrentControlSet\Services\InetInfo\
Parameters**
Contains keys controlling the functionality of the Internet Information Server adminis-
trative service.

Appendix

**HKEY_LOCAL_MACHINE\SYSTEM\CurrentControlSet\Services\MacFile\
Parameters**
This key contains values specific to the Service for Macintosh service. These values can be set using the Server Manager, the File manager, or directly in the Registry. See Knowledge Base article Q102996 for more information.

★ **HKEY_LOCAL_MACHINE\System\CurrentControlSet\Services\LanManServer\
Parameters**

Value	Data
AutoShareServer	1 = Create hidden administrative shares (c$, etc.). Specific to NT Server. This value can be set in the Windows NT Network\Sharing\Create hidden drive shares (server) section of the System Policy Editor
AutoShareWks	1 = Create hidden administrative shares (c$, etc.). Specific to NT Workstation. This value can be set in the Windows NT Network\Sharing\Create hidden drive shares (workstation) section of the System Policy Editor.
EnableFCOpens	1 = Combine MS-DOS file control blocks into a single open. May be necessary for older MS-DOS network applications.
EnableSoftCompat	1 = Map compatibility open request to normal open request. Some MS-DOS network applications may require this.
IRPstackSize	Allocated stack size for the SRV service to share to NT clients. Not present = default (4). Gradually increase this value if you get Not Enough Server Storage is Available to Process This Command errors.
Lmannounce	1 = Enable browser announcements to Lan Manager 2.x clients.
NullSessionPipes	List of null session pipes that are exempt from anonymous use restrictions.
NullSessionShares	List of shares that can be attached to by anonymous (null session) clients.
OplockBreakWait	Seconds to wait for client to respond to an oplock break request. Lower values detect dead clients faster but risk losing cached data. (35)
ScavTimeout	Time that the scavenger remains idle before waking up to service requests.
ThreadPriority	Server thread priority in relation to base priority.

★ **HKEY_LOCAL_MACHINE\SYSTEM\CurrentControlSet\Services\LanmanServer\ Shares**

Controls sharing of directories and printers on this system.

Value	Data
<Share Name>	String parameter list of maximum users, path to share, share permissions, and share type.

HKEY_LOCAL_MACHINE\System\CurrentControlSet\Services\LanmanWorkstation\ Parameters

This key contains values relating to the network redirector. Most of these values pertain to file locking and caching operations and should only be changed by application developers to tune their applications.

Value	Data
BufFilesDenyWrite	(1) = Buffer shared files opened only for read access.
BufNamedPipes	(1) = Buffer character named pipe operations.
BufReadOnlyFiles	(1) = Buffer shared read-only files.
CacheFileTimeout	Maximum time a close file will be left in the cache. (10)
CharWait	Time to wait for a named pipe to become available. (3,600)
CollectionTime	Maximum time that write cached data will remain in a character mode pipe. (250)
DormantFileLimit	Maximum files to leave open on a share after an application has closed them.
IllegalDatagramResetTime	Window for merging illegal datagrams into one log entry. (60)
KeepConn	Maximum time a connection can be dormant. (600)
LockIncrement	Rate at which the redirector ramps back failed lock operations from OS/2 applications. (10)
LockMaximum	Maximum number of nonblocking requests a server will receive from an application.
LockQuota	Maximum read bytes for applications using lock-and-read operations (4,096)
LogElectionPackets	1 = Generate events when browser receives election packets.

Appendix

Value	Data
MailSlotsBuffers	Maximum mailslot buffers. (5)
MaxCmds	Maximum work buffers. Increase for applications that use more simultaneous network operations. (15)
MaxCollectionCount	Writes smaller than this number of bytes are buffered to improve performance. (16)
NumIllegalDatagramEvents	Maximum number of illegal datagram events to log within IllegalDatagramResetTime. (5)
OtherDomains	Other LAN Manager domains to be listed for browsing.
PipeIncrement	Rate at which Workstation service backs off failing nonblocking pipe reads. (10)
PipeMaximum	Maximum time to back off failed non-blocking pipe reads.
ReadAheadThroughput	Throughput required before cache manager enables read-ahead buffering.
ServerAnnounceBuffers	Maximum buffers used to process server announcements. (20)
SessTimeout	Maximum short-term outstanding operation time. (45)
SizCharBuf	Bytes written into character mode buffers. (512)
Use512ByteMaxTransfer	(0) = Use server negotiated buffer size rather than a maximum of 512 bytes per request.
UseLockReadUnlock	(1) = Carry out automatic locks and unlocks after read and write operations.
UseOpportunisticLocking	(1) = Use opportunistic locking.
UseRawRead	(1) = Use raw reads.
UseRawWrite	(1) = Use raw writes.
UseUnlockBehind	(1) = Use opportunistic unlocking on the client.
UtilizeNTCaching	(1) = Use cache manager to cache the contents of files.

**HKEY_LOCAL_MACHINE\SYSTEM\CurrentControlSet\Services\MSFTPSVC\
Parameters**

Parameters pertaining to the FTP service.

Value	Data
AllowGuestAccess	1 = Allow guest access.
AnnotateDirectories	1 = Enable directory annotation. This displays the contents of the file named .ckm located in the annotated directory.
EnablePortAttack	Undocumented.
InstallPath	Installation path of the IIS services.
MajorVersion	IIS version.
MinorVersion	IIS Minor version.

**HKEY_LOCAL_MACHINE\SYSTEM\CurrentControlSet\Services\MSFTPSVC\
Parameters\Virtual Roots**

Contains the list of FTP service virtual root directories.

Value	Data
<Directory Root>	Path to directory Root.

HKEY_LOCAL_MACHINE\SYSTEM\CurrentControlSet\Services\Nbf\Parameters

This key contains values specific to the NetBEUI protocol.

Value	Data
AddNameQueryRetries	Times NBF will retry add_name_query and add_group_name_query packets. (3)
AddNameQueryTimeout	Time between AddNameQueryRetries in 100ns units.
AllRoutesNameRecognized	00000000.
DefaultT1Timeout	Time to wait for a response after sending LLC poll packet before retrying.
DefaultT2Timeout	Delay to respond after receiving LLC poll packet.
DefaultTiTimeout	Inactive link-alive poll delay.
GeneralRetries	Times to retry status_query and find_name packets. (3)
GeneralTimeout	Time between GeneralRetries in 100ns units.

Appendix

Value	Data
InitAddresses	Initial NetBIOS name memory allocations. (0) = No limit.
InitAddressFiles	Initial NetBIOS address files. (0) = No limit.
InitConnections	Initial connections to allocate. (1) = Automatically allocate.
InitLinks	Initial LLC link allocations. System will adjust as necessary. (2)
InitReceiveBuffers	Initial receive buffer allocation. (5)
InitReceivePackets	Initial receive packet buffers to allocate. (10)
InitRequests	Initial requests to allocate. (5)
InitSendPackets	Initial send packet buffers to allocate. (30) Increase if "send packets exhausted" counter increases in Performance Monitor.
InitUIFrames	Initial UI frames to allocate. (5)
LlcMaxWindowSize	LLC I frames to send before polling and waiting for a response. (10) Adjust if NBF communicates over a highly unreliable network.
LlcRetries	Number of polling retries after a T1 timeout before closing the link. (8)
MaxAddresses	Maximum NetBIOS name allocations for this machine. (0) = No limit.
MaxAddressFiles	Maximum NetBIOS name address files for this machine. Files correspond to connections. (0) = No limit.
MaxConnections	Maximum connections. (0) = No limit.
MaximumIncomingFrames	Maximum frames before ACK. (2)
MaxLinks	Maximum links for this computer. (0) = No limit.
MinimumT1Timeout	Mandatory wait time for poll response packet.
NameQueryRetries	Name_query packet retries. (3)
NameQueryTimeout	Time between NameQueryRetries.

Value	Data
NbProvider	Identifies the NetBIOS provider. ("_nb")
QueryWithoutSource Routing	Send queries without source routing info to support Token Ring bridges that cannot forward source-routed packets.
UseDixOverEthernet	Use DIX encoding vice IEEE 802.3 MAC frames over Ethernet. (0) = False.
WanNameQueryRetries	Name_query retries over RAS. (5)

★ **HKEY_LOCAL_MACHINE\SYSTEM\CurrentControlSet\Services\NDIS\Parameters**

The solitary value in this key determines how deferred procedure calls (DPCs) generated by interrupts are handled in multiprocessor systems. Because DPCs are cascading events from interrupts, the local processor cache will already contain the local processor information required to handle the DPC in many cases. For this reason DPCs should usually be handled on the processor that handled the interrupt for maximum efficiency.

Value	Data
ProcessorAffinityMask	Bit mask for processors that will handle shared interrupts in a multiprocessor system. (0xFFFFFFFF) = Distribute DPCs across all processors. (0) = Handle DPCs on the processor that handled the source interrupt.

HKEY_LOCAL_MACHINE\SYSTEM\CurrentControlSet\Services\NetBT\Adapters\ <Adapter>

This key contains values specific to the NetBIOS over TCP/IP driver and a specific network interface.

Value	Data
DhcpNameServer	IP address of WINS server as provided by DHCP. Not user configurable.
DhcpNameServerBackup	As above, secondary WINS server.
NameServer	IP address of the primary WINS server. Overrides DCHP parameter if present.
NameServerBackup	As above, secondary WINS server.

HKEY_LOCAL_MACHINE\SYSTEM\CurrentControlSet\Services\NetBT\Parameters
This key contains values that are specific to the NetBIOS over TCP/IP driver.

Value	Data
BcastNameQueryCount	Times to retry broadcast name queries. (3)
BcastQueryTimeout	Time between BcastNameQueryCount in milliseconds. (750)
BroadcastAddress	Global parameter to set the broadcast address for all subnets.
CacheTimeout	Time to cache names in the remote name table in milliseconds. (600,000)
DhcpNodeType	DHCP provided NodeType. Not user configurable.
DhcpScopeId	DHCP provided ScopeID. Not user configurable.
EnableDns	1 = Query DNS for names after other lookups fail. (0)
EnableLMHOSTS	1 = Search LMHOSTS for name resolution. (0)
EnableProxy	1 = Act as proxy name server for bound NetBT networks. A proxy name server allows broadcast client. (0)
EnableProxyRegCheck	1 = Deny name broadcast name registrations that are different than the existing name to address mapping.
InitialRefreshTimeout	Initial name registration refresh timeout.
LmhostsTimeout	Timeout value for DNS and LMHOSTS name queries in milliseconds. (6)
MaxDgramBuffering	Maximum memory to use for outstanding datagram transmits. (0x20,000) (128K)
NameServerPort	TCP/IP port to listen for name service packets. (137)
NameSrvQueryCount	Times to retry name queries to a WINS server. (3)
NameSrvQueryTimeout	Time between NameSrvQueryCount. (1,500)
NbProvider	RPC parameter indicating the transport used by NetBT. ("_tcp"). Do not change this value.
NodeType	Node type for name resolution: 1 = b-node 2 = p-node 4 = m-node 8 = h-node

Value	Data
RandomAdapter	1 = Randomize IP address in responses to name queries to load balance between two adapters on the same net.
RefreshOpCode	Force NetBT to use a specific name refresh packet opcode. This key is not well documented and should be left in its default state.
ScopeID	NetBIOS DNS name scope for the node. "*" = Null scope. Overrides DHCP.
SessionKeepAlive	Interval between keep-alive packets in milliseconds. 0xFFFFFFFF = Disable keep-alives. (3600000) (1h)
SingleResponse	1 = Only supply IP address from a single interface in name query responses.
Size/Small/Medium/Large	Size of the name table used to store local and remote names. (1) 1 = 16 (small) 2 = 128 (medium) 3 = 256 (large)
TransportBindName	Partial path to the transport object. Do not change this value. ("\Device\")
WinsDownTimeout	Time to wait before retrying to contact a WINS server in milliseconds. (15,000)

HKEY_LOCAL_MACHINE\SYSTEM\CurrentControlSet\Services\Netlogon\Parameters

Values specific to the NetLogon service.

Value	Data
DBFlag	Enable logging of NetLogon service to netlogon.log in the NetLogon share directory. Used only for debugging builds of Netlogon.dll.
DisablePassword Change	1 = Disable weekly machine account password change initiation from workstations or member servers. Machine accounts normally change passwords automatically every seven days. See Knowledge Base article Q154501 for information. (0)

Value	Data
ExpectedDialupDelay	Seconds before interactive logons timeout declaring domain controller cannot be found.
PulseInterval	Frequency at which Domain controllers transmit changes to the SAM in seconds. Decrease this value for cost/per/transmit WANs. (3,600) (1h)
Randomize	Wait seconds before BDCs should respond to PDC update messages. This is a form of collision avoidance. (30)
RefusePassword Change	1 = Refuse requests for weekly machine account password change from workstations or member servers. (0)
RequireSignOrSeal	(0) = Require Signed or Sealed channel. This should only be set if all domain controllers in all trusted domains support signing and sealing (i.e. are updated to SP4)
Scripts	Location of logon scripts. ("%SystemRoot%\system32\repl\import\scripts")
SealSecureChannel	(1) = Encrypt all outgoing secure channel traffic if domain controller supports it
SignSecureChannel	(1) = Sign all outgoing secure channel traffic if domain controller supports it
TrustedDomainList	List of domains that this domain controller trusts.
Update	"Yes" = Fully synchronize the SAM among domain controllers upon start-up. ("No")

HKEY_LOCAL_MACHINE\SYSTEM\CurrentControlSet\Services\NWCWorkstation\ networkprovider

Network provider values for the gateway or client services for NetWare (CSNW).

Value	Data
Class	Bitflag determining the network services provided by this redirector. (11)
DeviceName	Object name of the device driver. ("\Device\nwrdr")
Name	Provider description ("NetWare or Compatible Network")

Value	Data
NWCompatible-Authentication	(1) = Use NetWare compatible authentication.
ProviderPath	Path the network provider DLL. ("%SystemRoot%\System32\nwprovau.dll")

HKEY_LOCAL_MACHINE\SYSTEM\CurrentControlSet\Services\NWCWorkstation\ parameters

Values for the gateway or client services for NetWare redirector.

Value	Data
CurrentUser	SID of the logged-on user.
DisablePopup	1 = Disable NetWare broadcast messages equal to CASTOFF ALL in the NetWare redirector.
MaxBurstSize	Maximum packets to burst before requiring acknowledgement. 0 = Burst mode off.

HKEY_LOCAL_MACHINE\SYSTEM\CurrentControlSet\Services\NwlnkIpx\NetConfig\ <Adapter>

Values specific to the NWLink IPX compatible TDI compliant transport protocol for each installed network adapter.

Value	Data
AdapterName	Name of the NWLink adapter.
BindSap	Ethertype for Ethernet II frame types. (33,079)
EnableFuncaddr	(1) = Use IPX Functional Address for Token Ring adapters.
MaxPktSize	0 = Automatic
NetworkNumber	IPX network number for this adapter.
PktType	MAC frame type. 0 = Ethernet II 1 = Ethernet_802.3 2 = 802.3 3 = Ethernet SNAP 4 = Arcnet

Appendix

Value	Data
SourceRouteBcast	Source route to transmit packets to the broadcast MAC address. (0) = single-route 1 = All-routes broadcast
SourceRouteDef	Source route to transmit packet to a unique MAC address that does not appear in the source routing table. (0) = Single route 1 = All-routes broadcast
SourceRouteMcast	Source route to transmit packets to the multicast MAC address. (0) = Single route 1 = All-routes broadcast
SourceRouting	(1) = Enable source routing for Token Ring adapters.

HKEY_LOCAL_MACHINE\System\CurrentControlSet\Services\NWLinkIPX\Parameters

Values specific to the NWLink IPX compatible TDI compliant transport protocol.

Value	Data
ConnectionCount	Number of times an SPX probe will be sent when connecting to a remote node before an error occurs.
ConnectionTimeout	Time in half seconds between connection probe transmissions.
DedicatedRouter	1 = Computer is dedicated to router and has no services running on it.
DisableDialinNetbios	1 = IPX does not forward NetBIOS type 20 packets over RAS connections. Some NetBIOS applications may require enabling to operate properly.
DisableDialoutSap	1 = IPX does not transmit SAP announcements and responses on RAS connections.
EnableWANRouter	1 = Route IPX broadcasts over RAS links.
EthernetPadToEven	1 = Pad Ethernet frames to even length for older ODI cards. (1)
InitDatagrams	Number of datagrams initially allocated by IPX.
KeepAliveCount	Retry keep-alive probe before timing out. (8)

Value	Data
KeepAliveTimeout	Time between KeepAlive transmits in half-seconds. (12)
MaxDatagrams	Number of datagram buffers allocated by NWLink. (50)
RipAgeTime	Delay before requesting RIP update in minutes. (5)
RipCount	Retry RIP request before giving up. RIP is the IPX automatic routing table update protocol for IPX similar to RIP for IP. (5)
RipRoute	(1) = Enable IPX RIP updates.
RipTableSize	Number of entries in the RIP table. (7)
RipTimeout	Time between RIP requests in half-seconds. (1)
RipUsageTime	Delay before deleting old routing table entry in minutes. (15)
SingleNetoworkActive	1 = Both RAS and network adapter cannot be active at the same time. Allows CSNW to locate NetWare servers through RAS link. (0)
SocketEnd	End range for auto-assigned sockets. (24575)
SocketStart	Start range for auto-assigned sockets. (16384)
SocketUniqueness	Number of sockets to reserve when auto-assigning a socket. (8)
SourceRouteUsageTime	Delay before deleting Token Ring source routes. (15)
VirtualNetworkNumber	Computer's virtual network number.
WindowSize	Seed value for SPX allocation field. (4)

HKEY_LOCAL_MACHINE\SYSTEM\CurrentControlSet\Services\NwlnkNb
Parameters

NWLink NetBIOS values. This key was named NWNBLink in versions before NT 4.0.

Value	Data
AckDelayTime	Start value of the delayed acknowledgement time. Default or no entry is 250.
AckWindow	Frames to receive before acknowledgment. Can be set to zero for fast links. (Default or no entry is 2).

Appendix

Value	Data
AckWindowThreshold	Specifies how many milliseconds an Ack roundtrip should take. If the time exceeds the threshold, automatic acknowledgements are necessary. If set to zero, AckWindow is relied upon. (500)
BroadcastCount	Number of times to transmit a broadcast. (3) Broadcast count is doubled if Internet is enabled.
BroadcastTimeout	Time between transmission of find-name requests in half-seconds. (1)
ConnectionCount	Number of times to send a connection probe. (5) Doubled if Internet is set enabled.
ConnectionTimeout	Half seconds between connection probes during session initiation. (2)
EnablePiggyBackAck	1 = Reciever automatically acknowledges upon detecting the end of an inbound NetBIOS message. (1)
Extensions	1 = Use NWNBLink extensions.
InitialRetransmissionTime	Milliseconds between initial transmission retries. (500)
Internet	1 = Packet type is 0x14 (WAN broadcast) rather than 0x04. Also doubles the timings of numerous connection flow control settings.
KeepAliveCount	Number of attempted session-alive packets before timing out. (8)
KeepAliveTimeout	Half-seconds between session-alive packets. (60)
NbProvider	Object name of the NetBIOS network provider ("_ipx"). Do not change this value.
RcvWindowMax	Number of packets that can be received before acknowledgment. (4)
RetransmitMax	Retries before timing out due to bad link. (8)

**HKEY_LOCAL_MACHINE\SYSTEM\CurrentControlSet\Services\NwlnkSpx\
Parameters**

Values for the SPX services of the NWLink transport driver.

Value	Data
ConnectionCount	Times to probe when connecting to a remote node before erroring out. (5)
ConnectionTimeout	Time between probe attempts in half-seconds. (2)
InitialRetransmissionTime	Wait for acknowledgement delay before sending probe in milliseconds. (500)
InitPackets	Initial packet buffer allocations. (5)
KeepAliveCount	Keep-alive probes before timing out. (8)
KeepAliveTimeout	Time between keep-alives in half seconds. (12)
MaxPackets	Maximum packet buffers that SPX will allocate.
MaxPacketSize	Maximum packet size that SPX will negotiate with a remote node. (4096)
RetransmissionCount	Probes to send waiting for data ACK. (8)
SpxSocketEnd	Auto-assigned socket end boundary. (32767)
SpxSocketStart	Auto-assigned socket start boundary. (24576)
WindowSize	Seed value for SPX socket allocation field. (4)

**HKEY_LOCAL_MACHINE\SYSTEM\CurrentControlSet\Services\NwlnkRip\
Parameters**

Values for the NWLink RIP routing information protocol.

Value	Data
NetbiosRouting	Controls IPX NetBIOS broadcast forwarding. 0 = None (2) = Forward from RAS client to the network 4 = Forward from network to the RAS client 6 = Both 2 and 4

**HKEY_LOCAL_MACHINE\SYSTEM\CurrentControlSet\Services\RasMan\
Parameters**

Values for the RAS Manager.

Value	Data
Logging	1 = Log all RAS communications to %systemroot%\system32\device.log.

Appendix

★ **HKEY_LOCAL_MACHINE\SYSTEM\CurrentControlSet\Services\RasMan\PPP**
Values for the Point-to-Point protocol.

Value	Data
DisableSoftware Compression	1 = Disable software compression. (0)
ForceEncrypted Password	(1) = Use CHAP for authentication. 0 = Use PAP.
Logging	1 = Log all PPP events to %systemroot\system32\ras\ppp.log.
MaxConfigure	Times to retry configure_request packets before giving up. (10)
MaxFailure	Times to retry configure_nak packets without sending a configure_ack packet before assuming that a ppp session cannot be established. (10)
MaxReject	Times to retry config_rejects before assuming that a ppp session cannot be established. (5)
MaxTerminate	Times to retry terminate_requests before giving up. (2)
NegotiateTime	Window for ppp session establishment before giving up and disconnecting the line. 0 = Never hang up. (150)
RestartTimer	Window in seconds for transmission of configure_request and terminate_request packets before timing out and starting over. (3)

HKEY_LOCAL_MACHINE\System\CurrentControlSet\Services\RemoteAccess\Parameters
Values for the Remote Access service.

Value	Data
AuthenticateRetries	Number of retries. This value can be set in the Windows NT Remote Access Maximum number of unsuccessful authentication retries section of the System Policy Editor. (2)
AuthenticateTime	Time in seconds to authenticate. (120)
AutoDisconnect	Idle time in minutes before disconnection. This value can be set in the Windows NT Remote Access Auto disconnect section of the System Policy Editor.

Value	Data
CallbackTime	Call back time in seconds. This value can be set in the Windows NT Remote Access wait interval for callback section of the System Policy Editor.
EnableAudit	(1) = Auditing to event log enabled.
NetbiosGatewayEnabled	(1) = Enable NetBIOS Gateway so RAS clients can access other internal network nodes.

HKEY_LOCAL_MACHINE\System\CurrentControlSet\Services\RemoteAccess\Parameters\NetbiosGateway

Values for the gateway function of the Remote Access service.

Value	Data
DisableMcastFwd WhenSessionTraffic	(1) = Multicast datagrams are only transmitted when the link is not in use for session traffic.
EnableBroadcast	1 = Forward broadcasts over RAS link. (0)
EnableNetbiosSessions-Auditing	1 = Enable auditing of sessions. (0)
MaxBcastDg Buffered	Gateway-buffered broadcast datagrams. (32)
MaxDgBuffered PerGroupName	Buffered datagrams per group name. (10)
MaxDynMem	Maximum memory to allocate per session. (640K)
MaxNames	Maximum unique names per client. (255)
MaxSessions	Maximum sessions per client. (255)
MultiCastForward Rate	Controls multicast forwarding to RAS clients. -1 = Disable forwarding. 0 = Guarantee delivery. $0<n<32767$ = Forward every x seconds.
NumRecvQueryIndications	Number of simultaneous network connections each client can establish. (3)
RcvDgSubmitted PerGroupName	Maximum Receive Datagram NetBIOS commands per group name. (3)
RemoteListen	RAS client accessibility to network clients. 0 = No Access. (1) = Server and Messenger services are open. 2 = All NetBIOS services open.
SizWorkBufs	Size of work buffers, optimized for SMB. (4,500)

Appendix

HKEY_LOCAL_MACHINE\System\CurrentControlSet\Services\RemoteAccess\Parameters\IP

IP related values for the Remote Access service.

Value	Data
AllowClientNetwork Access	(1) = Allow remote clients to access the remote network through the RAS server using TCP/IP.
AllowIPClientIP Address	1 = Allow remote clients to request a specific IP address.
IPAddressEnd	IP address of the end of the assignment pool.
IPAddressStart	IP address of the start of the assignment pool.
UseDHCPAddressing	1 = Use DHCP to assign client IP addresses.

HKEY_LOCAL_MACHINE\SYSTEM\CurrentControlSet\Services\Rdr\Parameters

Values for the Redirector (workstation) service.

Value	Data
ConnectionTimeout	Maximum seconds for connect or disconnect completion. (300)
LowerSearchBufferSize	Byte to use for small searches. (16K)
LowerSearchThreshold	Minimum search size. Smaller sizes are at least this large. (16K)
StackSize	Default IRP stack size. (4)
UpperSearchBufferSize	Bytes to use for large searches. (32K)
UseAsyncWriteBehind	(1) = Enable async–write-behind.
UseWriteBehind	(1) = Use write-behind.

HKEY_LOCAL_MACHINE\SYSTEM\CurrentControlSet\Services\RelayAgent\Parameters

Values for the DHCP Relay Agent service. These values are undocumented.

Value	Data
DHCPServers	IP address of known DHCP servers.
EnableTracing	1 = Enable tracing of relayed DHCP packets?
HopsThreshold	Max relays before dropping packet? (4)
LogMessages	1 = Log messages (to Event Viewer?)
SecsThreshold	Maximum seconds before dropping packet? (4)

HKEY_LOCAL_MACHINE\SYSTEM\CurrentControlSet\Services\Replicator
Parameters
Values used for the Replication service.

Value	Data
ExportList	Semicolon separated list of servers or domains to notify when the export directory is updated. Null = Local domain notified.
ExportPath	Path to the replication export share.
GuardTime	Minutes the directory must be unchanged before replication is initiated. (2)
ImportList	Semicolon separated list of servers or domains to notify when the import directory is updated. Null = Local domain notified.
ImportPath	Path to the replication import path.
Interval	Minutes between change checks by export server. (5)
PulseConcurrency	Times last update is sent. (3)
Random	The upper boundary of the seed value from the export server for wait time before import server requests an update. This is a form of collision avoidance. (60)
Replicate	Controls the replication service. This value should be changed only by the system. 0 = None 1 = Export 2 = Import 3 = Both

HKEY_LOCAL_MACHINE\SYSTEM\CurrentControlSet\Services\SimpTcp
Parameters
Values that control the simple TCP/IP services. These values are undocumented but fairly obvious.

Value	Data
EnableMultipleThreads	1 = Spawn new thread per connection.
EnableTcpChargen	1 = Enable chargen service over TCP.
EnableTcpDaytime	1 = Enable daytime service over TCP.
EnableTcpDiscard	1 = Enable discard service over TCP.

Appendix

Value	Data
EnableTcpEcho	1 = Enable echo service TCP.
EnableTcpQotd	1 = Enable quote service over TCP.
EnableUdpChargen	1 = Enable chargen service over UDP.
EnableUdpDaytime	1 = Enable daytime service over UDP.
EnableUdpDiscard	1 = Enable discard service over UDP.
EnableUdpEcho	1 = Enable echo service over UDP.
EnableUdpQotd	1 = Enable quote service over UDP.
IoBufferSize	Buffer size (per connection?) (8,192)
MaxIdleTicks	Maximum idle time (milliseconds?) before a non-responsive socket is killed. (600,000) (10m?)
MaxTcpClients	Maximum clients for all simple TCP/IP services. This prevents simple services from being exploited by certain denial of service attacks. (16)
QotdFileName	Filename containing quotes to serve. ("%SystemRoot%\ system32\drivers\etc\quotes")
SelectTimeout	0000012c

HKEY_LOCAL_MACHINE\System\CurrentControlSet\Services\SNMP\Parameters\ PermittedManagers

Contains incremental values starting at 1. Data is the text of a permitted manager. This value can be set in the System\SNMP\Permitted Managers section of the System Policy Editor.

HKEY_LOCAL_MACHINE\System\CurrentControlSet\Services\SNMP\Parameters\ TrapConfiguration\Public

Contains incremental values starting at 1. Data is the text of a trap configuration. This value can be set in the System\SNMP\Traps for Public Community section of the System Policy Editor.

HKEY_LOCAL_MACHINE\System\CurrentControlSet\Services\SNMP\Parameters\ ValidCommunities

Contains incremental values starting at 1. Data associated with each value is the text of the valid community. This value can be set in the System\SNMP\Communities section of the System Policy Editor.

HKEY_LOCAL_MACHINE\SYSTEM\CurrentControlSet\Services\Streams
Parameters
Values used by the Streams environment.

Value	Description
MaxMemoryUsage	Max memory the Streams environment will allocate before failing further requests.

HKEY_LOCAL_MACHINE\SYSTEM\CurrentControlSet\Services\Tcpip\Parameters
Values used by the TCP/IP TDI compliant transport protocol.

Value	Description
ArpAlwaysSourceRoute	1 = TCP/IP transmits ARP requests with source routing on Token Ring networks.
ArpCacheLife	Seconds for arp entries to die in arp cache. (120) = Unused entry. (600) = Used entry.
ArpTRSingleRoute	1 = Send Token Ring source routed broadcasts as single-route vice all-route. (0)
ArpUseEtherSNAP	1 = TransmitArp requests using Ethernet SNAP frames vice DIX frames. (0)
Class	(8) = TCP/IP provides name service.
DatabasePath	Path to Internet configuration files hosts, lmhosts, networks, protocols, services ("%SystemRoot%\ System32\drivers\etc")
DefaultTOS	Default type of service parameter for outgoing IP packets. See RFC 791. (0)
DefaultTTL	Default time to live value for outgoing IP packets. (128)
Domain	DNS Domain of local host.
EnableDeadGW Detect	(1) = Change to backup gateway if transmits through current gateway seem unresponsive.
EnablePMTUBH Detect	1 = Use protocol to detect black hole routers that fail to properly implement the IP. "Don't fragment" flag. (0)
EnablePMTUDiscovery	(1) = Use protocol to discover largest packet size (Maximum Transmission Unit) to remote host.
EnableSecurityFilters	1 = Security filtering enabled. (0)
ForwardBroadcasts	Ignored parameter.

Appendix

Value	Description
ForwardBuffer Memory	Initial router buffer size. (74,240)
Hostname	DNS name of local host.
IGMPLevel	Multicast support. 0 = No support. 1 = Transmit only. (2) = Transmit and receive.
IPEnableRouter	1 = This host acts as a router. (0)
KeepAliveInterval	Milliseconds between unacknowledged keep-alive packets. (1000) (1s)
KeepAliveTime	Milliseconds between acknowledged keep-alive packets. (7,200,000) (2h)
MaxForward Pending	Maximum simultaneous IP packets waiting to be forwarded to a specific interface. (20)
MaxForwardBuffer Memory	Maximum router buffer size. (0xFFFFFFFF) (4GB)
MaxNumForward Packets	Maximum packet headers allocated for the router packet queue.
MaxUserPort	Highest port number to be used when any available port is requested. (5,000)
MTU	Maximum packet size. NT uses auto MTU detection, so modifying this value is not recommended.
NameServer	List of space-separated IP addresses of name servers.
NumForward Packets	Number of IP packet headers allocated for the router packet queue. (50)
PPTPFiltering	1 = Enable PPTP filtering (only PPTP packets are accepted by the host).
PPTPTcpMaxData Retransmissions	PPTP packet retransmission retries. This value should be higher than TCPMaxDataRetransmissions to prevent slow links from appearing dead.
SearchList	List of DNS domains to append to failed simple name resolutions. Use "com net org" for Internet hosts if you don't use DNS for WINS resolution. ("")
TcpMaxConnect Retransmissions	TCP connection attempts before erroring out. Initial timeout of 3 seconds is doubled after each attempt. (3)

Value	Description
TcpMaxData Retransmissions	TCP retransmit packet attempts before erroring out. (5)
TcpNum Connections	Maximum simultaneous TCP connections.
TcpTimedWait Delay	Maximum time a connection will wait for closure. See RFC 793.
TcpUseRFC1122 UrgentPointer	1 = Use RFC1122 vice. 0 = BSD interpretation of urgent data mode. (0)
TcpWindowSize	Max bytes transmitted without ACK. Increased values improve Internet performance. (8,760)

HKEY_LOCAL_MACHINE\SYSTEM\CurrentControlSet\Services\Tcpip\Parameters\ PersistentRoutes

List of persistent routes programmed using the route command. The value contains all information and the data field is null. Value follows this syntax:

```
<destination address>,<mask>,<gateway>
```

HKEY_LOCAL_MACHINE\SYSTEM\CurrentControlSet\Services\Tcpip\ ServiceProvider

Value	Description
Class	(8) = TCP/IP provides name service.
DnsPriority	DNS name resolution priority versus other name resolvers. (2,000)
HostsPriority	Hosts file name resolution priority versus other name resolvers. (500)
LocalPriority	NetBIOS name cache name resolution priority versus other resolvers. (499)
Name	Transport name. ("TCP/IP")
NetbtPriority	NetBT (WINS) name resolution priority versus other resolvers. (2,001)
ProviderPath	DLL for name resolution. ("%SystemRoot%\System32\wsock32.dll")

HKEY_LOCAL_MACHINE\SYSTEM\CurrentControlSet\Services\UPS

The UPS service stores its parameters in the service key name rather than the parameter subkey. Additional values are the following:

Value	Description
BatteryLife	Life, in minutes, of the backup battery when fully charged. (2)
CommandFile	Name of command file to execute before shutting down.
FirstMessageDelay	Seconds to delay first message that is waiting for normal power restoration. (5)
MessageInterval	Seconds between messages. (120)
Options	Bit mask of selected options. 1 = Installed. 2 = Power fail signal. 4 = Low battery signal. 8 = Can turn off. 16 = Positive signal on power fail. 32 = Positive signal on low battery. 64 = Positive signal on shut off. 128 = Use command file.
Port	Com port to which UPS is attached. ("COM1:")
RechargeRate	Minutes till UPS is fully recharged. (100)

HKEY_LOCAL_MACHINE\SYSTEM\CurrentControlSet\Services\Wins\Parameters

Values used for the Windows Internet Name Service.

Value	Description
BackupDirPath	Path to the backup directory.
BurstHandling	1 = Use protocol to delay large number of short period name registrations. (0)
DbFileNm	Full path for the WINS database file.
DoBackupOnTerm	1 = Backup database on WINS service stop. (0)
DoStaticDataInit	1 = Initialize database with values listed under the \datafiles key. (0)
InitTimePause	1 = Pause until first replication. (0)
LogDetailedEvents	1 = Verbose log entries.

Value	Description
LogFilePath	Directory path for WINS log files. ("%SystemRoot%\System32\WINS")
LoggingOn	(1) = Log changes to jet.log.
McastIntvl	Seconds to announce presence to peer WINS servers. (2,400)
McastTTL	Router hops that announcement can make.
MigrateOn	Treat old static, unique, and multi-homed records as dynamic when a new registration or replica appears.
NoOfWrkThds	Number of worker threads that can be created to handle name queries.
PriorityClassHigh	1 = WINS is high-priority service. (0)

HKEY_LOCAL_MACHINE\SYSTEM\CurrentControlSet\Services\Wins\Parameters\ConsistencyCheck

Values used to enable automatic WINS database consistency checking among WINS servers.

Value	Description
MaxRecsAtATime	Maximum records to replicate in a single consistency check cycle. (30,000)
SpTime	Day time for first consistency check. (2:00:00)
TimeInterval	Seconds between consistency checks. (86,400) (24h)
UseRplPnrs	1 = Contact only pull partners vice record owner. (0)

HKEY_LOCAL_MACHINE\SYSTEM\CurrentControlSet\Services\Wins\Parameters\Datafiles

Data files use by the WINS server to initialize its dynamic database.

HKEY_LOCAL_MACHINE\SYSTEM\CurrentControlSet\Services\Wins\Partners\Pull

List of servers that this server pulls replica names from and from which it can expect updates.

Value	Data
OnlyDynRecs	1 = Only dynamic records can be replicated.
RefreshInterval	Minutes between client name reregistrations. (5,760) (96h)

Appendix

Value	Data
RplOnlyWCnfPnrs	(1) = Replicate only with servers listed under push/pull keys.
TombStoneInterval	Delay before extinction of a released entry. (5,460) (96h)
TombStoneTimeout	Delay before extinct entries are removed from the database. (5460) (96h)
UseSelfFndPnrs	1 = Auto find other WINS servers and configure as push/pull partners through routers that support multi-casting. (0)
VerifyInterval	Interval to verify that unowned old names are still active. (2,073,600) (24 days)

HKEY_LOCAL_MACHINE\SYSTEM\CurrentControlSet\Services\Wins\Partners\Push

List of servers to which this server pushes replica names.

Value	Data
InitTimerReplication	1 = Inform partners of database status on start-up.
MemberPrec	1 = High relative address precedence in an Internet name group.
RplOnAddressChg	1 = Inform partners when address changes in mapping record.
UpdateCount	Number of changes to locally owned records before partners are informed.

HKEY_LOCAL_MACHINE\SYSTEM\CurrentControlSet\Services\WinSock\Parameters

Values pertaining to the Windows Sockets Interface.

Value	Data
Transports	List of bound transports.

★ **HKEY_LOCAL_MACHINE\SYSTEM\DISK**

This key stores information about disks, partitions, and volumes as maintained by the Disk Administrator. This key is backed up onto the emergency backup disk. Values under this key should never be directly edited.

HKEY_LOCAL_MACHINE\SYSTEM\Select

This key identifies which control set is current and which is LastKnownGood.

Value	Data
Current	ControlSet that is current. (1)
Default	ControlSet that is the default start-up control set. (1)
Failed	ControlSet that failed and caused fallover to LastKnownGood. (0)
LastKnownGood	ControlSet last known to boot completely besides the current control set. (2)

HKEY_USERS

This key contains all active loaded user profiles. HKEY_CURRENT_USER is a pointer to one of these profiles. See values under HKEY_CURRENT_USER.

HKEY_Users\<UserSID>\Software\Microsoft\Windows\CurrentVersion\Policies\ System

Value	Description
NoDispAppearancePage	1 = Appearance Page of the Display Control Panel is not available.
NoDispBackgroundPage	1 = Background page of the Display Control Panel is not available.
NoDispCPL	1 = Display Control Panel is not available.
NoDispScrSavPage	1 = Screen Saver Page of the Display Control Panel is not available.
NoDispSettingsPage	1 = Settings Page of the Display Control Panel is not available.

Appendix

Index

Note to Reader: Throughout this index **boldfaced** page numbers indicate the primary discussion of a topic. *Italicized* page numbers indicate illustrations.

Symbols & Numbers

Index

X

Z

Index

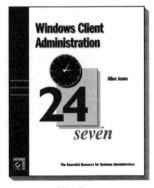

How to...